TRAVEL FACT AND TRAVEL FICTION

BRILL'S STUDIES IN INTELLECTUAL HISTORY

TUTA SUB AEGIDE PALLAS · 1683 ·

STANDARD LOAN

TRAVEL FACT
AND
TRAVEL FICTION

Studies on Fiction, Literary Tradition,
Scholarly Discovery and Observation
in Travel Writing

EDITED BY

ZWEDER VON MARTELS

E.J. BRILL
LEIDEN · NEW YORK · KÖLN
1994

The paper in this book meets the guidelines for permanence and durability of the Committee on Production Guidelines for Book Longevity of the Council on Library Resources.

Library of Congress Cataloging-in-Publication Data

Travel fact and travel fiction : studies on fiction, literary
   tradition, scholarly discovery, and observation in travel writing /
   edited by Zweder von Martels.
      p.   cm. — (Brill's studies in intellectual history : v. 55)
   Includes bibliographical references and index.
   ISBN 9004101128 (cloth)
    1. Travel writing.   2. Travelers' writings—History and criticism.
   3. Fiction—Technique.   I. Martels, Z. R. W. M. von. II. Series
   G161.T67   1994
   809'.93355—dc20   94-27051
                                     CIP

Die Deutsche Bibliothek – CIP-Einheitsaufnahme

Travel fact and travel fiction: studies on fiction, literary
tradition, scholarly discovery and observation in travel writing
/ed. by Zweder von Martels. – Leiden ; New York ; Koln :
Brill, 1994
   (Brill's studies in intellectual history ; Vol. 55)
   ISBN 90-4-10112-8
NE: Martels, Zweder von [Hrsg.]; GT

ISSN 0920-8607
ISBN 90 04 10112 8

PRINTED IN THE NETHERLANDS

CONTENTS

PLATES

Engraving by Theodorus de Bry from *Americae pars quarta, sive insignis et admiranda Historia de reperta primum Occidentali India a Christophoro Columbo anno MCCCCXCII scripta ab Hieronymo Bezono mediolanense* (Frankfurt, 1594), plate XX

[Text beneath engraving:] Indi Hispanis aurum sitientibus, aurum liquefactum infundunt. Indi Hispanis offensi propter nimiam eorum tyrannidem et crudelitatem, atque avaritiam, quoscumque capiebant vivos, militares praesertim duces, revinctis manibus, pedibusque proiiciebant in terram; mox auro in os iacentis infuso, cum hac exprobatione auaritiae: 'Ede, ede aurum Christiane'; ad maiorem cruciatum ac probrum cultellis lapideis, alius brachium Hispani, alius humerum, alius crus, abscindebant et subiectis prunis torrentes mandebant.

[Translation:] The Indians pour liquid gold into the gold-hungry Spaniards.
The Indians hated the Spaniards for their tyranny and cruelty and also for their avarice. Those whom they took alive, especially the generals, they would bind hand and foot and throw them to the ground. Then they would pour gold into their mouths as they lay and taunt them for their greed saying: 'Eat, Christian, eat this gold', and after this they made his suffering and disgrace even worse: with knives of stone, a first cut off the Spaniard's arm, another his shoulder, again another his leg, and roasting them on charcoal they ate them.

[Photograph: Trinity College, Cambridge]

From Isidore of Seville's *Originum sive etymologiarum libri xx.*
University of Groningen, MS 8, fo. 220ᵛ (Xth century)
[Photograph: Grafisch Centrum, University of Groningen]

Engraving by Theodorus de Bry from *Americae pars quarta* (op. cit. under I), plate VI

[Text beneath engraving:] Columbus primus inventor Indiae Occidentalis.
Columbus trans Gades in Portugalliam, et omnem illam Oceani oram nauigans, saepenumero animadvertit, et diligenter observauit, uentos quosdam statis anni temporibus ab occasu flare, qui multos dies constanti tractu spirarent; quos quum non aliunde, quam ex transmarina ora proficisci posse iudicaret, tamdiu circa eam rem cogitando animum versavit, ut eius certitudinem quaerere aliquando constitueret. Quapropter et Reipub. Genuensi, et Principibus aliquot suam operam obtulit, ut illam oram indagaret; sed ab omnibus neglectus, tandem sumptibus Ferdinandi et Isabellae Regum Hispaniae, navigationem instituit.

[Translation:] Columbus discoverer of the West Indies.
When Columbus sailed past Cadiz to Portugal and the length of the Atlantic coast, he

frequently observed and carefully noted, that at fixed times of the year, winds blew from the west, and that they remained constant for many days. This matter occupied him for a long time, and since he supposed that the winds could only come from a coast on the other side of the sea, he decided to verify his observations. He therefore offered his service to the Republic of Genoa and certain other Princes, hoping to investigate that coast. However nobody took up his cause, until he finally set sail financed by King Ferdinand and Queen Isabella of Spain.
[Photograph: Trinity College, Cambridge]

PREFACE

The idea for this volume of articles on travel writing developed from an interest in the sixteenth-century humanist Augerius Busbequius whose epistles on his embassy to the Ottoman empire were widely read in the seventeenth and eighteenth centuries. His writings are an interesting object of study in their own right; on the other hand, the author's deep knowledge of classical and contemporary literature and the influence of his work on later writers have made his work an ideal bridge between Antiquity and modern times.

My reading of different examples of travel books turned up four coherent themes which can be regarded as characteristic, and these return in the title of the conference 'Travel descriptions: Fiction, literary tradition, scholarly discovery and observation', held at the University of Groningen on February 27 and 28, 1992. The papers of the conference ranged from Herodotus to Goethe and Dickens; nine are here published together with eight other invited contributors. In this way a satisfactory overview could be given over the 2300 years separating the first and last authors. Besides, this spread offers a good representation of the different genres used for travel writing. Nevertheless, the reader will see that there is a clear emphasis on the period after the Middle Ages. In this period human mobility increased and the stream of travel writings became a wide river with many branches seeking new directions, and finding a wide range of sophistications.

The editor is grateful to the contributors for their efforts and pleasant cooperation, to Mr Peter Black (Cambridge) who corrected the English of a number of articles, and to Dr Arjo Vanderjagt for his advice and encouragement during the organisation of the conference and the further preparation of this volume. I also wish to thank Trinity College Cambridge, where, as a Visiting Fellow Commoner, I was enabled to complete the editing of this book, and to the Royal Netherlands Academy of Arts and Sciences (KNAW) for the research fellowship in which this project was initiated and brought to a conclusion.

Zweder von Martels

CONTRIBUTORS

Professor W.J. AERTS, Klassiek Instituut, University of Groningen, Oude Boteringestraat 23, 9712 GC Groningen, The Netherlands

Mr I. BEJCZY, Instituut Middeleeuwse Geschiedenis, Catholic University Nijmegen, Erasmusplein 1, 6501 HD Nijmegen, The Netherlands

Dr J. BEPLER, Herzog August Bibliothek, Postfach 1364, 3340 Wolfenbüttel, Germany

Professor D. Fehling, Stückenberg 43, 24226 Heikendorf bei Kiel, Germany

Professor V.I.J. FLINT, Department of History, University of Auckland, Private Bag 92019, Auckland, New Zealand

Professor M. GOSMAN, Vakgroep Romaanse Talen en Culturen, University of Groningen, Oude Kijk in 't Jatstraat 26, 9712 EZ Groningen, The Netherlands

Professor M.A. HARDER, Klassiek Instituut, University of Groningen, Oude Boteringestraat 23, 9712 GC Groningen, The Netherlands

Dr A.J.E. HARMSEN, Vakgroep Nederlandse Taal- en Letterkunde, University of Leiden, Gebouw 1167, Posbus 9515, 2300 RA Leiden, The Netherlands

Dr P. JACKSON, Department of History, University of Keele, Keele ST5 5BG, Staffordshire, England

Professor J.H.A. LOKIN, Vakgroep Rechtsgeschiedenis, University of Groningen, Turftorenstraat 19, 9712 BM Groningen, The Netherlands

Dr Z.R.W.M. VON MARTELS, Klassiek Instituut, University of Groningen, Oude Boteringestraat 23, 9712 GC Groningen, The Netherlands

Professor M. MUND-DOPCHIE, Department of Greek and Oriental Studies, University of Louvain, 1348 Louvain-la-Neuve, Belgium

Dr A.N. PALMER, Department of the Study of Religions, School of Oriental and African Studies, University of London, Thornhaugh Street, Russell Square, London WC1H 0XG, England

Professor R.C. PAULIN, Trinity College, Cambridge CB2 1TQ, England

Professor P. SKRINE, Department of German, University of Bristol, 21 Woodland Road, Bristol BS8 1TE, England

Dr C.C. VAN STRIEN, Witte de Withlaan 10, 2341 SR Oegstgeest, The Netherlands

Dr G.H. TUCKER, Downing College, Cambridge CB2 1DQ, England

INTRODUCTION: THE EYE AND THE EYE'S MIND

Without roots, unlike the trees, man is bound to wander over the earth like the beasts in quest for food and shelter. But the pleasure of learning and knowing distinguishes him from the latter. What nature denied him, he built for himself: boats to sail the sea and wings to fly so as to conquer the world.

Through history many have dreamed of journeys to the outer corners of their world. But inevitably most stayed at home, out of necessity or fear, and satisfied their curiosity with the writings of those who had really gone away, or of those who had never gone but had travelled in their imagination. These readers soon discovered that those books could help them travel further than any living man could go.

Travel writing seems unlimited in its forms of expression, but though we may therefore find it hard to define the exact boundaries of this genre, it is generally understood what it contains. It ranges from the indisputable examples such as guidebooks, itineraries and routes and perhaps also maps to less restricted accounts of journeys over land or by water, or just descriptions of experiences abroad. These appear in prose and poetry, and are often part of historical and (auto)biographical works. Sometimes we find no more than simple notes and observations, sometimes more elaborate diaries. The letter written during the journey itself, or composed long afterwards with literary skill is another much favoured form. But often it is subject to discussion whether we may still speak of travel writing, for instance, where the distinction between travel writing and fiction becomes small, and the novel comes into being.

In ancient literature we find early examples of much of all this: Pausanias's guidebook to Greece, and the geographical works of Strabo, another experienced traveller; history books like that of Herodotus and the accounts of military campaigns by Xenophon and Caesar; the purely practical road-books such as the Antonine Itinerary and the Peutinger map; and, of a totally different character, travel poetry like Horace's witty satire known as the *Iter Brundisium*, or the epics of Homer and Virgil in which travel is an important element, or Ovid's *Tristia* on his true or fictitious exile in Tomi; in prose we may mention the adventurous stories of Alexander's travels, Lucian's *True History*, and Apuleius's *Golden Ass*; and, finally, almost at the end of the ancient classical tradition Egeria's early pilgrimage to the Holy Land.

This and much more forms a huge corpus of travel literature that came into being over the centuries[1] and has attracted large numbers of readers. In it one

---

[1] For a catalogue of the endless forms of travel writing see Percy G. Adams, *Travel Literature*

finds countless examples of what one may call fiction, literary tradition, observation, and scholarly discovery—four terms which define important features of this genre. However, as this collection of essays shows, the relation between these terms is not fixed, but has many facets.

In studies on travel writing we are often reminded that travel authors borrow much of their material from predecessors. Examples of this practice are the journals kept by travellers during their travels through Europe as part of their education. Many of these authors had not spared their eyes reading traditional advice and information, but, it seems, they hardly looked around for themselves.

By the comparison of travel books and other forms of literature we may reach similar general conclusions and these may be of help in further study. On the other hand, they must not distract our attention from the differences which exist between individual works. For readers must be grateful that travellers, being only human, are often unpredictable. This unpredictability is partly the result of different educations and training, partly of the traveller's personality and of the motives and stimuli that urged him or her to leave home and take on the risk of journeying. Merchants, sailors, soldiers, students, explorers, pilgrims, or those seeking alienation from the world - they and others, all used their five senses and their talents in different ways as they travelled. So there is a world of difference between Herodotus's explorations of the then-known world, Marco Polo's description of his journey as a young merchant to the court of the Kubilai Khan at Peking, Columbus's keen observations as a sailor on the Great Ocean to the other side of the world, and Goethe's romantic search for the living past.

Readers from each generation ask themselves again why these people travelled, what they observed and experienced. Their answers vary according to the perspective of each reader and his general knowledge which, in its turn, depends on the investigations of scholars into the circumstances of each journey. In general, the imagination of the public has always been captivated by the real, positive achievements of these travellers. There was great interest in the new ideas and discoveries they brought back, the progress and change they could help to bring about on the return from an inspiring journey. In short, the talent of observation has always been regarded as of chief importance in a traveller, and if it is lacking it causes disappointment. This appreciation surfaces in Samuel Johnson's judgment of Thomas Pennant, whom he characterises as 'the best traveller I ever read; he observes more things than anyone does'.[2] In our age, the focus on observation is without comparison, as television, the public eye, leaves nothing unscrutinized and the camera is able to record things as tiny and hidden as the

---

and the Evolution of the Novel (Lexington, Kentucky, 1983), 38-80.

[2] See Samuel Johnson & James Boswell, *A Journey to the Western Islands of Scotland. The Journal of a Tour to the Hebrides*, Penguin, ed P. Levi (Harmondsworth, 1987), p. 14 (Introduction).

movements of insects under the ground, describing life and matter through pictures, making us almost forget to what extent our observations are influenced by words and concepts.

This culture of the eye was institutionalized during the Renaissance through collections of all sorts of curiosities, plants and animals, gathered over a long period of time by enterprising men, who had travelled widely. Collecting had a long tradition but it became conspicuous through the activities of the Medici family and the founders of similar collections. The sixteenth-century 'Wunderkammer' is another step in the direction of the later Museum. A similar innovation to bring *realia* under the eyes of the public, was the creation of botanical gardens, the first of which was planted in Padua before the middle of the sixteenth century. Together with the anatomical theatre they reformed medical teaching, since demonstration instead of reading became the essence of scientific training.

A not less important facet of this intellectual movement was the foundation of libraries and the systematic study of ancient literature which had become and would remain for a long time the standard for imitation and emulation. With this went the struggle to purify language and to define the exact meaning of words - first in Latin, soon followed by the vernacular languages. Thus the best possible tool for achieving general understanding of all aspects of life was created. That students of Latin shared a desire to go and look around with their eyes is clear from their fondness of making descriptions of persons, landscapes, towns, objects and events. In this way language was forced to its very limits. Characteristic, too, was the use of metaphors that remind us of painting and sculpture, stressing the importance of the eye and the imagination.

Nonetheless, it has been suggested that students of ancient texts were only looking backwards, and that they were less interested in the future. For this reason, philological study was even rejected by a few men whose quick apprehension could no longer bear a literary tradition full of inadequate and incongruous examples—men, who hated the loss of time caused by the study of Latin and Greek texts. In a single word, they wished to pass by the natural course of intellectual and cultural development. Protests of this kind by Paracelsus and Pomponazzi had no immediate effect. Descartes was fortunate to live in a time almost ripe for his ideas. Yet the traditional philological approach, which has to some the appearance of a detour, was, in fact, as essential for the intellectual growth and the advancement of society as the learning of speech for a child. For in many respects, the acquisition of a language that could be trusted in all circumstances supported the emerging sciences in their battle against prejudices, misconceptions, and the old superstitious belief in monsters and unnatural forces.

To the modern reader it can come as a surprise to realise that explorers often expressed themselves in words that reflect their reading of literature instead of what they actually saw. A famous example is Columbus's attractive but unrealistic description of the islands and the population he discovered. About a century later such cases were scornfully rejected with the words: 'Travellers, poets and liars are three words of one significance'[3].

If this is the verdict which travel writers deserve, it ought to be said that it can be easily applied to a much wider group. But, as I will show, caution is needed in the use of this judgment.

In our age, the gap between observation and scholarly discovery on the one hand and fiction and literary tradition on the other seems greater than ever before. Both observation and discovery are connected with originality and reality, with truth and sparkling results; fiction and literary tradition rather with fancy, with imagination and the world of books and the mind. But any sharp division between these terms is artificial and becomes untenable as soon as we look closely at the examples where authors rely on their observation. For even if the author's reality deviates from our 'truth', this does not automatically mean that there is a deliberate attempt to deceive the reader. I shall try to classify a number of cases, in order to find reasons for the lack of 'truth' in particular observations. Besides others, a number of examples are derived from Augerius Busbequius' *Turkish Letters*,[4] which is a rich source both because of the author's dependence on literary tradition and his trust in the use of his own eyes.

It would be cynical to doubt the honest intention of any author in advance. When, however, an account of particular events or facts is untrue in our eyes, an explanation is needed. One might be that the author had no clear insight into the essential elements or did not understand the working of what he described, and as a result made false conclusions.

This happens in Pietro Bembo's *De Aetna* (Venice, 1495), in which we have an account of a (fictitious?) dialogue with his father, Bernardo Bembo. He describes his ascent of Mount Etna in about 1494 and his observations of volcanic activities. But what he saw near the mouth of the crater and thought was happening in the bowels of the earth, was so much interwoven with ancient and medieval theory that to our mind his report has become an interesting mixture of fact and fiction, though to contemporaries it must have been quite real.

Another example of ignorance as the cause of misunderstanding is the attempt by medieval botanists to find the Sweet Flag (Acorus calamus) which had been described by the ancient physician Dioscurides. Platearius Mathaeus of the medical school of Salerno (around the middle of the twelfth century) believed he had found the plant in the Yellow Flag (Iris pseudoacorus), with which it had much in common, for instance the stiff and erect leaves and the fact that it fringes rivers and lakes; but it lacked the medical qualities which Dioscurides said the Sweet Flag should possess. On this basis generations of pharmacists sold this plant more or less fraudulently as medicine to their customers, turning a blind eye to its weak

---

[3] Cf. Richard Brathwaite, *The English Gentleman* (1631).
[4] For Busbequius, see Preface and pp. 140–57 of this book.

medicinal power. Eventually this problem was solved by Pier Andrea Matthioli, the author of an influential mid-sixteenth-century commentary on Dioscurides. Following the text of the Greek physician, he asked Busbequius during his stay in Constantinople around 1554, to search for the Sweet Flag in a place in Asia Minor, where it was supposed to grow. The ambassador's physician William Quackelbeen carried out this request and in a letter to Matthioli described how the plant was found, and how he studied the growth and qualities of a sample which was taken to the embassy.[5]

Bembo and the botanists before Matthioli may have been aware that their explanation was not fully satisfying, and, as long as the matter remained uncertain, they were forced to complete the picture from knowledge derived out of the literary tradition or from their own imagination.

In the sixteenth century when people learned to rely more and more on their own observation and were even prepared to test the veracity of statements which had come down to them through literature, verification was still often hard to obtain.

For this reason, belief in legendary animals like unicorns, dogheads and many others remained unshaken. We find much on them in Conrad Gesner's *Historia Animalium*. Concerning the unicorn ('Monoceros')[6] he provides us with all the particulars found in ancient, medieval and contemporary authors. He stated that the animal did not occur in Europe, and that no living example had ever been brought there. Even otherwise it was rarely seen. But the horn of the unicorn had sometimes been preserved. Gesner himself had seen pieces of it, and he quoted contemporary authors who mentioned that churches including the San Marco in Venice held such horns among their treasures. Gesner also speaks of a specimen of two ells long, which was found in the river 'Arula' in Switzerland, and taken to a nearby nunnery ('monasterium virginum'). That event, which had taken place in 1520, was reported to him by a friend who possessed fragments of the same horn. Finally there is a picture of the unicorn which helps the reader envisage what the animal looked like, though even without this picture, one can easily see it in the mind's eye thanks to the detailed information collected by Gesner.

Dependence on ancient authorities was great, the respect and admiration for them was in proportion. It took time to accept that great Greek, Roman and medieval authors could be wrong on specific points. Are we to be astonished about this, when signs of equal reverence still occur in modern books? It happens, for instance, that unrealistic facts in classical texts by important authors need explanation, for instance Caesar's vague remarks about elks living deep in

---

[5] P. A. Matthioli, *Epistolarum medicinalium libri quinque* (Prag, 1561), 172–3: William Quackelbeen to Matthioli, letter of July 26, 1557. See also K. Rüegg, *Beiträge zur Geschichte der offizinellen Drogen: Crocus, Acorus Calamus und Colchicum* (Stetten & Basel, 1936), 133–207.

[6] Conrad Gesner, *Historia animalium liber I de quadrupedibus viviparis* (Zurich, 1551), pp. 781–6.

'Germania', which had never been seen by the author.[7] Still scholars found that the great author could not have written this passage and they regard it as an interpolation by another mediocre writer. Often, too, passages containing apparent 'mistakes' are ascribed to errors caused by scribes who copied the text.[8]

Real observation requires training, not only for analysis and comparison, but for expressing new findings in words and concepts. Explorers often have no words to describe their discoveries, and are at first literally speechless. They must try to circumscribe by metaphors, create new words, or borrow from other languages, and inevitably they risk misunderstanding. How this works can be seen with children, when they give new names to unfamiliar objects: sometimes we grasp what they mean, more often not. So travellers, too, introduced new words and ideas, exciting our curiosity and imagination.[9]

An author who intends to record his observations and experiences faithfully may still go astray because he is misguided by others.[10] This might even be deliberate, for it is an old tactic in war and peace to show the beautiful sides and to hide the ugly. Unfortunately, it is not always easy to see through this play. Yet, it is especially rewarding in journalism when such conduct is exposed.

Vagueness or inaccuracy is often caused by external influences. Distortion in the description of real facts or events can also occur as a result of the chosen literary form. An example of this is in Busbequius's fictitious *Turkish Letters* in which the author summarizes the experiences of many years. The first letter, for example, contains a description of his first journey to Constantinople in late autumn 1554 but it also incorporates the experiences of later travels along the same route. In this letter, then, he refers to the tulip, a flower unknown before the middle of the sixteenth century. For a long time this passage has been regarded as the first mention of the tulip in European literature and consequently the author was reputed to have introduced the plant to Europe. But it was never noticed that Busbequius's tulips would have flowered at an odd time of the year, because the author states that he saw them near Edirne about the middle of December—an exceptional early season for spring flowers. Busbequius, however, also made daffodils and rice to grow at the coldest moment of the year. In order to cover the incongruity, he lulled the reader asleep with the following words: 'We were very much surprised to see them [*i.e.* tulips] blooming in midwinter, a season which does not suit flowers at all.'[11]

---

[7] Caesar, *De bello Gallico*, vi. 27: 'animals which resemble goats in shape and in their piebald colouring, but are somewhat larger, and have stunted horns and legs without joints or knuckles' (translation S. A. Handford in: Caesar. The Conquest of Gaul (Harmondsworth, 1952), p. 37.

[8] For an example, see Detlev Fehling on page 5 of this book.

[9] See Mary B. Campbell, *The Witness and the Other World: Exotic European Travel Writing, 400-1600* (Ithaca & London, 1988), pp. 222–38: 'The problems of words'.

[10] For an example, see Andrew Palmer on pp. 163–4 of this book.

[11] See Charles Thornton Forster's & F. H. Blackburne Daniell's *The Life and Letters of Ogier*

Especially in writings composed many years after events had taken place, we must be on guard against errors caused by lapses of memory, which can have very serious consequences for the contents. Often the author is not aware that in his memory the sequence of events is confused, or that his depiction of what had happened is coloured by his particular likes or dislikes, or his wish to emphasise the role he himself played.[12]

Finally, we have reached a point where descriptions do not correspond with our reality and at the same time none of the excuses mentioned so far seems valid, so that it appears as if the author does not fulfil the obligation, as we see it, to tell the 'truth'. But before we call him an impostor—and this, of course, he might be—we ought to analyse on what grounds he acted as he did.

From a rhetorical standpoint, the author's main task is to convince his readers. Since a travel writer has to report about the unknown, he is not always in an enviable position. His observations and experiences do not always meet with the public's expectations. For instance, they may be too good to be true, or the other world, about which he wishes to speak, may turn out not to contain the treasures or monsters imagined by the people at home. So whether he likes it or not, he must sometimes either disappoint his readers or (like Columbus) in order not to endanger his own position and future expeditions he must embellish the truth. For this, considerable skill is needed, and only with help of fictional elements—or 'white lies', if one prefers—can the writer attain the necessary verisimilitude for creating a bridge of understanding between his own wide knowledge of the subject and the narrower expectations of the reader.[13]

Not unlike real travellers, scholars and scientists put trust in their originality and their observation, and though it is their greatest desire to make progress in their field, they, too, have to follow the paths set out for them by earlier generations. They can only advance as far as others can follow them or they lose contact with popular knowledge.

Human society possesses a strong inclination to preserve what has been built up over the centuries and to protect itself from new influences. For this reason, most readers in the first place seek confirmation of old values dressed with a certain amount of novelty.

This tension between conservatism and unorthodoxy often reveals itself in many ways in travel writing. Mandeville, for instance, in the first part of his book follows the pattern of the traditional pilgrimage, but where he reached the extremities of the known world, he bursts out in an avalanche of marvellous

---

Ghiselin de Busbecq, Seigneur of Bousbecque, Knight, Imperial Ambassador (2 vols., Londen, 1881; repr. Geneva, 1971), vol. i, p. 107. For the Latin, see Augerius Busbequius, *Legationis Turcicae Epistolae Quatuor* (Paris, 1589), fos. 17ᵛ–18ʳ. For a critical edition of the *Turkish Letters*, see p. 140 (n. 2) of this book.

[12] For an example, see the author's article on page 151 ff. of this book.

[13] See, for example, the articles on Herodotus and Columbus in this book.

stories.[14] Busbequius, who is useful here as well, followed Strabo and Polybius in his descriptions of Asian cities (Constantinople, Nicea and Amasya), but elsewhere, dealing with less well-known themes such as the customs of the Turks, he is much freer in the treatment of his subject.[15]

Fiction, literary tradition, observation and scholarly discovery are useful categories with which to assess any travel writing. However, this introduction is intended to show that they have a relative value because so much of our reality is built up out of fiction; often what is fiction for the public at home is reality for the author who had been far away, and *vice versa*. In addition, the articles collected here show that these terms—either in connection to each other, or individually—allow different equally valid approaches; literature is not exactly as science. Our sole generalisation is that the writing of each individual author is defined by what he received from the world and what he himself added to it.

Zweder von Martels

---

[14] Christian K. Zacher, *Curiosity and Pilgrimage. The Literature of Discovery in Fourteenth-Century England* (Baltimore & London, 1976), 130–57.

[15] Busbequius (op. cit. n. 11), fos. 25ʳff. (Constantinople), fo. 31ʳ (Nicaea), fo. 38ᵛ (Amasya).

THE ART OF HERODOTUS
AND THE MARGINS OF THE WORLD

DETLEV FEHLING[*]

Unlike several other contributors to this book, I hardly need introduce the author who is my subject. Suffice it to remind the reader that Herodotus presents, in a work of about 800 printed pages, a comprehensive (though in some respects select) account of that short span of world history he had any knowledge about, presenting it as a development which led directly up to, and culminated in, the two great wars in which the Greeks vindicated their liberty against the Persian empire. In this work are included many digressions on the geography and ethnology of the more remote countries of the world. Herodotus' work is the first prose composition in Greek literature which has come down to us complete. The first part of my paper will consist in general remarks on some aspects of Herodotus' methods of collecting and using information. Inevitably, I shall have to repeat much that is contained in my earlier and somewhat more technical book on Herodotus,[1] and other publications of mine.[2] The second part of this paper will briefly survey the information Herodotus gives on the remotest parts of the world. We shall see that the last-named expression is more clearly defined for Herodotus than we should expect.

Any discussion of Herodotus' methods will necessarily have to begin with a basic problem, which has been seen clearly by all serious scholars for more than a century. (Later on I shall have to qualify this statement a little). There are no direct autobiographical statements in Herodotus (except that he calls himself a citizen of Halicarnassus, a small town on the coast of Asia Minor, but that counts as part of his name). But there are distributed over his work quite a number of passages where he says that he is reporting what is said in diverse places: 'The Egyptians say ...', 'the Spartans say ...' etc. There is also a smaller number of passages which, if what Herodotus states is correct, unequivocally imply his presence at the place he is talking about: 'I heard from ..., I asked ..., I saw ... , they told me ...', and in one exceptional case even: 'I went to Tyros in order to ascertain ...' (ii.44.1). I do not count these as autobiographical, because they are clearly not meant to tell about Herodotus himself, but are closely bound up with

---

[*] University of Kiel, Germany.

[1] D. Fehling, *Herodotus and his 'Sources'. Citation, Invention and Narrative Art*, translated from the German by J. G. Howie, Arca, 21 (Leeds, 1989); originally: *Quellenangaben Herodots* (Berlin, 1971).

Quotations by section and subsections as § 1.1 are valid for both editions.

[2] Especially: D. Fehling, *Die sieben Weisen und die frühgriechische Chronologie. Eine traditionsgeschichtliche Studie* (Bern, 1985).

the information he is presenting. Now the problem with these remarks—and I repeat: a problem recognized by everybody—is that much of what Herodotus tells us precisely in these places cannot be taken at face value, mainly for two or three reasons. (1) In many cases he makes non-Greeks tell stories that have nothing to do with their own traditions, as we know them from other sources, and are clearly products of Greek thought, i.e. based on ideas current in Greek literature before Herodotus. Thus, in the very first chapters of his work, Herodotus makes Persians and Phoenicians tell a story about the origin of what Herodotus calls the enmity between Greeks and Asiatics, and this story is wholly developed from Greek mythology. (2) In many cases information (objectively untrue), which purports to come from widely separated places, fits so neatly together as to betray a common origin. An example is ii. 54 ff, where Herodotus claims to have heard in Thebes, Upper Egypt, that the oracles of Dodona in the far North-West of Greece and of Siwa in the Libyan desert had been founded each by a Theban priestess who had been kidnapped by Phoenician pirates and sold to the mentioned places. In Dodona he was told the same story only with the difference that the part of the priestesses was played by black doves gifted with human speech, and coming from Thebes. The relation between the two versions is that of a miraculous story to a rationalized one, i.e. a version stripped of the miraculous element (the doves in the Dodonean version are black because Herodotus imagines the Egyptians to be blacks, a fact to which I shall return). It is impossible that these two versions are independent of each other, as they would have to be, if Herodotus heard them in the two places. The almost ridiculous idea of Phoenician pirates kidnapping women in Thebes, 400 miles from the sea as the ibis flies, and their selling one of them to Siwa deep in the desert, is an additional stumbling-block. For Herodotus, on the other hand, Phoenician pirates kidnapping persons and selling them to distant countries was a familiar idea; the motif occurs several times in the *Odyssey*. (3) There is also the analogous problem of certain material or factual proofs quoted by Herodotus for his stories, story and object or putative fact being likewise implausible and as nicely attuned to each other as the two versions about the oracles just mentioned. A simple example occurs in the same passage: Herodotus claims that the practice of giving oracles is the same in Thebes and in Dodona.

My own interest in the problem began when I realized that the explanations given by scholars for all these observations were not satisfactory. These explanations were based on an axiomatic belief that Herodotus' statements must be at least subjectively true. The most important ways out were (and with many scholars still are): that the stories look Greek, because the informants were influenced by earlier contacts with Greeks, or Herodotus just asked for confirmation of stories which actually (although this is never explicitly mentioned) had sprung from his own mind, and his 'informants' obligingly nodded assent whenever they felt it was expected from them, whether they understood Herodotus' Greek or not. In other words, rather make Herodotus an imbecile than a liar. For several years I was completely puzzled myself. Then (about thirty years ago) I saw in two cases that no other solution was possible but that the source-citations were simply made up by Herodotus himself. I still had no idea where the thing would lead me when I began to study the complete material. In the end, a clear-cut result emerged. Negatively, it became clear that the excuses used by most scholars would have to be applied on so gigantic a scale as to make them look even more ridiculous than the more extravagant examples of them looked already at first sight, and further, that cases exist where even the most desperate theories failed.

One such example of a hopeless case is the story of the foundation of Dodona, mentioned above. The first problem here is where to start. Shall we assume Herodotus to have come to Dodona with the Egyptian story in his baggage or vice versa? I mentioned the difficulty of the Egyptian story, and Egyptians could hardly have known Dodona even existed. On the other hand, who would believe that the priestesses of a proud Greek sanctuary would derive its origin from Egypt? So the theory of the leading questions would have to be used for both versions. But even this is precluded by the fact that the two versions are not the same, but are related in the way indicated above. We would have to suppose that during the journey from Egypt to Dodona (or vice versa) Herodotus had second thoughts about the story he had elicited nods in confirmation of in the other place, and changed it (either embellishing it by mythicizing it, or, in the other case, making it more acceptable by de-mythicizing it) and presented the story in its new attire to the partners of another telling-and-nodding-session.

Another example is iii. 12 where Herodotus mentions a battle, which had been fought a couple of years earlier between Egyptians and Persians, and says that he was led by natives in the neighbourhood to the battle-field in order to be shown a striking phenomenon—the bones of the dead were still lying around, separated by nationality for the convenience of observation—: the skulls of the dead Egyptians were harder than those of the Persians. It is well known that there is a clear connection between this story and physiological theories current in Greece at least roughly in Herodotus' own time. A Greek source (leading questions of Herodotus included) is, however, incompatible with the circumstances as Herodotus relates them.

So much for the negative side. On the positive side, I noted that Herodotus' source-citations follow rigid rules. There is always a close connection between source-citation and content, so that the former is predictable from the latter. There are three rules. The first and basic rule is what I call the rule of the obvious source. That is, Herodotus always quotes as his source those people who in the nature of things would know about the matter, provided (and here comes the snag in an otherwise innocent-looking observation) the story was historical fact. It is as if the Bible quoted the Babylonians for the story of the Babylonian tower, or the Egyptians for Joseph and the children of Israel in Egypt. Thus in Herodotus ii. 112–20 it is the Egyptians who can tell him about a visit of Paris and Helen to Egypt which is implied in the *Odyssey*: they claim that they kept the abducted Helen in Egypt, and for that reason the Trojans were unable to hand her over to the Greeks, and the Trojan war had to be fought to the bitter end. After the war, they say, Menelaos came to Egypt and collected her. All this we are told notwithstanding the fact that actual Egyptians knew nothing about Troy, Paris and Helen whatsoever. It is especially revealing that Herodotus makes the Egyptians say that they did not know what became of Menelaos after he had left Egypt (in the *Odyssey* he returns safely home). Thus the appearance of historical knowledge from original immediate eyewitnesses is kept up down to the last detail. I may add here that such nice detailed considerations about who should know or not know what are one of the finest elements of Herodotus' art, and are badly spoilt by those who imagine they must save his honour by defending the subjective truth of his statements.

The second rule is regard for party-bias. Herodotus avoids making his sources say anything that would be detrimental to the reputation of their own nation. Again, the rule can be as unrealistic as it seems natural. For instance, in the introductory chapters, which I briefly mentioned above, the Persians tell a long and elaborate story based wholly on Greek myth about the origin of the enmity between Asiatics and Greeks. This story leaves the Phoenicians as those who committed the first act of injustice; they abducted the Greek princess Io of Argos. Herodotus adds that the Phoenicians in general confirm what the Persians have said but they do not accept that Io was abducted by force. No, she had an affair with the captain of the Phoenician ship, and when she noted she was with child she went with him out of her own free will. The nodding-theory here implies that Herodotus thought of this excuse himself, but, conscientious historian that he was, he travelled all the way to Phoenicia to have it confirmed in the usual way. To entertain such a notion is, I think, an insult to Herodotus.

The third rule I call regard for Herodotus' own credibility. It takes two forms. One of them is that Herodotus avoids telling miraculous stories in his own name. I can pass over it here. The second form, however, has a special relevance for the present subject: Herodotus never directly quotes information from very far-away countries, from countries on the margins of the world. Wherever he comments about such countries, his quotations are somehow marked as coming from indirect information, often in such an unobtrusive form that this fact was never noted before I drew attention to it. That is, instead of simply saying as elsewhere: 'The X say ...', he says: 'The X are said to say ...' or 'The X and those who have heard it from them say ...' or something to the same effect. Since Herodotus clearly never travelled to these countries, this fact seems (just as the other two rules) perfectly innocent at first sight and can even be mistaken for proof of his painstaking accuracy. But there are two reasons which show that these citations are no more simple statements of fact than are the others. (1) It appears again, in some cases, that the information given under these citations is actually developed from earlier Greek literature. This holds, e.g., practically for everything Herodotus says about the Ethiopians. (2) There is an argument *e contrario*: Herodotus never marks as indirect any information about less remote countries (less remote here means anything between Babylon in the East and Carthage in the West). But those who want to defend his citations as correct, in order to explain certain oddities, badly need the possibility to excuse statements of Herodotus' as being based on indirect, and therefore distorted information. So nobody can accept the view that Herodotus accurately distinguishes between direct and indirect information. In reality, this distinction has nothing to do with Herodotus' real sources.

Before I proceed to explain my view of all this, one passage must be mentioned. I said above that there is no direct autobiographical statement in Herodotus, and it is time to mention one apparent exception. He says in ii. 29. 1 that in Egypt he got as far as Elephantine (the southernmost place of Egypt under Persian rule in

Herodotus' day, near present-day Assuan). It is impossible that this statement is true. There are too many things Herodotus tells us about Egypt which he could never have said, if he really had made his way up the Nile through the whole country. A number of scholars have realized this at least for Upper Egypt, but actually it cannot be denied for the whole of it. Since this is a crucial point for any discussion on Herodotus' credibility, I mention three of the most glaring errors.[3] (1) Herodotus says (ii. 8) that after four days' sailing up the Nile from Memphis, Egypt becomes broad again (i.e. broad as it is in the Delta, the coastline of which Herodotus estimates as about 350 miles long), and there is much in the way he talks about Upper Egypt to show that he sincerely believes this. In order to get rid of this problem, earlier editors simply changed the text here, making it fourteen days instead of four, thus catapulting the broadening out of Herodotus' sight, but also out of Egypt. This idea has been generally abandoned now, but no other expedient has appeared.[4] (2) He imagines that the great pyramids are situated in the mountains, which is at least a rather odd description of their situation (ii. 8.), and he thinks they stand in a triangle (ii. 126), while in fact they form almost a straight line (and certainly no one who has seen them will be apt to forget that). I drew attention to the last-named fact in 1971 (some scholars had obscured it by misleading translation), and hitherto nobody has contradicted.[5] (3) Herodotus calls the Egyptians 'wool-haired and black-skinned', and this certainly means that he thinks of them as negroes of a sort.[6] So much for the impossibility of Herodotus' claim to have travelled through the whole of Egypt as far as Elephantine. As for its meaning, we should note that Elephantine is marked by it as the southernmost point of the known world. It is here that the boundary lies between that part of the world about which direct information can be had, and the margins from which only indirect information reaches us. And in fact Herodotus adds in so many words, that everything he will tell us about the parts beyond that point are based on mere hearsay. It thus becomes clear that the statement is made only for the sake of this sequel. The whole passage is just a generalized form of the usual

---

[3] For a much longer list, splendidly argued, see O. K. Armayor, 'Did Herodotus ever go to Egypt', *Journal of the American Research Center in Egypt*, 15 (1980), 59–73, especially pp. 69–71. For a sceptic survey of the literature see Friedrich Oertel, *Herodots ägyptischer Logos und die Glaubwürdigkeit Herodots mit einem metrologischen Beitrag und Anhang*, Antiquitas, R. 1, Bd. xviii (Bonn, 1970).

[4] A. Lloyd thinks that a slight local widening of the Nile valley 50 miles south of Cairo is the solution, although at the same time he admits that Herodotus thinks of Egypt in the form of a double-axe (thin in the middle and broad at both ends). See his commentaries ad loc.: ed. Alan B. Lloyd, *Herodotus Book II*. 3 vols. (Leiden, 1975–1988); *Erodoto, Le Storie. Vol. ii: Libro II, L' Egitto. Introduzione, testo e commento* (Milano, 1989), and *Classical Review*, xli (1991), p. 309.

[5] There is also a false statement about a small pyramid in the middle of the triangle. Only this point is addressed by Erbse, who implausibly argues that the statement is meant by Herodotus as part of the tall story he is recounting. Unfortunately Erbse presents this utterly new idea as if I had overlooked a self-evident fact. Cf. Hartmut Erbse, *Studien zum Verständnis Herodots*, Untersuchungen zur antiken Literatur und Geschichte, 38 (Berlin & New York, 1992), p. 150.

[6] There are frequent attempts in the literature to explain this away, but they are in vain. See Armayor (op. cit. n. 3), pp. 60–2 and pp. 17 f. of my book (op. cit. n. 1).

types of source-indication, combining the forms: 'The so-and-so say ...' (for on this side of Elephantine) and 'It is reported that ...' (beyond).

When I wrote my book a quarter of a century ago, I felt that the enormous amount of cogent arguments I could muster put me in the position of the child in Andersen's famous tale about the emperor's new clothes. I could prove that the emperor was naked, and I expected that it would be enough to present this mass of proofs as completely and clearly as I was able to do, and everybody would realize it. On the other hand, I only briefly touched the question (to follow up the comparison in a somewhat doubtful way), how the emperor came to be naked. I thought that a few hints (which I did give) would suffice, and everybody could make out the rest for himself. The reaction to my book showed that I was in error. Obviously proofs could have been doubled or trebled, and it would not have made any difference. Indeed, this doubling actually took place, for a few years later my voice was joined by another such child, that is, by the American Kimball Armayor, who came up with independent proof from quite different angles. He showed, *inter alia*, that there is no reality behind Herodotus' story of a certain wondrous and gigantic building in central Egypt, which he calls the labyrinth, and which he tells us lay on the shore of an (equally unreal) lake with a circumference of 350 miles, called Lake Moeris (ii. 148). Herodotus claims to have wandered through the 1.500 chambers of this building himself. It may be remarked in passing (because it is typical for the way Greek authors use each other) that Armayor also shows that the later description of the same building by the first-century geographer Strabo is another fantasy based on the same elements Herodotus uses, but combining them in a way which makes the whole of his account glaringly contradictory to Herodotus.[7]

I said at the beginning that every serious scholar was aware of the problem posed by Herodotus' source-citations but that I should have to qualify that statement later. It is at this point that I had best introduce this qualification. A good number of mainly English ancient historians of the last few years seem more or less to have forgotten about the whole subject. Although there is, as against the last two or three generations, a remarkable tendency to treat Herodotus as a creative writer, they tend to ignore not only Armayor and myself but also the preceding decades of headaches over the problem. They just treat it as solved and leave it to their readers to guess what the solution is. I have much sympathy with their unwillingness to go over the same ground over and over again, since they are obviously aware that they are not able to provide better arguments than their predecessors. I am less sympathetic when it is said that my approach is a naive and outmoded nineteenth-century one, and should not interest our more enlightened century.[8]

---

[7] O. Kimball Armayor, *Herodotus' Autopsy of the Fayoum. Lake Moeris and the Labyrinth of Egypt* (Amsterdam, 1985).

A. Lloyd (both commentaries ad loc., op. cit. n. 4) disposes of this fact by assuming that Herodotus saw only one half of the building and Strabo the other, the Herodotean half being demolished by then. Of course, one can account for the facts in that way, too.

[8] I consciously prefer not to back the statements made in this paragraph by quotations. Authors

It appears, then, that something more than an accumulation of proofs is needed, and so I shall now go into this matter in a little more detail. The answer can be found in a very trite and commonplace saying, frequently applied to Herodotus and others. I mean the common warning that ancient authors must not be judged by modern standards. The usual way this commonplace is applied to Herodotus is to maintain that we must put up even with the most incredible errors. (Sometimes Herodotean scholars should ask themselves if they believe that the great military leaders of antiquity continuously committed such errors in their reconnoisance; if such were the conditions of the age, there is no reason why they should have done better than Herodotus.) What we really should ask, however, is whether modern standards of scientific publishing are so self-evident as to have the status of eternal moral laws so that they must have been valid for even the first author who set out to write a book that contained scientific elements. We should not treat Herodotus as if he awoke one morning and said to himself: 'I have a splendid idea how to make my name famous for many a century: let me be the first historian. Of course, this puts me under the moral obligation to behave like a conscientious historian, but, being an honest man, I should be able to live up to that.' It has often been pointed out that the nearest thing to Herodotus' enterprise existing in Greek literature before his time were the Homeric epics. The Greeks used to believe that the war which was the subject of these epics was, in principle, historical, and yet no Greek could or did overlook the fact that they consisted for the most part of pure fiction. Such considerations should help us to solve the dilemma in which Herodotean scholars always found themselves enmeshed. They believed that they only had the choice between Herodotus the truthful scholar and Herodotus the liar and impostor. They simply thought that between these two *tertium non datur*. Given this, it is understandable that the second possibility never had many friends. Herodotus so obviously makes the impression of a morally responsible and serious personality that nobody felt happy about catching him in a lie. Rather scholars would feel that it was not decent to do so, and so many of them preferred to close their eyes firmly in front of obvious observations.

---

who have been at least open to my approach or have even built on it, include Reinhold Bichler ('Die "Reichsträume" bei Herodot'. Eine Studie zu Herodots schöpferischer Leistung und ihre quellenkritische Konsequenz, *Chiron*, 15 (1985), 125–47), Adolf Köhnken ('Herodots falscher Smerdis', *Würzburger Jahrbücher für die Altertumswissenschaft*, N.F. 6a (1980), 39–50), Stephanie West ('Herodotus' epigraphical interests', *The Classical Quarterly*, 35 (1985), 278–305) (the titles mentioned are only examples). Very harsh criticism (and a full measure of examples) of the usual subterfuges is found in: R. Rollinger, *Herodots babylonischer Logos, eine kritische Untersuchung der Glaubwürdigkeitsdiskussion*, Innsbrucker Beiträge zur Kulturwissenschaft, Sonderheft 84 (Innsbruck, 1993), and P. Froschauer, *Herodots ägyptischer Logos, die Glaubwürdigkeitsdissussion in kritischer Sicht* (in print).

For a defense (largely) of my arguments, see Franz Hampl, 'Herodot, ein kritischer Forschungsbericht nach methodischen Gesichtspunkten', *Grazer Beiträge*, 4 (1975), pp. 97–136; repr. with addendum in: *Geschichte als kritische Wissenschaft. iii: Probleme der römischen Geschichte und antiken Historiographie sowie ein grundsätzlicher Rückblick*, ed. Ingomar Weiler, (Darmstadt, 1979), pp. 221–66. For a summary and discussion in English: Carolyn Dewald & John Marincola, 'A Selective Introduction to Herodotean Studies', *Arethusa*, 20 (1987), 9–40, especially pp. 27–32.

We should admit, then, that the use of literary devices which seem to us inadmissible in scholarly literature cannot be excluded a priori. Yet even if this is granted, we are not yet out of the dilemma; in a way, we are still caught in the same net. For we then have to answer the question: Does Herodotus want the reader to understand that his source-citations (and many other elements of his narrative besides) are fictive? Or does he want his fictions to go unnoticed? Again both sides of this dilemma seem to lead to unpleasant consequences. There are, of course, many possible reasons why an author should say one thing and wants the reader to understand another, mainly irony. But that is out of the question here. There are neither the signals for the reader which make the intention clear, nor is there anything like the special message irony must carry, if it is to make any sense. On the other side, it should be noted that the way Herodotus goes about his fictions is not the best method to conceal lies. We need only remember that it is Herodotus' methodical procedure which makes it possible to uncover his fictions. For the proof basically consists in pointing out that the picture Herodotus presents is time and again too good to be true. Had he been more erratic in his procedures, it would be much more difficult to find him out. I am sure Herodotus would have avoided this mistake, if his intention was to deceive his reader as best he could.

Is there a third way here, also? I think there is. I believe that Herodotus was not so much concerned whether he would be found out or not; he was rather concerned with what he would think of as the correctness of his methods. This will seem an enigmatic statement at first sight. Let me explain what I mean. Nobody will deny that Herodotus' work contains elements of science. But neither would anybody deny that it is also, and perhaps primarily, a work of art. It follows that Herodotus' methods could only partially be methods of science; they were, and had to be, also methods of art. But here we must be very careful to understand what 'art' should mean in this connection. Our usual view is to see science and art in conflict: science is for truth, and art for entertainment, fancy, fiction, and better selling of a book. The element of art thus appears as a concession of science, grudgingly admitted. I do not think that this would be Herodotus' view of the matter. His formula would rather be: science for truth, and art for verisimilitude. And here is the point where the above-mentioned commonplace should come in: We must understand Herodotus from the background of his situation, in his time. Herodotus knew that truth was not attainable for him in most parts of his enterprise; indeed he probably knew his limits better than many a contemporary student of ancient history does.[9] The rules of the source-citations which I discussed are rules of verisimilitude, and when I say that Herodotus was concerned with the correctness of his methods, I mean that he followed them conscientiously, even meticulously. A striking example is found in the passage, mentioned above, where Herodotus makes the native Egyptians show him the different nature of Persian and Egyptian skulls (iii. 12). Herodotus makes the

---

[9] Illusions in modern scholarly papers on the limits of possible knowledge are usually signalled by the phrase: 'We must proceed here with great caution' or something to the same effect. Invariably what follows is a reckless hypothesis mitigated only by an exceptionally generous measure of probablies, perhapses etc.

Egyptians explain that Egyptian skulls are hard because the Egyptians shave their heads and expose them to the hardening influence of the sun. It is clear that this explanation is only complete if a corresponding reason for the Persians is adduced. And sure enough this follows: the reason given is that they wear feltcaps and do not permit the sun to burn their skulls. But here two interesting observations can be made: (1) Herodotus avoids making the natives give the second, Persian part of the explanation; instead, he gives it in his own name. And (2) he very obviously avoids drawing the reader's attention to this change; on the contrary, he deliberately conceals it. He begins by saying: 'The natives said that the Egyptians, on one hand, ...', and the first part of the explanation follows, the expression 'on one hand' (Greek *mén*) making us expect that the second part will follow. But before that there is an intervening sentence. After this Herodotus recapitulates, quietly dropping the form of indirect speech: 'This, then, is the cause for the hardness of the Egyptians' skulls', and then he adds the other half in the same, independent form. Obviously, his rules of verisimilitude absolutely forbade him to make Egyptians pronounce any opinion on a foreign affair as Persian skulls: they do not know about the Persians' feltcaps. But he prefers the reader not to notice this artificial arrangement.

We can go even further. Verisimilitude and truth are not contrasts. Verisimilitude can often be thought to give an even better (because simpler and clearer) picture of deeper truths than is furnished by reality, where the fundamentals can be obscured and complicated by any amount of irrelevant detail. I therefore think that Herodotus' fictions contain a didactic element. They are meant to teach the reader lessons about typical human attitudes in transmitting information. They can, for instance, show how error and misinformation arise. A striking example of this is the following: according to the Scythians, Herodotus tells us, the far North is impenetrable, because earth and air are full of feathers (iv. 7). Several pages later he comes back to this and says that he thinks the Scythians really mean the snow (iv. 31). In v. 10 there is a similar story: the Thracians say that stinging bees make the country beyond the Danube uninhabitable. The two stories are obviously twins; Herodotus' explanation for the one (doubtless correct) is equally valid for the other. Stories and explanation are attuned to each other, and the whole is clearly contrived. It is probably not accidental that Herodotus gives the explanation only in one of the two cases and separates it there from the first mention of the story. The reader is supposed to decode the distorted message himself, but for safety Herodotus helps in one of the two cases.[10]

A last point I touch only very briefly, although it is perhaps more fundamental than any other. There is a rule, so strict that it can almost be called a law, that those who tell stories in which fact and fiction are mixed never must admit their own part in the creation of them. They must avoid any discussion with their audience about their sources, and the usual way to preclude such discussion is to give a simple and global answer which renders any further questioning useless. The Muses of the rhapsodes belong in this category, and so does the usual old

---

[10] Compare also the frequent juxtaposition of a mythical version of a story with its rationalization (as in the case of Dodona, mentioned above) See pp. 109–12 of the author's book (op. cit. n. 1).

grandmother of the teller of fairy-tales (although in this case it is not a matter of fact versus fiction but of adherence to tradition versus invention). I call this phenomenon 'mythical authorship'. The difference with Herodotus is that his global answer ('what I am telling I always know from those in whose country the thing happened') is never mentioned in so many words but is, so to speak, particularized and adapted to the individual case.[11]

Coming now to the second part of this paper, we may begin by stating that it is also part of Herodotus' art of verisimilitude that he does not claim to have any direct information from beyond the limits of the known world (in other words, he has not visited those parts), and that anything he says is based on hearsay. The negative part of this claim obviously has not only verisimilitude, but is also true; this, however, must not induce us to take the positive part also at face value. When Herodotus says that he travelled in Egypt as far as Elephantine, and adds that everything he can say about the parts beyond is known from hearsay, one gains the impression that that information was collected by him in Elephantine. There is a somewhat similar passage where the route by which such 'hearsay' travelled is specified. A point of geography which is very important for Herodotus (I shall come back to it) is relayed by three intermediate sources and reaches the known world in Cyrene; again our impression is that Herodotus collected the information in that place (iii. 32. 1–3). He speaks similarly about the North: the Scythians have contact with the remote Bald Men, a fairy-tale tribe, but this contact is mediated by seven interpreters and seven languages (iv. 24). Once more, the natural conclusion is that Herodotus heard about the Bald Men from the Scythians or even from Greeks in the Greek towns on the Black Sea coast.[12] But if we take all this seriously, we once more make the mistake of expecting truth where we are given verisimilitude. The actual sources are quite different. On one hand Herodotus had an inheritance of notions which came in part from earlier Greek literature, and in part (at least ultimately) from Near Eastern literary sources.[13] On the other hand, in that age of general progress in which Herodotus lived, new information poured in incessantly and widened the Greeks' horizon. As a third element, however, Herodotus' own imagination always plays an important part. It works on closing gaps but also on adapting earlier notions to the author's own taste and naturally had a freer hand than elsewhere in those passages where he speaks of remote regions about which genuine knowledge was unattainable anyway. I must mention here one factor which scholars have always tended to

---

[11] For my view on 'mythical authorship', see also *Die ursprüngliche Geschichte vom Fall Trojas*, Innsbrucker Beiträge zur Kulturwissenschaft, Sonderheft 75 (Innsbruck, 1991), pp. 83–5.

[12] For a complete collection of similar passages see pp. 96–104 (= § 2.6.2) of my book (op. cit. n. 1). My statement on p. 100 that except for 4.24 interpreters are never mentioned in Herodotus is erroneous.

[13] I cannot repeat here the reasons why I do not reckon with stable oral traditions; they are laid out in other publications of mine, mainly my monograph *Amor und Psyche ... Eine Kritik der romantischen Märchentheorie*, Abh. d. Mainzer Akademie (Mainz, 1977). Of course, Herodotus' immediate sources for literary traditions can always have been oral. Oral sources in general are by their very nature ephemeral, and as a rule nothing reliable can be established about them. There is a large sphere where they cannot, on principle, be distinguished from Herodotus' own contribution.

overlook (treated by me elsewhere in some detail). Since Herodotus knew well that things which were said in existing books were also purely conjectural, he was not bound to repeat his sources faithfully; he could always replace one conjecture by another or vary it. And he had to, since books were still few and nobody saw any use in the repetition of things that had been mentioned by others.[14]

And now I shall discuss some of the individual notions on remote countries we find in Herodotus.[15] Already the Babylonians had made the world circular and put themselves in the centre of it. We know this, if not from other sources, from a famous clay tablet not very much older than Herodotus, which shows Babylonia and adjacent countries (only very few details are given) surrounded by a circular stream, and, in a symmetrical arrangement, purely mythic regions beyond. The circularity of the world could not have been suggested to them by any special features of Mesopotamian geography. But it is always the most natural assumption for people to imagine themselves as living in the centre of a circle. You know you can move away from your home in any direction, and there is no reason to think that the end of the world is nearer on one side than on any other. Of course, the assumption is also flattering. It confirms that your group is the most normal and typical or even the best type of the human race. In a similar way, man will think of his environment as the most normal part of the world; the mere fact that he is familiar with it makes it appear so. This holds even for dangers. Lions and snakes look very different for those for whom they are part of their everyday life. They know how to deal with them, and at the worst they are looked upon as one of the plagues which the gods have inflicted on mankind. If they learn that there are countries free of them, their absence there will be considered a feature of paradise. With this, I have come to the other half of the picture: the world beyond the horizon (a circular notion again) is believed to be full of unknown dangers, of all sorts of abnormal people and things, and, as I said, of wondrous blessings also.

The Greeks took the circular picture of the world with a surrounding river from the Babylonians, by and by replacing the river by the oceans (the details of this process are not clear), and, of course, they placed themselves in the centre. Basically, this is what we find in Herodotus, although there is a famous passage (iv.36) where he expresses dissent with those who make maps which show the ocean-river 'as if drawn with a pair of compasses'. From Hecataeus, who had written on geography, perhaps two generations before, Herodotus seems to have taken the division of the whole circle into four equal sectors, each separated from its neighbours by a body of water: the Nile in the south, the Danube (believed to run due south in the last part of its course) in the north, the straits of Gibraltar in the west, and in the east a small stream named Phasis (from which the name of the pheasant is derived, as coming from *Phasiané* or the Phasis-valley), in the eastern recess of the Black Sea, or modern Georgia. The choice of the insignificant

---

[14] See pp. 176–8 (= § 3.2) of the author's book (op. cit. n. 1). It is a very general phenomenon that later authors do not copy earlier ones but vary them. The most frequent mistake of classical *Quellenforschung* is the assumption that x cannot be the source of y, if y differs from x.

[15] For a recent survey of Greek notions on the margins of the world see James S. Romm, *The Edges of the Earth in Ancient Thought. Geography, Exploration, and Fiction* (Princeton N.J., 1992).

Phasis is probably determined by its role in the lost epic about the Argonauts, a literary creation which in its turn was closely connected with the beginnings of Greek seafaring in the Black Sea some two or three centuries before Herodotus. A special feature which goes together with the circularity of the world in Herodotus is the notion that many things were similar in different directions of the wind-rose; the west is often excepted, because Herodotus has generally little to say about it. Thus since in North Africa the known world is clearly bounded by deserts, those deserts that can be found in the East are believed to fulfill the same function, and in the North deserts are hallucinated. Then there is the belief that much gold exists in the same three directions. In the North it is guarded by griffins (iv. 27), in the East by ants of prodigious size, and it is collected there with great danger by the Indians (iii. 105; cf. iii. 101–2: one of the miraculous ants is kept in the Persian king's palace). Surely one of these stories is modelled after the other. As to the South, however, it is merely said that the peaceful Ethiopians have gold in such abundance as to think it proper to make chains from it for their prisoners.

There is also a special relationship in symmetry and contrast between the North and the South. I mentioned the supposed southward course of the Danube, which has obviously to do with the fact that its counterpart the Nile runs northward. But since there was not getting round the fact that further upstream the Danube runs eastward, Herodotus expects the same of the Nile. It is this expectation which is confirmed by the news mentioned above which got to Cyrene through three intermediate sources: far in the south of Libya there is a river with crocodiles. Of course, there are such rivers south of the Sahara. Yet I think there can be little doubt that the story is simply made up. Herodotus also believes that crocodiles are found in the river Indus in the East.

Homer had said that the Ethiopians, that is, the black race, are twofold, one half living in the East, and the other in the West. This erroneous notion, of course, originated from the view (half correct) that black people are black because they are burnt by the sun, and the expectation (wildly wrong) that the regions which are nearest to either the rising or the setting sun must be the ones most exposed to its rays. Herodotus has the Ethiopians in the south where they belong, but he thinks that the Indians are also black (iii. 101); even their semen is black.

And here I have to mention one of the funniest passages in the work. Herodotus seems to assume that in early times there was also some traffic along the borders of the world (perhaps there is here some influence of Argonaut epic again). Thus, for instance, he imagines (v. 9) that a certain tribe beyond the Danube, named the Sigynnai (the only tribe in those parts he has anything to say about), wear Median dress and say they originated from the Medes (the Medes, it is true, are still within the known world but near its borderline). In the passage I want to introduce here (ii. 103–5), it is said that the Colchians, who live by the river Phasis, share many characteristics with the Egyptians. Among other things, they are black—as Herodotus imagines the Egyptians to be—and they practice circumcision. There is clearly not the least basis of fact for all this; the whole idea is developed merely on the basis of the special role that the Nile and the Phasis play in Herodotus' picture of the world. What is particularly interesting here is the immense show of inquiry and confirmation Herodotus displays, which made this passage one of the strongest proofs for me when I contended that Herodotus' source-citations are fictive. At first, Herodotus says, he noticed himself that the Colchians must be Egyptians. Then he asked both, and it appeared that the Colchians had originated, many centuries ago, from a small detached body of troops of the Pharaoh Sesostris, who had been a great conqueror and had campaigned in the most distant countries. Here comes an especially nice touch of verisimilitude. Although Herodotus says that both peoples confirmed his impression, he adds that the Colchians remembered their Egyptian origin better than the Egyptians remembered their relation with the Colchians. This makes obvious sense, because it seems natural that the Colchians would remember the origin of their nation, while the Egyptians had less reason to remember the loss and the whereabouts of a small detachment of their army. (Strictly speaking, they had no reason at all, but Herodotus does not want to forego their confirming voice.) Since, of course, there is not the slightest bit of history behind the whole story, those scholars who still believe in the authenticity of Herodotus' source-citations are especially hard put to explain, how by mere accident such a beautiful touch of verisimilitude arose.[16] Herodotus goes on to explain his argument on circumcision. It is true, he says, that there are five other peoples who practice it, but two of them, the Jews among them, say they have learnt it from the Egyptians (of course, no Jew ever said such a thing!), and two had it from the Colchians. This leaves the Ethiopians, and here Herodotus says he cannot tell whether they learnt it from the Egyptians or the Egyptians from them. This is verisimilitude again: the Ethiopians are a mysterious people far beyond the limits of the known world. Access to them is always indirect. When the Persians wanted to get into contact with them, they had to use intermediaries; they sent a party of Fish-Eaters, a tribe, itself probably mythic, living around Elephantine (iii. 19). And when the Persian king leads an army against them, they suffer from hunger, before they have covered a fifth of the distance, and never reach their destination (iii. 25).

Peoples living beyond the limits of the known world are believed to have two special characteristics: they are more numerous than others, and many of them are peaceful and 'just'. The Indians are the most numerous people in the world, followed by the Thracians (iii. 94; v. 3). If the Thracians were to unite themselves under one king, they would be stronger than any other people; fortunately they do not. Tacitus transferred this idea to the Germanic peoples, and from him the nineteenth century took the topos of the 'unselige deutsche Zwietracht' (ill-fated German discord) and the strength of a united Germany. The Scythians are, according to some, very numerous; others say they are few, if only true Scythians are counted (iii. 81; the meaning is that the true Scythians are not peripheral). Finally, the Ethiopian king says to the Persian envoys that the Persians ought to be glad that the Ethiopians are not inclined to embark on conquests (iii. 21). The topos has a long later history, and some notions which are familiar from modern times derive from it, e.g. concern about the immense numbers of Russians and the danger this could mean for their western neighbours. Testimony earlier than Herodotus seems to be lacking; in Greek literature, at least, there is nothing. The

---

[16] Nobody has tried as yet, at least in print.

simple geometrical fact that the area of a circle grows with the square of the radius may have, to some extent, provided a psychological basis.

The other topos I mentioned, the friendly character of peripheral peoples, does have older precursors. Homer knows the Abioi, who are the justest of all mankind (their name has sometimes been interpreted as 'the remote ones'). Several poets had things to tell about the Hyperboreans, a legendary tribe in the far North, which has special relations with the gods and leads a blissful life in a mild climate (there was never good reason to doubt the obvious etymology of their name: 'those beyond the north wind'). Herodotus' contribution to the topos consists mainly in his representing the Ethiopians as a peaceful race, and in the story he tells about the Hyperboreans' connection with Delos and Apollo (iv.32–6), but he throws doubt on their existence: if they exist, there should be people beyond the south wind also.[17]

There are also features which are just strange. The Ethiopians are long-lived, their life-span is 120 years (iii.23). There is a desert route which runs westward from southern Egypt and marks the southern boundary of the known world, and along this route strange peoples live: there are those who do not know individual names, those who have no ordinary language but squeak like bats, those who do not dream, and others who live in houses of salt (iv.181–5). There are also teratological features: in the far North live the Bald Men, the One-eyed, and a goat-footed tribe (iv.25ff.). Finally, there are some definitely disagreeable people: the Neuroi who turn into wolves (iv.105) and the Androphagoi or man-eaters (iv.100, but only the name is given). There is remarkably little in the way of miraculous animals. Egypt has the wonderful Phoenix (ii.73), and flying snakes, originating from Arabia, try to invade the country (ii.75, iii.107). In one place on the desert route, mentioned above, are cattle with such long horns that they are unable to move forward when grazing (iv.183). We usually have no means of knowing how these fantasies arose. In some of the examples from the North Herodotus' immediate source is Aristeas, an older poet whom he quotes; in most other cases Herodotus himself is our oldest source.

It would take too long to enumerate everything. But there is one last point that should not go unmentioned. There are some cases where a remote people (not necessarily one that is strictly outside the known world) is quoted for a custom which is unusual and perhaps shocking, but recommended by some sort of internal logic. The Trausoi mourn when a child is born, and rejoice over their dead (v.4). The origin of this notion is clear: the Greeks often express pessimistic views about life in general, so these people have drawn the necessary conclusions. Another example is the funny method ascribed to the Babylonians of marrying off their girls (i.196). They are auctioneered, the more beautiful ones to those who pay most, the ugly ones to those who demand least, and the money which comes in from the former is used to pay for the latter. Such things are just plays of fancy. The mind experiments with possibilities, and it is nicer to present them in the form

---

[17] This argument is, I think, much more reasonable than usually supposed. Herodotus does not really mean the people but the physical feature, that is, the point of origin of the wind and the region beyond this point. He surmises a symmetry of causation.

of narrative than to discuss them in theory. Plato has done a similar thing with his Atlantis. Such is Herodotus' art, and if this means that Herodotus is a liar, I for one would not give such a liar in exchange for a hundred truthful and tedious pedants.

TRAVEL DESCRIPTIONS IN THE *ARGONAUTICA* OF APOLLONIUS RHODIUS

M. A. HARDER[*]

1. INTRODUCTION

In the third century BC, the Alexandrian poet Apollonius Rhodius wrote his *Argonautica*, an epic in four books, in which he told of Jason's journey to Colchis to bring back the Golden Fleece. This journey was long and full of perils and adventures. On the outward journey the Argonauts followed the traditional route across the Aegean Sea and into the Black Sea. On the homeward journey, after securing the Golden Fleece with the assistance of the Colchian princess Medea, they took a different route to escape from the Colchians who chased after them. They went along the Ister and passed through many strange and distant places in the far West, and in North-Africa before they eventually reached their home in Iolcus again. This story, in which travel descriptions obviously play a part, is placed in the distant mythical past, before the Trojan War, and told by an external narrator long after the event. In this article I wish to investigate some aspects of the nature and importance of the travel descriptions in the *Argonautica* and the way in which they are presented to the reader.[1]

2. TRAVEL DESCRIPTIONS IN THE *ARGONAUTICA*

Generally speaking, Apollonius' travel descriptions are a bookish mixture of scientific Alexandrian geography and the fabulous geography of Homer.[2] Apollonius concentrates on description of the features of the landscape and peoples. Other items which might figure in a travel description, like towns, buildings or monuments receive little attention.[3]

---

[*] Department of Greek and Latin, University of Groningen, The Netherlands.

[1] For a detailed survey of the geography of Apollonius see E. Delage, *La géographie dans les Argonautiques d' Apollonios* (Paris, 1930). For the route through the Pontus Euxinus in general, see also A. Baschmakoff, *La Synthèse des Périples Pontiques* (Paris, 1948); I have not seen M. F. Williams, 'Landscape in the Argonautica of Apollonius Rhodius' (Diss. Univ. of Texas Austin 1989; microfilm: *DA* 50,1989,1650a–1651a). For Apollonius' narrative technique, see in general P. Händel, *Beobachtungen zur epischen Technik des Apollonios Rhodios,* Zetemata 7 (Munich, 1954); M. Fusillo, *Il tempo delle Argonautiche* (Rome, 1985). Translations of Apollonius are from R. C. Seaton, *Apollonius Rhodius. The Argonautica* (London & Cambridge, Mass., 1967), where necessary adapted to the text of H. Fraenkel, *Apollonii Rhodii. Argonautica* (Oxford, 1961).

[2] See Delage (op. cit. n. 1), *passim* and his summary on 290 ff.

[3] Towns are generally just briefly mentioned in the course of a story; see, for instance, i. 609 ff. (Lemnos); i. 965 (town of Doliones); ii. 760 (town of Lycus); iii. 210 ff. (Colchis); iv. 1068 (town and palace of Alcinous). Apart from the palace and garden of Aeëtes (iii. 215–48) other palaces are

As to the descriptions of landscape, when the Argonauts are sailing along unhindered, the landscape is usually described in conventional terms and appears only as a kind of background to the travelling, to which sometimes a few details are added. A typical example of such a passage is the first stage of the journey in i. 580–6:

> Αὐτίκα δ' ἠερίη πολυλήιος αἶα Πελασγῶν
> δύετο, Πηλιάδας δὲ παρεξήμειβον ἐρίπνας
> αἰὲν ἐπιπροθέοντες, ἔδυνε δὲ Σηπιὰς ἄκρη·
> φαίνετο δ' εἰναλίη Σκίαθος, φαίνοντο δ' ἄπωθεν
> Πειρεσιαὶ Μάγνησσά θ' ὑπεύδιος ἠπείροιο
> ἀκτὴ καὶ τύμβος Δολοπήιος. ἔνθ' ἄρα τοίγε
> ἑσπέριοι ἀνέμοιο παλιμπνοίησιν ἔκελσαν

(And straightaway the misty land of the Pelasgians, rich in cornfields, sank out of sight, and ever speeding onward, they passed the rugged sides of Pelion; and the Sepian headland sank away, and Sciathus appeared in the sea, and far off appeared Piresiae and the calm shore of Magnesia on the mainland and the tomb of Dolops; here in the evening, as the wind blew against them, they put to land ...)

Typical features of this passage, which recur in the other passages of quiet travelling,[4] are: the insistence on the speedy passing of places,[5] the steady pattern of departure and arrival and the way in which the landscape figures merely as something which is seen by the Argonauts.[6] The landscape in such passages is described by its general characteristics, which are rarely more colourful than ὑπεύδιος and εἰναλίη in the passage just quoted.[7] Sometimes a detail of geographical interest is added, like the description of the shadow of Mount Athos reaching as far as Lemnos (i. 601–4),[8] the entrance to Hades near the Acheron (ii. 727–51), or the mouth of the river Thermodon (ii. 970–84).[9] In other cases a brief mythological excursus is added, for instance, about the mouth of the river Callichorus (ii. 904–10) or about the river Parthenius (ii. 936–9). Many of these passages may be accounted for by the antiquarian or literary preoccupations of the scholar-poet.

There is a tendency to describe the landscape in detail only when it is important

---

merely mentioned, like that of Lycus (ii. 759) or given a few conventional details, like that of Hypsipyle (i. 785–9). For monuments, see, for instance, i. 585 (tomb of Dolops); ii. 911–29 (tomb of Sthenelus).

[4] See, for instance, i. 592–609; 922–35; ii. 345–407 (instructions of Phineus); 720–51; 1241–70; iv. 562–76; 1622–37; 1778–81.

[5] Indicated by verbs like παρεξέθεον (i. 592), θέοντες (i. 600); παρεμέτρεον (i. 595; 1166), παρήμειβον (i. 933), παρανεῖσθε (ii. 357), παραμειβόμενοι (ii. 382) etc.

[6] See the frequent use of verbs like ἐσέδρακον (i. 598), εἰσορόωντες (i. 1166), δερκόμενοι (ii. 725) of the Argonauts and verbs like ἀνέτειλε (i. 601), προυφαίνετ' ἰδέσθαι (i. 1113), φαίνετο (i. 1114) etc. of the landscape.

[7] See, for instance, i. 593 δυσήνεμον, 595 πόντῳ κεκλιμένην, 597 πολυκλύστους, 927 αἰπά, 932 ἠμαθόεσσαν etc.

[8] This phenomenon was often mentioned in antiquity; see F. Vian, *Apollonios de Rhodes. Argonautiques* (Paris, 1976), ad loc.

[9] See H. Fraenkel, *Noten zu den Argonautika des Apollonios* (Darmstadt, 1968), on *Argonautica*, ii. 972–84 on the artificial and literary character of the description.

in the story,[10] either because the Argonauts make a longer stop at a place, like Cyzicus or Corcyra, or when the landscape plays an active part in the story, like the Symplegades or the Syrtis. The second category is described in greater and more vivid detail than the first, as can be seen when we compare the description of Cyzicus in i. 936–40 with that of the Syrtis in iv. 1235–49. The description of Cyzicus, where the Argonauts arrive after a quiet journey (i. 922–35), can be regarded as an objective description of the geographical and topographical situation (i. 936–40):

> Ἐστι δέ τις αἰπεῖα Προποντίδος ἔνδοθι νῆσος
> τυτθὸν ἀπὸ Φρυγίης πολυληίου ἠπείροιο
> εἰς ἅλα κεκλιμένη, ὅσσον τ' ἐπιμύρεται ἰσθμός
> χέρσῳ ἔπι πρηνὴς καταειμένος· ἐν δέ οἱ ἀκταί
> ἀμφίδυμοι, κεῖται δ' ὑπὲρ ὕδατος Αἰσήποιο·

(there is a lofty island inside the Propontis, a short distance from the Phrygian mainland with its rich cornfields, sloping to the sea, where an isthmus in front of the mainland is flooded by the waves, so low does it lie. And the isthmus has double shores, and it lies beyond the river Aesepus ...)

The Syrtis, on the other hand, is reached because a storm lasting nine days sweeps the Argonauts helplessly along and is immediately described in its most frightful aspects (iv. 1235 f.):

> ... Σύρτιν, ἵν' οὐκέτι νόστος ὀπίσσω
> νηυσὶ πέλει, ὅτε τόνδε βιῷατο κόλπον ἱκέσθαι.

(Syrtis, wherefrom is no return for ships, when they are once forced into that gulf ...)

It is then explained why no return is possible: the Syrtis is an endless stretch of sand, with only a little water, impossible to navigate, where there is no drink or food or animal life (iv. 1237–44). This explanation by the narrator is followed by a description of the first reaction of the Argonauts, who see the endless, empty landscape and are filled with anxiety (iv. 1245–9). In iv. 1250–79 the Argonauts utter their despair in direct speech and repeat in their own words the earlier description of the desolation of the place. After this, we are told how they spent the rest of the day and eventually laid down to die and how Medea and the servants given to her by Arete spent the night lamenting their fate (iv. 1280–1304). Thus we see that the Syrtis, which in the *Argonautica* is one of the greatest dangers, is described on three different narrative levels, each emphasizing its gruesome aspects: (a) described by the narrator, (b) described by the narrator as it is seen through the eyes of the Argonauts, (c) described by the Argonauts in direct speech.[11]

As to the descriptions of peoples, or individuals living along the route taken by the Argonauts, the same can be said of the description of the landscape: their character and / or history are described in detail when they play an important part in the story, like the Lemnian women or the Doliones, Amycus or Phineus.[12]

---

[10] See also Delage (op. cit. n. 1), p. 282.

[11] These levels correspond to those distinguished for the *Iliad* in I. J. F. de Jong, *Narrators and Focalizers* (Amsterdam, 1987): simple narrator-text, complex narrator-text and character-text.

[12] For peoples, see, for instance, i. 609–32 (Lemnian women); 942–52 (Doliones); ii. 752–5 (Lycus and Mariandyni); iv. 891–903 (Sirenes); 991–2 (Phaeacians); 1309–11 (Libyan heroines); for

Other peoples receive less attention, although there are exceptions, where, as with the description of the landscape, antiquarian or literary preoccupations may account for the description. Notable among the exceptions in this respect are the descriptions of the habits of the Chalybes, Tibareni and Mossynoeci, which occur twice, once in the instructions of Phineus, who tells the Argonauts the route they have to follow to Colchis, and once in the travel description following it.[13] Here, ethnographical interest may explain the excursus. Another striking exception is the description of Thrinacia and the cattle of Helius (iv. 968–78), which the Argo passes uneventfully. Here an allusion to the *Odyssey* may be thought to explain the description, as there it was the eating of Helius' cattle at Thrinacia which brought the death of Odysseus' companions (*Odyssey*, xii. 260 ff.).

The distribution of the travel descriptions, and the way in which they are related to the adventures of the Argonauts, show that on the whole the descriptions of peoples and landscapes play a subordinate part in the *Argonautica*.[14] Although it is a work about a long journey into distant regions, the main points of interest in the story are the *adventures* of the Argonauts in foreign places and among foreign people. Generally speaking—and allowing for some exceptions, as discussed above—we may say that the descriptions are offered to introduce the reader to the role of certain people or landscapes as actors in the story. The emphasis on action instead of description is also apparent in the summary of the first part of the *Argonautica* in ii. 762–71. Here Jason offers Lycus a catalogue of Argonauts and tells him about their *adventures* so far, not about the sights they have seen. The way in which Lycus reacts may be thought to suggest the reactions of the ideal reader of the epic (ii. 771–95):[15] he is much pleased by the eventful story, and mourns the loss of Heracles.

There is, in the *Argonautica*, a difference between the travel descriptions in books i–ii and a large part of those in book iv. During the outward journey in books i and ii the Argonauts are still in a world of which they are more or less in control, and where they are able to solve their problems with a little help from characters like Phineus and the sons of Phrixus, and occasionally from the gods. The descriptions of the landscape are of a conventional character: it has well-known and reassuring qualities, like being wooded or sandy or steep (see note 8). If a description is a little more elaborate, like that of Cyzicus or the river Thermodon, it is still limited to geographical or topographical details presented

---

individuals ii. 1–7 (Amycus); 178–193 (Phineus); iv. 662–84 (Circe and her animals); 1638–48 (Talos).

[13] In ii. 311–407 Phineus offers his instructions to the Argonauts and describes the habits of the Chalybes (374–6), Tibareni (377–8) and Mossynoeci (379–383). Their unusual habits are again, with slightly different emphasis, described in ii. 1001–29. On this passage, see Fraenkel (op. cit. n. 9), on ii. 1001–29; R. L. Hunter, *The Argonautica of Apollonius. Literary Studies* (Cambridge 1993), 90–5.

[14] Differently Delage (op. cit. n. 1), pp. 9 ff., who states on p. 9: 'L' épopée d' Apollonios est surtout géographique.' Although he may be right in thinking that geographical interest prompted Apollonius in collecting the material for his story (but this cannot be verified), this is not reflected in the way in which the journey is presented to the reader.

[15] See Fraenkel (op. cit. n. 9), on ii. 761–72.

without any suggestion of danger or strangeness. Even the Acherusian headland, though grim, is not seen in all its grimness by the Argonauts, because the entrance to Hades is on a slope *behind* the cape, and the reader is comforted by the mention of the Megarians, who later called the mouth of the Acheron Σοωναύτης (ii. 729–48). In ii. 537–620 the Argonauts pass through the Symplegades, which are described in fearsome detail, but thanks to the instructions of Phineus, and with the help of Athena, they survive, and this makes them hopeful for the rest of the journey. Thus, one may summarize, the landscape in books i–ii is on the whole reassuring, its grim aspects not being visible to the Argonauts or being successfully overcome by—at least partly—their own efforts.

Also in their confrontation with people along the route we see that in books i–ii the Argonauts are able to help themselves, as in the Lemnian episode (i. 609–910), where Heracles urges them to leave the island and they obey his orders, or in the story of Amycus and the Bebrycians (ii. 1–163), where Polydeuces is able to defeat the king in a boxing-match, and the Argonauts subsequently defeat the people. When the Argonauts receive help, this takes the form of travel instructions, like those of Phineus (ii. 311–407) or the sons of Phrixus (ii. 1197–215), or companions they acquire on the way, like the sons of Phrixus or Dascylus (ii. 802–5). All this is on a human level and the Argonauts are the main agents in the story; divine help is kept in the background.

In these books, on the whole, the Argonauts are optimistic and hopeful about their journey, especially after sailing through the Symplegades, when Jason tests the morale of his companions and is convinced of their courage and confident that it will see them through all the perils of the journey and, besides, that as long as they follow the instructions of Phineus, they will encounter nothing as bad as the Symplegades (ii. 620–47).

In book iv, which contains the homeward journey, the beginning and end are in the same style as books i–ii, but in between, the Argonauts make an excursion into strange and dangerous regions. In a large part of book iv the Argonauts travel through regions which are presented as exotic and fabulous, reminiscent of the landscape of the travels of Odysseus. In the descriptions of the landscape much emphasis is placed on its frightening and dangerous aspects, both in the narrator-text and in the eyes of the Argonauts, whose fear is frequently described and voiced (as in the description of the Syrtis discussed above).[16] Several times the Argonauts are at the end of their resources and depend largely on divine intervention: in contrast with books i–ii there is a great deal of divine action in book iv: Argonauts are often frightened and dispirited, and gods and demi-gods help them to overcome the dangers of the journey. To illustrate this, let us compare the story of the Symplegades in ii. 537–647 with that of the Planctae, and Scylla and Charybdis in iv. 753–963. In the first, the Argonauts are eventually helped by Athena, but there is also repeated mention of their own activity, as in ii. 573 f.:

---

[16] See also, for instance, iv. 682 (wonder about Circe); 920 (anguish about Sirens); 958–60 (extreme fear of Hera on behalf of the Argonauts when they pass through the Planctae and Scylla and Charybdis).

... ἐρέται δὲ μέγ' ἴαχον. ἔβραχε δ' αὐτός
Τῖφυς ἐρεσσέμεναι κρατερῶς·

(and the rowers gave a loud cry. And Tiphys himself called to them to row with might and main)

In the second the Argonauts are carried through the dangerous place by the Nereïds, who are instructed by Thetis and Hera, and they are the object rather than the subject of the action (iv. 948–55):[17]

αἱ δ', ὥστ' ἠμαθόεντος ἐπισχεδὸν αἰγιαλοῖο
παρθενικαί, δίχα κόλπον ἐπ' ἰξύας εἰλίξασαι,
σφαίρῃ ἀθύρουσιν περιηγέι· + ἡ μὲν ἔπειτα +
ἄλλη ὑπ' ἐξ ἄλλης δέχεται καὶ ἐς ἠέρα πέμπει
ὕψι μεταχρονίην ἡ δ' οὔ ποτε πίλναται οὐδει—
ὣς αἱ νῆα θέουσαν ἀμοιβαδὶς ἄλλοθεν ἄλλη
πέμπε διηερίην ἐπὶ κύμασιν, αἰὲν ἀπωθεν
πετράων· περὶ δέ σφιν ἐρευγόμενον ζέεν ὕδωρ

(and the Nereids, even as maidens near some sandy beach roll their garments up to their waist out of their way and sport with a shapely rounded ball; then they catch it one from another and send it high into the air; and it never touches the ground; so they in turn one from another sent the ship through the air over the waves, as it sped on ever away from the rocks; and round them the water spouted and foamed)

While all this happens Hera, the helper and protectress of the Argonauts, cannot bear to watch, and throws her arms around Athena (iv. 958–60). This may also be contrasted with the cheerful scene of the departure of the Argo in i. 547–58, when the gods are watching proudly and happily.[18]

The indications about the route in book iv are far less clear than in books i–ii. On the outward journey, for example, the Argonauts are given detailed instructions by Phineus in ii. 311–407.[19] On the homeward journey, Phineus is rather vague (ii. 411–25), but Argus offers some information about the route along the Ister, based on the study of maps (iv. 253–93). After this, their information comes from (semi)divine sources, like the voice of the Argo (iv. 580–91) or Thetis, who offers instructions to Peleus (iv. 851–65).[20]

3. ASPECTS OF THE PRESENTATION OF THE STORY

In accordance with the difference in landscapes, Apollonius chooses different means to present his story of the outward and homeward journeys. In books i–ii he presents the story in such a way that one can detect the use of literary devices to make it seem part of the world known to the narrator and his readers, and therefore it seems plausible and convincing. The narrator's message seems to be

---

[17] For similar situations, see also iv. 557–61; 640–51; 1232–5.

[18] See Fraenkel (op. cit. n. 9), on i. 519–79. On iv. 958–60, see also A. Hurst, *Apollonios de Rhodes. Manière et cohérence* (Rome, 1967), 120 about the gods as: '"spectateurs interposés", porteurs d' émotions que le spectacle décrit dans les vers suivants devrait faire éprouver au lecteur.'

[19] Other passages of travel instructions in books i–ii are: i. 982–4 (Cyzicus); ii. 1197–215 (Argus). In ii. 802–5, Lycus sends his son Dascylus with the Argonauts to assure them of a friendly reception among the people they will pass. Further, see Fraenkel (op. cit. n. 9), pp. 178 ff.

[20] See also iv. 1305–79 (Libyan heroines); 1406–48 (Hesperides); 1551–85 (Triton). On these passages of travel information in general, see Fraenkel (op. cit. n. 9), pp. 178 ff.

that everything one reads can be verified. He has various means to achieve this, one of which is the extensive use of *aitia* (literally: 'stories which tell the cause or origin of something'), through which he draws attention to historical monuments or rituals dating from the passage of the Argonauts and—as it were—proving that the journey really took place and can still be verified.[21] Another means is the addition of learned details, suggesting a well-informed narrator, and the use of anonymous spokesmen, suggesting, too, a narrator who is not only well-informed, but also careful, because he offers the information, but refrains from taking responsibility for what he has from hearsay.[22]

In this article I shall discuss only the use of *aitia*, which is the most conspicuous and least traditional (when compared to the early Greek epic) of the narrative means just mentioned. These *aitia* often conclude an episode, thus emphasizing its effects in the present, but they also appear frequently in the course of a narrative section, almost casually drawing attention to the fact that traces of the the Argonauts' passage can still be observed.[23] In the course of the *Argonautica* one finds several types of *aitia*: many of them offer proof that the Argonauts have been at a certain place, because they describe the consequences of the events (names, altars or temples, tombs, rituals), others prove to the readers that the places visited by the Argonauts were as described by the narrator. A third group of *aitia* is more loosely connected with the story, and serves to confirm details not immediately connected with the route or achievements of the Argonauts, but concerning the world at large.

The first category, which one could call 'Argonautic *aitia*', is the largest, as most of the *aitia* describe the traces of Argonaut activities. These traces may be names, as in, for instance, i. 591:[24]

τὴν δ' ἀκτὴν ᾿Αφέτας ᾿Αργοῦς ἔτι κικλήσκουσιν.

(And even now men call that beach Aphetae of Argo)

or some sort of monument as in, for instance, i. 957 ff.,[25] where it is said that the Argonauts cast away their small anchor-stone and left it beneath the fountain of Artacie:

... ἕτερον δ᾿ ἕλον, ὅστις ἀρήρει,
βριθύν· ἀτὰρ κεῖνόν γε θεοπροπίαις ᾿Εκάτοιο
Νηλεῖδαι μετόπισθεν ᾿Ιάονες ἱδρύσαντο
ἱερόν, ἣ θέμις ἦεν, ᾿Ιησονίης ἐν ᾿Αθήνης.

(and they took another meet for their purpose, a heavy one; but the first, according to the oracle of the Far-Darter, the Ionians, sons of Neleus, in after days laid to be a sacred stone, as was right, in the temple of Jasonian Athena)

---

[21] On aetiology in the *Argonautica*, see, for instance T. M. Paskiewicz, 'Aitia in the second book of Apollonius' Argonautica', *Illinois Classical Studies,* 13 (1988), 57–61; M. Valverde Sanchez, *El aition en las Argonáuticas de Apolonio de Rodas* (Murcia, 1989).

[22] For some examples of this technique, see Fraenkel (op. cit. n. 9), p. 45 (n. 53).

[23] For *aitia* concluding episodes, see, for example, i. 1075 ff.; 1354 ff; ii. 718 ff.; 841 ff.; iv. 658; iv. 1727 ff.; 1770 ff. For *aitia* occurring in the course of an episode, see, for example, i. 957 ff.; i. 1019 f.; ii. 296 f.; iv. 250 ff.; 480 f.; 534 ff.

[24] See also i. 988; 1019; 1148 f.; ii. 296 f.; 686 f.; 929; iv. 658; 1153 f.; 1620; 1717.

[25] See also i. 1061 f.; 1068 f.; ii. 717 ff.; 841 ff.; iv. 250 ff.; 651 f.; 1217 ff.; 1476 f.

or a ritual as in i.1072 ff.,[26] where the Doliones are grieving for their king and queen and fasting:

> ... οὐδ' ἐπὶ δηρόν
> ἐξ ἀχέων ἔργοιο μυληφάτου ἐμνώοντο,
> ἀλλ' αὔτως ἄφλεκτα διαζώεσκον ἔδοντες.
> ἔνθεν νῦν, εὖτ' ἂν σφιν ἐτήσια χύτλα χέωνται
> Κύζικον ἐνναίοντες 'Ιάονες, ἔμπεδον αἰεί
> πανδήμοιο μύλης πελανοὺς ἐπαλετρεύουσιν.

(nor for a long time by reason of grief did they take thought for the toil of the cornmill, but they dragged on their lives eating their food as it was, untouched by fire. Here even now, when the Ionians that dwell in Cyzicus pour their yearly libations for the dead, they ever grind the meal for the sacrificial cakes at the common mill).

Sometimes an episode results in the founding of a city; thus in iv.515 ff. and iv.1210 ff. we hear how the Colchians, who have been persecuting the Argonauts in vain decide not to return to Colchis, but to found cities along the coast of the Adriatic and on and near the island of the Phaeacians.

The second category is less well represented. For example ii.746 ff.[27] about the river Acheron:

> τὸν μὲν ἐν ὀψιγόνοισι Σοωναύτην ὀνόμηναν
> Νισαῖοι Μεγαρῆες, ὅτε νάσσεσθαι ἔμελλον
> γῆν Μαριανδυνῶν· δὴ γάρ σφεας ἐξεσάωσεν
> αὐτῇσιν νήεσσι, κακῇ χρίμψαντας ἀέλλῃ.

(In after times the Megarians named it Soönautes when they were about to settle in the land of the Mariandyni; for indeed the river saved them with their ships when they were caught in a violent tempest).

i.26 ff.[28] is an example of the last category: at the beginning of the catalogue of Argonauts the narrator speaks about Orpheus:

> αὐτὰρ τόνγ' ἐνέπουσιν ἀτειρέας οὔρεσι πέτρας
> θέλξαι ἀοιδάων ἐνοπῇ ποταμῶν τε ῥέεθρα.
> φηγοὶ δ' ἀγριάδες κείνης ἔτι σήματα μολπῆς
> ἀκτῇ Θρηικίῃ Ζώνης ἔπι τηλεθόωσαι
> ἐξείης στιχόωσιν ἐπήτριμοι, ἃς ὅγ' ἐπιπρό
> θελγομένας φόρμιγγι κατήγαγε Πιερίηθεν

(Men say that he by the music of his songs charmed the stubborn rocks upon the mountains and the course of rivers. And the wild oak trees to this day, tokens of that magic strain, that grow at Zone on the Thracian shore, stand in ordered ranks close together, the same which under the charm of his lyre he led down from Pieria).

Here, in the first *aition* of the *Argonautica*, the idea that extant remains show what happened in the past is stated explicitly: the rumours of anonymous spokesmen (the subject of ἐνέπουσιν) are confirmed by visible proof (σήματα), still (ἔτι) available to the narrator.[29] One gets a picture of a narrator who, in a critical way, is putting to the test what he hears from others by comparing his own observations

---

[26] See also i.1048 f.; 1138 ff.; 1354 ff.; ii.849 f.; iv.1727 ff.; 1770 ff.
[27] See also ii.909 f.; iv.599 f.
[28] See also i.624 ff.; 1304 ff.; ii.526 f.; 713.
[29] For σήματα, see iv.554 and 1620 σήματα νηός, about songs, and material remains proving the passage of the Argo. On the *aition* as proof see also Fraenkel (op. cit. n. 9), p. 45 (n. 53).

and looking for proof in the same way that historians look for τεκμήρια.[30] In other *aitia* the idea of proof is not expressed explicitly, but in all groups of *aitia* one may observe certain fixed elements of phrasing which underline the relation between past and present:

(1) a clear indication of the narrator's presence, by an expression such as καὶ εἰσέτι νῦν,[31] or of the fact that the result of the action was permanent, by a word like ἐσαιεί.[32] A combination of these expressions is found in i. 1075 f. ἔνθεν (Fraenkel: ἔνθ' ἔτι codd.) νῦν ...|... ἔμπεδον αἰεί. Sometimes there is a foreshadowing of later events without explicit conclusions as to the present; so, for instance, i. 957 ff. (quoted above), where μετόπισθεν (strictly speaking) indicates only a date after the events of the narrative,[33] but may include the present as in i. 1061 f.[34]

> ... πεδίον Λειμώνιον, ἔνθ' ἔτι νῦν περ
> ἀγκέχυται τόδε σῆμα καὶ ὀψιγόνοισιν ἰδέσθαι.

(the meadow-plain, where even now rises the mound of his grave to be seen by men of a later day).

In other instances we find merely the present tense, as in i. 988

> ἥδε δ' Ἰησονίη πέφαται Ὁδός, ἥνπερ ἔβησαν

(and the path they trod is named the path of Jason).[35]

(2) Frequent use of a demonstrative pronoun drawing attention to the fact that it is *this* particular feature of the Argonaut story which accounts for the current state of affairs. So, for instance, iv. 534 ff.[36]

> τοὔνεκεν εἰσέτι νῦν κείνη ὅδε κεύθεται αἴη
> ἀμφὶ πόλιν Ἀγανὴν Ὑλληίδα, πολλὸν ἔνερθεν
> οὔδεος, ὥς κεν ἄφαντος ἀεὶ μερόπεσσι πέλοιτο

(Therefore even now this tripod is hidden in that land near the pleasant city of Hyllus, far beneath the earth, that it may ever be unseen by mortals).

Alternatively, or in combination with a demonstrative pronoun, the cause of the present situation may be emphasized by words like τοὔνεκεν.[37]

There was a great deal of interest in *aitia* in the Hellenistic period. Callimachus, for instance, devoted his major work, the *Aetia*, to this subject. The story of the

---

[30] On the differences between poets and historians concerning fact and fiction in ancient literary criticism see, for instance, R. Meijering, *Literary and Rhetorical Theories in Greek Scholia* (Groningen, 1987), 54 ff.; M. Puelma, 'Der Dichter und die Wahrheit in der griechischen Poetik von Homer bis Aristoteles', *Museum Helveticum*, 46 (1989), 65–100.

[31] See for (καὶ) εἰσέτι νῦν (γε or περ) i. 1354; ii. 717; 850; iv. 534; 1153; for ἔτι νῦν (περ) ii. 526; iv. 480; 599; 1770; for ἐξέτι κείνου iv. 250; for ἔτι i. 591; 1019; 1047; ii. 853; iv. 1217.

[32] See i. 1138 ἐσαιεί; ii. 605 νωλεμές; iv. 652 ἔμπεδον.

[33] See also i. 1309 μετὰ χρόνον; 1346 μέλλεν; ii. 746 ἐν ὀψιγόνοισι; iv. 1216 στείχοντος ... αἰῶνος.

[34] See also i. 1148 f. ἐνέπουσιν |... ὀπίσσω; ii. 842 σῆμα δ' ἔπεστι καὶ ὀψιγόνοισιν ἰδέσθαι.

[35] See also i. 1068; ii. 296; 910; 929; iv. 515; 658; 1476; 1729.

[36] See also for forms of ἥδε i. 988; 1019; 1062; ii. 687; 713; for forms of κεῖνος i. 958; 1149; iv. 481; 1153; 1727 f.; for an article with demonstrative connotation i. 591; ii. 297; 746; iv. 599; 651.

[37] For τοὔνεκεν, see, for instance, i. 1354; iv. 534; ἐξ οὗ ii. 909; ἐκ τοῦ ii. 929; τοῖο ἕκητι ii. 524.

Argonauts was particularly suited to this aetiological treatment as it was considered an event which left many traces; see Strabo i.2.39 (C46):

καὶ μὴν καὶ περὶ Σινώπην καὶ τὴν ταύτῃ παραλίαν καὶ τὴν Προποντίδα καὶ τὸν Ἑλλήσποντον μέχρι τῶν κατὰ τὴν Λῆμνον τόπων λέγεται πολλὰ τεκμήρια τῆς τε Ἰάσονος στρατείας καὶ τῆς Φρίξου· τῆς δ᾽ Ἰάσονος καὶ τῶν ἐπιδιωξάντων Κόλχων καὶ μέχρι τῆς Κρήτης καὶ τῆς Ἰταλίας καὶ τοῦ Ἀδρίου, ὧν ἔνια καὶ ὁ Καλλίμαχος ἐπισημαίνεται.

(... in the area of Sinope, the seacoast there, the Propontis and the Hellespont as far as the region of Lemnos one tells about many signs of the travels of Jason and Phrixus. Of the journey of Jason and the Colchians who persecuted him also as far as Crete and Italy and the Adriatic, some of which are also mentioned by Callimachus)

This idea might owe something to the large number of τεκμήρια collected by Apollonius, but it is clear from the references in the scholia on Apollonius that most of these *aitia* were also attested in authors whom Apollonius used as his sources.[38]

Like many elements in the *Argonautica*, Apollonius' use of *aitia* may also be regarded in relation to Homer, in particular his narrative technique, and to ancient views on the subject. There are no examples for Apollonius' use of *aitia* in Homer,[39] but in one passage in the *Iliad*, the narrator tells at some length what will happen after the events of his story. This is *Iliad*, xii.3 ff. about the destruction of the Greek wall after the Trojan War,[40] concluded in 34 f.

Ὣς ἄρ᾽ ἔμελλον ὄπισθε Ποσειδάων καὶ Ἀπόλλων θησέμεναι

(thus Poseidon and Apollo were to arrange it in after times)

(with words later recurring in such lines as *Argonautica*, i.1309

καὶ τὰ μὲν ὡς ἤμελλε μετὰ χρόνον ἐκτελέεσθαι

(these things were thus to be accomplished in after times).

The scholiast states that Homer had invented this wall, and that in order to prevent his fiction from being detected he added the story of its destruction; see the bT-scholion on *Iliad*, vii.445

ἀναιρῆσαι τὸ πλάσμα τοῦ τείχους σπουδάζων ὁ ποιητὴς ὥσπερ ἀπὸ μηχανῆς βοήθειαν πορίζεται εἰς τὸ μηδένα ἐπιζητεῖν ὕστερον τὰ τῶν τειχῶν ἴχνη

(the poet, eager to destroy the fiction of the wall, provides himself with help, as it were from the machine, in order that no one will afterwards try to find traces of the wall)

(see also the bT-scholion on *Iliad*, xii.3–35).[41] According to this interpretation

---

[38] For a brief survey, see P. M. Fraser, *Ptolemaic Alexandria*, i (Oxford, 1972), 627 f. (with notes).

[39] Aetiology in Homer is restricted to a few etymological explanations of names; see Valverde Sanchez (op. cit. n. 21), pp. 37 f.

[40] For a recent discussions of the passage, see De Jong (op. cit. n. 11), pp. 88 f. with further references.

[41] The scholia on the Iliad are edited by H. Erbse, *Scholia Graeca in Homeri Iliadem* (Berlin, 1969–83). For similar comments of scholia on passages in the *Odyssey*, see the scholion on *Od.*, x.3 (about the floating island of Aeolus) ἴσως τερατεύεται ἵνα μὴ ζητῶμεν πῶς κεῖται ('perhaps he talks marvels in order that we shall not try to find out how it is situated') and xiii.152 (about Poseidon's plan to bury the town of the Phaeacians) ἵνα μὴ ζητῶμεν νῦν ὅπου οἱ Φαίακες εἰσιν· φαίνεται γὰρ τὰ περὶ αὐτῶν ('in order that we shall not try to find out now where the

of Homer's technique this is the opposite of what Apollonius is doing: whereas
Homer was regarded by later critics as having tried to prevent future investigators
from looking for traces of his stories, Apollonius' narrator—at least in books
i–ii—almost invites his reader to undertake a journey in the footsteps of the
Argonauts, providing him with a series of clear markations along the route so that
he can find proof that it was no mere fiction.

In book iv the Argonauts enter a strange and dangerous world similar to that of
the travels of Odysseus in the *Odyssey*. It should be noticed first of all that
Apollonius does not make use of the first-person narrative used in the *Odyssey*
(the so-called *Apologoi*). This way of presenting a travel description may be
regarded as a means of making the story plausible and convincing. When, as in
the *Odyssey*, the first-person travel description is inserted into a narrative presented
by an external narrator this *also* has the effect of relieving the external narrator
from the responsibility for the truth of the travel description.[42] Apollonius
presents this world through narrative means which are more sophisticated than
those used in the *Odyssey*. In contrast to book i–ii, there is in book iv a conspicuous lack of attempts to prove that the story has really happened or even that it was
plausible. This seems to be underlined by Apollonius' treatment of 'Argonautic
aitia' in the passage between iv.522 and iv.1622 Two points are worth noticing:

(1) the passage is framed by comparable 'Argonautic *aitia*': the last two *aitia* in
the introductory passage before the Argonauts really embark on the more exotic
and 'Odyssean' part of their journey concern the tripod of Apollo hidden in the
land of the Hylleans (iv.522–51) and the Argonaut remains and Argoan Harbour
at Aethalia (iv.657–9). When the Argonauts arrive in the land of the Hylleans,
they seem almost certain of their safe return (iv.522), but soon after their course
is changed by Hera, according to Zeus' wish that they shall be purged of the
murder of Apsyrtus. The passage about the anger of Zeus is introduced by a
request to the Muses to explain why there are Ἀργῴης ... σήματα νηός to the
West (iv.552–6), and we hear how the Argonauts are carried back from the
Adriatic Sea to the Eridanus, almost end up miserably in the streams of Oceanus
and eventually enter the Tyrrhenian Sea after sailing through the Rhodanus. This
dangerous trip ends at Aethalia, where some traces of the Argo are described.
After Aethalia the Argonauts pass through regions known from the *Odyssey*, the
island of Circe, the Sirens, the Planctae and Scylla and Charybdis, Thrinacia with
the cattle of Helius, and eventually the island of the Phaeacians, called Drepane
(iv.990 and 1223), but identified as Corcyra by the scholion on iv.982–92. The
whole passage until the Argonauts reach the island of the Phaeacians is devoid of

---

Phaeacians live, because the story about them is mere fiction'), discussed by Meijering (op. cit. n.
30), p. 254 (n. 125).

[42] See W. Suerbaum, 'Die Ich-Erzählungen des Odysseus', *Poetica*, 2 (1968), 150–177, esp. 175:
'Die Abenteuer im Lande der Zauber-und Märchengestalten ... bilden eine Welt für sich, deren
Glaubwürdigkeit nicht so sehr vom eigentlichen Erzähler, dem Dichter, sondern von dem Ich-
Erzähler Odysseus verbürgt wird. Der Kunstgriff, den Helden selbst in der Ich-Form erzählen zu
lassen, könnte somit an sich eine Distanzierung des Er-Erzählers Homer ... von dem Stoff der
Apologoi sein; paradoxalerweise wird dadurch jedoch eher eine höhere Beglaubigung der
märchenhaften Fahrten erreicht.'

'Argonautic *aitia*'.[43] At the island, however, a Cave of Medea (iv. 1153–5) is registered and the *aition* may be thought to mark the intermezzo in the inhabited world. From Phaeacia, the Argonauts are swept in nine days to the wild regions of the Syrtis in North Africa, and it is only when they emerge from that area that we find two 'Argonautic *aitia*' again, which correspond to those at the beginning of the fabulous part of the journey, and seem to mark the return to civilization. In iv. 1547–91 the second tripod of Apollo is offered to the gods of the country and Triton in return explains how the Argonauts can find a way to leave the Tritonian Lake and reach the Mediterranean Sea again. When the Argonauts reached the sea, the point is marked by another Argoan Harbour and traces of the Argonauts' stay (iv. 1620–2). From here onwards the Argonauts are back in the world of books i–ii. Thus the exotic travels in the West and in North Africa are marked by a lack of 'Argonautic *aitia*', and framed by corresponding *aitia* in ring-composition. This means that, on the one hand, they are located in places which are related to certain markation points in the known world (instead of in the *Oceanus*), but that, on the other hand, the reader is not offered the evidence to check how much freedom the narrator allowed himself in his descriptions of this area.

(2) In several passages one is reminded of the scholiasts' interpretations of the passages of Homer mentioned above: whereas in books i–ii the reader was, as it were, invited to follow the tracks of the Argonauts through a series of *aitia*, here the treatment of *aitia* is such that this wish is frustrated:

- the mention of the *aitia* of the tripods of Apollo is, on closer scrutiny, not very useful if one wants to 'prove' the passage of the Argonauts: in iv. 534 ff. one tripod is hidden in the ground

... ὥς κεν ἄφαντος ἀεὶ μερόπεσσι πέλοιτο

(that may be ever unseen by mortals) (iv. 536),

whereas in iv. 1590 f. the other tripod disappears together with Triton:

... μετὰ δ' οὔ τις ἐσέδρακεν, οἷον ἄφαντος
αὐτῷ σὺν τρίποδι σχεδὸν ἔπλετο

(but thereafter did no one mark how he vanished so near them along with the tripod);

- as in book ii, there is a passage about two Argonauts dying in close succession, but when the Argonauts Canthus (iv. 1485–1501) and Mopsus (iv. 1502–36) die in Syrtis, there is no mention of their tombs to be seen in later days, as of the tombs of Idmon (ii. 815–50) and Tiphys (ii. 851–7), which are mentioned in ii. 853 δοιὰ γὰρ οὖν κείνων ἔτι σήματα φαίνεται ἀνδρῶν ('for still are to be seen two monuments of those heroes');

- in iv. 645–8 Hera helps the Argonauts to sail undamaged through the regions of the Celts and Ligyans by making them invisible, i.e. they pass through the area unnoticed and leave no traces.

---

[43] See also Valverde (op. cit. n. 21), pp. 250 f., who also relates the lack of *aitia* to the fantastic nature of this part of the journey.

4. CONCLUSION

In summary, one may say that in books i–ii the travels of the Argonauts are along the route of the well-known commercial *periplus*, whereas those of a large part of book iv are of an exotic and fabulous nature. In books i–ii the narrator seems to make efforts to make his travel descriptions plausible and to suggest that what he is telling is true and can be verified. The means he uses, in particular the use of *aitia*, suggest the critical attitude of a scholar who wants to be plausible and trustworthy and draws attention to the fact that this is 'literature', a story told and documented long after the event.[44] In the exotic parts of book iv, the narrator generally refrains from such efforts, but in such a way that the attentive reader is made aware of what is missing.

The means Apollonius is using, or not using, may be regarded in the light of the tradition of learned Alexandrian poetry and of the current literary criticism of the period, which to a large extent overlapped with Homeric criticism. As regards the homeward journey of the Argonauts, Apollonius combined several versions of the route they had taken[45] and for the Western part of the route relied very much on the innovations of Timaeus and Timagetus. In doing so, and at the same time giving this part of the journey an 'Odyssean' character, Apollonius seems to challenge the view represented by Eratosthenes and others, who insisted that the travels of Odysseus took place in *Oceanus* and that one should not attempt to identify them with known locations, as did also Callimachus.[46] Apollonius draws attention to this by emphasizing that the Argonauts, although travelling through the regions visited by Odysseus, did *not* enter *Oceanus*, and by marking the Western route by the 'Argonautic *aitia*' at Aethalia and Lake Triton and suggesting the identification of the island of the Phaeacians with Corcyra. At the

---

[44] See also R. Heinze, *Virgils epische Technik*, third edition (Leipzig & Berlin, 1915), 373.

[45] For details on this subject, see Delage (op. cit. n. 1), pp. 51 ff.

[46] See Apollodorus *Fragmente griechischen Historiker,* ii, ed. F. Jacoby (Berlin, 1930), 244 F 157 (apud Strabo, i. 2. 37 (C44) = Callimachus, *Fragmenta nuper reperta*, ed. R. Pfeiffer (Bonn, 1923), 13) Ἀπολλόδωρος δὲ ἐπιτιμᾷ Καλλιμάχῳ, συνηγορῶν τοῖς περὶ τὸν Ἐρατοσθένη, διότι, καίπερ γραμματικὸς ὤν, παρὰ τὴν Ὁμηρικὴν ὑπόθεσιν καὶ τὸν ἐξωκεανισμὸν τῶν τόπων, περὶ οὓς τὴν πλάνην φράζει, Γαῦδον καὶ Κόρκυραν ὀνομάζει ('Apollodorus, agreeing with Eratosthenes and his school, censures Callimachus, because, though a scholar, Callimachus names Gaudos and Corcyra as scenes of the wanderings of Odysseus, in defiance of Homer's fundamental plan, which is to transfer to Oceanus the regions in which he describes the wanderings as taking place'; tr. Horace Leonard Jones, Loeb ed.) and Eratosthenes fr.1 A 14 Berger (i.e. H. Berger, *Die geographischen Fragmente des Eratosthenes* (Leipzig 1880)) (apud Strabo, i. 2. 19 (C26)) ... ὑπολάβοι τις ἄν, φησί [sc. Eratosthenes], τὸν ποιητὴν βούλεσθαι μὲν ἐν τοῖς προσεσπερίοις τόποις τὴν πλάνην τῷ Ὀδυσσεῖ ποιεῖν, ἀποστῆναι δ' ἀπὸ τῶν ὑποκειμένων, τὰ μὲν οὐκ ἀκριβῶς πεπυσμένον, τὰ δὲ οὐδὲ προελόμενον οὕτως, ἀλλ' ἐπὶ τὸ δεινότερον καὶ τὸ τερατωδέστερον ἕκαστα ἐξάγειν ('... for he [Eratosthenes] says, one may suppose that the poet wished to place the wanderings of Odysseus in the far west, but abandoned his purpose, partly because of his lack of accurate information, and partly because he had even preferred not to be accurate but rather to develop each incident in the direction of the more awe-inspiring and the more marvellous'; tr. Horace Leonard Jones, Loeb ed.). See also Eratosthenes' famous statement that one can only hope to locate the travels of Odysseus, when one finds the maker of Aeolus' bag of winds in fr. 1 A 16 Berger (apud Strabo, i. 2. 15 (C24)).

same time he rather emphatically refrains from offering further evidence for the passage of the Argo between the 'markation points'. Thus we may detect in Apollonius' presentation of his poetic material, in particular in his travel descriptions, an ambiguity which we find also in Callimachus, who was criticized by Apollodorus because he identified Calypso's island with Gaudos, and the island of the Phaeacians with Corcyra (see note 47). In his *Aetia* and hymns, Callimachus took great care to make his tales agree with his sources,[47] but in *Hymn* i.65 ψευ-δοίμην, ἀίοντος ἅ κεν πεπίθοιεν ἀκουήν ('let me produce fiction in such a way that it would convince the ears of those who listen'), he seems to accept 'fiction', provided that it should at least be convincing.[48] Although the subject requires more detailed research than has been possible within the compass of this article, the work of both poets seems to give evidence of an ambiguous attitude towards facts and fiction. The travel descriptions in the *Argonautica* seem to be not only subordinate to the description of the adventures of the Argonauts, but also to serve a meta-poetic purpose. Through the way in which he presents them to his readers Apollonius seems to show a certain awareness of the discrepancies between facts and fiction.

---

[47] Also his famous words ἀμάρτυρον οὐδὲν ἀείδω ('I sing nothing that is not attested'; Callimachus, Fragmenta incertae sedis 612; tr. C. A. Trypanis, Loeb ed.) may be regarded as a statement against unlimited poetic licence (although lack of context should prevent us from making too much of it).

[48] In a similar vein Aristotle, *Problemata* (tr. W. S. Hett, Loeb ed.), xviii. 10 (917b, 15) remarks Διὰ τί ἡδόμεθα ἀκούοντες τὰ μήτε λίαν παλαιὰ μήτε κομιδῇ νέα; ἢ διότι τοῖς μὲν πόρρω ἀφ' ἡμῶν ἀπιστοῦμεν, ἐφ' οἷς ἀπιστοῦμεν, οὐχ ἡδόμεθα, τὰ δὲ ὥσπερ ἔτι αἰσθανόμεθα, καὶ περὶ τούτων ἀκούοντες οὐχ ἡδόμεθα ('Why do we enjoy hearing of events which are neither very old nor quite new? Is it because we disbelieve what is far away from us and we do not enjoy what we disbelieve, but the present is still within our observation and we do not enjoy hearing of it'). See on poetic fiction also Aristotle, *Poetica* (tr. W. Hamilton Fyfe, Loeb ed.), xxiii. 2 (1460b), ... ἀνάγκη μιμεῖσθαι τριῶν ὄντων τὸν ἀριθμὸν ἕν τι ἀεί, ἢ γὰρ οἷα ἦν ἢ ἔστιν, ἢ οἷα φασιν καὶ δοκεῖ, ἢ οἷα εἶναι δεῖ; ('... he must always represent one of three things—either things as they were or are; or things as they are said and seem to be; or things as they should be'). See further the literature mentioned in n. 30.

ALEXANDER THE GREAT AND ANCIENT TRAVEL STORIES

W. J. AERTS[*]

Travelling is one of the fundamental activities of man and is recorded in Greek literature as early as in the epics of Homer. When in the fourth century BC the boundaries of the known world were drastically expanded by the expeditions of Alexander the Great, a literary tradition immediately developed around his deeds and travels.[1] This tradition includes legends collected in the *Alexander Romance*, on which we will focus much of our attention. This work,[2] as we know it in its

---

[*] Department of Greek and Latin, University of Groningen, The Netherlands.

[1] On Alexander see, for instance, Peter Morris Green, *Alexander of Macedon, 356–323 BC. A Historical Biography* (second revised and enlarged edition, Harmondsworth, 1974) (with full bibliography); W. W. Tarn, *Alexander the Great II: Sources and Studies* (London, 1950); W. J. Aerts, J. M. M. Hermans & E. Visser, *Alexander the Great in the Middle Ages. Ten Studies on the Last Days of Alexander in Literary and Historical Writing. Symposium Interfacultaire Werkgroep Mediaevistiek, Groningen 12-15 October 1977* (Nijmegen, 1978).

[2] Texts and studies of the *Alexander Romance* (= AR) used for this article:

a = *Historia Alexandri Magni*, ed. W. Kroll (Berlin, 1926)

b = *Der griechische Alexanderroman, Rez. b*, ed. Leif Bergson (Stockholm etc., 1965)

c = I. *Der griechische Alexanderroman, Rezension γ. Buch I nach der Handschrift R herausgegeben*, Beiträge zur klassischen Philologie, 4, ed. U. von Lauenstein (Meisenheim am Glan, 1962)
II. *Der griechische Alexanderroman, Rezension γ. Buch II nach der Handschrift R herausgegeben*, Beiträge zur klassischen Philologie, 12, ed. H. Engelmann (Meisenheim am Glan, 1963)
III. *Der griechische Alexanderroman, Rezension γ. Buch III nach der Handschrift R herausgegeben*, Beiträge zur klassischen Philologie, 33, ed. F. Parthe (Meisenheim am Glan, 1969)

e = *Vita Alexandri Regis Macedonum*, Bibliotheca scriptorum Graecorum et Romanorum Teubneriana, ed. J. Trumpf (Stuttgart, 1974)

l = *Leben und Taten Alexanders von Makedonien: Der griechische Alexanderroman nach der Handschrift L*, Texte zur Forschung, 13, ed. & tr. H. van Thiel, sec. ed. (Darmstadt, 1983)

Byz. = *Das byzantinische Alexandergedicht, nach dem codex Marcianus 408*, Beiträge zur klassischen Philologie, 13, ed. Siegfried Reichmann (Meisenheim am Glan, 1963)

Pseudo-Callisthenes, ed. C. Müller (Paris, 1846)

W. Walther Boer, *Epistola Alexandri ad Aristotelem ad codicum fidem edita et commentario critico instructa*, Beiträge zur klassischen Philologie, 50 (The Hague, 1953)

Kleine Texte zum Alexanderroman: Commonitorium Palladii, Briefwechsel zwischen Alexander und Dindimus, Brief Alexanders über die Wunder Indiens / nach der Bamberger Handschrift, Sammlung vulgärlateinischer Texte, 4, ed. Fr. Pfister (Heidelberg, 1910)

FGH = *Fragmente der griechischen Historiker*, ed. F. Jacoby (Berlin 1927): *iiB 1: Theopompos und die Alexanderhistoriker*, iiiC §688 on Ctesias.

U. Moennig, *Die spätbyzantinische Rezension *ζ des Alexanderromans* (Cologne, 1992)

oldest form (*a*), is generally dated around 300 AD, but much of it is earlier, for instance, the story that Alexander was the son of the last Pharaoh Nectanebo and Olympias. This story can only have had relevance for the period in which the Ptolemies set up and consolidated their power in Egypt, and was probably meant as propaganda to create a link between the Ptolemaic dynasty and the Pharaohs. It will be clear, however, that most of the reports on Alexander's expedition and the countries conquered come from the first generation of historians after Alexander.[3]

In the first part of this article, I will demonstrate with a number of passages that apart from the destruction of Persian power, the exploration of the unknown world was an important goal of Alexander's expedition. This desire to explore became also a characteristic feature of literature which developed around the theme of Alexander's travels. Some examples of this can be found in the two following sections. The second part of the article will give examples of how the authors of stories about Alexander borrowed from a long literary tradition. The third part deals with a number of stories that appear in the *Alexander Romance* which must already have been in circulation, perhaps in a '*proto-Alexander Romance*' form. It is clear from Lucian's *Verae Historiae* (*c*. 120– *c*. 180 AD)[4] that the author was acquainted with sources also used by the anonymous author(s) of the Romance.

1. There can be no doubt that Alexander's campaign against Persia served in the first place a military purpose. His actions in Greece were designed to prevent an attack from the rear. And even if his aim was only the liberation of Greek cities in Asia Minor, he must soon have realized that this could only be achieved by a direct attack on the enemy.[5] According to Plutarch and also the author of the anonymous text of the *Alexander Romance*[6], Persian envoys were sent by Darius to Philip to claim tribute. Since the Macedonian king was on campaign, they were received by his son Alexander, who, according to Plutarch,[7] made inquiries not only about distances and important centres in the Persian empire, but also about

---

The transmission of the texts of the *Alexander Romance* is complex. In short, *b* dates from late Antiquity or the early Byzantine period; *c* is a contamination of *b* and *e* dating from the middle Byzantine period, and the Byzantine Alexander Poem from the thirteenth century, whereas *l* has the most ample text from the late Byzantine period. See also below in the text of this article. For a discussion of the sources, see R. Merkelbach & J. Trumpf, *Die Quellen des griechischen Alexanderromans*, Zetemata, 9 (revised sec. ed., Munich, 1977).

[3] *The Alexander Romance*, Penguin Classics, tr. & introd. Richard Stoneman (Harmondsworth, 1991), Introduction.

[4] On Lucian see, for instance, Graham Anderson, *Lucian. Theme and Variation in the Second Sophistic*, Mnemosyne, Suppl., 41 (Leiden, 1976), and Id., *Studies in Lucian's Comic Fiction*, Mnemosyne, Suppl., 43 (Leiden, 1976).

[5] On Greek-Persian relations, and the motives for a Greek attack on Persia in the early fourth century BC, see A. R. Burn, *Alexander the Great and the Middle East* (revised third edition, Harmondsworth, 1973), pp. 31–9: 'The Men and the Hour' (Greece and Persia, 401–340). Protection of the Greek area's in Asia Minor served as a starting-point.

[6] Plutarchus, *Alexander*, v. 1–3; *AR*, i. 23, 2–5 (*a*); the portrait motive in *ibid*. 8 (*b*, *l*).

[7] For the conception of this story in the *Alexander Romance*, see p. 37.

the power of the Persian king and his customs. As a result the envoys had the impression that Alexander might become a more dangerous adversary than his father, and therefore they had his portrait made for their own king. It is unlikely that the envoys gave answers containing military information, but perhaps Alexander—as Aristotle may have taught him—phrased his questions as a prospective 'tourist' would have done, asking them about mountains, fauna, tribes, climates, and satraps, so as to learn indirectly what he wanted to know.

That Alexander had an ardent wish to explore unknown parts of the world appears from the organization of his staff. It consisted not only of military advisers but also of geographers, botanists, zoologists, mathematicians, astronomers and architects, and, of course, a 'propaganda section' for writing down his *faits et gestes* under the directorship of the historian Callisthenes, Aristotle's nephew.

The same Callisthenes accompanied Alexander on his visit to the oracle of Ammon in the Siwah oasis. Alexander's motive for this journey was certainly not of military, but rather of a more personal character. One possible reason was given by Callisthenes (fr. 14 = *FGH*, iiB, p. 645): a pilgrimage in the footsteps of his forefathers Heracles and Perseus. Another might have been Alexander's wish to consult also this famous oracle after he had visited Delphi and other cult places. According to Callisthenes, Alexander was addressed as 'Son of Zeus', a detail which fits with the later Ptolemaic propaganda: the oracle had only to hail Alexander as Ammon's son and he could be ranged into the Egyptian tradition and put on a par with a former *cosmocrator*, Sesonchosis.[8]

Interesting also is the story that after many hardships during the march through the hills of Bajaur and Swat on his way to the river Indus (after his defeat of the formidable Porus, king of the Paurava), his soldiers refused to go on with the expedition from the Indus towards the Ganges or even further.[9] The general was deeply shocked by the mutiny of his Macedonian troops, who ascribed their survival to the good fortune of their general, but thought that further risks could only bring a catastrophe. For many days Alexander sat sulking in his tent, until he reluctantly retreated to Babylon—a terrible march through the Makran (or Gedrosian) desert,[10] causing the loss of two thirds of his troops. The reason why he wanted to make new conquests in India can hardly have been the consolidation of the lands already conquered—further conquests would have brought no end to this need to consolidate!—, but it must have been his yearning to visit countries behind the horizon, or, to quote Peter Green: 'His main impulse, however, seems to have been sheer curiosity, a pathos for the unknown, coupled with his determination to achieve world-dominion in the fullest sense. When he stood by

---

[8] Sesonchosis 'cosmocrator' is mentioned in *AR*, i. 33. 6 (*a*). On the visit to the oracle of Ammon in the Siwah oasis, see Tarn (op. cit. n. 1), pp. 347–59.

[9] For this dramatic event, see Peter Green (op. cit. n. 1), pp. 409–10.

[10] It is said that one of Alexander's reasons for taking this route was that it had previously been chosen by Queen Semiramis and the Persian King Cyrus I. From Semiramis' army only twenty people survived, of Cyrus's not more than seven! Arrian, *Anabasis*, vi. 24. 2-6 = Nearchos, *FGH*, iiB c (§133), p. 707, 21 ff. The same story is in Strabo, xv. 1. 5.

the furthest shore of Ocean, that ambition would be fulfilled.'[11]

Something similar is suggested in a *Letter of Aristotle to Alexander* (*AR*, iii.26 (127.27 (*a*)), where Aristotle states that Alexander has proved to be the best general, possessing the judgement of Nestor and the valour of Odysseus, who πολλῶν ἀνθρώπων ἴδεν ἄστεα καὶ νόον ἔγνω ('saw the cities of many peoples and learnt their ways.')[12]

2. Traditionally Alexander is said to have borrowed his strategic insights from Homer's *Iliad*, which he kept with a dagger under his pillow at night. But it is probable that he was acquainted with a range of authors such as Herodotus, Thucydides, Ctesias of Cnidus[13] (early part fourth century BC) and Xenophon, experienced in warfare on Persian territory. But it must soon have become clear that reality was often different from what Aristotle had taught and what he had read in other Greek authors. He crossed plain after plain in a firm belief that finally, as Xenophon had described in his *Anabasis*, the sea would appear before his eyes. But the idea that fabulous plants and beasts such as the 'Dogheads' and 'Breasteyes' were behind the horizon gradually moved up as the horizon yielded. And since the Macedonian conqueror never reached the Ocean in the East, it remained possible for historians and story tellers to seek inspiration in traditional lore. Examples of new literary inventions are Alexander's adventures in the diving-bell and the griffin-balloon.[14] Others, such as the story about Alexander's march into the realm of darkness with the prophetic trees of the Sun and the Moon, are based on myths of heroes descending into the underworld in order to learn the future (Odysseus), to bring a loved one back to life (Hermes for Demeter's daughter; Orpheus), or to fight against death himself or his dog (Heracles).

There are other proofs that stories about Alexander were influenced by literary tradition. As to the story of Alexander and the Amazons,[15] it is not surprising that the operations in the Kabul region brought to mind Herodotus's episode on the Amazons (iv.110, 1 ff.).[16] Reports of historians such as Clitarch, Plutarch and Arrian on an affair between the Queen of the Amazons and Alexander were inspired by a myth told by Herodotus (iv.8 and 9) that the Scythians were

---

[11] Peter Green (op. cit. n. 1), p. 380.

[12] Homer, *The Odyssey*, Penguin Classics, tr. E. V. Rieu (Harmondsworth, 1946).

[13] This author on Persian matters and the first writer of a separate work on India, invented the 'Cynocephali people', the 'Dogheads', who held their place in descriptions of the world at least until the time of Marco Polo (see below).

[14] The descent in the diving-bell is told in *AR*, ii.38 (*b, c, l, Byz.* etc). On Alexander's flight, see V. M. Schmidt, *De luchtvaart van Alexander de Grote in de verbeelding der Middeleeuwen* (Groningen, 1988), with a detailed bibliography on the subject. See also I. Michael, *Alexander's Flying Machine: the History of a Legend. An inaugural Lecture Delivered at the University of Southampton, 29th January 1974* (Southampton, 1974).

[15] *AR*, iii.25.2 ff.; Diodorus, xvii.77.1 ff; Curtius, vi.5.24 ff; Justin, xii.3.5 ff.

[16] This was either the region next to the Caucasus or next to the Caspian Gates. See Michael Grant, *Ancient History Atlas, 1700 BC to AD 565* (third edition, London, 1986), 38.

descendants of Heracles and a local female chthonic deity.[17] In the *Alexander Romance*, we find that Alexander even started a correspondence with the Amazons. These Amazons lived on an island, and were only visited once a year—probably during the horse sacrifice festival—by their men on the mainland.[18] These habits form the counterpart of those of the Brahmans, described in the *Booklet of Palladius on the peoples of India and the Brahmans*.[19]

It is worth mentioning that the events of these stories follow Alexander's main conquests. At the same time they present lessons in modesty or herald his death. Lessons in modesty were already an important feature of Herodotus. His story of the confrontation of the Persian king Cyrus and Tomyris, the queen of the Massagetes [i. 204 ff], formed the inspiration for the famous Candace story in the *Alexander Romance*. According to Herodotus, Cyrus propagated 'the legend of his superhuman origin and the success [εὐτυχίη = *fortuna*] of all his previous campaigns'[20]; but despite his cunning in capturing Tomyris's son (who soon afterwards committed suicide), Cyrus was rapidly defeated, and died. In the *Alexander Romance*, Alexander himself is cunningly captured by Queen Candace, who knowing that Alexander often played his own envoy in disguise, recognized him by means of a portrait she had made of him earlier. In this case Alexander's life is saved because he had helped one of Candace's sons to get his wife back.

Finally, Herodotus's influence can be detected in the descriptions of marvellous flora and fauna in the different versions of the *Alexander Romance*; they are either in the form of letters to Aristotle and Olympias, or occur in the story itself.[21]

---

[17] On a possible historical starting point of the Amazon episode, see Tarn (op. cit. n. 1), 326ff. See also E. Mederer, *Die Alexanderlegenden bei den ältesten Alexanderhistorikern*, Würzburger Studien zur Altertumswissenschaft, 8 (Stuttgart, 1936), 84–93.

[18] See *AR*, iii. 25. 7 (*a*). Though there is a lacuna in the text between the passage on the festival and on the 'man-hunting' of the Amazons, it is probable that both are connected. The Armenian version adds explicitly that during the festival, the women cross over to the men and remain with them for 30 days. The words ἐπὶ ἡμέρας λ′ in the Greek text are perhaps a reminiscence of this custom. Stoneman (op. cit. n. 3) translates 'the festival lasts six days' without any explanation of the origin of this figure. In the case of the Brahmans visiting their wives in the 'coldest' months, July and August, the limit of their stay is 40 days, which should probably be interpreted as the period necessary to establish pregnancy.

[19] *Pseudo-Callisthenes* (op. cit. n. 2), iii. 9; cf. *Byz.*, 4810 ff.

[20] Herodotus, *The Histories*, Penguin Classics, tr. Aubrey de Sélincourt (Harmondsworth 1954), 96.

[21] Merkelbach & Trumpf (op. cit. n. 2), pp. 66–7 see 'soldiers' folklore' in the stories of the fights with the half-men-half-beasts. This explanation is not sufficient for creatures such as the Cynocephali, whose history can be traced back to earlier Greek authors, and followed through the Middle Ages. The 'Dogheads' mentioned by Herodotus (iv. 191) were animals (probably a species of monkeys), not men. Moreover Herodotus only reproduces a piece of information given him by the Lybians. Ctesias (*FGH*, §588, iiic, pp. 501–2) thinks of them as a people numbering 120.000, living in India (R. Shafer, 'Unmasking Ktesias' Dogheaded People', *Historia*, xiii (1964), 499–503 argues that Ctesias misunderstood some Persian interpretation of an old version of the Mahabharata). Medieval literature offers many examples: Johannes de Plano Carpini (first half of the thirteenth century), for instance, places them in Siberia beyond the Samojedes, Marco Polo near Sumatra. Apparently, they formed a traditional element in descriptions of the world without which these

3. Such legends as they appear later in the *Alexander Romance* have apparently acted as a catalyst to set off grotesque histories such as those written by Lucian. This author mentions as 'sources' for his jokes Homer, Herodotus, Ctesias, but his parody applies in the first place to the genre of the romance. Lucian pokes fun at the Alexander's fantastic adventures, especially in his *True Histories*. A number of examples will show the relation between the *Alexander Romance* and Lucian.

In the *Verae historiae* (i.5), the narrator explains the reason for his journey, which fits exactly Alexander's (unspoken) aim to explore Indian territory: 'the motive and purpose of my journey lay in my intellectual activity and desire for adventure, and in my wish to find out what the end of the ocean was, and who the people were that lived on the other side.'[22] If we substitute the words 'what the end of the mainland was' for 'what the end of the ocean was', and the words 'near the ocean' for 'on the other side', we will find that the text corresponds with what Alexander intended when he planned his further expeditions in India.

Lucian's story of the (unintentional) journey by ship to the states of the moon and the sun may be interpreted as an extrapolation of the story about Alexander's exploration of the sea and sky (which in turn is to be regarded as an extrapolation of his 'cosmocratorship'!). The long voyage in the darkness in Lucian (*VH*, i.6) recalls a similar account in the *Alexander Romance* (*AR*, ii.29 (*b*)). The bronze stele which indicated that 'Heracles and Dionysus came as far as this point' (*VH*, i.7) reminds us of a similar stele erected by Alexander, and described in the *Booklet of Palladius*[23], at the frontier of the territory of the Seres

ἔνθα οἱ Σῆρες τὸ μέταξον τίκτουσι, κἀκεῖ λιθίνην στήλην στήσας ἐπέγραψεν· Ἀλέξανδρος ὁ Μακεδόνων βασιλεὺς ἔφθασα μέχρι τούτου τοῦ τόπου.

where the Seres (= Chinese) produce the silk, there, too, Alexander erected a memorial stone, on which he had the following text inscribed 'I, Alexander, King of the Macedons, came as far as this place'.

A more direct relation between Lucian and the Alexander stories is to be found in the Latin *Letter to Aristotle*, where it is told that Porus after his defeat by Alexander, had become his ally, and had brought him to two monuments (τρόπαια) of solid gold erected by the gods Heracles and Dionysus. The Indians who accompany him explain that the land between these monuments and the Ocean offers nothing else of interest, but Alexander wants to continue despite warnings that mortals cannot surpass the deeds of gods like Heracles and Dionysus. When, near the country of the Ichthyophagi and the Cynocephali, his camp is ravaged by a thunderstorm, his soldiers regard this as a sign that the gods were not willing to allow human beings to pass beyond the footsteps ('vestigia') of Heracles and Dionysus.[24] Generally Lucian's parody of the erection of such

---

descriptions were incomplete and consequently untrustworthy. See Johannes de Plano Carpini, *Storia dei Mongoli*, ed. P. Daffinà, et al. (Spoleto, 1989), p. 272; Marco Polo, *Von Venedig nach China: die grösste Reise des 13. Jahrhunderts*, ed. Theodor A. Knust (fifth edition, Tübingen & Basel, 1979), iii.18.

[22] For the translations of Lucian, see A. M. Harmon, *Lucian* (Cambridge, Mass., & London, 1979).

[23] *Pseudo-Callisthenes* (op. cit. n. 2), iii.7.19.

[24] Walther Boer (op. cit. n. 2), 35.8. It should be noticed that the combination of Dionysus and Heracles is a typical feature of the *Alexander Romance*. In *AR*, vii.9 and viii.3 (*a*) Nectanebo

a monument is connected with a passage in Diodorus (ii.38 and 39) (based on Megasthenes), where previous expeditions of Dionysus and Heracles were described. But Diodorus does not mention the erection of any such monument by either Dionysus or Heracles, whereas Lucian speaks about ἴχνη δύο, two footprints of large but different size, the smallest of which belonged to Dionysus, the other to Heracles; this reference is usually seen as a parody of Herodotus iv.82, where the Scythians show Heracles's footprint measuring two cubits. Here, too, Lucian and the *Alexander Romance* have motives in common, which must originate from either the first generation of Alexander historians or a *proto-Alexander Romance*, or both.

Herodotus and Ctesias mention many fantastic beasts; the *Alexander Romance* (Letters to Aristotle and Olympias) adds new ones and it is not surprising that Lucian's rich fantasy also makes its own contributions.[25] His 'Ant Dragoons' (ἱππομύρμηκες) are not very different from the family of the gold digging (super)ants of Herodotus iii.102, even though they are much bigger. Cynocephali, once in the form of Cynobalani ['Puppycorns', *VH*, i.16], are also found: 'dog-faced men who fight on the back of winged acorns'; elsewhere they are transformed into 'Codheads' (θυννοκέφαλοι) [*VH*, i.35]. Whereas in these cases there is no reason to presuppose an Alexander story as source of inspiration, Lucian's story told in *Verae historiae*, ii.2 does have a connection with the *Alexander Romance*, ii.14 (*a*). In Lucian's the narrator and his crew are overtaken at sea by north winds, which rapidly transform the sea into thick layers of ice, six fathoms deep; yet after a five-day sleigh ride with the boat, the ice melts again in the sudden warmth. The *Alexander Romance*, more specifically, tells that the river Strangas [in *AR*, ii.14 (*a*)] quickly freezes 'so that its surface becomes as firm as a stone road, and beasts and wagons can cross over it. Then a few days later it melts and becomes fast-flowing again ...'[26]

Another story in Lucian (*VH*, i.36) presents a scene similar to one in the *Alexander Romance*: after an enormous whale had swallowed the narrator's ship complete with the crew, they lived in his belly together with a Cypriot who was obliged to pay 'the Solefeet a tribute of five hundred oysters a year.' When he did not fulfil this obligation, the Solefeet and other peoples who lived in the belly now considered a battle:

---

announces the appearance of the begetting god: Ammon, Heracles, Dionysus. In the episode on Thebes the poet Ismenias tries to restrain Alexander from destroying the city by putting forward Heracles and Dionysus as its protectors (*AR*, lv.5 ff (*a*)). Elsewhere [*AR*, iii.4.8 ff. (103.10–11 ff. (*a*))] Alexander finds a way to bring the mountain Aornos under his control, which Heracles had vainly attempted before him. Finally, after the birth of the monstrum that presages his death, Alexander prays to Zeus to take him up as the third mortal under the gods, after Heracles and Dionysus, in honour of his brave deeds (*AR*, iii.30.15–16 = 133.4 ff (*a*)).

[25] See, for instance, *VH*, i.13 ff with Ἱππόγυποι ('Vulture Dragoons'), Λαχανόπτεροι ('Grassplumeriders'), Κεγχροβόλοι ('Millet-shooters'), Σκοροδομάχοι ('Garlic-fighters') etc. In *AR*, ii.17.20 (109.21 ff (*a*)) Alexander meets with ταυρελέφαντες ('Bull Elephants'), κυνοπέρδικες ('Dog Partridges' (?)), νυκτάλωπες (or: νυκταλώπεκες ('Nightfoxes') etc.

[26] Translation Stoneman (op. cit. n. 3), p. 101.

Αἰτία δὲ τοῦ πολέμου ἔμελλεν ἔσεσθαι τοῦ φόρου ἡ οὐκ ἀπόδοσις, ἤδη τῆς προθεσμίας ἐνεστώσης. καὶ δὴ οἱ μὲν ἔπεμπον ἀπαιτοῦντες τὸν δασμόν· ὁ δὲ ὑπεροπτικῶς ἀποκρινάμενος ἀπεδίωξε τοὺς ἀγγέλους.

The cause of war was to be the withholding of the tribute, since the date for it had already arrived. They sent and demanded the tax, and he gave the messengers a contemptuous answer and drove them off.

Lucian's description of these circumstances recalls the story in the *Alexander Romance* (i. 23), that Persian envoys came to collect taxes. So does the terminology: answering Alexander's question 'What do those strangers want?', his servants say: 'τοὺς συνήθεις φόρους ἀπαιτοῦντες τὸν πατέρα σου' ['demanding the usual taxes from your father']; Alexander's answer to the envoys is full of contempt: since he is Philip's son, Philip will not pay any more, and he himself will in due time take back the taxes already paid: Οὕτως εἰπὼν ἀπέπεμψε τοὺς φορολόγους μηδὲ γραμμάτων ἀξιώσας τὸν ἀποστείλαντα αὐτοὺς βασιλέα ['with these words he dismissed the tax-gatherers without deigning to give them any letter to the king who had sent them']. Remarkably, the Cypriot in Lucian's story is able to give his haughty answer because he knows himself to be supported by the narrator and his men (which is, in fact, an inversion of the motive as used in the *Alexander Romance*). Moreover, neither story of the Persian envoys, in Herodotus (v. 17 ff.) nor the one in Plutarch's *Alexander* (5), shows the same pattern as that in Lucian and the *Alexander Romance*.[27]

Perhaps Lucian's whale episode is itself an extrapolation of a passage like that found in the *Alexander Romance* [AR, iii. 17 (a, Letter to Aristotle)], where Alexander's attention is drawn to an island, which is in fact a monster. When local people state that there is the tomb of a king on the island, Alexander wants to visit it. His friend Phidon offers to inspect the place, using the topical argument that if he should die Alexander would still have other friends, whereas if Alexander would perish, the whole world would mourn. And Phidon's words were justified: as soon as he had set foot on 'land', the monster dived to the bottom of the sea, and Phidon and the soldiers who accompanied him drowned.[28]

Another episode where Lucian may have had an Alexander passage in mind is the description of the city in the land of the blessed (*VH*, ii. 11). Though the scholiast saw it as a parody of New Jerusalem,[29] it is rather to be regarded as a parody of Heliopolis described in *Alexander Romance*, iii. 28.3 ff (a): 'its circumference was 120 stades, and there were fourteen towers raised of gold and emerald. The wall was made of Indian stone. In the middle was an altar built also of gold and emerald ...' In Lucian (*loc. cit.*) we read: 'The city itself is all of gold and the wall around it of emerald. It has seven gates—an allusion to Thebes—all of single planks of cinnamon. The foundations of the city, and the ground within

---

[27] For the motives of the envoys throughout the *Alexander Romance*, see Merkelbach & Trumpf (op. cit. n. 2), p. 24 (n. 36).

[28] In *Batrachomyomachia*, 82 ff. (a poem, probably written in the first century, and also full of parody) the mouse rides on the back of the king of the frogs, but drowns when the frog sees a water-serpent and dives to the bottom of the pool.

[29] See Harmon, *Lucian* (op. cit. n. 22), p. 313 (n. 4): Lucian's city is not necessarily a parody of the New Jerusalem, though the scholiast understood it to be so.

its walls, are ivory. There are temples of all the gods, built of beryl, and in them great monolithic altars of amethyst ... '

In an article in the *National Geographic Magazine* of January 1968, Helen and Frank Schreider described how they had travelled in Alexander's footsteps by Land-Rover, on foot and horseback, covering about 25.000 miles. Even in the twentieth century, extreme endurance and the will to succeed were needed to overcome the many difficulties caused by climate and nature. But in Alexander's days a journey of about 25.000 miles was an even larger distance: it was equal to ten years of campaigning 2.500 miles a year, that is about seven miles a day. And if reports of sieges like that of Tyre, which took three months, are true, and if we calculate the necessary days for rest, then on many days more than 20 or 25 miles were covered. In the meantime, enemies were defeated, and the foundations of a large empire were laid. This helps to understand why Alexander, the charismatic leader of the campaign, his expeditions and the distant regions he had (or could have) visited, continued to appeal to the imagination. Already the first generation of historians mixed what they had witnessed with traditional stories, or pure fantasy. Later historians found it even more difficult to discern what was right or wrong; stories like those of the *Alexander Romance* were appealing illustrations of what a 'cosmocrator' had looked like, and of the wonderous world he had lived in. It was the world that tickled the imagination of readers of romances like those of Achilles Tatius and Heliodorus. Travelling by 'book' had the same fascination for them as films about foreign countries and moonscapes for us. And whereas Greek novelists like Achilles Tatius remained within the framework of the imaginable, the hero of the *Alexander Romance* could tread in the footsteps of his ancestor Heracles and settle with monsters. Lucian's fantastical and satirical pen transformed these stories almost into 'science fiction'.

EGERIA THE VOYAGER,
OR THE TECHNOLOGY OF REMOTE SENSING
IN LATE ANTIQUITY

ANDREW PALMER[*]

INTRODUCTION

In the twelfth century Jerusalem was in the hands of Crusader kings, and western pilgrims flooded to visit Palestine. Back in Italy, evidently in response to their needs, Peter the Deacon, the librarian of the abbey of Monte Cassino, compiled a book about the Holy Places from ancient authorities. One of these was the venerable Bede; another was a woman pilgrim of the fourth century, whose name, Egeria, we know from the seventh-century Galician monk Valerius.[1] When Peter consulted this woman's letter, it was still complete; the manuscript he used has survived, but many of its pages are now lost. At some stage it was taken from Monte Cassino to Arezzo; and it was at Arezzo that G. F. Gamurrini rediscovered it in 1884. Since his publication in 1887 the Latin text has been edited fourteen times and translated, often repeatedly, into the following languages: Russian, Italian, English, Danish, Greek, German, Spanish, French, Polish, Portuguese, Rumanian, Catalan and, most recently, Dutch. The bibliography on Egeria stands presently at about 450 titles. Evidently, this is no ordinary letter. It has been seen as the earliest surviving first-person description of a journey undertaken for the sake of the personal experience of travelling. Indeed, Mary Campbell's recent study of 'exotic European travel writing' begins with this text. Besides this book on exotic travel, there are two recent articles on Egeria by Hagith Sivan.[2]

---

[*] Department of the Study of Religions, School of Oriental and African Studies, London.

[1] The most convenient edition in which to consult the text of Egeria is that of Pierre Maraval in *Égérie, Journal de Voyage (Itinéraire)*, Sources Chrétiennes 296 (Paris, 1982), including an edition of Valerius's letter by Díaz y Díaz, in addition to good introductions to both texts and annotated translations into French. It is to this edition that I refer in this article. The basic edition, however, is E. Franceschini and R. Weber, *Itinerarium Egeriae*, Corpus Christianorum: Series Latina, clxxv (Turnhout, 1958), 27-103. John Wilkinson, *Egeria's travels to the Holy Land*, second edition (Jerusalem & Warminster, 1981) collates an English translation of Egeria's letter with other authors, such as Peter the Deacon, whose twelfth-century compilation gives us an idea of the original contents of the damaged manuscript, and with the Armenian Lectionary (an early arrangement of the Scriptures as they were read at Jerusalem to suit every occasion in the calendar of the Church), which provides a good control on Egeria's observations of the Jerusalem liturgy. This book has a rich apparatus which has not been sufficiently assimilated by the writers who have consulted it, perhaps because of the fragmented presentation. It is from Wilkinson that I have taken the translations of Egeria and of Peter.

[2] For the bibliography of Egeria see: C. Baraut, 'Bibliografía egeriana', *Hispania sacra*, 7 (1954), 203-15; M. Starowieyski, 'Bibliografía egeriana', *Augustinianum*, 19 (1979), 297-318; C. Renoux, 'Hierosolymitana', *Archiv für Liturgiewissenschaft*, 23 (1981), 1-29 (on Egeria: 10-15); P. Devos,

The first part of my paper is devoted to the questions addressed in these articles: who was Egeria? What was her geographical and social background? How must we envisage the sisters for whom she wrote? The second part uses the headings of fiction, form, research and observation to examine Egeria according to criteria applied to travel writing in general. In the last part, I ask with what success Mary Campbell has depicted Egeria as an exotic travel writer.

1. WHO WAS EGERIA?

The monk Valerius says nothing of the Old Testament sites which figure so prominently in Egeria's letter, nor does he mention her sojourn in Jerusalem. Nevertheless, there can be little doubt that he was referring to this text, when he celebrated the devotion which had made the nun he calls Egeria climb so many steep mountains, despite her 'feminine fragility'. The fact that this seventh-century Galician monk singled Egeria out for praise has led some to suppose that she was his countrywoman. According to Sivan, 'the archaeological evidence excludes Galicia from the zone of early conversion to Christianity'. Sivan does not explain what kind of archaeological evidence can positively rule out 'early' Christianity from Galicia. But we may agree that Egeria need not have been a Galician.

Valerius says that Egeria 'started out from the shore of the furthest western Ocean and made herself known to the East'. Sivan dismisses this as a rhetorical antithesis. But Egeria knew the Atlantic coast; she compared the Red Sea with 'the Ocean' and 'the Italian Sea':

> This sea has the name 'Red' not because the water is red or muddy. Indeed, it is quite as sparkling clear and cold as the Ocean. Its shellfish are excellent, and unusually sweet, and all types of fish from this sea taste as good as the fish in the Italian Sea. You have all the sea-food you could want: there are trumpet-shells and oysters of various kinds, white-shells, and several kinds of large snail. And the different things you find along the shore are bigger and prettier than by any other sea. Also there is a great deal of coral on this shore. The Red Sea is a part of the Ocean.[3]

This passage is preserved only by Peter the Deacon; but it bears Egeria's hallmark. She showed a particular interest in the sacred fish at Edessa: 'I have never seen fish like them, they were so big, so brightly coloured, and tasted so good' (Egeria 19.7; tr. Wilkinson, p. 116). Earlier, she had been appreciative of the taste of the

---

'Egeriana', *Analecta Bollandiana*, 105 (1987), 159-66 and 415-24; S. Janeras, 'Contributo alla bibliografia egeriana', *Atti del convegno internazionale sulla Peregrinatio Egeriae nel centenario della pubblicazione del Codex Aretinus 405 (già Aretinus VI, 3), Arezzo 23-25 ottobre 1987* (Arezzo, 1990), 355-66, with the list of contents of that volume. Add Mary B. Campbell, *The Witness and the Other World: Exotic European Travel Writing, 400-1600* (Ithaca & London, 1988); F. Ledegang, *Als pelgrim naar het Heilige Land: de pelgrimage van Egeria in de vierde eeuw*, Christelijke bronnen, 4 (Kampen, 1991); Andrew N. Palmer, 'King Abgar of Edessa, Eusebius and Constantine', in: Hans Bakker (ed.), *The Sacred Centre as the Focus of Political Interest* (Groningen, 1992), 3-29; Hagith Sivan, 'Who was Egeria? Piety and pilgrimage in the age of Gratian', *Harvard Theological Review*, 81 (1988), 59-72; Hagith Sivan, 'Holy Land Pilgrimage and Western Audiences: Some Reflections on Egeria and Her Circle', *Classical Quarterly*, 38 (1988), 528-35; I. Higgins in *Speculum. A Journal of Medieval Studies*, 65 (1990), 625-28: review of Campbell (1988), listing a number of recent books on pilgrimage.
[3] Peter the Deacon, *On the Holy Places*, Y10, translated by Wilkinson (op. cit. n. 1), p. 207.

water out of the rock which Moses struck in the desert (Egeria 11.2; tr. Wilkinson, p. 106). Unlike the other writers used by Peter the Deacon, she certainly saw the Red Sea (Egeria 7.2-3; tr. Wilkinson, p. 101). The second person plural and the lively style are characteristic of her letter. We need not doubt that it was originally Egeria who wrote this for her countrywomen; nor that their country was on the Atlantic coast of Europe.

In describing the Euphrates, Egeria compares it with the Rhone, as if she shared the knowledge of the latter river with her readers (Egeria 18.2; tr. Wilkinson, p. 115). But this does not mean that we have to assume, as Sivan does, that she and they were from a city on the Rhone. Sivan paints a picture of Egeria as a member of the commercial bourgeoisie of Arles, enjoying throughout her travels in the East the human contacts supplied by the business network of her family and friends. But there is no evidence for this in the text. Egeria may be referring to a description she had shared with her sisters in a previous letter, not to the experience of their own senses; for she must have crossed the Rhone on her journey from the Atlantic coast towards the East.

Bordeaux, from which a pilgrim had made his way to the Holy Land in AD 333, could provide Egeria with an alternative urban setting. The itinerary of the Bordeaux Pilgrim is a literary antecedent of Egeria's letter.[4] Monasticism of the Egyptian kind was practised in the nearby Diocese of Tours in the fourth century, so it may have spread also to Bordeaux. Valerius tells us, after all, that Egeria was a 'nun' (sanctimonialis).

Sivan might concede the point of the Atlantic coast and simply transpose the bourgeois milieu she posits for Egeria from Arles to Bordeaux; but could a nun have been seated in a worldly salon? Sivan thinks not; she claims that Egeria was no nun. The words 'venerable' and 'sisters', by which Egeria sometimes addresses her correspondents (Egeria 12.7 and 46.1; tr. Wilkinson, pp. 107 and 144, for example) could be applied to laywomen as well as to nuns. But Sivan is not content to be cautious; she denies that a consecrated virgin or an abbess could have made a pilgrimage from Gaul to the Holy Land in the fourth century. She alleges that the religious calling and managerial responsibility of such a person would have been incompatible with the freedom of movement and the prolonged absence of Egeria.[5]

The deaconess Marthana, who was in charge of a convent of virgins in Isauria, at the shrine of St Thekla, certainly did make the pilgrimage to Jerusalem. It was there that she met Egeria, to whom she became very much attached. Indeed, Egeria's detour to the shrine of Thekla was probably motivated as much by the hope of meeting up with Marthana again as by the desire to see yet another holy site; for, with the exception of Edessa, she does not otherwise visit 'apocryphal' or non-biblical shrines. It is obvious that Egeria identifies with Marthana more

---

[4] Published in *Itineraria et alia geographica: i. Itinerarium Burdigalense*, eds. P. Geyer & O. Cuntz, Corpus Christianorum: Series Latina, clxxv (Turnhout, 1965); translated by Wilkinson (op. cit. n. 1), pp. 153–63.

[5] Sivan's arguments for her view of Egeria and her circle are scattered throughout the two articles cited in n. 2, above.

than with anyone else she met on her journeys. Perhaps they had more in common than their female sex, their sexual abstinence and their desire to pray in the Holy Places. Of all the people Egeria met, Marthana was the only one she thought suitable to be introduced by name to her sisters. This fact suggests that Egeria's correspondents were nuns, like Marthana; and the equality of status implicit in the close friendship between Marthana and Egeria might suggest that the latter was herself also the head of a convent. As for the freedom with which Egeria decided to visit Marthana, if it had been an absolute freedom, she would not have felt obliged to justify the detour to her sisters (Egeria 22.2; tr. Wilkinson, p. 121).

Egeria belonged, then, to a community of virgins. That explains her long visit to the monks of the Egyptian desert and her consuming interest in the monks and nuns of every place (Egeria 3.7, 11.1, 16.3, 23.3 and 49.1; tr. Wilkinson, pp. 94, 106, 111-12, 121 and 146-47; and note especially Egeria 13.1, tr. Wilkinson, p. 108, where the report of *monks* who had been to the memorial of Job is cited as Egeria's reason for going there also). The holy men of Edessa are the first of her reasons for undertaking the journey there (Egeria 17.1; tr. Wilkinson, p. 113). (This unplanned detour to Edessa, like that to the shrine of St Thekla, is carefully justified to her sisters by a number of different arguments.) At Harran she 'had the unexpected pleasure of seeing the holy and truly dedicated monks of Mesopotamia, including some of whose reputation and holy life we had heard long before we got there' (Egeria 20.6; tr. Wilkinson, pp. 118-9). She had conversations with these men (Egeria 20.7; tr. Wilkinson, p. 119); and all such conversations, she is at pains to assure her sisters, were 'either about God's Scriptures or the deeds of the great monks' (Egeria 20.13; tr. Wilkinson, p. 120).

Sivan notes, however, that Egeria 'transmits neither their miracles nor their edifying conversations'. But then, she was not writing an *historia monachorum*, at least not in the letter that we have. She might well have done so in another letter; for, as Maraval argues in the introduction to his edition, there must have been at least one letter before this one, and Egeria promised to write more later (Egeria 23.10; tr. Wilkinson, p. 122). The way Egeria saves up everything she has to say about the Jerusalem liturgy for a separate chapter is proof that she had sufficient discipline, as a composer of prose, to omit certain details, however natural it might be to mention them in the piecemeal way that she observed them, in order to write about them with more thematic cohesion elsewhere. The subjects noted by Sivan for their absence would have lent themselves well for such separate treatment, perhaps in her lost account of the visit to the holy ascetics of Egypt.

It is an intriguing 'novelistic' speculation, that Egeria might have been seen by John Cassian while he was a novice monk in Bethlehem. If she was intending to write (as others would do around 400) a separate tract on the discipline and conversation of the monks in Mesopotamia, the Holy Land and Egypt, her detailed questioning of these monks might have left the young John (supposing that he was among them) with a strong impression of the desire that existed in distant Gaul for knowledge about the way of life he himself had chosen. Cassian would, in fact, later go as a self-appointed teacher of the monastic life for men and women to Marseilles, the port from which, in all likelihood, Egeria had first set out to sea.

A point in favour of the picture of Egeria the religious, as opposed to that of

Egeria the layperson, is that she herself contrasts the laypeople in her narrative with the religious, rather than (as is usual) with the clergy (Egeria 49.1-2; tr. Wilkinson, p. 147). Another strong argument that Egeria and her sisters belonged to a religious community is their insatiable thirst for information about new and better ways of performing the Christian liturgy. It is difficult to imagine a salon of more or less worldly women poring over all the rituals so meticulously recorded in the second half of our text.

Maraval thinks that Egeria 'travelled in the best conditions' and 'enjoyed a mount and an escort';[6] for Sivan, the fact that Egeria spent more than three years away from home (Egeria 17.1; tr. Wilkinson, p. 113) 'indicates either affluence or the existence of contacts within local financial circles'. She finds further evidence of wealth in the detours to Edessa and to the shrine of St Thekla: 'She made frequent (sic) departures from her original plan, again without apparent regard for economic or time factors.'[7]

We have already seen that Egeria's freedom was circumscribed by her obligations to the sisters to whom she reported so diligently; and she did not 'consider the possibility of never returning to the West' (Sivan, loc. cit.), except in the sense that she knew it was possible that she would die before she got there (Egeria 23.10; tr. Wilkinson, pp. 122-3). The way she justifies her detours to Edessa (Egeria 17.1; tr. Wilkinson, p. 113: no pilgrim to Jerusalem 'misses going also on the pilgrimage to Edessa') and to the shrine of St Thekla (Egeria 22.2; tr. Wilkinson, p. 121: 'especially since it was so close') as being well worthwhile, and not far from the route she had to take on her way back to the patria, might suggest that the community, or its protecting bishop, was supporting her pilgrimage. Sivan herself has a similar idea: 'Perhaps we are dealing with a "reading circle" of devout and pious women who met regularly to study and discuss the Scriptures and who supported a member on pilgrimage, asking in return for a written report of it.'[8]

Nor need the expense have been crushing. Egeria needed few companions and in Palestine she sometimes dispensed even with these when she could get a local escort, as when she went to Carneas (Egeria 13.2; tr. Wilkinson, p. 108). Wherever she went she enjoyed the hospitality of monks, nuns and bishops (Egeria 5.12; tr. Wilkinson, p. 98). Nuns were doubtless exempt from tolls and taxes in the Christian Empire; and Egeria's tastes were simple, though she obviously looked up to the 'ascetics' (a new word for her: Egeria 10.9; tr. Wilkinson, p. 106), and, more realistically, admired the custom of fasting according to one's individual strength without boasting or disparagement of others. Her utter amazement at the silk and gems displayed in the churches of Jerusalem at Epiphany does not speak of a familiarity with affluence (Egeria 25.8-9; tr.

---

[6] P. Maraval, 'Le Temps du pèlerin (IVe-VIIe siècles)', in Le Temps chrétien de la fin de l'Antiquité au Moyen Âge - IIIe-XIIIe siècles. Paris, 9–12 mars 1981, ed. Jean-Marie Leroux, Colloques internationaux du Centre National de la Recherche Scientifique, 604 (Paris, 1984), 479-88.

[7] Sivan, 'Who was Egeria? ...' (op. cit. n. 2), p. 70.

[8] Sivan, 'Holy Land Pilgrimage ...' (op. cit. n. 2), p. 531.

Wilkinson, p. 127); and she expects her sisters to be equally impressionable. She finds her admiration somehow inappropriate and breaks it off as suddenly (and as artificially) as she had called herself to order after describing her meeting with Marthana—another (intentional) revelation of inordinate emotion.

As for Maraval's remarks, they are misleading. Egeria only enjoyed an escort on the Sinai peninsular, where she was travelling with a large caravan of other pilgrims, accompanied by Roman soldiers and considerable numbers of the clergy (Egeria 7.2 and 9.3; tr. Wilkinson, pp. 101 and 103).

Egeria's Latin is not at all obviously that of a noblewoman. Sivan postulates a class of petit-bourgeois pious snobs, imitating the true aristocrats with their salons of devout women and their patristic education, but not quite 'making the grade'.[9] Such pretentions might have made Egeria drop a few patristic names from time to time, or show some interest in politics or commerce, but she does none of these things. There is no evidence that this middle class of half-educated laywomen existed; but there is good evidence that nuns were educated in Latin up to the level necessary for reading the Bible and singing hymns. Egeria's style is most obviously the product of such a monastic education, in spite of the discipline already remarked on, and the almost epic quality of her repetitions. But there is no reason why the nun should not have been of a good family.

Valerius, then, was right, whether he read an explicit statement as to Egeria's *patria* and vocation in the superscript or subscript of his complete exemplar of the text, or simply inferred them, as we have just done, from the text. She was a nun, probably the head of a monastic community situated on the Atlantic coast of Gaul.

Egeria is not obviously the product of an urban environment. She completely ignores the spectacular urban architecture of Antioch, treating it simply as a place to stock up on supplies for the journey to Constantinople. If she had described Antioch at length in an earlier letter, she might have been expected to refer back to the impressions shared with her sisters in that letter. By contrast, she never wearies of describing the countryside, something uncommon in classical authors of urban origin, unless they are writing a set-piece as a literary exercize.

Egeria delights in every garden, orchard and spring (Egeria 4.7 and 9.4; tr. Wilkinson, pp. 96 and 103), invariably shows an interest in the water-supply (Egeria 11.1-2 and 13.2; tr. Wilkinson, pp. 106 and 108), admires the monks of Sinai for their labours in tilling the soil (Egeria 3.6; tr. Wilkinson, p. 94), shows no fastidiousness about the practicalities of travel and climbs right up the steep side of a mountain on foot without noticing the effort (Egeria 3.2; tr. Wilkinson, p. 91). If she had social status to maintain, we might have expected her to be carried in a litter, instead of riding a donkey and dismounting on difficult terrain. She herself remarks that 'even ladies and even lords' go on foot in the Palm Sunday procession at Jerusalem (Egeria 31.4: 'pedibus omnes, sed et si quae matrone sunt aut si qui domini'; mistranslated by Wilkinson, p. 133). But in speaking of herself she never makes it appear that walking was a concession

---

[9] Sivan, 'Who was Egeria? ...' (op. cit. n. 2), p. 66–7.

to the holiness of the occasion or the place; it was simply a practical necessity. Nowhere does a remark on civic amenities (such as baths, theatres, hippodromes and markets) intrude, not even in Constantinople, where she makes the round of all the churches (Egeria 23.9; tr. Wilkinson, p. 122); and it is difficult to believe that Egeria's sense of what is appropriate in this 'holy' narrative could have been such an effective filter against the world, if she had felt herself to be a part of it.[10]

2. FICTION, FORM, RESEARCH AND OBSERVATION IN EGERIA

a) Fiction

With regard to fiction, we may quote Robin Lane Fox: 'Biblical tours have a very long history: seeing, maybe, is believing, but believing also ensures that there is plenty to see.'[11] Egeria is willingly deceived; but she only 'deceives' in the sense that she idealizes, and then she deceives herself as much as her correspondents. Egeria was also one of those—and not the least influential one, I suspect—who created the powerful myth of sacred geography by which the world-pictures of the Middle Ages were formed.[12]

Another 'fiction' is that the pilgrim herself experienced only the appropriate emotions of gratitude and satisfaction, or of sorrow at Passiontide; never annoyance, scepticism, suspicion, fear, homesickness, loneliness, physical attraction - hardly ever even deeply felt friendship, except towards her correspondents (whom she calls 'animae meae' = 'my souls' and 'lumen meum' = 'my light'). The closest she gets to presenting her individuality is in describing her curiosity (Egeria 16.3; tr. Wilkinson, pp. 111-12: 'ut sum satis curiosa' = 'for I am extremely inquisitive') and her desire to be reunited with her friend Marthana (Egeria 23.3; tr. Wilkinson, p. 121: 'amicissima michi' = 'who is my very dear friend'; significantly, as I have already remarked, the only person in her narrative to whom she puts a name). We have seen already how she disciplines herself and returns abruptly to the subject, signalling a departure from what is deemed to be appropriate. Besides, this revelation of human love serves in the context implicitly to justify Egeria's detour to the shrine of St Thekla.

Egeria never insults her sisters with a tall story about amazing things never actually seen by her. The bishop of Edessa told her such a story, which she passed on credulously to her sisters (Egeria 19.5-19; tr. Wilkinson, pp. 115-17). But if she had not been at pains to record accurately the very words used by the bishop, it would not have been so easy for us to detect his deception.

---

[10] As P. Maraval (op. cit. n. 6) says, the Bordeaux Pilgrim (who is translated by Wilkinson (op. cit. n. 1), pp. 153-63) 'contents himself with mentioning the staging-posts, the frontiers and the distances, hardly referring to the beauty of the cities he passes through, however important, nor to that of the landscape he encounters,' but changes his attitude as soon as he reaches the Holy Land.

[11] Robin Lane Fox, *The Unauthorized Version: Truth and Fiction in the Bible* (London, 1991), at the beginning of Chapter 14 ('Digging and travelling'), which, with Chapter 15 ('Fifth Gospels'), is relevant to our subject.

[12] Pierre Maraval, *Lieux saints et pèlerinages d'Orient: histoire et géographie, des origines à la conquête arabe* (Paris, 1985).

Briefly, what happened is this: the bishop led Egeria around the interior of the city, from the springs below the citadel on the south side to the channel outside the wall on the north side, then out through the great gate on the east side and round the back of the citadel to the palace on top, from the ruins of which the modern visitor looks down on the springs. This view down onto the town is one of the most memorable things about Urfa, in modern Turkey, the site of Edessa. Procopius remarks on it (*Buildings*, II.vii.13); but Egeria says nothing about it. The view would have formed a splendid climax to her tour, instead of which she concludes rather lamely that the bishop 'showed us all the other things there were to see'.

Had Egeria seen the view, she would have detected the bishop's deception, which was to make her believe that the river which flowed through Edessa issued from the springs at which her tour began. From the citadel the former course of the river above the city can be seen; and it is unlikely (as Maraval suggested in a note to his edition) that it went underground, though rivers do so from time to time in porous limestone, before Egeria's visit in 384. At any rate, it was above ground in 413, when it flooded disastrously. The river (much diminished) now flows through the channel outside the north wall, the channel which was cut after 303 to drain the floodwater which had destroyed the city in that year for the second time. But when Egeria saw it, the channel was dry; and the bishop made sure that she took note of this. The month was April, so the river was surely full. Egeria crossed over it and compared it to 'a great river of silver'. But the bishop took care that she should not see where it came from.

He avoided the west side of the city, which meant leaving on the left the acropolis with its ancient temples and the Roman-style stadium outside the west wall onto which the acropolis looked down; if Egeria had asked about the monuments on this side, he could have said, with truth, that they were all pagan or secular. He mounted the southern citadel from the back (Edessa had two citadels, the original acropolis and another one outside the southern wall) and made sure that Egeria saw the interior of the palace whose exterior she had seen from below, without however getting the opportunity to enjoy the panorama afforded by the windows on the north side of the palace.

The purpose of this elaborate deception was to impress upon the pilgrim the 'truth' of a story which the bishop told her: about a king who was blessed by Jesus in a letter; about an enemy who attacked the city of this king, which was Edessa; about the channel cut by this enemy to divert the city's only water-supply, the river, away from the inhabitants; and about the miracle by which the river dried up, once and for all, leaving the enemy waterless, while simultaneously within the city superabundant springs welled up where no springs had ever been before. That this story is fiction is proved by an archival record preserved at Edessa from *circa* 205, which shows that the springs were tributaries to the river and antedated the channel.[13] But Egeria's account of what she saw and heard at

---

[13] This record opens the *Chronicle of Edessa*, ed. I. Guidi in: I. Guidi (ed.), *Chronica minora*, part 1; Corpus Scriptorum Christianorum Orientalium: Scriptores Syri, ser. 3. vol. 4 (Paris, 1903).

Edessa is nonetheless meticulous and exact. She cannot herself on any account be accused of deliberate fiction.

b) Form

The *itinerarium* was, by origin, no art-form, but a substitute for a map, designed exclusively for military use. Kai Brodersen's work on Roman mental maps, *Terra cognita*, which is now in preparation, will soon be the best reference for this. The Bordeaux Pilgrim (AD 333) took this written, but unliterary, form, and made it an instrument for those 'soldiers of Christ' who would follow in his footsteps. Roman generals plotted their routes from the imperial city to the periphery of the inhabited world (or so they fondly imagined); this pilgrim plotted the reverse: a route from the periphery to the centre. And that centre was not Rome, but Jerusalem. Whereas the curiosity of the Romans was greatest at the furthest limits of their territory, it was only when the pilgrim neared his goal that he began to register the significance of what he saw, like a space-probe containing instruments programmed to come alive once the targeted planet is approached.

Egeria writes in the tradition of the Pilgrim from Bordeaux, who preceded her by fifty years; yet she is alive and personal in a way that he is not. Her chatty style is reminiscent of Cicero, but there is no politics, no malice, no vanity. Perhaps I should qualify this last: there is no overt, boyish boasting, but there is, on closer inspection, a certain artifice in the way Egeria presents herself. She does not say she is on intimate terms with all the holiest people in the East, but that is the impression one gains from her narrative. She does not say that she underwent horrendous ordeals of endurance and braved great risks, but she gives us the information from which we can conclude this. She does not stress the fragility, under so many labours, of her feminine sex, yet this is the aspect of her narrative which made the greatest impression on Valerius. The closest she comes to boasting openly is when she displays her knowledge of the Bible to the bishop of Harran, himself a great expert on the Scriptures, and obliges him to admit that one detail in his story is apocryphal (Egeria 20.10; tr. Wilkinson, p. 119).

Latin offered many models for the letter-writer, but their influence has not, so far as I am aware, been detected in Egeria. As I have already said, she has at times an almost epic style, but without a clear debt to any epic poet.[14] She is not entirely without Herodotean curiosity, but this was a natural trait with her, not a literary mannerism. Any parallels with Horace's witty 'Journey to Brundisium' (*Satires,* i.5) are fortuitous; the contrasts are revealing and pervasive. Her foremost literary model was probably the Old Latin version of the Bible; in closing the account of her journey she consciously models herself on one of St Paul's epistles (Egeria 23.10; tr. Wilkinson, p. 123).

---

[14] Compare L. Spitzer, 'The Epic Style of the Pilgrim Aetheria', *Comparative Literature,* 1 (1949), 225–258.

c) Research

Egeria's contribution to the knowledge of her correspondents lies above all in her identification and sensual presentation of biblical sites and her description of the Jerusalem liturgy.[15] Both represent the fruit of long research, carefully assembled and ordered; and the fact that this research was undertaken *in odore sanctitatis* does not detract from the clarity of the results.

Historians of eastern monasticism and, to a lesser extent, those of the Roman army, can make very good use of her observations as well, while taking account of exaggerations designed to enhance her presentation (e.g. Egeria 19.1; tr. Wilkinson, p. 115). However, it may be that she reduced the information about monks and nuns to externals, reserving her knowledge of their life, which must have been extensive, for another letter which is lost or which she did not live to write. It is important, in any case, to take account of Egeria's ability to report selectively and thematically, and not to judge her on the silences in the preserved portion of her treatises.

She communicates her surprise and delight at what is new to her as well as her recognition of what is familiar (Egeria 27.1 and 44.1; tr. Wilkinson, pp. 128 and 143). This enables us to gauge the difference between her culture and that which she observed. Egeria always wants to know the reason for things being as they are; and she expects the same curiosity to live in the mind of her sisters (Egeria 16.3 and 46.1; tr. Wilkinson, pp. 111-12 and 144). The description of the seafood provided by the Red Sea (quoted in Part One, above), which is preserved by Peter the Deacon, and that part of her narrative which describes the way the Faranites, a camel-herding tribe on the Sinai peninsular, travel under cover of darkness without losing their way, are examples of the incidental way in which her narrative could have been used to increase encyclopaedic knowledge. But such tit-bits invariably served to fill out the narrative of a section of Egeria's journey which offered too few biblical associations. It was no part of her purpose in travelling to record facts, regardless of their relevance to Scripture and the Liturgy.

Occasionally a scriptural tag is used to 'consecrate' a merely geographical observation, as in Egeria's description of the river Euphrates: 'The Bible is right to call it "the great river Euphrates". It is very big, and really rather frightening since it flows very fast like the Rhone, but the Euphrates is much bigger. We had to cross in ships, big ones, and that meant I spent maybe more than half a day there' (Egeria 18.2-3; tr. Wilkinson, p. 115). Yet Egeria's purpose is actually to supply her correspondents with images to conjure with in reading the Bible, because they were obliged to do so without the benefit of first-hand observation. Even the Red Sea was described only to underline with a plethora of detail that it forms part of the same encircling Ocean to which the coast of the Atlantic also belongs; for this observation enhances the position of Jerusalem at the sacred centre. As for the Faranites, their nomadic existence serves Egeria as a

---

[15] See Wilkinson (op. cit. n. 1); E. David Hunt, *Holy Land Pilgrimage in the Later Roman Empire, AD 312-460* (Oxford, 1982); Peter W. L. Walker, *Holy City, Holy Places? Christian Attitudes to Jerusalem and the Holy Land in the Fourth Century* (Oxford, 1990).

vivid evocation of the wanderings of the Hebrews in the wilderness (Egeria 6.2 and 7.3; tr. Wilkinson, pp. 100 and 101).

d) Observation

Egeria's method of observation involved taking shorthand notes, as is shown by her interview with the bishop of Edessa; nor can we imagine her remembering without notes all the details of her other journeys, and particularly of the Jerusalem liturgy. That she does not name the bishop of Edessa, or the bishop of Jerusalem, or any other bishop or monk, but only her friend Marthana, may be due either to a desire to portray them as ideal types, or to a reluctance to overburden her readers with non-biblical particulars. On one occasion she excuses herself for burdening them with a large amount of topographical detail, at the same time implicitly inviting praise of her own phenomenal memory (Egeria 5.8; tr. Wilkinson, p. 97). Non-literate people do sometimes have an amazing memory; but Egeria's narrative of her visit to Edessa suggests that her note-taking method made her all the more ready to forget what she had not made a note of. For example, the journey from the bridge over the river to the channel is a complete blank, though it took her through the whole city. This could, however, be an intentional economy.

Egeria's five senses all contributed to her vivid presentation. No doubt that was one of the things that made it obvious that she was most fitted to function as the eyes, the ears, the nose, the mouth and the hands of all her sisters. Another was her ability to write lucid and lively prose, without stylistic pretentions and without such mistakes of grammar as might obscure her meaning. She is unlikely to have mastered shorthand herself; there was probably a professional scribe in her party when she went to Edessa, as well as an interpreter. Note that she sometimes speaks for her companions and is evidently not travelling with her social equals on such occasions. This is not incompatible with her probable status as a leader of nuns.

It seems improbable, in spite of her occasional mention of Greek words and place-names, that she could entirely do without an interpreter, even after three years in Jerusalem. She speaks of people who are bi-lingual in Greek and Latin without giving any hint that she was one of them (Egeria 47.3-5; tr. Wilkinson, p. 146); and her vanity, although not blatant, is, as we have seen, a strong characteristic, so that it is difficult to suppose she suppressed information from which we might have concluded that she had learned Greek well. Instead, she suggests this, by dropping occasional Grecisms, whereas she does not appear (though we must allow for textual corruption) even to have known the genitive of 'Anastasis' (Egeria 25.8; tr. Wilkinson, p. 127).

Altogether, Egeria seems to have been sufficiently equipped to function, for the benefit of her Atlantic-bound sisters, as an instrument of 'remote sensing'. We can detect in several passages the preparation which Egeria underwent in the circle of her sisters, before she undertook her journey. They seem to have read through the whole Bible, comparing notes with the records of other pilgrims, such as the one from whom Egeria got her copy of the correspondence between Jesus and the King of Edessa (Egeria 19.19; tr. Wilkinson, p. 117), and drawing up a list of

places where important events had occurred. It is very telling that Egeria's sisters
expected her to find the pillar of salt which had been Lot's wife (Egeria 12.7; tr.
Wilkinson, p. 107); and she was only too glad when the local clergy provided her
with an explanation for its absence. Meanwhile, the local clergy obviously made
a note of this desideratum. Later pilgrims would not be disappointed![16]

It is doubtful whether Egeria's circle had much understanding of typology, for
although it is clear from her narrative that typological relations between the Old
Testament and the New, and even perhaps between the believing King of
Edessa[17] and the Christian Roman Emperor, were built into the topographical
structures of pilgrimage which she followed, she does not seem aware of them,
nor is there any indication that her sisters had told her to look out for them.

One such subtlety was the fish-barbecue which she took with the bishop on
Sunday morning beside the sacred pool at Edessa (Egeria 19.7; tr. Wilkinson, p.
116). A few years before, in his hymns on the pearl, Ephrem had suggested to his
Edessene congregation the analogy between this pool and Lake Galilee.[18]
Egeria's guide was acting out a typological reference in cooking the sacred fish
for her to eat. The Apostles' breakfast with their resurrected Lord had been
described by the evangelist as an allegory of the mission to the Gentiles;[19] and
Thomas, who (for the bishop known to Egeria) had been the Apostle of Edessa,
was present at that breakfast. All this, however, passed Egeria by; though she did
note the size and the colour of the fish, and their excellent savour. Perhaps the
bishop explained his actions while Egeria's interpreter had his mouth full; or, not
being typologically minded, Egeria forgot the complicated details. It is also
possible that the bishop enacted this allegory wordlessly for such as 'had eyes to
see'. In a similar way, as we shall see, Egeria was presented with a silent
typological allegory in gesture and geography when she visited 'Opu Melchisedech' (Egeria 13.2-15.6; tr. Wilkinson, pp. 109-11). On this occasion, too, she
missed the point.

The metaphor of a space-probe, which lies behind the wording of my title, is
misleading as well as helpful; one might even say that it is helpful by the very
fact that it suggests a contrasting model. The 'Voyager' space-probe was sent out
from earth to the outer reaches of the solar-system to beam back pictures of a
planet which men had never seen. Egeria was sent out from the furthest edge of
the inhabited world towards the very centre of that world, Jerusalem, to bring alive
for her compatriots what they knew only through the written word and to bring
them up to date on the development of Christianity at the very hearth from which
the first fire sprang.

---

[16] See Wilkinson (op. cit. n. 1), pp. 219 f.

[17] See the end of section a, above; Egeria and her fellow-pilgrims were encouraged to visit Edessa
before Constantinople, as the Christian Kingship of the latter was foreshadowed in the former.

[18] Implicit in *Hymni de fide* 81: 14 and *Hymni de fide* 85: 9-10, on which see now Andrew N.
Palmer, 'The Merchant of Nisibis: Saint Ephrem and his Faithful Quest for Union in Numbers', in
Early Christian Poetry (*Vigiliae Christianae*. Supplements), eds. Jan den Boeft & Anton Hilhorst
(Leiden, 1993), 167–233.

[19] *The Gospel According to St John,* 21: 1–14. The number of the fish, one hundred and
fifty-three, is the number of the Gentile nations, according to certain Jewish sources.

If they possessed the itinerary of the Bordeaux Pilgrim, their appetite will have been whetted, but no more, making them all the more conscious of their hunger. This hunger was sensual and not to be satisfied by such a laconic narrative. Perhaps the approved masculine taste of that period eschewed such dependence on the senses. In that case, the necessary corrective would have had to have been written by a woman. Egeria's pilgrimage was a quest for a spiritual home, undertaken as a joint venture by a group whose religion made them strangers in their own country. It is this fact which distinguishes Egeria from the 'eurocentric' tradition of later European travel. In the last part of my paper I shall take issue with Mary Campbell on this point.

3. EGERIA AND EXOTIC TRAVEL

Campbell associates Egeria with an exoticizing tradition: in her introduction she talks about alienated experience, about the contrasted images of 'Home and the Other World', though it is difficult to rhyme this with her statement that Egeria 'was not prepared to be shocked, and she was not shocked'. Egeria was 'the most naïve of writers'—'a clean slate'. Herodotus and Ctesias wrote in order to record 'the data accumulated during their journey',[20] whereas for Egeria her own self is 'necessary as a rhetorical presence', because her journey is a personal quest. Campbell speaks of 'a special kind of blindness and vision'; Egeria and her kind 'read in the stones and fountains and caves of Palestine the narrative that had lured them there, the story of the Jewish people, whose holy places the Christian Church was already beginning to appropriate'. Here she sees another difference between Egeria and the classical travellers: 'The customs of alien people, recorded by Herodotus thoroughly and usually objectively, are irrelevant or demonic in this new kind of Holy Land which is inhabited mostly by unbelievers.' Egeria procedes according to 'an agendum of moments of perception'. 'Her horizons were not widened.' She was 'a woman of average intelligence', whose 'work is not an attempt at art'. 'She is not writing to amuse or fascinate, but almost as clearly she is not writing to inform her venerable sisters.' Rather, she takes advantage of the power of the written word 'to arrest and fix the reader's consciousness, even as hers is being arrested by the holy places themselves.' 'Her pleonastic repetitiveness gives to this account of what must have been high adventure something of the quality of a rosary being recited.'

The letters of her female contemporaries, so far as they are known to us, lead us to expect more emotion; by contrast, 'Egeria's composition is an anomaly, a document of deep reserve'. It reflects 'no inner process of transformation and no gradual accumulation of insight or depth of feeling'. Her literary allegiance is to the itinerary: 'a river of significance running through insignificant and consequently unmapped space'. This, according to Campbell, is what makes her draw a veil over virtually all human detail, except for certain incidents from sacred history, which have been burned, as it were, into the landscape. 'There are no

---

[20] That Herodotus may have been doing something rather different is a detail that escaped Mary Campbell (op. cit. n. 2). See Detlev Fehling, 'The Art of Herodotus and the Margins of the World', in this book.

"places", only "places where"'. On one occasion, she mentions 'an ecstatic meeting with an old friend' (Marthana). This, and another passage in which she enthuses about the gorgeousness of Jerusalem at Epiphany, are signalled as 'breaches of decorum' by the abrupt interruption: 'But let me get back to the subject.' Campbell concludes her treatment of Egeria with some general statements: 'It is not just Egeria's self-effacement and purely devotional orientation that separate her from the tradition she helped to engender. It is finally her ecstatic *contemptus mundi*.' By the very act of resisting it, Egeria heralds the 'interest in the external world' evinced by later travel-writing (e.g. *Mandeville's Travels*). The same applies to 'the subjective and autobiographical capacities of the form', which would be developed in *The Booke of Margery Kempe*, for example. Egeria is 'working continually to elevate her raw sense experience into a form of communion with that sacred world which *in illo tempore* merged for a while with this one.' 'The celestial Jerusalem is the object of her desire, and its geographical shadow only a spur to meditation.' Here Mary Campbell abandons Egeria and goes on to describe Adamnan's *De locis sanctis*, which 'displays a much greater concern with the physical presences of the Holy Land and exploits our interest in the traveler in significant, if fleeting and subtle ways.'

Campbell has many valuable insights; I particularly like her phrase: 'there are no places, only places where'. My favourite example of this is Opu Melchisedech, the place where Melchisedech offered bread and wine (Egeria 13.2-15.6; tr. Wilkinson, pp. 109-11). Next to it, up a hill reminiscent of the mountain of Paradise, at the source of a stream like that which flows through Scripture and down the whole duration of the Divine Dispensation, is the Garden of Saint John, where John the Baptist was said to have operated. Nothing could be more blatantly typological than to remove John the Baptist from the river Jordan, where Scripture places him (hence Egeria's uneasy 'appeared to have operated', Latin: 'parebat fuisse operatum'; compare Egeria's caution at 8.3 and 20.10, tr. Wilkinson, pp. 102 and 119), and place him in an orchard next to Salem. Egeria is unaware of this and, consequently, unaware also of the deeper meaning of the gesture by which she is dismissed: the monks who live in that garden offer their chaste woman visitor apples for a blessing. Each apple was a token that the harm done through the apple Eve gave Adam had been healed.

To see Egeria as an exotic traveller is to distort the most evident truth, that she was journeying towards the centre of her universe. This, surely, rather than the filter of decorum, is the explanation for her lack of homesickness, of paranoia, of xenophobia. She feels at home in the lands where the Christian Faith is strongest. Unlike many Greek writers on Syria, she felt no need to underline the eccentricities of the hermits in that land, only to praise their sanctity in general terms. Her only moment of alienation is when she observes that the city of Harran is entirely inhabited by pagans, in spite of the fact that it is associated with Abraham. At Harran, she was close to Persia, the country from which Abraham had come. As she looks out across the frontier, the bishop who stands next to her reinforces the sensation she receives of a great gulf fixed between herself and the pagan world: he tells her, inaccurately, that Roman citizens are not allowed to enter Persia. It is reassuring, then, that the 'blessed city' of Edessa, the brightness of which is accentuated by the artificially absolute contrast with its 'entirely pagan' neighbour, Harran (an entirely pagan city would not have had a Christian bishop), stands out as a bulwark against incursions from the Empire of the Infidel. If she had gone into Persia, her account of the journey surely would have satisfied Campbell's criterium for exoticism.

Since she did not, her narrative cannot be said to inaugurate the tradition by which western Europe confirms and consolidates its own sober self-image by contrasting it with the alien, enticing, dangerous and corrupt world of the East.[21] Instead it represents the Holy Land as the norm: an ideal which westerners should strive to attain. By saying that the Red Sea is 'also a part of the Ocean', Egeria made it clear that by travelling beyond Jerusalem, she had travelled southwards beyond the mid-point of the world. By not travelling beyond Edessa, except to see the liminal Harran, redolent of that Other World, she indicated that, in her mind's eye, the further East was a land of darkness, for her sun rose in Jerusalem and shone only on those countries perceived as Christian. Her journey was not a voyage to the frigid outer reaches of the solar system, but a trusting, quasi-baptismal plunge into the fire at the centre of her universe.

---

[21] I do not intend, by evoking this tradition, either to suggest that western Europe differed in its 'ethnocentrism' from other regional entities, such as Islam, or to subscribe to the anti-Orientalist rhetoric of Edward Said, the weakness of whose argument in *Orientalism* (1978) is exposed by B. Lewis in 'The Question of Orientalism', first published in *The New York Review of Books*, 12 June 1982, 49–56, and reprinted in B. Lewis, *Islam and the West* (New York & Oxford, 1993), 99–118, 192–194.

WILLIAM OF RUBRUCK IN THE MONGOL EMPIRE: PERCEPTION AND PREJUDICES

PETER JACKSON[*]

The Franciscan Friar William of Rubruck has often been described as an envoy of King Louis IX of France, but in fact he made his journey from Palestine to the Mongols (or Tartars, as they were commonly known in the West) early in 1253 in a missionary capacity and, as he told his Mongol interlocutors more than once, in accordance with the Rule of his Order. News had reached Louis' crusading army that the Mongol prince Sartaq was a Christian, and so the friar's first goal was Sartaq's encampment on the western banks of the Volga. He also intended to make contact with some Germans who had been enslaved by the Mongols during the invasion of Hungary in 1241–42 and to bring them spiritual comfort. The letter he and his colleague carried from the king to Sartaq was simply one of recommendation, in which Louis in addition sent felicitations to the Mongol prince on his conversion: ironically, it was this which was misinterpreted by the Mongols as a request for an alliance against the Islamic world and so prolonged the friars' journey.[1] Sartaq despatched Rubruck and his colleague to his father Batu, the ruler of the so-called Golden Horde, who in turn forwarded them to the court of his cousin, the great khan (*qaghan*) Möngke (1251–59). There they arrived in December 1253 and stayed until July 1254, when Möngke sent Rubruck back with a letter ordering King Louis to accept his place in the Mongol world-empire and to submit. On his arrival in Syria in 1255, Rubruck found that Louis had left the country well over a year previously. As the Franciscan provincial minister would not allow him to travel to France, he was obliged to send his report to the king, with the request that Louis ask the minister to release him. Since the English Franciscan Roger Bacon, who was in Paris a few years later, records having met Rubruck, we can assume that Louis's intercession was successful. After this, Rubruck disappears from view.[2]

Because Rubruck's *Itinerarium* was in the nature of a private letter and not the account of an official embassy, it seems to have barely circulated, and we may have Bacon to thank that it was preserved at all, for the four principal surviving

[*] Department of History, University of Keele, England.
[1] Jean Richard, 'Sur les pas de Plancarpin et de Rubrouck: la lettre de saint Louis à Sartaq', *Journal des Savants*, (1977), 49–61, reprinted in his *Croisés, missionnaires et voyageurs: les perspectives orientales du monde latin médiéval* (London, 1983).

[2] For what is known of Rubruck, see the translation of the *Itinerarium* by Peter Jackson, introduction, notes and appendices by Peter Jackson with David Morgan, *The Mission of Friar William of Rubruck: His Journey to the Court of the Great Khan Möngke*, Works issued by the Hakluyt Society, Sec. Ser., clxxiii (Cambridge, 1990), 39–47.

manuscripts are all English. Indeed, it looks very much as if, until Rubruck was rediscovered by Richard Hakluyt, in the late sixteenth century, the material in the *Itinerarium* was available only in abridged form through the medium of Bacon's *Opus maius*.[3] The comparison with the report of Rubruck's fellow Franciscan John of Plano Carpini, who had visited the Mongols as the ambassador of Pope Innocent IV in 1246–47, is instructive. The surviving manuscripts of Plano Carpini's *Ystoria Mongalorum* are numerous: there are variant recensions, of which one at least, the so called 'Tartar Relation', was composed in eastern Europe even before Carpini had rejoined the pope.[4] In terms of its contents, moreover, the *Itinerarium*, which reads for the most part like Rubruck's memoirs and is accordingly rambling and laced with digressions, has been compared unfavourably with Carpini's *Ystoria*—admittedly a systematic dossier composed by an experienced diplomat and administrator whose task was to assess the extent of the Mongol danger and to propose a means of countering it.[5]

But the comparison can be misleading. Rubruck's report is undeniably a more human document than is Plano Carpini's. In the first place, it has a certain quality of intimacy, since a remark in the epilogue suggests that the friar numbered Louis among the 'spiritual friends' whom he was anxious to see once more.[6] And secondly, the king had told Rubruck to write down for him everything he had seen among the 'Tartars'.[7] Rubruck seems to have interpreted this commission fairly broadly, and one wonders what Louis made of a report which contained material not only on the Mongols—the way they constructed their tents, the way they made *qumis* ('comos', fermented mare's milk), the rituals that surrounded sickness and death, their various taboos—but also on languages, geography, Korean costume, Chinese medicine, and Inner Asian fauna (Rubruck is the first European writer to mention the *ovis Poli*, or *arghali*, the great horned sheep which of course takes its name from a Venetian adventurer who sighted it twenty years or so later). Unsystematic Rubruck's report may be for the most part (at least after chapters II–VIII, which are devoted to specific aspects of Mongol life), and lacking in any overall practical purpose. But it is full of personal reactions to the trying and alarming situations in which Rubruck and his colleague found themselves. It is for

---

[3] Jarl Charpentier, 'William of Rubruck and Roger Bacon', in: *Hyllningsskrift tillägnad Sven Hedin på hans 70-årsdag den 19. Febr. 1935* (Stockholm, 1935), 255–67.

[4] See pp. 91–2 of Peter Jackson, 'William of Rubruck: a Review Article', *Journal of the Royal Asiatic Society of Great Britain and Ireland*, (1987), 91–7.

[5] For a slightly unfair comparison of the two reports, see vol. II, pp. 375–81 of C. R. Beazley, *The Dawn of Modern Geography. A History of Exploration and Geographical Science from the Conversion of the Roman Empire to AD 900 (c. AD 900–1260 - AD 1264–1420) ... With Reproduction of the Principal Maps of the Time*, 3 vols. (London, 1897–1906).

[6] Rubruck, *Itinerarium*, Epilogue, 1, in Anastasius van den Wyngaert (ed.), *Sinica Franciscana, i. Itinera et relationes fratrum minorum saeculi XIII et XIV* (Quaracchi-Florence, 1929), 330; tr. Jackson & Morgan (op. cit. n. 2), p. 276. For Louis's friendship towards the Mendicants, see Lester K. Little, 'Saint Louis's involvement with the friars', *Church History*, xxxiii (1964), 125–48; William Chester Jordan, *Louis IX and the Challenge of the Crusade: a Study in Rulership* (Princeton, 1979), 129–30.

[7] Rubruck (op. cit. n. 6), Preface, 2, p. 164; tr. Jackson & Morgan (op. cit. n. 2), p. 59.

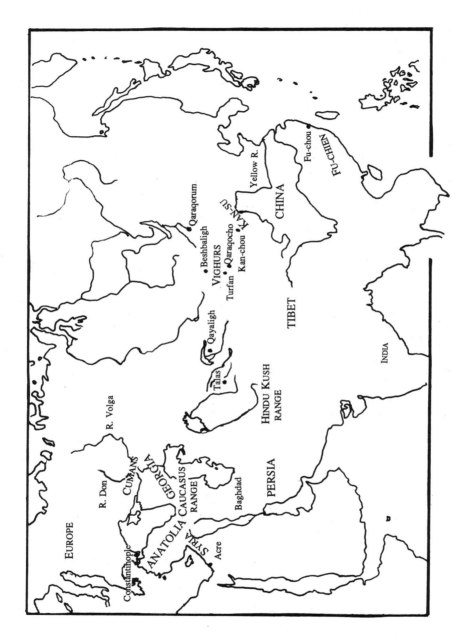

II. RUBRUCK'S JOURNEY THROUGH ASIA, 1253–55

these reasons that the authors of a recent French translation could say: 'It is a film as much as a book.'[8]

It is true that Rubruck does not emerge from his narrative as particularly erudite. He often misquotes Scripture, and he quotes the *Aeneid* once, incorrectly. As we shall see he was clearly familiar with St Augustine's writings against Manichaeism, though possibly only through the intermediary of that great text-book of twelfth-century theology, the *Sententiae* of Peter Lombard, which was one of the books he carried with him on his journey.[9] He appeals on several occasions to the *Etymologiae* of Isidore of Seville (d. 636), and once mentions the third-century author Solinus. Otherwise we do not know from what sources he culled his preconceptions about Asia: although he alludes to the Plano Carpini mission (and incidentally garbles his fellow Franciscan's name as 'Polycarpo'), there is no evidence that he had read Carpini's report. His information on the past history of Hungary and the Balkans is gleaned from unnamed chroniclers (though he may, it seems, have been citing Godfrey of Viterbo's *Pantheon*).

Apart from that, we know nothing—as he may have done. But there can be no doubt concerning his powers of observation, the curiosity that impelled him to seek further information, his keen critical sense and the scientific accuracy of his account. He is the first traveller to notice that the languages of the Russians, Poles, Bohemians, 'Slavonians' and Wends (here termed 'Vandals') were closely related,[10] and comments later on the kinship of the Cuman and Uighur languages, both of course belonging to the Turkish family.[11] To Rubruck goes the credit of correctly identifying the people of 'Great Cathay' (China) with the *Seres* of Classical Antiquity.[12] He does not hesitate to challenge the authority of learned men of bygone ages, not least Isidore. Regarding the Caspian Sea, Rubruck points out that it is not a gulf extending inland from the Ocean, as Isidore had asserted, but is completely landlocked.[13] Isidore, moreover, had spoken of dogs in the far north so large and so fierce that they would attack bulls and kill lions. Rubruck is more cautious. 'What is true, I learned from tales I heard,' he says, 'is that towards the Northern Ocean dogs are used, on account of their great size and strength, to draw wagons, like oxen.'[14] This is no credulous simpleton ready to purvey the old myths about the East. Where Plano Carpini's report had soberly listed fabulous races like the Parossitae and the Cynocephali among the nations of Asia subjugated by the Mongols,[15] Rubruck asked his Mongol hosts about these monsters mentioned by Isidore and Solinus: he was told that such creatures had never been sighted, 'which makes us doubt very much', he says, 'whether it is

---

[8] Claude & René Kappler (tr. and annot.), *Guillaume de Rubrouck envoyé de saint Louis. Voyage dans l'empire mongol, 1253–55* (Paris, 1985), 61–2.

[9] Rubruck (op. cit. n. 6), xvi. 3, p. 204; tr. Jackson & Morgan (op. cit. n. 2), p. 120.

[10] Rubruck (op. cit. n. 6), xxi. 4, p. 219; tr. Jackson & Morgan (op. cit. n. 2), p. 139.

[11] Rubruck (op. cit. n. 6), xxvi. 4, p. 234; tr. Jackson & Morgan (op. cit. n. 2), p. 159.

[12] Rubruck (op. cit. n. 6), xxvi. 8, p. 236; tr. Jackson & Morgan (op. cit. n. 2), p. 161.

[13] Rubruck (op. cit. n. 6), xviii. 5, p. 211; tr. Jackson & Morgan (op. cit. n. 2), p. 129.

[14] Rubruck (op. cit. n. 6), xix. 1, pp. 211–12; tr. Jackson & Morgan (op. cit. n. 2), p. 130.

[15] Plano Carpini, *Ystoria Mongalorum quos nos Tartaros appellamus*, v. 30, 31, 33, in Van den Wyngaert (op. cit. n. 6), vol. i, pp. 73, 74–5.

true'.[16] Only once or twice does he appear to have swallowed some new improbable story, as when he passes on without comment information he had received about a city in Cathay with walls of silver and battlements of gold; though he rejected, on the other hand, a tale concerning a country beyond Cathay where people remained at whatever age they were on entering it.[17]

One important consequence of Rubruck's voracious appetite for information is that it leaves the reader in no doubt as to the authenticity of the travelogue. It has been questioned whether Marco Polo's *Divisament dou Monde* provides conclusive testimony that the celebrated Venetian was ever in China;[18] and indeed the later Middle Ages would witness a number of reports of journeys that were, either totally or in part, imaginary.[19] Even Plano Carpini appears to have been afraid that his experiences would not be accepted as genuine; hence the list of persons whom he had met en route inserted at the end of the *Ystoria*.[20] Rubruck voices no such apprehensions; nor did he need to do so. His fear is not that he will not be believed, but that his report will be found wanting. He admits in his preface to being overawed by the task of writing to so exalted a monarch. The report begins with words from Ecclesiasticus concerning the wise man, 'He shall pass into the country of strange peoples; he shall try good and evil in all things'; and then continues, 'This task I have accomplished, my lord king, but may it have been as a wise man and not as a fool, for many do what a wise man does, yet not in a wise manner but foolishly rather, and I fear I am one of them.'[21] And when struggling to describe the Mongol tents, he pauses to exclaim: 'Indeed I should have drawn everything for you had I known how to draw.'[22]

Rubruck was no pacifist. One looks in vain for the qualities commonly associated with the founder of the Franciscan Order; and those scholars who have been at pains to stress that mission and crusade were by no means opposed to each other but were complementary[23] might well draw on Rubruck's *Itinerarium* for

---

[16] Rubruck (op. cit. n. 6), xxix.46, p. 269; tr. Jackson & Morgan (op. cit. n. 2), p. 201. See generally John Block Friedman, *The Monstrous Races in Medieval Art and Thought* (Cambridge, Mass., 1981).

[17] Rubruck (op. cit. n. 6), xxvi.8, and xxix.49, pp. 236, 270; tr. Jackson & Morgan (op. cit. n. 2), pp. 161, 202–3.

[18] John W. Haeger, 'Marco Polo in China: Problems with Internal Evidence', *Bulletin of Sung and Yüan Studies*, xiv (1978), 22–30.

[19] J. K. Hyde, 'Real and imaginary journeys in the later Middle Ages', *Bulletin of the John Rylands Library of the University of Manchester*, lxv (1982), 125–47. Jean Richard, 'Voyages réels et voyages imaginaires, instruments de la connaissance géographique au Moyen-Age', in: *Culture et travail intellectuel dans l'Occident médiéval*, Centre National de la Recherche Scientifique (Paris, 1981), 211-20, reprinted in his *Croisés, missionnaires et voyageurs* (op. cit. n. 1). For an example from the Islamic world, see Stephen Janicsek, 'Ibn Baṭṭūṭa's Journey to Bulghār: Is it a Fabrication?', *Journal of the Royal Asiatic Society of Great Britain and Ireland*, (1929), 791–800.

[20] Plano Carpini (op. cit. n. 15), ix.49–51, pp. 128–9.

[21] Rubruck (op. cit. n. 6), Preface, 2, p. 164; tr. Jackson & Morgan (op. cit. n. 2), p. 59.

[22] Rubruck (op. cit. n. 6), ii.4, p. 173; tr. Jackson & Morgan (op. cit. n. 2), p. 74.

[23] Elizabeth Siberry, 'Missionaries and Crusaders, 1095–1274: Opponents or Allies?' in: W. J. Sheils (ed.), *The Church and War. Papers read at the Twenty-First Summer Meeting and the Twenty-Second Winter Meeting of the Ecclesiastical History Society* (London, 1983), 103–10;

further evidence. He advocates sending crusading forces through Anatolia in view of the enfeebled condition of the Seljük Turks since the Mongol onslaught of 1243.[24] He believes that the Teutonic Knights could conquer Russia with ease, because were the Mongols to learn that the Pope was launching a crusade against them, they would surely flee back into their wilderness.[25] At one point the friar himself all but dons crusading armour. When he reached the *qaghan*'s encampment, he tells us, the Mongols were nonplussed at his arrival, since he had not come to make peace (which in their vocabulary meant submission). 'For they have already reached such a level of arrogance that they believe the whole world is longing to make peace with them. Certainly for my own part I would, if permitted, preach war against them, to the best of my ability, throughout the world.'[26]

Indeed the friar did not find the Mongols themselves unduly impressive. He was the first person from the Latin world to visit their 'capital', Qaraqorum, which he dismisses as smaller than the Parisian suburb of Saint Denis, and the *qaghan*'s palace, he tells us, was inferior in size to the abbey of Saint Denis.[27] Nor were the Mongols particularly formidable warriors. Rubruck was clearly struck by their organizational capacity, and at the very end of the *Itinerarium* he pays implicit tribute to their powers of endurance, with his observation that if Western armies were ready to put up with similar conditions they could conquer the world.[28] But earlier he comments that the Mongols had never conquered any country by force, only by subterfuge.[29] The general impression to be gleaned from his account of the Mongol world is one of poverty and meagre resources: prior to Chinggis Khan's time, at least, the Mongols had been a 'poverty-stricken tribe';[30] Mongol armour, made up of strips of boiled leather, was 'ill-fitting and unwieldy', and during his return journey through the Caucasus he noticed that his escort wore armour looted from their Alan enemies.[31] There is no trace of the Mongols' role as fearful harbingers of the Apocalypse, so often found in chronicle accounts of the great invasion of 1241-42.[32] Here they are seen not as some eschatological

---

eadem, *Criticism of crusading 1095-1274* (Oxford, 1985), 16-9, 207-8. For the Mendicants, see Benjamin Z. Kedar, *Crusade and Mission: European Approaches towards the Muslims* (Princeton, 1984), chapter 4.

[24] Rubruck (op. cit. n. 6), Epilogue, 3-4, pp. 330-1; tr. Jackson & Morgan (op. cit. n. 2), pp. 277-8.

[25] Rubruck (op. cit. n. 6), xiii.2, p. 195; tr. Jackson & Morgan (op. cit. n. 2), p. 107.

[26] Rubruck (op. cit. n. 6), xxviii.3, p. 244; tr. Jackson & Morgan (op. cit. n. 2), p. 173.

[27] Rubruck (op. cit. n. 6), xxxii.1, p. 285; tr. Jackson & Morgan (op. cit. n. 2), p. 221.

[28] Rubruck (op. cit. n. 6), xix.4, p. 213; tr. Jackson & Morgan (op. cit. n. 2), p. 131; Epilogue, 4, p. 331; tr. Jackson & Morgan (op. cit. n. 2), p. 278.

[29] Rubruck (op. cit. n. 6), xxxiii.3, p. 290; tr. Jackson & Morgan (op. cit. n. 2), p. 227.

[30] Rubruck (op. cit. n. 6), xvii.4, p. 207; tr. Jackson & Morgan (op. cit. n. 2), p. 124.

[31] Rubruck (op. cit. n. 6), xxxvii.17, pp. 317-18; tr. Jackson & Morgan (op. cit. n. 2), pp. 259-60.

[32] Davide Bigalli, *I Tartari e l'Apocalisse. Ricerche sull' escatalogia in Adamo Marsh e Ruggero Bacone* (Florence, 1971). Anna-Dorothee von den Brincken, 'Die Mongolen im Weltbild der Lateiner um die Mitte des 13. Jahrhunderts unter besonderer Berücksichtigung des *Speculum Historiale* des Vincenz von Beauvais O.P.', *Archiv für Kulturgeschichte*, lvii (1975), 117-40. G. A. Bezzola, *Die Mongolen in abendländischer Sicht [1220-1270]: ein Beitrag zur Frage der Völkerbegegnungen* (Berne & Munich, 1974), 100 ff., 128-9.

phenomenon but simply as the successors of the Huns (less powerful than the Huns, in the friar's view, because they did not advance as far as Gaul); and hence they can be placed squarely in the tradition of previous invaders of eastern Europe. At one point, he applies to them the words of Deuteronomy: they are 'no people and a foolish nation'.[33] Throughout Rubruck's narrative, then, the Mongols appear as human beings—greedy, cunning, boorish, and at times profoundly irritating, but human beings for all that. It is as if he is determined to reduce them to lifesize.

As a missionary, however, Rubruck's concern was primarily with religious matters, and it is to those that I want to devote most of this paper. The friar met many Christians in the course of his stay in Mongol territory. Although he was unable to make contact with the German slaves of whom he had gone in search, he nevertheless came upon a number of other European slaves who had been taken prisoner by the Mongols over a decade previously: those he singles out for especial mention at or near Qaraqorum include the Parisian goldsmith William Buchier, whose adopted son would serve Rubruck as interpreter during the religious debate.[34] But much of Rubruck's time was spent with non-Latin Christians, in particular an Armenian monk, Sergius (Sargis), who had arrived at Möngke's court one month before the friars, and Nestorian Christians belonging to what was of course the dominant Christian sect in Inner Asia. The gulf that separated the Franciscan—member of a newly founded order which represented the spiritual shock-troops of the Latin West—from these eastern Christians emerges strikingly from the narrative.

Some of the Nestorians' practices, those which harmonized with the usage of the Western church, clearly met with Rubruck's approval. He notes that at Qaraqorum on Easter Eve (1254) they baptized sixty souls 'in the most methodical fashion'.[35] And he reports that the Nestorians of these parts freely acknowledged the primacy of Rome.[36] But there were also divergences which tried his sense of Christian fraternity. He seems to have objected especially to the fact that the Armenian and Nestorian Christians had no use for the crucifix and employed only the cross without the figure of Christ: in fact, at one point, when Buchier brought to court a silver crucifix which he had manufactured for the *qaghan*, Sergius and the Nestorians removed from it the effigy of Christ, at which the friar was scandalized.[37] Rubruck inferred that these eastern Christians took a low view of the Passion or found it in some way embarrassing.[38] Yet at the same time he observed the great reverence with which the Nestorians worshipped the cross and

---

[33] Rubruck (op. cit. n. 6), xxi.2 and 4, pp. 219–20; tr. Jackson & Morgan (op. cit. n. 2), pp. 138–9. Bezzola (op. cit. n. 32), p. 181.

[34] See Leonardo Olschki, *Guillaume Boucher, a French artist at the court of the Khans* (Baltimore, 1946; repr. New York, 1969).

[35] Rubruck (op. cit. n. 6), xxx.14, p. 282; tr. Jackson & Morgan (op. cit. n. 2), p. 216.

[36] Rubruck (op. cit. n. 6), xxx.10, and xxxi.4, pp. 280, 283–4; tr. Jackson & Morgan (op. cit. n. 2), pp. 213–14, 218.

[37] Rubruck (op. cit. n. 6), xxix.62, pp. 275–6; tr. Jackson & Morgan (op. cit. n. 2), p. 208.

[38] Rubruck (op. cit. n. 6), xv.7, and xxix.34, pp. 203, 264; tr. Jackson & Morgan (op. cit. n. 2), pp. 117, 196.

taught others to worship it.[39] What he does not appear to have realized is that the cross the Nestorians revered (and presumably this applied also to an Armenian living under their influence) was not that on which Christ had suffered and died. For them the Passion was a single historical event in the past which was over and done with; their cross, rather, was that of the *Parousia*, the symbol of Christ's return in glory at the Last Judgement.[40]

Rubruck greatly deplored the fact that the Nestorian clergy tolerated pagan practices among those to whom they had access and who were sympathetic to the Christian faith, neglecting to teach them that such practices were wrong.[41] At one point he gives vent to a veritable diatribe against the Nestorians. Since a locality was visited by its bishop as seldom as once in fifty years, on such an occasion they had all their male children, even those in the cradle, ordained as priests, with the result that almost all their menfolk were priests. The priests were ignorant. They recited their office and had the scriptures in Syriac, a language they did not know, so that they chanted, he says, 'like the monks among us who know no grammar; and for this reason they are completely corrupt'. They married, some of them having several wives in the Mongol fashion, and those with one wife would marry again after her death. They were more active on behalf of their wives and families, and so had an eye less to spreading the faith than to making money. They practised usury and also simony, administering none of the sacraments without a fee. They were drunkards, and those of them who reared young Mongol princes alienated their charges through their immorality and greed, 'for the lives of the Mongols and even of the idolaters are more blameless than their own'.[42]

Some of these accusations are less than fair. Rubruck made little or no allowance for the predicament of Christian communities cut off by vast distances from their metropolitan authority in Baghdad and required to accommodate themselves to the exigencies of nomadic life. Ordination during rare episcopal visitations was doubtless a crucial precaution in the steppe in order to maintain the apostolic succession and to ensure the survival of a numerically adequate priesthood. Lacking, too, the tithes and landed endowments available to Latin ecclesiastical institutions, the Nestorian clergy would inevitably have been obliged to fall back on other sources of income such as fees, so that the charge of simony does not seem altogether appropriate to their situation.[43] As for the retention of pagan practices by new converts, the Western church itself in an earlier age, when

---

[39] Rubruck (op. cit. n. 6), xxix. 30–33, 35, pp. 262–4; tr. Jackson & Morgan (op. cit. n. 2), pp. 194–6; and see Jean Dauvillier's note in *Recherches sur les chrétiens d'Asie centrale et d'extrême-orient; en marge de Jean du Plan Carpin; Guillaume de Rubrouck; Màr Ya(h)-bʰallàhâ, Rabban Sàumâ et les princes Öngüt Chrétiens. Oeuvres posthumes de Paul Pelliot* (Paris, 1973), 169–70.

[40] Jean Dauvillier, 'Les croix triomphales dans l'ancienne église chaldéenne', *Eléona* (October, 1956), 11–17, and his 'Guillaume de Rubrouck et les communautés chaldéennes d'Asie centrale au moyen âge', *L'Orient Syrien*, ii (1957), 237–8; both reprinted in his *Histoire et institutions des Eglises orientales au Moyen Age* (London, 1983).

[41] Rubruck (op. cit. n. 6), xxix. 42, p. 267; tr. Jackson & Morgan (op. cit. n. 2), p. 199.

[42] Rubruck (op. cit. n. 6), xxvi. 12–14, p. 238; tr. Jackson & Morgan (op. cit. n. 2), pp. 163–4.

[43] Anna-Dorothee von den Brincken, *Die 'Nationes Christianorum Orientalium' im Verständnis der lateinischen Historiographie*, Kölner Historische Abhandlungen, 22 (Cologne, 1973), 304–6.

evangelizing the pagan Germanic peoples, had countenanced the survival of pre-Christian practices in order to ease the transition to the new faith. How much more likely was this to be the case at the time of Rubruck's visit to Central Asia, where a number of faiths had for centuries jockeyed for influence and syncretism was inescapably part of the religious landscape? Even 'one of the wiser among the Nestorian priests', says the friar, enquired of him whether the souls of animals were able to pass after death to a place where they would not be obliged to suffer.[44] Such penetration of Christianity by alien ideas—in this case Buddhist or possibly Manichaean—was not uncommon; nor was Christianity alone in undergoing contamination, as we shall see.[45]

Intellectually, the Nestorians with whom Rubruck associated at Qaraqorum come across as lightweight. The *qaghan* Möngke ordered the Christians, the Muslims and the Buddhists there to participate in a public debate on the merits of their respective religions. On the eve of the debate, Rubruck consulted with the Nestorians as to how best to proceed. They wished first to attack the Muslims, with whom the relations of the Nestorian communities throughout Western and Central Asia had doubtless been more strained than with the Buddhists. Rubruck pointed out to them that it was preferable to dispute with the Buddhists first, since the Muslims, like the Christians, were monotheistic and would thereby begin as their allies. When they next rehearsed arguments, and Rubruck asked them to prove the existence of God, the Nestorians could only catalogue scriptural texts, to which, as the friar observed, their opponents would simply respond with their own writings.[46] This discussion, as also the debate itself the following day when Rubruck took first turn at representing the Christian viewpoint, demonstrates the Westerner's superiority in dialectic over his eastern brethren.[47] Like the criticisms of Nestorian morality, it highlights the divergent paths taken by the two churches over the previous centuries. Rubruck represented a church that was the product of the eleventh-century Gregorian Reform movement and of other important developments in thought and letters during the twelfth. The picture he draws of the Nestorians strikingly evokes a church that shared many of the characteristics of the Latin ecclesiastical establishment in, say, the ninth or tenth century.

It is in any case important to see the friar's strictures in context. Rubruck met no Nestorian cleric above the rank of priest. The priest Jonas, whose father had been an archdeacon and who was regarded by his colleagues as one also, seems

---

[44] Rubruck (op. cit. n. 6), xxxiii. 15, p. 295; tr. Jackson & Morgan (op. cit. n. 2), p. 232.

[45] Wolfgang Hage, 'Christentum und Schamanismus: zur Krise des Nestorianertums in Zentralasien', in: Bernd Jaspert & Rudolf Mohr (eds.), *Traditio-Krisis-Renovatio aus theologischer Sicht: Festschrift Winfried Zeller zum 65. Geburtstag* (Marburg, 1976), 114–24. See generally Walther Heissig & Hans-Joachim Klimkeit (eds.), *Synkretismus in den Religionen Zentralasiens. Ergebnisse eines Kolloquiums vom 24.5. bis 26.5.1983 in St. Augustin bei Bonn*, Studies in Oriental Religion, 13 (Wiesbaden, 1987).

[46] Rubruck (op. cit. n. 6), xxxiii. 11, pp. 293–4; tr. Jackson & Morgan (op. cit. n. 2), p. 231.

[47] R. W. Southern, *Western views of Islam in the Middle Ages* (Cambridge, Mass., 1962), 51. Johannes Fried, 'Auf der Suche nach der Wirklichkeit: die Mongolen und die europäische Erfahrungswissenschaft im 13. Jahrhundert', *Historische Zeitschrift*, ccxliii (1986), 287–332, see esp. pp. 308–10, 312.

to have struck him as an exception, since he is described as 'a well-read man' and clearly won Rubruck's respect: it was unfortunate, perhaps, that his death occurred prior to the debate.[48] Nor does Rubruck seem at any time to have had contact with a Nestorian monk: although we are told of the arrival at Möngke's court, just before Rubruck's departure, of a monk who 'had the appearance of a man of sense', there is no indication that the friar ever met him.[49] Consequently we have no way of knowing what Rubruck would have made of a bishop or a monk of the unimpeachable scholarly or moral attainments of Rabban Sawma, who was to visit Western Europe as a Mongol envoy in 1287.[50]

The *Itinerarium* gives the impression that Möngke's court was haunted by different religious groups each trying to claim the *qaghan* as its own. Sometimes the confrontation could take an extreme turn: the Nestorian Jonas was apparently poisoned by the Armenian monk Sergius as part of a jostling for influence at court.[51] Nestorian clerics told Rubruck that Möngke had been baptized, and the Armenian monk assured him that Möngke put his faith exclusively in the Christians. Nevertheless, says the friar: 'he was lying, inasmuch as the khan believes in none of them … And yet they all follow his court as flies do honey, and he makes them all gifts and all of them believe they are on intimate terms with him and forecast his good fortune.'[52] Such optimism as to the possibility of winning over the *qaghan* was fuelled by the religious policy of the Mongol government. The Mongol sovereigns required all holy men—the religious class within each confessional group—to pray for them: such religious were in fact exempted from the head tax and from all forced labour. This policy seems to have sprung from the belief that all faiths were but different ways of worshipping the one god—the sky-god, Tenggeri, of steppe tradition.[53] Later Rubruck had the opportunity to hear the *qaghan*'s religious beliefs from his own mouth, during their final interview, when Möngke spoke of shamanistic practices as just one of the paths to God given to humanity.[54] In fact, Möngke remained strongly attached to his ancestral shamanism; though a few years after Rubruck's visit he is found

---

[48] Rubruck (op. cit. n. 6), xxix. 56, and xxxi. 2–7, pp. 273, 283–5; tr. Jackson & Morgan (op. cit. n. 2), pp. 206, 217–19.

[49] Rubruck (op. cit. n. 6), xxxvi. 17, p. 311; tr. Jackson & Morgan (op. cit. n. 2), p. 252.

[50] Jean Dauvillier, 'Les provinces chaldéennes "de l'extérieur" au moyen âge', in: *Mélanges F. Cavallera* (Toulouse, 1948), 312; repr. in his *Histoire et institutions* (op. cit. n. 40). Jean Richard, 'La mission en Occident de Rabban Çauma et l'union des églises', *XIIᵉ Convegno Volta. Oriente e Occidente nel medio evo* (Rome, 1957), 162–7; reprinted in his *Orient et Occident au moyen âge: contacts et relations* (London, 1976).

[51] Rubruck (op. cit. n. 6), xxxi. 2 and 7, pp. 283, 285; tr. Jackson & Morgan (op. cit. n. 2), pp. 217, 219.

[52] Rubruck (op. cit. n. 6), xxix. 15–16, pp. 256–7; tr. Jackson & Morgan (op. cit. n. 2), p. 187-8.

[53] Thomas T. Allsen, *Mongol Imperialism: the Policies of the Grand Qan Möngke in China, Russia, and the Islamic lands, 1251–1259* (Berkeley & Los Angeles, 1987), 121–2. D. O. Morgan, *The Mongols* (Oxford, 1986), 44.

[54] Rubruck (op. cit. n. 6), xxxiv. 2, p. 298; tr. Jackson & Morgan (op. cit. n. 2), pp. 236–7.

expressing the view that Buddhism stood in relation to other faiths as did the palm of the hand to the fingers.[55]

As for Sartaq, Rubruck was not convinced that his Christian faith was genuine. At one juncture he simply asserts that he does not know whether the prince was a Christian or not, but has the impression that Sartaq held Christians in derision, since he accepted gifts from Christian envoys as they passed through his headquarters on their way to his father Batu, but sent Muslims on more expeditiously if their gifts were superior.[56] Earlier he states categorically that Sartaq was not a Christian, and that rumours of his Christian faith, like those about Möngke himself and his predecessor, the *qaghan* Güyüg (1246–48), and like the still earlier stories about Prester John, had arisen from the tendency of the Nestorians to exaggerate: 'for', he says, 'they create big rumours out of nothing.'[57] And yet Sartaq's Christianity is in fact attested not only by Armenian and Syriac sources but also by Muslim authors, who surely had no interest in distorting the truth here.[58] In some measure, Rubruck's remarks may be connected with his reservations about the Nestorians in general; but another consideration may be more relevant. Before he left Sartaq's encampment, he was told by the prince's chancellor, Quyaq: 'Do not say that our master is a Christian: he is not a Christian; he is a Mongol.' Rubruck concluded that for the Mongols 'Christendom' denoted a people, 'and although', he says, 'they may perhaps have some belief in Christ they have no desire to be called Christians, since they want to promote their own name, Mongol, to a level above all others.'[59] The friar may well have been right about the ethnic content of the word 'Christian'. But perhaps the essential point to be grasped is a different one: whatever the religious sympathies of any individual Mongol prince or general, his first concern was the maintenance and extension of the Mongol empire.

Muslims were also to be found at the headquarters of Möngke and other Mongol princes. In so far as Rubruck has anything opprobrious to say about the Muslims, it seems to be at Batu's encampment, where they were possibly more numerous and enjoyed greater influence than further east. He refers to the Bulgars of the Volga region as 'the worst sort of Saracens' on account of their strictness in observing the faith; in answer to Batu's enquiry with whom King Louis was at war, he employs the customary formula that the 'Saracens' were profaning the house of God in Jerusalem; and here too there is a passing reference to a 'Saracen' who was supposed to take care of the friars at Batu's camp but neglected to

---

[55] Édouard Chavannes, 'Inscriptions et pièces de chancellerie chinoises de l'époque mongole', *T'oung Pao*, Sec. Ser., v (1904), 381–3.

[56] Rubruck (op. cit. n. 6), xviii. 1, p. 209; tr. Jackson & Morgan (op. cit. n. 2), p. 126.

[57] Rubruck (op. cit. n. 6), xvii. 2, p. 206; tr. Jackson & Morgan (op. cit. n. 2), p. 122.

[58] Juwaynī, *Ta'rīkh-i Jahān-gushā*, ed. Mīrzā Muhammad Qazwīnī, Gibb Memorial Series, xvi (Leiden & London, 1912–37), i, p. 223; J. A. Boyle (tr.), *The History of the World-Conqueror* (Manchester, 1958), 268. Jūzjānī, *Tabaqāt-i Nāṣirī*, sec. ed. ʿAbd al-Haiy Habībī (Kabul 1342–3 solar / 1963–4), ii, p. 217. For other references see Rubruck, tr. Jackson and Morgan (op. cit. n. 2), p. 126, n. 1.

[59] Rubruck (op. cit. n. 6), xvi. 5, p. 205; tr. Jackson & Morgan (op. cit. n. 2), p. 120.

provide them with any food.[60] Otherwise the report is free of polemic about Islam and the Muslims, and one has the impression that Rubruck felt more charitably towards them than towards the Buddhists or the shamans—and certainly than he did towards the Mongols. We have seen that he viewed the Muslims as allies initially in the public debate. When the Buddhists had been vanquished, he made way for the Nestorians, who wished to continue the disputation with the Muslims. But the Muslims, he tells us, declined to argue, conceding that the Christian faith was true, as was everything in the Gospel, and confessing that they wished to die a Christian death.[61] Either Rubruck's interpreter was in difficulties at this juncture (and it must be borne in mind that Buchier's son may have understood only Mongolian and not Persian, which was in all likelihood the language of the Muslims present[62]), or these were decidedly heretical Muslims. Perhaps the explanation is that they recognized, as did Rubruck himself, that they had more in common with the Christians than with the other religious groups.

Rubruck is the first western observer to provide a reasonably full account of Buddhism. He cites, albeit in corrupted form, the Buddhists' incantation *Oṁ mani padme hūṁ*; he describes the interior of their pagodas, their sometimes extraordinarily large idols, and the dress and lifestyle of the Buddhist monks (whom he calls *tuins*, from Chinese *tao-jen*, 'men of the path').[63] He refers to the existence of several sects,[64] but distinguishes only two: those who believe in only one god, whom he terms the Uighurs ('Iugurs') after a Turkish people dwelling in the Tarim basin,[65] and those who worship many. Monks in the former category he met at Qayaligh en route for Möngke's court and argued with them about their use of idols until his interpreter proved incapable of finding the right words.[66] It was a Buddhist of the polytheistic variety who was his opponent in the debate at Qaraqorum. For all its virtues, however, the material on Buddhism in the *Itinerarium* suffers from two defects. One is that the friar wrongly links the Uighur form of Buddhism with the shamanism practised among the Mongols, of which he furnishes a rather full description elsewhere.[67] The grounds for this false equation seems to be that in each case only one god was worshipped, and consequently Rubruck has the Mongols belonging to the Uighur sect.[68] In this context it looks as if the Franciscan's readiness to identify fellow monotheists in

---

[60] Rubruck (op. cit. n. 6), xix. 3, 5 and 8, pp. 212, 213, 215; tr. Jackson & Morgan (op. cit. n. 2), pp. 131, 133.

[61] Rubruck (op. cit. n. 6), xxxiii. 20–1, p. 297; tr. Jackson & Morgan (op. cit. n. 2), p. 234.

[62] Huang Shijian, 'The Persian language in China during the Yüan dynasty', *Papers on Far Eastern History*, xxxiv (Sept., 1986), 83–95.

[63] Rubruck (op. cit. n. 6), xxiv. 5, xxv. 1–6, pp. 228–31; tr. Jackson & Morgan (op. cit. n. 2), pp. 151–2, 153–5.

[64] Rubruck (op. cit. n. 6), xxiii. 7, p. 227; tr. Jackson & Morgan (op. cit. n. 2), p. 149.

[65] Rubruck (op. cit. n. 6), xxiv. 4, xxv. 7, xxvi. 1, xxxiii. 22, pp. 228, 231, 233, 297; tr. Jackson & Morgan (op. cit. n. 2), pp. 151, 155, 157, 234.

[66] Rubruck (op. cit. n. 6), xxv. 7–8, pp. 231–2; tr. Jackson & Morgan (op. cit. n. 2), pp. 155–6.

[67] For the shamans, see Rubruck (op. cit. n. 6), xxxv, pp. 300–5; tr. Jackson & Morgan (op. cit. n. 2), pp. 240–5.

[68] Rubruck (op. cit. n. 6), xxv. 9, p. 232; tr. Jackson & Morgan (op. cit. n. 2), p. 156.

the interests of spreading the Gospel may have blinded him to reality. The confusion may have arisen in part also because, as Rubruck mentions quite correctly twice when describing the Uighur sect, the Mongols had borrowed the Uighur script[69] and it would have been natural to assume that they had adopted the Uighurs' religion as well.

The other defect is that Rubruck ascribes to Buddhists in general the dualist beliefs associated with Manichaeism. On this, the fourth great religion established in Central Asia, the friar has relatively little to say. Manichaeism, founded in Persia in the mid-third century AD, had flourished in Central Asia and had reached China by 694. Its heyday had coincided with the era of the Uighur empire, whose *qaghans* had adopted Manichaeism as the state religion in 762.[70] Following the overthrow of the empire in 840, its influence may have waned somewhat in the two successor-states founded by Uighur princes, one in Kan-chou and the other in Qaraqocho and Beshbaligh. By the time the first of these principalities had been absorbed into the Hsi-Hsia empire of the Tangut in 1028, Manichaeism there had been eclipsed by Buddhism.[71] But the Uighur kingdom in Beshbaligh survived significantly longer. Contrary to the assumption of a recent writer on Manichaeism,[72] this kingdom was not destroyed by the Mongols. Far from it: the Uighur king (*iduq-qut*), Bawurchuq, brought over his people to Chinggis Khan—the first city-dwellers to recognize Mongol overlordship, as Rubruck points out—and was given the conqueror's daughter in marriage.[73] Indeed, the Uighur kingdom enjoyed a considerable degree of autonomy under Mongol overlordship, at least until the end of the thirteenth century, when the Mongol Yüan emperors were no longer able to defend it against rival Mongol princes in Central Asia and the *iduq-qut* had to withdraw into Kan-su.[74] How had Manichaeism fared in the Beshbaligh kingdom? To this question we can return no certain answer. Buddhism had evidently obtained a considerable hold on the region by the thirteenth century.[75]

---

[69] Rubruck (op. cit. n. 6), xxv. 5, xxvi. 1, pp. 231, 233; tr. Jackson & Morgan (op. cit. n. 2), pp. 154, 157.

[70] Hans-Joachim Klimkeit, 'Das manichäische Königtum in Zentralasien', in: Klaus Sagaster & Michael Weiers (eds.), *Documenta Barbarorum. Festschrift für Walther Heissig zum 70. Geburtstag*, Veröffentlichungen der Societas Uralo-Altaica, 18 (Wiesbaden, 1983), 225–43.

[71] Elisabeth Pinks, *Die Uiguren von Kan-chou in der frühen Sung-Zeit (960–1028)*, Asiatische Forschungen, 24 (Wiesbaden, 1968), 113–4.

[72] Samuel N. C. Lieu, 'Precept and Practice in Manichaean Monasticism', *The Journal of Theological Studies*, New Series xxxii (1981), 160.

[73] Rubruck (op. cit. n. 6), xxvi. 1, p. 233; tr. Jackson & Morgan (op. cit. n. 2), p. 157.

[74] Thomas T. Allsen, 'The Yüan dynasty and the Uighurs of Turfan in the 13th century', in: Morris Rossabi (ed.), *China among Equals: the Middle Kingdom and its Neighbours, 10th—14th Centuries* (Berkeley, Los Angeles & London, 1983), 243–80. Geng Shimin & James Hamilton, 'L'inscription ouïgoure de la stèle commémorative des iduq qut de Qočo', *Turcica. Revue d'études Turques*, xiii (1981), 10–54.

[75] Annemarie von Gabain, *Das Leben im uigurischen Königreich von Qočo (850–1250)*, Veröffentlichungen der Societas Uralo-Altaica, 6 (Wiesbaden, 1973), i (Textband), 175–99; more briefly in her *Das uigurische Königreich von Chotscho, 850–1250*, Sitzungsberichte der deutschen Akademie der Wissenschaften zu Berlin, Klasse für Sprachen, Literatur und Kunst, Jhrg. 1961, no. 5 (Berlin, 1961), p. 69.

But we know that there was still a Manichaean monastery (*mānestān*) in Turfan during the Mongol epoch, because a document has survived telling us how it was rebuilt after being destroyed: the editors suggest that the monastery may have suffered from the attentions of a ruler who inclined towards Buddhism.[76] Be that as it may, there is no reason to believe that at the time of Rubruck's visit, Manichaeism had been completely obliterated by the rival faith.

Commentators have restricted themselves to noticing that Rubruck provides some slight evidence for the persistence of Manichaean influences in Central Asia in the mid-thirteenth century. Although I can claim no expertise on the subject of Manichaeism, it seems to me that there is more to be extracted from the report, and this is what I should like to explore in the remainder of the paper, though what I have to say will tend to be speculative given the nature of the evidence. One of the difficulties attending a quest for Manichaeans in this period is the attitude of the Muslims. Rubruck himself met Muslims who recoiled even from talking about such pagans.[77] And medieval Muslim authors betray a similar reluctance to distinguish different groups of 'idolaters'. Thus Hamd-Allāh Mustawfī Qazwīnī, for example, writing in the early fourteenth century, says of the Chinese that 'they are idolaters who make images according to the faith of Mani'; and in the mid-thirteenth century the chronicler Juwaynī outlines the religious system of the one-time Uighur empire in terms that could just as easily relate to Buddhism as to Manichaeism.[78] It has to be said, therefore, in Rubruck's defence that he is not alone in confusing Buddhists and Manichaeans.

The confusion is understandable. Manichaeism had undergone considerable penetration in both doctrine and practice by Buddhist influences: Buddhist deities are named in Manichaean treatises and hymns; Mani himself is depicted as the Buddha or said to be in a state of *nirvana*; and so on.[79] That the *tuins* may have included Manichaeans is not inherently improbable. It was characteristic of Manichaeism to camouflage itself in this fashion. Two examples lie to hand. Only thirty years previously the Taoist adept Ch'ang Ch'un, en route to wait upon Chinggis Khan in the Hindu Kush, passed through Beshbaligh (in the Uighur kingdom, as we have seen), and claims to have met there not only Buddhists but also Taoists; though he was struck by the fact that they dressed quite differently

---

[76] Geng Shimin & Hans-Joachim Klimkeit, 'Zerstörung manichäischer Klöster in Turfan', *Zentralasiatische Studien*, xviii (1985), 7–11.

[77] Rubruck (op. cit. n. 6), xxiv. 2, p. 228; tr. Jackson & Morgan (op. cit. n. 2), p. 151.

[78] Hamd-Allāh Mustawfī Qazwīnī, *Nuzhat al-qulūb*, ed. and tr. Guy Le Strange, Gibb Memorial Series, xxiii (Leiden & London, 1915–19), text p. 257 (*butparastān bāshand bar dīn-i Mānī sūratgar*), tr. p. 250. Juwaynī (op. cit. n. 58), i, p. 44 (tr. Boyle, p. 60).

[79] Samuel N. C. Lieu, *Manichaeism in the later Roman Empire and Medieval China* (Manchester, 1985), 208–13. Hans-Joachim Klimkeit, 'Buddhistische Übernahmen in iranischen und türkischen Manichäismus', in: Heissig & Klimkeit (op. cit. n. 45), pp. 58–75. Helwig Schmidt-Glintzer, 'Das buddistische Gewand des Manichäismus: zur buddhistischen Terminologie in den chinesischen Manichaica', ibid., 76–90.

from their *confrères* in China.[80] As has been pointed out, these people, domiciled as they were so many hundreds of miles from China, are most unlikely to have been Taoists, and they were almost certainly Manichaeans: genuine points of contact between the two religions did exist.[81] Our other example comes from China itself. Several years after Rubruck's mission, Marco Polo reports finding a community of 'Christians' at Fu-chou in the southern Chinese province of Fu-chien who kept no idols, worshipped no fire, and observed neither Muslim nor Christian rites. If Polo is to be believed, they were subsequently adjudged the status of Christians by Qubilai at their own request—and despite opposition from the local 'idolaters' (i.e. Buddhists), who regarded them as part of the Buddhist community.[82] The general view today is that they were adherents of the Manichaean faith, which is in fact known to have been strongly entrenched in Fu-chien.[83] It is only fair to add that in passing themselves off as devotees of other faiths the Manichaeans were not guilty of simple subterfuge. We might cite one of the leading authorities concerning Mani and his missionaries: 'as exponents of the one truly universal and fully consummated religion they believed that all the suitable material they found in Christianity, in Zoroastrianism and in Buddhism was at their disposal.'[84] Syncretism, in other words, was built into the Manichaean world-view.

The 'Manichaean heresy' is mentioned twice in the whole of Rubruck's narrative, and each time only briefly. The first occasion is when Rubruck interrupts an argument between the Armenian monk Sergius and the Nestorian Jonas about the Creation. The issue was actually whether Man was created before Paradise or after, but in appealing to the friar's verdict Sergius asks, 'Did not the Devil, on the first day, bring earth from the four quarters of the world, make clay of it and then mould it into a human body, and God breathe a soul into it?' 'On hearing the Manichaean heresy', says Rubruck, 'and him uttering it publicly and without a blush, I gave him a sharp rebuke ...'[85] The other reference occurs in the context of the debate with the Buddhists at Qaraqorum. 'All of them', says Rubruck, 'belong to the Manichaean heresy, to the effect that one half of things is evil and the other half good, or at least that there are two principles; and as

---

[80] Li Chih-ch'ang, *Hsi-yü chi*, tr. Arthur Waley, *The Travels of an Alchemist: the Journey of the Taoist Ch'ang-ch'un from China to the Hindukush at the Summons of Chingiz Khan* (London, 1931), 80–1.

[81] P. Pelliot & Ed. Chavannes, 'Un traité manichéen retrouvé en Chine', part II, *Journal Asiatique*, 11e série, i (1913), 316–8.

[82] Marco Polo, (*Le divisament dou monde*), tr. A. Ricci, *The Travels of Marco Polo Translated into English from the Text of L. F. Benedetto* (London, 1931), 261–3: see P. Pelliot's review of the Benedetto edition on which this translation is based, in *Journal des Savants*, (1929), 42.

[83] P. Pelliot, 'Les traditions manichéennes au Foukien', *T'oung Pao*, xxii (1923), 193–208.

[84] Jes P. Asmussen, 'Der Manichäismus als Vermittler literarischen Gutes', *Temenos*, ii (1966), 8, cited in Klimkeit, 'Buddhistische Übernahmen', p. 73. In *X^uāstvānīft: Studies in Manichaeism* (Copenhagen, 1965), 147, Asmussen refers to their 'ingenious capability of accommodation' (cf. also p. 149). For further examples, see Lieu (op. cit. n. 79), pp. 206–17.

[85] Rubruck (op. cit. n. 6), xxix. 56, p. 274; tr. Jackson & Morgan (op. cit. n. 2), p. 206.

regards souls, they all believe that they pass from one body to another.'[86] One minor matter must be resolved at this juncture. In his commentary on Rubruck's report, published in 1900, W. W. Rockhill dismissed the idea that the transmigration of souls formed part of Mani's doctrine.[87] Subsequent research, however, brought to light conclusive evidence within Manichaean texts that this doctrine was indeed Manichaean and showed additionally that a wide range of mediaeval observers, both Christian and Muslim, knew that it was.[88] So Rubruck can be exonerated of error here.

Rubruck's opponent in the debate is described as a *tuin* who had come from 'Cathay'. But from the account of the confrontation it is clear that we are dealing either with a Buddhist who had assimilated Manichaean ideas on the Creation or with a Manichaean whose doctrine had been contaminated by Buddhist beliefs. The friar's own view, which I have just cited, is that it was the former; but perhaps the latter possibility should not be discounted. In any case, whatever the status of Rubruck's adversary, the friar employed against him arguments appropriate to a dispute with dualists; and it has been pointed out that for his line of reasoning he was greatly indebted to St Augustine, whose writings, notably the *De natura boni*, had included a powerful defence of Christianity against Manichaean teachings.[89] When invited to begin by discussing either how the world had been made or what became of souls after death, Rubruck opted instead, in true Augustinian fashion, to begin with God, because 'All things are from God'. When asked about the nature of his God, he issued a vigorous statement of God's omnipotence and omniscience. This provoked the question, 'If your God is as you say, why has he made half of things evil?' 'That is an error,' retorted Rubruck: 'It is not God who created Evil; everything that exists is good.' There followed the classic Manichaean question, 'Where does Evil come from?', to which the friar responded with the equally classic Augustinian statement, 'You ought first to ask what Evil is.' Shortly afterwards, Rubruck's part in the debate was abruptly curtailed when, if we can believe his version of events, he severely discomfited his antagonist and the Nestorians thereupon interposed in order to dispute with the Muslims.

There is an earlier episode in Rubruck's report which may possibly relate to an encounter with Manichaeism and which, so far as I know, has not been cited in that context. The friar is describing the idol temples in the town of Qayaligh ('Cailac' as he calls it), which lay on his outward route, and says that in one of these temples he met a man who had a cross on his hand in black ink, 'which led me', he says, 'to believe he was a Christian, since he answered like a Christian all

---

[86] Rubruck (op. cit. n. 6), xxxiii. 14, p. 295; tr. Jackson & Morgan (op. cit. n. 2), p. 232.

[87] W. W. Rockhill, *The Journey of William of Rubruck to the Eastern Parts of the World, 1253–1255*, Works issued by the Hakluyt Society, Sec. Ser., iv (London, 1900), 231, n. 1.

[88] A. V. Williams Jackson, 'The Doctrine of Metempsychosis in Manichaeism', *Journal of the American Oriental Society*, xlv (1925), 246–68.

[89] Samuel N. C. Lieu, 'Some themes in later Roman anti-Manichaean polemics: II', *Bulletin of the John Rylands Library of the University of Manchester*, lxix (1986–7), 248–50. Fried (op. cit. n. 47), pp. 310–11.

the questions I put to him.' Rubruck asked him why there was no cross or effigy of Christ in the temple and was told it was not their custom. 'From this,' he tells us, 'I concluded that they were Christians, and that the omission was due to faulty doctrine.'[90] It is curious that Rubruck, despite his seemingly insatiable appetite for knowledge, says no more on the subject. It is also tantalizing. The information we are given sets this particular establishment apart from anything else described in the entire narrative: it seems to have nothing to do either with the Buddhist temple described immediately afterwards or with the Nestorian church which the party came upon a mere three leagues from Qayaligh and which they entered joyfully because, Rubruck tells us, 'we had not seen a church for a long time'.[91] Can it be, therefore, that the building at Qayaligh was a *mānestān* and that the man to whom the friar spoke was a Manichaean? The brief description of the interior of the temple does not help us much, because we have no information as to how Manichaean establishments were decorated: such documents as we possess on individual monasteries relate to their economic base rather than to their spiritual or aesthetic aspects.[92] But we do know that the cross played a part in Manichaean iconography.[93] Rubruck also refers here to 'an image with wings rather like St Michael, and others resembling bishops, with their fingers held as if in blessing'.[94] Now this latter detail evokes the Buddhist teaching posture (*vitarkamudrā*), with the left hand raised, which is commonly found in Manichaean art;[95] and the winged figure of an archegos is also not unknown.[96] It would be ironic if at the very point where he may have entered a Manichaean temple and addressed a devotee of Mani the friar failed to recognize the fact.

It would be ironic, but not surprising. The Western religious, living in the shadow of St Augustine, was accustomed to dealing with Manichaean ideas, or what seemed to him to constitute Manichaean ideas even when the resemblance was hardly more than superficial. Thus the Cathars, and other, less important heretical groups before them in western Europe, were readily labelled Manichaean because their faith was essentially dualist;[97] though it is nowadays doubted

---

[90] Rubruck (op. cit. n. 6), xxiv. 1, p. 227; tr. Jackson & Morgan (op. cit. n. 2), p. 150.

[91] Rubruck (op. cit. n. 6), xxvii. 1, pp. 238–9; tr. Jackson & Morgan (op. cit. n. 2), p. 165.

[92] Peter Zieme, 'Ein uigurischer Text über die Wirtschaft manichäischer Klöster im uigurischen Reich', in: Louis Ligeti (ed.), *Researches in Altaic languages. Papers Read at the Meeting of the Permanent International Altaistic Conference Held in Szeged, August 22–28, 1971*, Bibliotheca Orientalis Hungarica, 20 (Budapest, 1975), 331–8. Geng Shimin, 'Notes on an ancient Uigur official decree issued to a Manichaean monastery', *Central Asiatic Journal*, xxxv (1991), 209–30.

[93] Hans-Joachim Klimkeit, 'Das Kreuzessymbol in der zentralasiatischen Religionsbegegnung. Zum Verhältnis von Christologie und Buddhologie in der Zentralasiatischen Kunst', *Zeitschrift für Religions- und Geistesgeschichte*, xxxi (1979), 99–115, see esp. p. 105 and Abb. 5.

[94] Rubruck (op. cit. n. 6), xxiv. 2, p. 227. The text, following MS C, reads *ymaginem*, which I accordingly translated (p. 151) as 'statue'; but I am now inclined to adopt the reading *ymaginationem* of MSS D, S and L, which might suggest, rather, a painting.

[95] Hans-Joachim Klimkeit, *Manichaean art and calligraphy*, Iconography of Religions, 20 (Leiden, 1982), plates 14b and 22, described at pp. 30, 35: both miniatures are from Qocho. At the latter place, Klimkeit describes the gesture as 'in a typically Manichaean fashion'.

[96] Lieu (op. cit. n. 79), p. 210.

[97] Steven Runciman, *The Medieval Manichee. A Study of the Christian Dualist Heresy*

whether the connection with Manichaeism can be sustained.[98] The Cathar movement had excited considerable anxiety in Western ecclesiastical circles during the previous hundred years, and the emergence of the new mendicant orders of friars was part of the response. Rubruck's intellectual background would have trained him to be on the alert for Manichaean doctrines; and in this respect, as in others we have examined, he appears very much a child of his time. We can be confident that he felt well equipped to deal with misconceptions, derived from Manichaeist teaching, about Creation or about the transmigration of souls. What he might not have been prepared to meet in the eastern steppe was a Manichaean in the flesh.

If I have been concerned in this paper to highlight areas of inaccuracy or misunderstanding in Rubruck's report, it is not out of any desire to denigrate that report generally. The *Itinerarium* is surely one of the most precious of medieval travelogues; in its vividness it does not simply tell us about the Mongol world but transports us there in person; the insights it provides into the religious situation in the empire are unmatched by any other source from the European side or from Western Asia. But it is important to remember that the report, for all its excellence, was still—like less meritorious writings—the work of an individual. The religious milieu it depicts is refracted for us through the lens of a thirteenth-century friar, one committed to voluntary poverty, preaching, and purity of doctrine. From such an observer, the standards of the Nestorian Church may have obtained less than their due; the hitherto unknown Buddhist faith may have met with only semi-comprehension; and Manichaeism—real Manichaeism rather than its shadowy vestiges in other religious systems or communities—may have escaped recognition altogether.

(Cambridge, 1947).

[98] Malcolm Lambert, *Medieval heresy: popular movements from Bogomil to Hus* (London, 1977), 13, 32–3, 63.

MARCO POLO'S VOYAGES: THE CONFLICT BETWEEN CONFIRMATION AND OBSERVATION

MARTIN GOSMAN[*]

During a banquet in honour of his safe return to Venice (1295), Marco Polo opened the hems and linings of his unsightly cloak, which had previously set his fellow townsmen laughing, and pulled out a quantity of precious stones, demonstrating the truth of at least some of his assertions about the Orient. This event, mentioned by the geographer Giovanni Battista Ramusio (1485–1557) in his *Navigazioni e viaggi*[1], is not to be found in the account Marco is said to have dictated, in 1298, to Rustichello of Pisa while imprisoned in Genoa.[2] Whatever the circumstances in which his text was written, this exhibition of precious stones is not only at the heart of Marco's story, but also highlights the problem of the reception of his rather remarkable account. It is not surprising that contemporaries called Marco a 'braggart': his story was too extraordinary. Whether or not Marco was aware of the possibility that he might not be believed, his account ends with the traditional protestations of reliability one finds in many medieval travel stories. In the last paragraph Marco insists not only on the exceptional nature of his adventure (nobody had ever seen so much of the inhabited world), but also on the truth and completeness of his information (everything that could be said about the

[*] Department of Romance Languages, University of Groningen, The Netherlands.

[1] See vol. iii, pp. 29–30 of Giovanni Battista Ramusio, *Navigazioni e viaggi*, ed. Marica Milanesi, 6 vols. (Turin, 1978–88).

[2] The genesis of Marco's account is confused and complex. According to the legend, Marco dictated his story to Rustichello who wrote it down in a Franco-Italian dialect. Italo M. Molinari is convinced of this ('Un articolo d'autore cinese su Marco Polo e la Cina', *Annali (Istituto Orientale di Napoli). Supplemento, 30*, 42, fasc. 1 (Naples, 1982)). A version of this text, probably corrected by a certain Grégoire, was given by Marco himself to Thibault de Cépoy. The oldest Tuscan version must be ascribed to Niccolò degli Ormanni (who died in 1309); the Latin text seems have been written by Francesco Pino around 1320. But there are other important sources of information about Marco's adventures. The first is Pietro Abano's *Conciliator differentium philosophorum et medicorum* (written before 1310). According to Pietro, Marco himself had provided him with many interesting details. See Michel Mollat, *Les explorateurs du XIIIe au XVIe siècle. Premiers regards sur des mondes nouveaux* (Paris, 1984), pp. 32. Another source is Ramusio mentioned above. In this paper, I mainly use Ruggero M. Ruggieri's edition of Polo's adventure: *Marco Polo. Il Milione. Introduzione, edizione del testo toscano («Ottimo»), note illustrative, esegetiche, linguistiche, repertori onomastici e lessicali* (Florence, 1986). The *Ottimo* redaction has less *fioritura* than the French one, though it is possible that the latter is closer to *an* original. Ruggieri's rather chaotic introduction is not really relevant. In order to obtain a 'reliable' image of the text, I shall refer from time to time to the translation of Marco's text into modern French by Louis Hambis, *La Description du Monde. Texte intégral en français moderne avec introduction et notes* (Paris, 1955). Hambis' scholarly work definitively outranks Ruggieri's.

Mongols, the Saracens as well as about many unknown regions of the world, could be found in his book). That is to say, as far as he had listed everything he thought his listeners needed to hear; he had not judged it worthwhile to mention a number of details concerning the countries around the Black Sea, and he suppressed other well-known facts: did not Venetians, Genoese and Pisans regularly visit those parts of the world? Was not their information already available to everyone?

There is no long list of sources of the kind found in John of Plano de Carpini's travel story.[3] Marco, however, produces some other protestations of veracity in what one could consider the first paragraph of his book. It would hardly be necessary to comment on that fact, were it not that he distinguishes facts registered by himself from those borrowed from reliable sources. The difference between the two kinds of observation, he says, will be stated clearly 'acciò che'l ... libro sia veritieri e sanza niuna menzogna' (p. 103). We are dealing here with a deliberate selection of elements which—at least that is what the opening line of the texts suggests—have some anthropological bias: Marco wants to discuss the 'diversità delle regioni del mondo' as well as the 'diversitade delle genti' living in those regions. Everything is told in good order. The concept of diversity, however, though frequently used in medieval texts, remains rather vague. Later on, I shall come back to it.

From reading the accounts of John of Plano de Carpini and William of Rubruck, and the reasons they give for their journeys into Mongol country, it is evident that the two Franciscans were sent eastward (the former by Innocent IV, the latter by Saint Louis) with a clearly defined mission: they were to analyse and describe the military power of the Mongols as well as convert them to Christianity.[4] There is nothing of this in Marco's account. There is no real explanation why the Polos wanted to return to the East, this time with Marco. Some indication can be found in chapters 2–17, where Marco not only summarizes the voyage of his father and uncle, but also his own. This last journey is presented as a kind of answer, given by the Polos, to a request from Khubilai Khan (1260–94) to the Pope, to send him six men

> che sapessero bene mostrare a l'idoli e a tutte altre generazioni di là che la loro legge era tutta altramenti e come ella era tutta opera di diavolo, e che sapessero mostrare per ragioni come la cristiana legge era migliore. Ancora pregò [= the Khan!] li due frategli che li dovessero recar l'olio de la làmpana ch'arde al Sepolcro di Cristo in Gerusalemme (pp. 108–9)

These details, mentioned again in chapters 10–11, are interesting. Marco suggests that, because of their very special relationship with the Mongol Khan, the Polo brothers were acting as ambassadors of the Holy See. There is no word—and this is significant—on the motivation for Khubilai Khan's request. It looks as if the latter were just waiting to be illuminated by the Christians. However, taking into account Rubruck's description of the religious orientation of the Mongols, one

---

[3] See Jean de Plan Carpin, *Histoire des Mongols*, tr. and annot. by Dom Jean Becquet & Louis Hambis (Paris, 1965), 130–2.

[4] Becquet & Hambis (op. cit. n. 3), p. 23; Claude & René Kappler, *Guillaume de Rubrouck. Envoyé de saint Louis. Voyage dans l'Empire Mongol (1253–1255)* (Paris, 1985), 83.

learns that their rulers adopted a tolerant attitude toward other religions. One could belong to whatever cult one wished, provided that in every prayer the salvation of the Khan's soul was addressed.[5] And that Khubilai Khan had never seen a *Latino*, that is to say a European, as Marco pretends (p. 106) is quite wrong: large numbers of European slaves and prisoners in the Mongol encampments had been seen by the missionaries mentioned above.

I have already mentioned that Marco gives no reason whatsoever for his journey to the Mongol empire. Moreover, he reveals almost nothing about the activities of his father, uncle and himself in the Far East. This is surprising, as commerce must have been their motive for returning to Khubilai Khan's court. After all, they were merchants. The Italian version mentions that Marco's father and uncle stayed for about three years in Chiapciu (p. 150), but there is no mention of what they did there. The French version adds (p. 75) that (according to Marco) their activities were of little interest and therefore not recorded. Thus, the account is characterized not only by selection of information put forward (as said before, Marco offered no information at all about the countries bordering the Black Sea), but also by a certain manipulation of facts as well as of character portrayed.

Marco is also rather cautious. Though we cannot really accuse him of the traditional eurocentrism that assumed the superiority of Latin Christian civilization, we must admit that, taking into account Mongol tolerance of religious diversity, it would be rather curious to suppose that the Khan should have admitted that his own religion was inferior to the Christian faith (he speaks of '... opera di diavolo ...'). Psychologically this is highly improbable: the Mongols were a strong military power, and too arrogant to give this possibility any serious thought. The truth must be either that Marco thought this was the case or—and this seems more plausible—that he simply could not afford to pretend that a serious discussion between Christianity and Mongol heathenism could be organized. That undoubtedly would have led to difficulties with the church. In discussions with Muslim theologians, Christians never abandoned their claim to superiority nor the hope of conversion of those 'idolatrous people' (did not the vernacular epic tradition mention several Islamic 'idols'?).[6]

There is another interesting detail in these paragraphs which, together, constitute a kind of prologue ('pròlago'; p. 115): Marco does not dwell upon the physical difficulties of his long journey. He just remarks that the second trip to Khubilai Khan's court took 'tre anni, per lo mal tempo e per gli fiumi, ch'erano grandi e di verno e di state' (p. 111), and is only interested in 'divisare delle provinci e

---

[5] See Kappler (op. cit. n. 4), pp. 158–66; 212–5; Morris Rossabi, *Khubilai Khan. His Life and Times* (Berkely, Los Angeles & London, 1988), 152.

[6] For the layman's view in vernacular literature, see, amongst other texts, J. Bédier's (ed. and tr.) *La Chanson de Roland publiée d'après le manuscrit d'Oxford* (Paris, s.d.), vv. 2580–90. For the regular attempts to convert Muslims by rational arguments, see Robert I. Burns, *Muslims, Christians and Jews in the Crusader Kingdom of Valencia. Societies in Symbiosis* (Cambridge, 1984), 80–8; 91–4, as well as B. Hamilton, *Religion in the Medieval West* (London, 1986), 145–50.

paesi ov'egli fu' (p. 111). The Franciscan missionaries, on the other hand, did complain about the hardships they suffered.[7]

Marco's explicit desire to discuss the 'diversità delle regioni del mondo' is traditional,[8] and though his travel story differs considerably from those of his predecessors, its actual shape and wording still remains within the boundaries of tradition. Here Rustichello's contribution must not be forgotten. He may be responsible for the 'epic' elements in, for instance, the elaborate descriptions of the great battles fought by Mongols (see below). Marco left Venice at the age of 15, and would probably not have remembered, some 25 years later, the standard formulaic presentation of heroism in literature and historiography, if ever he had read this kind of texts in his youth.

Epic elements in documents considered as empirical and presented as such are not uncommon in medieval writing. In those days *mimesis* never was the author's goal. He just concentrated on the conformity of his style. As a result, epic and historiographic texts are often very similar in presentation. They were sometimes even 'performed' in the oral society of those days. This is a significant feature of the *General istoria* of Alfonso the Wise, and the *Grandes Chroniques de France*. These informative texts incorporate many epic texts as if they were 'historical' documents. (In fact texts integrated for their 'historical' value are sometimes the only witnesses of specific epic traditions now lost). Stylistically speaking, Marco's account, although characterized by many literary and epic accents, is traditional too. He (or Rustichello, or both) wanted the account to conform with others; otherwise it would have been unreadable. Thus, Marco's presentation contains a number of stylistic techniques derived from literary tradition. This is particularly noticeable in the formulaic redaction of his travel story.

Before giving some examples, two points need to be stressed:

1) No analysis of Marco's text can ignore the fact that his absence lasted twenty five years; that fact must have affected his memory. Though many historical studies have shown that Marco gives us a fairly reliable description of his journey, his memory may sometimes have failed him.

2) In addition to the traditional, Christian prejudice against other cultures and religions in Marco's account (though we must admit that he does not exaggerate), there is a certain egocentricity: Marco does push himself to the forefront. Whether this specific aspect of his account contributed to his being seen as a 'braggart' in medieval (Venetian) society, which thought collectively, cannot be determined.

As mentioned before, Marco planned to describe the diversity (the text speaks of 'diversità' / 'diversitade') of the regions he passed through, and the peoples he saw. The use of that particular word already betrays the traditional focus of medieval travel writing and geography. This is not surprising: medieval authors, as well as their readers were interested in the *difference* between their society and

---

[7] See Becquet & Hambis (op. cit. n. 3), p. 62; Kappler (op. cit. n. 4), p. 172.

[8] This is not surprising: everybody seems to act in the same way. Herodotus himself was only interested in differences between his own society and the ones he visited or heard about. See Philippe Ariès, *Le Temps de l'Histoire* (first edition, 1954; second edition, Paris, 1986), 90.

those of others. They only sought confirmaton of their superiority. Differences are
introduced with precise formulas, which can be positive: 'In that country there is
...', or negative: 'They do not have ...'; 'We (i.e. the Europeans) do not ...',
etc.[9] In what way this particular registration-technique corroborated European self-
assurance is difficult to ascertain. It is possible that a certain uneasiness due to
confrontation with the unknown or unfamiliar plays a part here.

Differences registered could never be thoroughly analysed by the travel writer.
This is hardly surprising, as he was a stranger in the territories he passed through,
and did not know the local languages. So he could see no more than the external
elements of foreign society. A traveller never understood the mechanisms of
societies whose language he did not speak, or with whom he could not communi-
cate in the *lingua franca* (Latin in Europe, or some Persian dialect in Asia).[10]
This was true for early travellers like the abbess Egeria who visited the Sinai and
the Holy Land around 400, but even travellers who made the *Grand Tour* in the
eighteenth century, still followed tradition, for various reasons.[11] What these
travellers noticed, and sometimes described, in a rather correct and empirical way,
are mainly ritual and other external elements. They never penetrated the mysteries
below the surface. A *real* description apparently gave the information the author
and his readers wanted to have.

Marco's aim was not to enumerate possible military or religious actions against
the Mongols (as the Franciscan missionaries before him). His writing is not based
on any antagonism towards Mongol power, although it does contain the traditional
animosity towards Islam. Marco regularly notes that all Muslims are 'nemici d'i
cristiani' (p. 285), or that Christians are ... migliore gente per arme che non sono
i saracini ... (p. 284).[12] On the other hand, infidels—generally covering all
peoples outside Islam—are far better off: they never function in the antagonistic
perspective Muslims are seen in. Besides, they are potential proselytes. Sometimes,
however, Marco hesitates. Speaking of the idols worshipped on islands he visited,
he prefers not to describe the unpleasant and abominable ritual connected with
these idols.[13] But generally his attitude towards infidels is moderate. This will
still be the case in Pigafetta's description of the inhabitants of the Pacific.[14]

From this point of view Marco's account is traditional and beyond suspicion in
the eyes of his contemporaries. Despite this, he was considered a liar mainly
because he contradicted the traditional image of the Mongols. People just could
not believe that those barbarians who had threatened to destroy Europe in

---

[9] See the author's 'Le royaume du Prêtre Jean: l'interprétation d'un bonheur', in: *Actes du Colloque 'L'idée de bonheur au Moyen Age. Actes du colloque d' Amiens, 1984*, ed. Danielle Büschinger (Göppingen, 1990), 213-23.

[10] See Hambis (op. cit. n. 2), p. viii.

[11] See the author's 'Viaggiatori olandesi in Italia (1500–1700)', in: *Bulletin van het Belgisch Historisch Instituut te Rome*, 61 (1991), 37–58.

[12] Medieval men did not (could not) see the difference between Shi'ites and Sunnites; cf Claude Cahen, *Orient et Occident au temps des croisades* (Paris, 1983), 10–20.

[13] See Hambis (op. cit. n. 2), p. 237.

[14] See L. Peillard, *Antonio Pigafetta. Relation du premier voyage autour du monde par Magellan (1519–1522)* (Paris, 1984), 138, 159–60.

1240–41, had reached the level of civilization and organization Marco described in his book. Nothing of the kind was known. Was not Europe the last of the *regna* announced in the Bible, and, as all Augustinian historiographers pretended, the final stage of humanity?[15] Psychologically, the publication of Marco's travel story was miscalculated. For European readers a civilized Mongol society was simply unimaginable. Their approach has nothing to do with philosophical, moral, religious or even scientific truth. It rejects any socio-political system that makes traditional, antagonist structures redundant. John of Mandeville was well aware of how people thought. He composed a very intelligent 'travel account' in accordance with current European perceptions of the Middle and the Far East. The story of this 'armchair-traveller' was accepted as truth: 'empirically' nothing had been verified, but it was based on traditional notions and prejudices.[16]

Although a great part of Marco's account was unacceptable, because it did not have the necessary clear-cut distinction between good and evil, his style was not. His text gives the standard inventory of relevant knowledge, and presents it as a kind of catalogue. Other travel stories were organized in the same way. The reconstruction of an itinerary always goes step by step; halting-places mentioned, are its natural markers. This explains the 'chronological' character of many travel stories. The fact that Marco, who was writing 25 years later, had to dig deep in his memory must also have contributed to the paragraphic organization of his account: every paragraph forms a stage in the whole of the journey. Formulaic approaches are the logical consequence of all this. Generally speaking a paragraph 'opens' with the mention of a name, place, region: 'Chingitalis ('Gengis Khan') ...' (p. 148); 'Egli è vero che sono due Ermenie, la Piccola e la Grande ...'(p. 117); 'In Georgia ...' (p. 120), etc. Closing formulas are a little more precise: 'Abbiamo contato ...'; 'or diremo ...' (p. 121); 'Or lasciamo ...' (p. 153); 'Or ci partiamo di ...' (p. 281).

It is not certain whether our traveller had kept records of important events. Anyway, tradition forced him to organize the account of his journey stage by stage. This explains its chronological order. There is, however, one remarkable detail. The introduction to his description of Seilla (Ceylon, present-day Sri Lanka) goes as follows: 'E dirovvi che ella gira dumilia quattrocento miglia, secondo che dice lo mappamundo' (p. 257). This is curious. Did Marco use or see a map (the

---

[15] For the different theories about the *regna*, see, among others, Walter Baumgartner, 'Zu den vier Weltreichen von Daniel', *Theologische Zeitschrift*, 1 (1945), 17–22; Werner Goez, *Translatio Imperii. Ein Beitrag zur Geschichte des Geschichtsdenkens und der politischen Theorie im Mittelalter und der frühen Neuzeit* (Tübingen, 1958), *passim*.

[16] The text has been edited by Malcolm Letts (ed. and tr.), *Mandeville's Travels, Texts and Translations*, 2 vols., Works Issued by the Hakluyt Society, Sec. Ser., ci (London, 1953). See also Christiane Deluz, *Le Livre de Jehan de Mandeville. Une 'géographie' au XIVe siècle*, Publications de l'Institut d'Études Médiévales (Université Catholique de Louvain). Textes études, congrès, viii (Louvain-la-Neuve, 1988), *passim*. It is rather surprising to see that, in the sixteenth century, Mandeville's travel story becomes a subject of discussion for the Inquisition: the *diversitas* described by Mandeville sometimes referred to 'unorthodox' religious attitudes; see Carlo Ginzburg, *The Cheese and the Worms. The Cosmos of a Sixteenth-Century Miller*, tr. John & Anna Tedeschi (London, 1982), 44–5.

French texts confirms the passage in the Italian text, speaking—but this is a minor difference—of a map used by sailors in that region, p. 250), during his return to his native city, or is he here referring to a European *mappamundo* used during the reconstruction of his journey and his explanations to Rustichello? Or did he provide a map together with his account as did many other travellers or authors of *itineraria* like Matthew Paris?[17] I am unable to answer this question. However, it is important that Marco bases his description on a map which could have helped him with determining wind directions (he uses the traditional eight winds found on medieval maps). So we read: '... verso tramontana ...'; '... tra levante e greco ...' (pp. 132 and 140) or combinations of time and direction: '... sessanta giornate verso tramontana ...' (p. 150). Sometimes he provides his reader with the distances from place to place, following a traditional technique that, as far as I can see, stems from Roman cartographical traditions, of which the famous *Tabula Peutingeriana* is an interesting witness.[18] The Bordeaux pilgrim, who travelled to the Holy Land in 333 AD, gives us, in good Roman tradition, a list of stopping places (*mansiones*) and stages (*mutationes*) together with the distances. No directions are given.[19] This need not surprise us: every traveller could obtain on the spot the necessary information for the next part of his journey. Guides were available practically everywhere, even in the Orient where distances were much greater. Marco's extensive descriptions of the efficient Mongol courier and postal services, as well as of their sophisticated signposting (by, for example, the planting of trees along the trails) are very telling. But Marco is not really interested in the factual details of his long journey. From time to time he gives practical information in the form of a modern travel guide: travellers should take special supplies when passing through deserts or uninhabited regions.

The formulaic character of the text reveals itself in the practical details just mentioned, but also in the description of the different stages before and after Marco's sojourn in the actual Mongol Empire. Here is the description of Little Armenia:

> ... Nella Piccola è signore uno che giustizia buona mantiene, ed è sotto lo Gran Cane. Quivi ha molte ville e molte castella, e abbondanza d'ogni cosa, e havvi ucellagioni e cacciagionis. Quivi soleva già essere di valentri uomini: ora sono tutti cattivi; sono rimaso loro una bontà: che sono grandissimi bevitori ... sopra mare hae una villa ch'ha nome Laias, la quale è di grande mercanzia ... e gli mercatanti di Venegia e di Genova e d'altre parti quindi levano loro mercanzie ... Ora conteremo di Turcomania (p. 117)

In this fragment—and the same goes for many other paragraphs of Marco's

---

[17] For the (very few) Polo-manuscripts with maps, see Raleigh A. Skelton, *Explorers' Maps. Chapters in the Cartographic Record of Geographical Discovery* (London & New York, 1958), 3–9; Anna-Dorothee von den Brincken, 'Mappa Mundi und Chronographia. Studien zur "Imago Mundi" des abendländischen Mittelalters', *Deutsches Archiv für Erforschung des Mittelalters namens der Monumenta Germaniae Historica*, 24 (1968), 118–86. For other maps in travel accounts, see Margaret Wade Labarge, *Medieval Travellers. The Rich and Restless* (London, 1982), 12–3.

[18] See Ekkehard Weber, *Tabula Peutingeriana. Codex Vindobonensis 324. Vollständige Faksimile-Ausgabe im Originalformat*, 2 vols. (Graz, 1976), 13 ff.

[19] Published in *Itineraria et alia geographica: i: Itinerarium Burdigalense*, Corpus Christianorum: Series Latina, clxxv (Turnhout, 1965), 12.

text—we meet several formulaic and traditional elements. Like his predecessors, Marco gives the approximate directions of the winds, the name of the region or town, its size, its local ruler, its eventual subordination to Mongol rule as well as its religious orientation. Subsequently the paragraph mentions the numerous towns and castles, thus indicating a power structure, the natural richness, and the abundance of food. All this belongs to tradition. The legendary Orient is urbanized, it is a horn of plenty, and it can feed innumerable people. The Other World (and this is also true for the Celtic world, or the Land of Cockaigne) is always built on hyperboles. Marco's account also generates its own clichés, its own formulas: after having been mentioned and commented upon, the existence and use of paper money (pp. 192–3), for example, becomes a constituent part of a formula. As soon as the situation becomes different, there will be some explicitness: in the province of Toloma small change is not of paper, but 'di porcellane' (p. 222).

Fortunately formulas do not exclude creativity; they do permit a certain elasticity, as we saw in the description of Little Armenia. Marco's interest in the Armenians is noteworthy; he remarks that in ancient times they had a reputation for courage, but that now they are just a bunch of drunks. He may have been influenced by preconceived ideas on Christian sects, who did not recognize Rome's authority. Crusaders regularly showed their dislike for the Armenians.[20] But it also cannot be excluded that, in passing through the Middle East, he picked up some current antipathy towards the Armenians. If so, it is possible that the denigratory remarks about the Armenians are formulaic, too. Another example of Marco's dislike of towards Christian sects can be found in the paragraphs about the Georgians who observe the 'legge di greci' (p. 120), and the inhabitants of Mosul who respect the 'legge cristiana, ma non come comanda la Chiesa di Roma' (p. 122). These are examples of superficial diversities observed from the outside—note that rituals are easy to describe, but hard to interpret. Sometimes Marco keeps his promise to mention the differences between the things he saw personally and the reports of others. But credibility always conditions his approach. In the paragraph on the fire worshippers with their strange religious customs, for instance, Marco keeps his distance: the text (always in the third person) says that reliable spokesmen 'tutto questo dissono a messer Marco Polo, e è veritade' (p.126).

In the part of the book dedicated to the Mongol power structure, things change considerably. It is evident that his presentation has been influenced a) by his long service to and protection from the Khan, and b) his knowledge of Persian and, especially, Mongol (he did not know Chinese) permitting him to sense many

---

[20] The Augustinian concept of *ordo naturalis* explains the crusaders' dislike of Greek and other non-Latin Christians in the Middle East. In 1098 the commanders of the crusading army wrote to Urban II: '... nos enim Turcos et paganos expugnavimus, haereticos autem, Graecos et Armenos, Syros Iacobitasque expugnare nequivimus ....', see: H. Hagenmeyer, *Epistulae et Chartae ad historiam primi belli sacri spectantes. Die Kreuzzugsbriefe aus den Jahren 1088–1100* (first edition, Innsbruck 1901; Hildesheim & New York, 1973), 161–5, especially p. 164. See also J. Tyerman, 'The Holy Land and the Crusades of the Thirteenth and Fourteenth Centuries', in: ed. Peter W. Edbury, *Crusade and Settlement. Papers read at the first Conference of the Society for the Study of the Crusades and the Latin East and presented to R. C. Smail* (Cardiff, 1985), 105–12.

things 'below the surface'. Marco's exact status in the Mongol empire is unclear. Here his egocentrism causes some difficulties. It is hard to believe that he was a kind of civil servant—in the course of time the Mongol recruiting system had come rather close to the elaborate, hierarchical Chinese system[21]—or that he could have been 'governatore' of Tigni (= Yangtchou?) as he states (p. 230). It is probably wise to ignore this 'window-dressing': so far no corroboration for this has been found.

Marco's descriptions of the palaces and the complicated court ceremonial as well as the many countries under Mongol rule, are always given in relation to Mongol power. The remark in the paragraph on Little Armenia, that the country belonged to ' ... lo Gran Cane ... ' sets the tone. This explains why all information is organized around what Marco considers essential: the Mongol empire. Khubilai Khan's court is the psychological focus of the narrative. On page 210, Marco explicitly states that all the countries mentioned in his book come under the rule of the Khan.

Marco's admiration is practically without limits. There is no criticism. His description gives us the impression of an empire in which controlled violence and authoritarianism produce permanent harmony. Of course, this is just an impression. At the end of the account, he mentions rebellions, lost battles and abandoned expansionist projects (for instance, an expedition to Japan). But he never associates these political and military setbacks with the decline in power, which Christian authors would see as inevitable. From this perspective his account differs considerably from those of his predecessors, probably because he stayed longer than they did among the Mongols.

And here we meet an interesting detail. As said before, Marco's travel story is purely factual and it does not pretend to give a moralizing interpretation of the events registered. Whenever there is some shading in the descriptions of the Mongol system—here the word 'criticism' should be avoided—it occurs in the presentation of conflicts among the Mongols. The historical description of Gengis Khan's dynasty shows us that concord and union amongst the Mongols disappeared rapidly:

> ... ora vi dico che sono molti i bastardi, ché quegli che usano a Ucara se mantengono gli costumi degli idoli e hanno lasciato loro legge, e quegli che usano in levante tengono la maniera di saracini. La giustizia vi si farà com'io vi dirò (p. 158).

Without entering into details, Marco here makes a connection between separation on the 'religious' and political level. This is understandable: in the Christian world, the Augustinian idea of 'natural order' implied respect for the socio-political and religious establishment (hence the ferocious attack on heretics). Although in the Mongol empire the divergence of opinions inevitably also led to discord, Marco registers this without any analytical comment. An example is the following: two 'signori ... amendue discesi della ischiatta di Cinghi Cane; ma

---

[21] Rossabi (op. cit. n. 5), pp. 129, 185; D. O. Morgan, 'Who ran the Mongol Empire', *Journal of the Royal Asiatic Society*, (1982), 124–36, especially 129–30. See also Wiet Idema & Lloyd Haft, *Chinese Letterkunde. Inleiding, historisch overzicht en bibliografieën* (Utrecht & Antwerp, 1985), 55–6, 65–70.

divisi, ché l'uno è signore del Levante en l'altro del Ponente ...' fight each other to the death (p. 299). And here follows Marco's (or Rustichello's?) description of the decisive battle between these 'signori':

> Tutto il campo era pieno d'uomeni mort e di fediti. Poi missoro mano alle ispade: quella era tale tagliata di teste e di braccia e di mani di cavalieri, che giammai tale non fu veduta né udita; e tanti cavalieri a terra, ch'era una maraviglia a vedere da ciascunaparte; ne giammai non morí tanta gente in un campo, che niuno non poteva andare per terra se no su per gli uomeni morti e fediti. Tutto il mondo pareva sangue, che gli cavagli andavano nel sangue insino a mezza gamba. Lo romore e i'pianto era sì grande di fediti ch'erano in terra, ch'era una maraviglia a udire lo dolore che facevano (p. 299).

One immediately recognizes the traditional hyperbole of the vernacular epic. The image of horses up to their knees in the blood of the dead and wounded is well known.[22] But the author fails to analyse the description of this discord, and does not even consider a possible relation of cause and effect between the divergent (religious) opinions and an internal struggle for power. Perhaps there was no link: the war between the lords of the 'Levante' and the 'Ponente' did not necessarily have a religious motivation. In the Middle Ages, however, any breach of religious homogeneity inevitably led to socio-political disruptions; one can think here of Jesus warning the Pharisees: 'a house divided against itself shall not stand.'[23] But Marco is silent; he maintains his vision of a monolithic, well organized Mongol empire. It is uncertain, whether this is the result of conscious thought.

In his account, Marco oscillates between what tradition demands and his own conflicting observations. Although his approach was pragmatic in, for instance, his reference to the ancient Christian cosmology, he still wrote in a traditional antagonistic way: the diversity mentioned in the opening lines of his book can only imply a psychological comparison between two socio-political systems: the divided (Latin) Christian world versus the centralistic Mongol empire.

In medieval travel accounts, comparisons are made without comment on the situation and position of the society with which the Christian world is compared. Comments on the (Latin) Christian world occur, for instance, in theological, moralistic and legal treatises. But (European) travellers had no access to views stemming from foreign societies through ignorance of their languages. There was also an arrogant assumption of European superiority. When, in the sixteenth century, Fray Bernardino de Sahagún tries to read and interpret such sources, he still does it from a 'European' viewpoint.[24] In the same way, geographic descriptions of the earth and travel books tend to be eurocentristic and strongly influenced by tradition. For instance, the influence enjoyed by Isidore's

---

[22] Raymond of Aguiler's gives an identical description of the taking of Jerusalem by the crusaders. See eds. J. Hugh Hill & Laurita L. Hill, Le 'Liber' de Raymond d'Aguilers, Documents relatifs à l' histoire de croisades, 9 (Paris, 1969), 15 ff.

[23] See Matthew, 12:25: '... Omne regnum divisum contra se desolabitur; et omnis civitas vel domus divisa contra se, non stabit.'

[24] His text is available in the edition of J. Rose, Fray Bernardino de Sahagún, Histoire générale des chose de la Nouvelle-Espagne (Paris, 1981). The translation from Spanish into French is by D. Jourdanet and R. Siméon.

Etymologiae explains the navel-gazing attitude of the European traveller. Another important point is that Asia was known to the majority only through descriptions and *mappaemundi*. Until the thirteenth century, Europeans had seen little of Asia (apart from the Middle East), even though they were absolutely fascinated by this distant world.[25]

So, Asia (as well as other unknown regions) was not even granted a real existence: often practical experience lost out to sacrosanct tradition. Petrarch (1304–74) still accepted the *Graphia aurea* and the *Mirabilia Romae* as reliable documents. But he had to admit that he knew nothing of the Chinese or Indians.[26] Giovanni Cavallini, however, showed a significant advance. In his *Polistoria* (written between 1343 and 1352) he referred to early literary sources in order to identify ancient remains.[27] Scientific evolution, however, is not a linear process: Fra Mauro, the famous Venetian cartographer (d. 1460), still maintained that he preferred St Augustine's authority to modern empiricism, which he considered too dangerous for the natural order.[28] But in the sixteenth century, cartographers like Mercator and Ortelius followed a more scientific procedure, as they only used traditional knowledge when empirical information was not available.[29]

Polo's story ignores the traditional, normative prejudices that characterize, for instance, the accounts of contemporary missionaries who went to Asia. Plano de Carpini's dislike of the Mongols, whom he regarded as killers, looters, fornicators, insulters, etc., is a good example.[30] An identical perception colours the accounts of John of Montecorvino (d. 1328), the first Bishop of Khanbaliq (Pekin), and the naive Odoric of Pordenone (d. 1331).[31] Marco's animosity, in contrast, is restricted to Islam, which in itself is not surprising.

To conclude, Marco's story, a strange story in the eyes of his contemporaries, is based on a long sojourn in the Mongol empire where he lived under the protection of Khubilai Khan. This fact and his knowledge of Mongol and Persian explain the difference between his and other contemporary reports about the Mongols. The

---

[25] Of course, merchants had already visited much of the continent (for instance, into Russian territory), but their experiences were not normally written down. See Pierre Chaunu, *L'Expansion européenne du XIIIe au XVe siècle* (second edition, Paris, 1983), 90. For the fascination exercised by 'Asia', see, amongst others, Annie Angrémy, 'La *Mappemonde* de Pierre de Beauvais', *Romania*, civ (1983), 316–50 and 457–98.

[26] F. Fernández-Armesto, *Before Columbus. Exploration and Colonisation from the Mediterranean to the Atlantic, 1229–1492* (London, 1987), 121.

[27] See Roberto Weiss, *The Renaissance Discovery of Classical Antiquity* (second edition, Oxford, 1988), 30, 42–3.

[28] Tullia Gasparrini Leporace & Roberto Almagià, *Il Mappamondo di Fra Mauro* (Venice, 1966), plate XXXIII, p. 56.

[29] See Numa Broc, *La géographie de la Renaissance*, Comité des Travaux historiques et scientifiques, 1 (Paris, 1986), 159–85.

[30] Becquet & Hambis (op. cit. n. 3), pp. 39–40. Plano de Carpini travelled in 1245–46.

[31] See J.-P. Roux, *Les explorateurs au Moyen Age*, Le temps qui court, 25 (Paris, 1961), 74–84; J. Favier, *Les grandes découvertes. D'Alexandre à Magellan* (Paris, 1991), 174–8.

precious stones he conjured from his unsightly cloak during the banquet are concrete proof of his successes in the Far East. Instead of complaints about shortage of food and ill-treatment like in Rubruck's report, Marco, according to his account, had been treated well, and he regularly boasts about the high administrative functions he held in the Mongol empire. The sophisticated, age-old Mongol-Chinese tradition of the training of civil servants, however, must have made such an impressive career impossible. On the other hand, linguistic studies have shown that Marco did not know Chinese. So we assume that he may only have occupied lower ranks of Mongol-Chinese administration. In Marco's account, the centralistic Mongol empire is presented as a kind of socio-political Eldorado. No setback, be it political or military, diminishes his appreciation of the Mongol system.

Here we have come upon the essential difference between Marco's account of the oriental world and the many traditional descriptions of the thirteenth century. Though any specific comment on his book is lacking, we may presume that because of its traditional character, the information about the first part of his journey and about the return-trip was not what provoked the rejection of his story. As a matter of fact, these parts contain much factual information, which may have been useful to merchants and travellers,[32] and they were certainly not the reason for his nickname: 'Il Milione'. That part was not strange at all. The real reason for the disbelief of his fellow townsmen (and others) must lie in Marco's claim that he had become part of the Mongol system and had been the guest of the Great Khan himself, whereas all earlier stories presented them as barbarians. Marco's integration in a society considered hostile to Christians, who regarded themselves as the final and perfect stage in the evolution of mankind, made his story unbelievable. The idea that barbaric Mongol society was better organized than the Christian, and that it was tolerant in religious matters, seemed ridiculous.

Marco's account did not assume Christian superiority, and was hardly conditioned by traditional oriental lore, but was conceived as a pragmatic and empirical record of a journey, and did not confirm the ideas that had taken root in (Latin) European thinking. His story has no didactic programme (as in Plano de Carpini's account) nor critical comments. It should rather be considered as a concrete proof of his observations. Venetians were merchants, and therefore Marco's thinking was—if I may use the metaphor—as practical as the portulans used by navigators. He never explicitly linked the stages and events of his trip to the constituent details of cosmological *mappamundi* as his scholarly contemporaries did: there is no Garden of Eden conditioning the whole of his perception. The few *mirabilia* mentioned in the account can be considered as a sacrificial gesture to tradition. That is why Marco's account differs so much from thirteenth-century tradition, where geographical writing still carried undertones: the Hereford and the Ebstorf *mappaemundi* considered Jerusalem as the geographical and cosmological navel of the world, even as the touchstone of (Christian) perfection. Hence, those who lived far from Jerusalem, that is to say far from perfection,

---

could only be close to bestiality.[33] And the Mongols lived far from Jerusalem and the civilized Christians.

The whole socio-political organization of the Christian world of the Middle Ages was based on the doctrine of redemption. From that perspective, a Mongol empire, governed by idolatry, could not exist as Marco Polo had explained. It may not have been his intention to disturb traditional views about non-Christian people, but being without any prejudice against the Mongols, he, being a Christian, had accepted a temporary integration in their society, and had valued them. This was unacceptable to his contemporaries: Europeans never talked *with* strangers, always *about* them. Their aim was to maintain the 'diversità' / 'diversitade' already mentioned, and to respect the traditional moral view of God's creation: non-Christians could not be allowed to rule the world. By talking and even living *with* barbarians that according to medieval cosmology lived on the edge of the world, Marco became a stranger in his own society.

---

[33] See Jörg G. Arentzen, *Imago Mundi cartographica. Studien zur Bildlichkeit mittelalterlichen Welt- und Oekumenekarten unter besonderer Berücksichtigung des Zusammenwirkens von Text und Bild,* Münstersche Mittelalter-Schriften, 53 (Munich, 1984), *passim.*

BETWEEN MANDEVILLE AND COLUMBUS:
TVOYAGE BY JOOS VAN GHISTELE

ISTVÁN BEJCZY[*]

Tvoyage, by Joos van Ghistele, is the most extensive traveller's tale in Middle Dutch literature, and also one of the most engaging in its genre. Nevertheless, it has so far received little attention.[1]

Joos van Ghistele's book stands between the writings of John Mandeville and Christopher Columbus. His journey took place from 1481 to 1485, while the account of it was recorded around 1490, shortly before Columbus's first journey to America and almost a century and a half after the appearance of Mandeville's popular work. In its contents, too, *Tvoyage* shows a striking affinity with the writings of Mandeville and Columbus. I intend to make this clear by commenting on *Tvoyage* from various points of view. First I shall give a short account of Joos van Ghistele, and his work.

Joos van Ghistele was born in Ghent in 1446, of patrician parents. His father, Gerard van Ghistele, had made a career in Ghent as a Councillor. In 1441, he was a member of the Bench of Aldermen and in 1449 he became Grand Bailiff for the Burgundian duke, Philip the Good. Joos, too, found employment with both duke and city. He attended the court of Charles the Bold, after which he was knighted, between 1464 and 1467. In 1477, the year in which the duke died, he was elected Chief Alderman of the Bench of the Keure, and was re-elected in 1480. In September 1481, a few months after he had finished his chairmanship, Joos began his journey. Accompanied by a group of his countrymen,[2] he visited the Holy

---

[*] Catholic University of Nijmegen, The Netherlands.

[1] Some useful information on Joos van Ghistele and his journey is in the general, and rather dilettantish study by P. Dieleman, *De groote reiziger Mer Joos van Ghistele* (Middelburg, 1932) (without annotations). For a summary of the travel account, see: *Voyage naar den lande van belofte, in modern Nederlands naverteld door A. Demaeckere* (Amsterdam, 1936). M. Vanberghen, 'Mer Joos van Ghistele, de grote reiziger', *Ghendtsche Tijdinghen*, 8 (1979), 343–5, is a cursory sketch. *Tvoyage* recently received attention in two articles in: eds. W. P. Gerritsen, Annelies van Gijsen & Orlanda S. H. Lie, *Een school spierinkjes. Kleine opstellen over Middelnederlandse artes-literatuur* (Hilversum, 1991): H. van Dijk, 'Reizigers naar het Heilige Land en het middelpunt van de wereld', pp. 49–52; and T.-M. Nischik, 'Zur definitorischen Bestimmung der "Fachliteratur"', pp. 127–30. A Dutch version of this article, 'Jan van Mandeville overtroffen: *Tvoyage* van Joos van Ghistele. Boekenwijsheid en persoonlijke beleving in een laat-middeleeuws reisverhaal' appeared in *Literatuur. Tijdschrift over Nederlandse letterkunde*, 10 (1993), 146-53. A critical edition of *Tvoyage* by R. Gaspar will probably appear around 1995 (under the auspices of the Nederlands Historisch Genootschap).

[2] *Tvoyage van Mher Joos van Ghistele, oft anders, Texcellent, groot, zeldsaem ende vremd voyage,*

Land and North Africa (his route will be discussed below). On his return in the summer of 1485 the town of Hulst organized a banquet in his honour, a fact recorded in the civic accounts, and one which provides proof of his journey. Once more he took up his official career. In 1486 he was reinstated as Chief Alderman, and in his father's footsteps he acted as Grand Bailiff of Ghent from 1492 to 1494. Joos must have died around 1520, presumably in Zuiddorpe, the seat of the Ghistele family in Zeeuws Vlaanderen.[3]

The account of Joos van Ghistele's journey was written in about 1490 by Ambrosius Zeebout, a priest, who had not taken part in the journey. Although we know little about Zeebout, he certainly left a distinct mark on *Tvoyage*. Apart from what Joos and his men told him, he used written sources—some of which are specifically named—, continued the account to include statements about events after Joos's return, and provided the book with a preface. He also added an introductory chapter for future travellers to the Orient, in which he gives practical advice concerning the journey itself and descriptions of various Islamic, eastern Christian, and Jewish communities and customs. The latter served, in the first place, to inform travellers how they could avoid arguments and swindling. As a whole they form an extensive ethnographic survey of the Middle-East itself worthy of study.

Tvoyage is a comprehensive tale, and it is strikingly precise. The 1557 edition, including Zeebout's first chapter, is 348 pages long and densely printed. There are three manuscripts, and three editions were printed in Ghent, in 1557, 1563 and 1572. The editions are based on a manuscript owned by Filips van Liedekerke, a nobleman, married to one of van Ghistele's granddaughters.[4] The book must have been popular, for Henric van den Keere, the printer of the 1557 edition, commented in the preface that the work was very famous and had been popular in Flanders for many years.[5] This fact is attested by Laurens van Haecht's 1595 Antwerp edition of Jan Aerts's travel account (1484), in which he wrote that Joos's travels were well-known in his country.[6]

---

ghedaen by wylent Edelen ende weerden Heere Mher Joos van Ghistele ... (Ghent, 1557), ii.1, p. 38, gives four names in the rubric: Jan van Conijnghshaud (van Quisthout, Joos's chaplain), Joris van Ghistele, Jan van Vaernewijck and Joris Palijngh.

[3] The information in this paragraph is from Dieleman (op. cit. n. 1). Vanberghen (op. cit. n. 1), gives 1477 as the year in which Gerard van Ghistele was elected alderman and Joos knighted. A claim that Joos had introduced buckwheat is unfounded; this plant was known in the Low Countries by the end of the fourteenth century: see K. A. H. W. Leenders, 'De boekweitcultuur in historisch perspectief', *Koninklijk Nederlands Aardrijkskundig Genootschap. Geografisch Tijdschrift*, Nieuwe Reeks 21 (1987), 213–27.

[4] Manuscripts and printed editions are mentioned in R. Jansen-Sieben, *Repertorium van de Middelnederlandse artes-literatuur* (Utrecht, 1989), 135, 148–50 (printed editions), 247, 272, 418 (manuscripts).

[5] *Tvoyage* (op. cit. n. 2), 'Den Drucker tot den Lezer', fo. V[r]: 'tselue uoyage in desen lande van Vlaanderen ghenoug vermaerd / bekend ende menighfuldelic ghecopieerd / gheschreuen end verbreed is gheweest van ouer veel iaren.'

[6] (Jan Aerts), *Cort verhael eender heerlijcker Reysen gedaen byden machtigen Factoor des Conincx van Portugael Emanuelis die xiiijste*, ed. Laurens van Haecht (Antwerp, 1595), fo. Aij[v].

Possibly this popularity of *Tvoyage* owes something to its language and imagery which were attuned to readers in the Low Countries. The novelties Joos witnessed during his journey are often compared with things and events in his fatherland. The old centre of Cairo is as large as Ghent, the Sultan's palace alone as big as Dendermonde, and the Nile as wide as the Scheldt at Antwerp. In parts of the Arabian desert, dunes are found like those near The Hague. And, finally, ships departing from the Red Sea are required to dock at Aden like those setting sail from Dordrecht.[7] Joos also mentions when he visited fellow-countrymen. In Cairo, he stayed with Francisco Tudisco, a merchant and goldsmith from Mechlin; in the Greek town of Modon with a barber from Biervliet.[8] Joos (or Zeebout) also makes a number of surprising references to the Low Countries, for instance the anecdote attributed to anonymous poets about Hippocrates's daughter whom the goddess Diana had turned into a dragon, and imprisoned on the island of Kos, where she was waiting to be rescued by a knight from the Low Countries.[9]

But the main reason for the popularity of his work was probably the wide range of Joos's travels. Both Ambrosius Zeebout and Henric van den Keere stressed in their prefaces that Joos did not stay away the usual six to nine months of a journey to Jerusalem, but for four years, and that he had not only visited the Holy Land like so many pilgrims, but had travelled more widely than most others.[10] In addition, the story of his journey is interlarded with information about biblical, ancient and contemporary history.

Nevertheless, as I will show, *Tvoyage* is the record of a not completely successful journey. The fact is that Joos van Ghistele had two destinations. Apart from his main aim which was to visit the Holy Land, he also wanted to find the land of Prester John (Ethiopia). In Cologne, Joos happened to have read 'in a book'—presumably the *Historia trium regum* by Johannes von Hildesheim—that 'all christians from the Low Countries who enter the land of Prester John, and carry with them some jewels which have been brought into contact with the bodies of the Three Kings, of which they have evidence in the form of letters and authentic seals, would be very welcome there, and be received with gladness'.[11] Joos's reading of Johannes von Hildesheim must have been somewhat inaccurate for in his tale details are confused. The Middle Dutch versions of the *Historia trium regum*—those most closely related to Joos's account—tell that Indian pilgrims liked to purchase jewels that had been brought into contact with the Three Kings in Cologne, and that pilgrims and merchants 'from this country' take advantage of this. They take jewels along with them to India, saying they are from

---

[7] *Tvoyage* (op. cit. n. 2), iii.5, p. 138 (Ghent); iii.7, p. 140 (Dendermonde); iii.19, p. 156 (Scheldt); v.2, p. 190 (dunes); iv.12, p. 206 (Dordrecht).

[8] *Tvoyage* (op. cit. n. 2), iii.5, p. 137 (Tudisco); viii.19, p. 320 (barber).

[9] *Tvoyage* (op. cit. n. 2), viii.7, p. 302.

[10] *Tvoyage* (op. cit. n. 2), 'Epistre de l'Imprimeur', fo. ij^v.; 'Den Drucker tot den Lezer', fo. V^v; 'Voor-reden des Autheurs' (without page indication).

[11] *Tvoyage* (op. cit. n. 2), ii.1, p. 38: 'alle Christenen uut nederlanden commende in tland van Pape Jan met hemlieden brijnghende eenighe iuweelen … ghetouchiert an de lichamen van den dry Conijnghen ende daer af ghetughe hebbende by letteren ende zeghelen autentijck / daer zeer willecomme wezen zauden ende blidelick ontfanghen werden.'

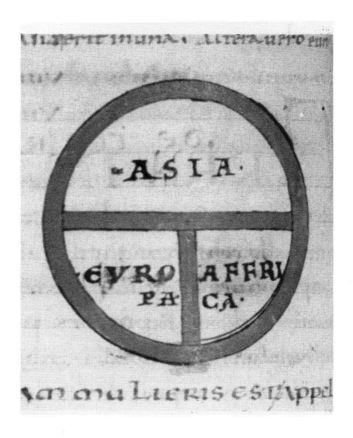

III. T-O WORLD MAP
From Isidore of Seville 's *Originum sive etymologiarum libri xx.*
University of Groningen, MS 8, fo. 220^v (Xth century)

Cologne. The same Indian pilgrims also send all news connected with the Three
Kings in sealed letters to Prester John.[12]

Anyway, Joos asked permission from the Dean of the Cathedral in Cologne to
bring some jewels into contact with the bodies of the Three Kings, which were
preserved there, 'for he was actually planning to visit the land of Prester John, and
especially the grave and memorials of the apostle St Thomas'.[13] This request was

---

[12] T. J. A. Scheepstra, *Van den heilighen Drien Coninghen. Middelnederlandse teksten* (Groningen,
1914), 209 (from a fifteenth-century manuscript); *Historien der heiligher drie coninghen* (Delft,
1479), fo. i 4^{v-r}.

[13] *Tvoyage* (op. cit. n. 2), ii.1, pp. 38–9: 'want hy warachtighe meenijnghe hadde tland van den

granted in a solemn ceremony after which Joos and his men set off with the jewels carefully wrapped.

Without great difficulty, Joos arrived in the Holy Land. From Venice he took a ship to Beirut, and from there continued his journey to Jerusalem and beyond, accompanied by other travellers. Paulus Walther from Guglingsheim records that for a part of his journey, he had travelled with Joos and his men.[14]

Joos never reached his second destination, the land of Prester John. In a first attempt he travelled from the Holy Land to Alexandria and Cairo, in order to proceed south across the Red Sea. He had already gone some distance when his passage was impeded by the Emir of Aden. His travel permit from the Egyptian Sultan was of no avail, because the King of Aden did not recognize the Sultan as his lord. Joos now returned to Egypt and travelled to Tripoli by way of Cyprus, hoping to travel east, around the Arabian peninsula. After visiting Syria, and Persia as far as Tabriz, this plan was also abandoned due to exhaustion. Joos had been informed by merchants of dangers ahead, and of a sinister disease that was about to break out. So he decided to head home, but not by the shortest route. After a second visit to Tripoli, he sailed past Crete to Constantinople, then around Greece, crossing the Mediterranean to Tunis, then back again to Genoa; from there he travelled overland to Venice, and finally home to Flanders.

His desire to visit Prester John must have been strong. He only abandoned his plan after travelling half way round the world, because of inaccurate reading of the *Historia trium regum.* It is certainly peculiar that after he had finally begun his return journey, Joos should have made such a large detour. What can have been the reason for this?

A solution may be found in the imaginary line which links the places Joos visited: first in a southerly direction, a line runs from Flanders to the Holy Land; then, further to the south from the Holy Land to Aden, and back again in the direction of the Holy Land via the same line to the north; next, in an easterly direction, to Tabriz in Persia, and back again in the direction of the Holy Land via the same line to the west; then, further to the west, ending up in Tunis. Finally the line returns to Flanders.

The picture of a cross develops, with the Holy Land in the centre. It is the same cross that lies at the basis of the so called T-O world maps, in which Jerusalem occupies a central position.[15]

As a guiding principle derived from medieval Christian cartography, the idea of the cross probably directed the contents of *Tvoyage*, perhaps even to such an extent that parts were invented to meet the needs of the model. Joos certainly visited the Holy Land, and very likely Egypt, too, (as he was seen in those

---

Pape Jan te besouckene / ende principalic te visiteren tgraf ende de memorie van den Apostel Gods S. Thomaes.'

[14] *Fratri Pauli Waltheri Guglingensis Itinerarium in Terram Sanctam et ad Sanctam Catherinam,* ed. M. Sollweck (Tübingen, 1892), 141, 149–51. In his notes, Sollweck criticizes Joos's account; also on pp. 163–5.

[15] On medieval cartography, see A. Verrycken, *De middeleeuwse wereldverkenning,* Dossiers Geschiedenis, 15 (Louvain & Amersfoort, 1990); P. D. A. Harvey, *Medieval Maps* (London, 1991).

regions), but his journeys beyond are less certain. In other words, as far as possible, he may have seized the opportunity to reproduce the cruciform picture of the world in the account of his travels, using cartographic models, and his pretended quest for Prester John as principal motive. Zeebout also intended *Tvoyage* to be a geographical reference book, mentioning in his preface that he had divided *Tvoyage* into eight books, and that its contents were concisely described 'in order that the country, the town, the place or whatever readers found of interest might be better and more easily found'. And he indicated that he, in order to be complete, had described places not visited by Joos, but which were known from other travellers.[16]

If this hypothesis is correct, *Tvoyage* by Joos van Ghistele is similar to the work of John Mandeville, which was also a description of nearly the whole world. Mandeville visited at most the Holy Land and Egypt, but presented his stories as though he had seen all countries mentioned in his book.[17] His work is essentially a popular geography book rather than a traveller's tale.[18] Perhaps the same is true for *Tvoyage*. In this respect it may be significant that, at least once, the author apparently wanted to improve on Mandeville's geographical insights, though without mentioning him.[19]

Yet *Tvoyage* reads like an account of a real journey. Joos's descriptions are remarkably precise and detailed, and appear to be based on actual experiences. But unlike Mandeville Joos avoids fantastic tales about marvellous animals or monstrous human beings. Joos did not see such monsters, though he had expected to.

Joos twice questioned other travellers about the existence of monsters, with the explicit intention of verifying reports which he had heard in Flanders. Remarkably this investigation begins in Aden, and again in Tabriz, which are respectively the most southerly and most easterly points of his journey. So at the very moment when he finds himself furthest from home, monsters come to his mind. Or in other words, beings that, from a cultural perspective, are furthest from him are placed at the greatest distance from Flanders in his geographical description. Twice he made inquiries about monsters, twice he received similar answers. The traditional expectation that there were monsters living in the Orient was not fulfilled. On the contrary, in Aden, Joos and his men said

---

[16] *Tvoyage* (op. cit. n. 2), 'Voor-reden des Autheurs' (without page indication): 'op dat men te bet ende ghereedelicker zaude moghen vinden / tland / de stede / plecke oft ander zake danof een yeghelic belieuen zal te lesene.'

[17] For the original French text and a number of English translations, see Malcolm Letts (ed. and tr.), *Mandeville's Travels. Texts and Translations*, 2 vols., Works Issued by the Hakluyt Society, Sec. Ser., ci (London, 1953). For the Middle Dutch translations, see N. A. Cramer (ed.), *De reis van Jan van Mandeville, naar de Middelnederlandsche handschriften en incunabelen* (Leiden, 1908).

[18] For this supposition, see W. P. Gerritsen, 'Mandeville en het astrolabium', *De Nieuwe Taalgids. Tijdschrift voor neerlandici*, lxxvi (1983), 481–95.

[19] This refers to the inquiry into the centre of the world; see H. van Dijk, 'Reizigers naar het Heilige Land' (op. cit. n. 1); cf. I. P. Bejczy, 'De wereldkaart van Jan van Mandeville', *Millennium. Tijdschrift voor Middeleeuwse studies*, iii (1989), 99–105.

to those who had joined them that they had been told before that there were various monsters in those regions, and savages as well, asking how much truth there was in these reports. The others told them that they did not know, and had never heard of such things; but that strange species of animals exist in great numbers in the great desert between Egypt and Abyssinia, where Prester John dwells, and that they live in troops or herds, looking quite similar to apes, as big as ten-year-old children, fierce and blood-thirsty, seeming to possess human intelligence, having ruddy-coloured hair from the shoulders up, with long tails, and they are named baboons or magots, which can be called savages.[20]

Something comparable occurred in Tabriz:

They also asked whether any people with a strange appearance or other peculiarities lived anywhere in the locality of Tartary, or on the Indian islands. They were told that occasionally various monsters had been found (sometimes here, sometimes there), but not locally, and also that they had never heard tell that there was a specific country or region ... [*some words appear to be missing here*], but they were told that the people in those countries do have various peculiar customs and traditions which would seem very strange here.

Joos's informants then went on to say that people from India sometimes catch long-tailed monkeys that are skinned and cooked and sold to foreign merchants who are told that what they buy are actually pygmies. Unfortunately, they were unable to provide any other information. Here the author of *Tvoyage* added: '... nevertheless, it can be assumed that this has some truth in it as the Scriptures mention it in several places.'[21] Then follows another supposedly true story about salamanders that could live in fire.

Thus, wild stories about monsters are rejected in *Tvoyage*—they are even partly treated as products of the Indian 'tourist industry'—but though the author cannot find any confirmation of their existence, and his informants know nothing, they nevertheless do believe that savage and very peculiar people live near the land of Prester John and in India—unfortunately, just in those regions that remain beyond Joos's reach. It is important to add that the informants were indigenous. In Aden, they were the guides by whom Joos and his men were shown around in the town,

---

[20] *Tvoyage* (op. cit. n. 2), iv.15, p. 209: 'tot den ghenen die met hemlieden ghijnghen / dat zy tanderen tiden hadden hooren zegghen / dat in die maertsen ende landen waren diuerssche monstren / ende ooc wilde lieden / vraghende watter waer af wesen moghte. Men zeyde hemlieden dat mer daer niet af en wiste te spreken / noch noyt ghehoort en hadde maer dat in tgroote desert dat leyt tusschen Egypten ende Abassien daer Pape-Jan woond / waren manieren van dieren in grooter menighten / hem met troppen of cudden tsamen haudende / ghenouch den Schemijnkelen ghelijc / wel alzo groot als kinderen van tien iaren / fel ende bloedghier / schynende recht verstand hebbende van menschen / ruudachtich van hare van den schauderen opwaert / met langhen steerten ghenaemt Babewynen oft Magocs / de welke men Wilde lieden zegghen magh.'
[21] *Tvoyage* (op. cit. n. 2), vii.15, p. 281: 'Ooc zo vraeghden zy oft daer omtrent yewers in Tartarien oft in eylanden van India eenighe lieden woonden van vremden maecsele oft van eenigherande wonderlicke fatsoene: men andwoordde hemlieden dat men wel zomwylen by auontueren nu in deen plecke dan in een ander diuersche Monstren ghevonden hadde / maer en wisten gheen plecken daer omtrent noch ooc en hadden noyt hoore zegghen datter eenighe landen oft plaetsen waren ... maer zeyden dat in dien landen tvolc wel diuersche wonderlicke zeden ende manieren hebben die in deze landen zeer vremde zauden wezen om hooren ende om zien'; 'zo en wisten zy daer af niet te spreken / nochtans zo is wel te bemoeden datter wat af wezen moet mids datter de schrifture af zeyd ten diuerschen plecken.'

and presumably they were the same merchants from the regions around the Red Sea, with whom they had arrived in Aden.[22] In Tabriz, Joos speaks with local merchants, who had accompanied him from Aleppo. Therefore the remark in *Tvoyage* that there must be some truth in stories about monsters because they also figure in the Bible cannot originate from the non-Christian informants, but must come either from Joos himself, or from Zeebout. It is just as likely that Joos and / or Zeebout had a hand in the meagre confirmation of the existence of monsters. They adopted a European viewpoint as regards the remarks made in Tabriz 'that the people in those countries do have various peculiar customs and traditions that seem very strange here.' And the story about salamanders living in fire, which are known from western medieval literature, is another example. By giving statements such as these to Orientals, the western ideas about monsters were, at least partly, confirmed. In this way, Joos peopled the edges of the world, the regions that remained unknown to him, with a number of strange creatures already figuring in European literature.

Exactly the same happens in Christopher Columbus's travel accounts. On 11 October 1492, Columbus believed he had reached India. Armed with western knowledge about the Orient, which he had acquired mainly from Pierre d'Ailly's *Ymago mundi*[23], he, like Joos, expected to find monsters. To his surprise he did not; and he wrote at the end of his first expedition: 'So far I have encountered no monstrous people on these islands such as many thought; rather, the populace is extremely deferential.'[24] According to his log-book Columbus only encountered Indians who were well-formed in every respect. These Indians told him about cannibals living on neighbouring islands or on the mainland, a one-eyed people with dog heads, who ate human flesh.[25] One wonders how, without knowledge of their language, Columbus could have understood these Indians. Probably he makes them relate traditional, European, views about cyclopes and *cynocephali*, situating them just beyond the regions he had visited himself. Yet, when, at the end of his journey, he did meet a few Indians who were uglier and more warlike, he thought they must have been related to those cannibals.[26] Another clearer example of such a projection of western belief in monsters on the basis of attestations by the Indians is to be found in Columbus's description of what he heard about the island of Matinino: the island was inhabited solely by women, who, during a certain period of the year, allowed males of a cannibal tribe from another island to visit them. Boys born out of those unions, were sent to their

---

[22] *Tvoyage* (op. cit. n. 2), iv.13, p. 206.

[23] On Columbus's scholarly knowledge and the way he made use of it, see Valerie I. Flint, *The Imaginative Landscape of Christopher Columbus* (Princeton, 1992).

[24] Cristóbal Colón, *Textos y documentos completos. Relaciones de viajes, cartas y memoriales*, ed. Consuelo Varela (Madrid, 1982), doc. V: Carta a Luis Santagel (15 February 1493), p. 144: 'en estas islas fasta aquí no he hallado ombres mostrudos, como muchos pensavan, más antes es toda gente de muy lindo acatamiento' (see, however, note 26).

[25] Colón (op. cit. n. 24), doc. II: 'Diario del primer viaje', pp. 51, 62, 65, 72, 78, 84, 115–9.

[26] Colón (op. cit. n. 24), doc. II: 'Diario del primer viaje', pp. 115–19; in his letter referred to above he also mentioned that the cannibals or the Caribs were the only monsters he had seen himself (Carta, p. 145).

fathers. Girls would stay behind with their mothers.[27] In this story, elements of the myth of the Amazons can easily be recognized. This shows that Columbus, like Joos van Ghistele, composed a typically 'European' picture of what he thought to be the Orient using information from local sources about neighbouring areas—information that in the eyes of their contemporaries would confirm the fables about monster-races, and compensate for the disappointing absence of real monsters.

So, *Tvoyage* by Joos van Ghistele is an intriguing document, comparable in design to Mandeville's travel account, and demonstrating a similar attitude towards fantastic beings to that of Columbus. And rightly, Henric van den Keere, the publisher of the 1557 edition of *Tvoyage*, remarks in his preface: 'we people from Ghent and Flanders, yes all people from the Low Countries have no less reason to exult in this [traveller] than the Germans and French have done in theirs and still daily do.'[28]

---

[27] Colón (op. cit. n. 24), doc. II: 'Diario del primer viaje', p. 119.

[28] *Tvoyage* (op. cit. n. 2), 'Den Drucker tot den Lezer', fo. V^r: 'ende en hebben wy Ghentenaers ende alle Vlamijnghen / ia / alle Nederlanders niet min causen om met desen te triumpheren / dan de Duudschen ende Fransoysen met den hueren en hebben ghedaen ende noch daghelics doen.'

TRAVEL FACT AND TRAVEL FICTION
IN THE VOYAGES OF COLUMBUS

VALERIE I. J. FLINT[*]

Factual information about the travels and discoveries of Christopher Columbus poured from the presses in 1992. For this and allied reasons, I shall say comparatively little here about real travel; about the admiral's voyages, that is, as they in fact slowly unfolded, from the islands of the Caribbean to the mainlands of South and Central America. And I shall hardly mention the actual discoveries at all. The principal preoccupation of this paper will be not with travel fact and travel fiction as we might see it now; with what we might call the objective reality of travel, that is, as opposed to imaginative tales about it, (the former, to serious travellers, taking precedence over the latter). It will be concerned instead with travel fact and travel fiction as Columbus saw it. Columbus's adventures will certainly still occupy the centre of the stage, but they will be discussed not as they happened, but as the account of them formed itself within the admiral's own head as he went along, and as it poured out in his reports to his sovereigns and supporters in Spain. I shall begin the enquiry with some reminders from our world of objective reality, but we shall then abandon this world and plunge instead into one in which our categories of fact and fiction give way to other categories; categories which were used, or (as I prefer to think) manipulated, by the admiral himself. We shall embark thereby upon a mental voyage quite as perilous as those physical ones whose strict account I am limiting so firmly; but it is one which may have, I hope, (providing we survive it) special rewards to offer.

The central enterprise will be, then, a two-fold one. In the first section of it, I shall treat of the great admiral's reading, and of the complex of fact and fiction, our style, to be found within this corpus; a complex which, it must be said, does tend towards the fictional. I shall do this in an attempt to reconstruct the pre-existing mental picture within which Columbus's real discoveries were set. Secondly, and crucially, I shall make some suggestions about how this reading was actually employed in the furtherance of the admiral's ambitions, and in his efforts to explain his accumulating experiences to his sovereigns and supporters; this with the aim of arriving at a partial assessment (for it can only be partial, given the current state of our knowledge) of the relative importance of our kind of travel fact and travel fiction to the admiral himself. There may be some surprises for us

[*] Department of History, University of Auckland, New Zealand.
For the preparation of this paper I am indebted to the award of Visiting Fellowships at Clare Hall, Cambridge, and at the Newberry Library, Chicago.

hidden in this second exercise. Columbus appears in some ways as skilled a direc-
tor of the newly invented printed word as he was of the caravel; and some of that
which *we* might, at first sight, be inclined to relegate to the ranks of travel fiction,
may turn out to have had a quite extraordinary importance in the prosecution of
the whole enterprise. It may, indeed, have been decisive in the pursuit and
eventual establishment of certain facts about the voyages.

First of all, however, the prefatory reminders. After the timely intervention and
support of Queen Isabella of Castille in 1492, Columbus undertook four voyages
to the 'Indies'. The first took place between August 3, 1492 and March 15, 1493,
and the second between October 13, 1493 and June 11, 1496. On these first two
voyages the admiral touched upon (and named) the major Caribbean islands,
including Hispaniola (now Haiti and the Dominican Republic), Cuba and Jamaica.
An abortive attempt was made to found a settlement, Navidad, on Hispaniola, and
Columbus refused to accept that Cuba was in fact an island, declaring it officially
part of the mainland of Cathay on 12 June 1494. After the acclaim and widespread
publicity which followed the first voyage, however, the appreciation of his efforts
began to decline, and the admiral had to wait until 1498 before undertaking a third
one. This occupied the period late May to late October of that same year. On this
voyage, the little fleet sailed southwards, via Trinidad, to the Gulf of Paria and the
mouths of the great Orinoco, then northwards again, back to Hispaniola.
Columbus's popularity reached a particularly low point at the end of this third
voyage. His methods of government were condemned by the Commendador
Bobadilla, sent out from Spain to Hispaniola to investigate them, and he was
carried back to Spain in chains. Columbus was restored to his sovereigns' favour
only with difficulty, and he never again regained his former position. The fourth
and final voyage took place between April 3, 1502 and November 7, 1504. On this
he sailed back in the direction of the South American continent (which he had
declared, at the end of the third voyage, to be at the edge of the Terrestrial
Paradise), and anchored off the coast of Honduras in late July 1502. The fleet
explored the Mosquito Coast of Nicaragua and the coasts of Costa Rica, Veragua
and Panama before being stranded on Jamaica through the loss of a caravel.
Rescue came late, and it was not until over a year later that the survivors left
Hispaniola for Spain.

This, then, is the outline of Columbus's journeys to the Caribbean and the South
American continent; journeys which he always maintained had taken him to the
ends of the east and Cathay.[1] There remain a few remarks to be made about the
admiral's personal situation. Despite the grandiose claims of his second (and
illegitimate) son, Ferdinand, Columbus came of humble parentage[2] and was
largely self-educated;[3] two circumstances which perhaps sharpened his sensitivity

---

[1] For all the recent literature upon the admiral, one of the best accounts of him is still Samuel E.
Morison, *Admiral of the Ocean Sea. A Life of Christopher Columbus*, 2 vols. (Boston, 1942).
[2] See the earliest biography by Antonio Gallo, printed and translated by John B. Thacher,
Christopher Columbus. His Life, His Work, His Remains . . . , i (New York & London, 1903), 192–3.
[3] For a good summary of recent literature upon the subject of Columbus's education see Pauline

to the power of the written word and the ability to read and write it, once he had acquired these skills for himself. They certainly sharpened his appetite for honours, and he was relentless in his search for these, and for more material rewards.[4] His expectations, however, were never adequately fulfilled, and as at the beginning, so to the end of his life in May 1506, Columbus was dependent upon external support (especially the support of the sovereigns of Castille) for the financing of his ventures and for the securing of those which he took to be his rights.

The admiral's known surviving library is pitifully small. Beyond the palimpsest manuscript copy of Seneca's *Tragedies*,[5] the Biblioteca Columbina in Seville preserves, and attributes to him as owner, nine printed books. Five of these have extensive marginal notes, many certainly written by Columbus himself.[6] These are, the compendium known as *Imago mundi*, put together between *c.* 1410 and 1414 by Cardinal Pierre d'Ailly (1340–1420) and printed in Louvain 1480–83,[7] the *Historia rerum ubique gestarum* of Aeneas Silvius Piccolomini (Pope Pius II, 1458–64), printed in 1477, an Italian translation of Pliny's *Natural History,* printed in Venice in 1489, a copy of Plutarch's *Lives*, this time translated into Castilian and printed at Seville in 1491,[8] and a Latin rendering of the *Travels* of Marco Polo, translated by Fra Pippino of Bologna (perhaps between the years 1302–14) as the *De consuetudinibus et conditionibus orientalium regionum*, and printed in Antwerp in 1485/6.[9] The admiral seems also to have owned and lightly annotated a copy of the *Geography* of Ptolemy (in a 1490 printed edition). He had an anonymous fifteenth century biblical concordance, and, it seems, the *Philosophia naturalis* of Albertus Magnus, printed in Venice in 1496, and the *Confessionale* of Antoninus Florentius, printed in Venice in 1476.[10]

M. Watts, 'Prophecy and Discovery: on the Spiritual Origins of Christopher Columbus's "Enterprise of the Indies"', *American Historical Review*, xc, 1–2 (1985), 74–102, see esp. pp. 74–5.

[4] Documents in which Columbus claimed titles for his family, and special privileges in the matter of trade with his discovered lands, are printed in translation in Samuel E. Morison (tr. and ed.), *Journals and Other Documents on the Life and Voyages of Christopher Columbus* (New York, 1963), 26–30, 299–302.

[5] This was assigned to Columbus by the late nineteenth-century librarian of the Biblioteca Columbina; Simon de la Rosa y Lopez, *Libros y autographos de D. Cristobal Colon* in: *Discurso leidos ante la Real Academia Sevillana de Buenas Letras*, i (Seville, 1891), 21.

[6] The annotations to them are printed, together with those portions of the original works to which they refer, in Cesare de Lollis, *Raccolta di documenti e studi pubblicati dalla R. Commissione Columbiana. i/2: Scritti di Cristoforo Colombo* (Rome, 1894), 291–523.

[7] A facsimile of this incunabulum has been published: *Imago mundi by Petrus de Aiaco with Annotations by Christopher Columbus* (Massachusetts Historical Society, Boston 1927). The Latin texts of d'Ailly's *Imago mundi, Epilogus mappae mundi,* and *Compendia cosmographiae Ptolomaei* have been edited and published, complete with Columbus's annotations and a translation into French, by Edmond Buron, *Ymago mundi de Pierre d'Ailly ...*, 3 vols. (Paris, 1930).

[8] No modern edition of these last three items as yet exists.

[9] There is a modern translation of this into Italian, together with Columbus's Latin *postille*: Luigi Giovannini, *Il Milione. Con le postille di Cristoforo Colombo*, Il fascino dell' ignoto, 3 (Rome, 1985).

[10] Lopez (op. cit. n. 5), pp. 20–1.

IV. 'COLUMBUS PRIMUS INVENTOR INDIAE OCCIDENTALIS'
Engraving by Theodorus de Bry (1592) (see page vii of this book)

He had access to, and may have owned, far more however. His quotations from the Bible are legion, and we may suppose that he accompanied his concordance with a Vulgate text. He certainly knew the immensely popular *Catholicon* of John of Genoa (d. *c.* 1298), for he takes sections (in part *verbatim*) from it for his annotations to the *Imago mundi,* (perhaps from a Venice edition of 1490).[11] He read the *Book of Sir John Mandeville,*[12] and I think I can prove also, and most interestingly, that he read the curious *Chronicle* of the Franciscan Friar John of Marignolli. John of Marignolli was sent as papal legate to the court of the Great Khan in 1338 and remained in the Khan's dominions until 1353.[13] John's *Chronicle* recounts some of his eastern travels and incorporates (briefly, but vividly for all that) descriptions of the cities and lands and peoples he found there.[14] The *Chronicle* was written between the years 1355–59, when John was in the service of the Emperor Charles IV of Bohemia, and so was close in time to Mandeville's famous, and much disputed, work.[15] It was close to this in spirit too, as I hope we shall shortly see. Columbus was, in addition, at least acquainted with the works of two other famous Franciscans: Nicholas of Lyra (1270–1349), whose commentary on the Bible was the first such commentary to be printed,[16] and Francis of Meyronnes (1285–1325), whose *Veritates theologicae* or *Compendium* upon St Augustine's *City of God* supplied the admiral with yet another postil to the *Imago mundi.*[17] And the admiral perhaps owned, and certainly had access to, the *City of God* itself, for he compiles from it in his own *Book of Prophecies* (as he does from a variety of Augustine's other works),[18] and appends a whole chapter from it (XVII, xxiv—the one to which he refers in his postil from Francis of Meyronnes

---

[11] The *verbatim* sections are noted by Buron (op. cit. n. 7), vol. i, pp. 165–8; vol. ii, p. 394; vol. iii, pp. 558–9, 562–64, 582, 634–66. The 1490 Venice edition of the *Catholicon* is in fact closer to the first postil than the two editions to which Buron refers.

[12] Andreas Bernaldez states that Columbus knew Mandeville's *Book.* The admiral's son, Ferdinand, certainly knew it, and implies that his father did. Cecil Jane (tr.), *Select Documents Illustrating the Four Voyages of Columbus, Including those Contained in R. H. Major's 'Select Letters of C. Columbus',* i, The Hakluyt Society, Sec. Ser., lcv (London, 1930), 130–1. Benjamin Keen (tr.), *The Life of the Admiral Christopher Columbus by his Son Ferdinand* (London, 1960), 42–4.

[13] The essential facts about John of Marignolli's career are given by Livarius Oliger, 'De anno ultimo vitae Fr. Iohannis de Marignollis missionarii inter Tartaros atque episcopi Bisinianensis', *Antonianum,* xviii (1943), 29–34.

[14] The *Chronicle* is edited by Josef Emler, *Fontes rerum Bohemicarum. iii: Kronika Marignolova* (Prague, 1882), 492–604.

[15] I set out the evidence for Columbus's knowledge of the *Chronicle* of John of Marignolli in V. I. J. Flint, 'Christopher Columbus and the Friars' in: eds. L. Smith & B. Ward, *Intellectual Life in the Middle Ages* (London, 1992), 295-310.

[16] Rome, 1471–72. Nicholas's work was especially well known in Spain; K. Reinhardt, 'Das Werk des Nicholas von Lyra im mittelalterlichen Spanien', *Traditio. Studies in Ancient and Medieval History, Thought and Religion,* xliii (1987), 321–58.

[17] Buron (op. cit. n. 7), vol. I, pp. 206–15. Columbus also quotes from Nicholas in his *Book of Prophecies*; De Lollis (op. cit. n. 6), pp. 78–9. 103–4, 136, 142–3, 146–51.

[18] De Lollis (op. cit. n. 6), pp. 144–5. See also especially pp. 97–103.

to the *Imago mundi*) to his copy of Pope Pius II's *Historia*.[19] He knew the *De antiquitatibus* of Josephus too, again perhaps directly. In his appended notes to the *Historia* he follows the section from Augustine's *City of God* with a section from the *De antiquitatibus* (Book VIII). Columbus used this same section once again in the so-called 'Lettera rarissima' he wrote to his sovereigns after the fourth voyage.[20]

My final contributions to the admiral's reading-list are two. The first springs from the identification of the so-called 'Great Carthusian' to whom Columbus refers in his long note to chapter XXIIII of the *Imago mundi*. The reference puzzled the text's editor, Edmund Buron,[21] but it must be, in fact, to the *Expositio in psalterium Davidis* of the Carthusian Ludolf of Saxony (d. 1377). Ludolf of Saxony was well known in Spain as 'El Cartujano', and his famous *Vita Christi* was translated into Catalan shortly after 1496, and then into Castillian.[22] The *Expositio psalterii* was printed in 1491. The second is *Le pèlerinage de vie humaine* of the mid-fourteenth century Cistercian Guillaume de Deguileville, after whom Columbus may have named the island 'El Romero' on his third voyage.[23]

Columbus's cartographic knowledge can hardly have been less extensive than his reading. He and his brother Bartholomew were trained as chart makers, and Genoa, their birthplace, was in the forefront of the production of portolan charts. As the admiral was leaving upon his first voyage in 1492, moreover, Martin Behaim in Nuremberg was building his famous globe. The impossibility of proving that Columbus ever met Behaim, or saw the globe, is one of the most infuriating failures of end to meet end in the whole of the history of Columbus's discoveries, but he certainly knew many of the sources upon which Behaim and his collaborators drew. Foremost among these is the work of Henricus Martellus. Henricus Martellus (*fl. c.* 1480–96, and sometimes known as Henricus Martellus Germanus) was a German cartographer active in the supplying of maps supplementary to Ptolemy's *Geography*; both world maps, that is, and 'tabulae modernae'. Martellus

---

[19] De Lollis (op. cit. n. 6), p. 366.

[20] Jane (op. cit. n. 12), vol. ii, pp. 104–5; De Lollis (op. cit. n. 6), pp. 366–7. No one, to my knowledge, has so far pointed to the connection between the note appended to the *Historia* and the 'Lettera rarissima'.

[21] Buron (op. cit. n. 7), vol. i, pp. 306–7.

[22] See Edgar Allison Peers, 'La epoca Fernandina y el comienzo del misticismo en Espana' in: *Fernando el Catolico y la cultura de su tiempo, V Congreso de Historia de la Corona de Aragon* (Saragossa, 1961), 67.

[23] The relevant passage, a part of Ludolf's exposition of Psalm 71: 10, reads: 'Vel ad litteram possit exponi de magis qui venerunt adorare Christum cum muneribus qui fuerunt de his provinciis ...' ('We might explain this literally as applying to the magi who came to adore Christ, and who came from these provinces.') Psalm 72: 10 speaks, of course, of the Kings of Tarshish and the Isles, and of Sheba and Seba (Vulgate, Saba). I reproduce it from a copy of the 1491 edition, held in the Wing collection of the Newberry Library, Chicago. I set out the case for Columbus's knowledge of *Le pèlerinage de vie humaine* in V. I. J. Flint, 'Columbus, "El Romero" and the so-called Columbus Map', *Terrae Incognitae*, 24 (1992), 19-29.

supplied Behaim with one of the prototype maps for his globe.[24] He may also
have known the work of Columbus's brother, Bartholomew.[25] One of Martellus's
world maps is thought, in addition, originally to have been designed to accompany
the *Historia* of Pope Pius II. It is overwhelmingly likely, then, that Columbus had
seen at least some of the maps of Martellus,[26] and that through them he came
close to Behaim. He came close in other ways as well. Behaim clearly drew upon
the famous letter, accompanying 'graphic sketch' and flawed short reckoning of
the distance westwards to Japan made by Paolo Toscanelli for the King of
Portugal in 1474, to tempt the latter to the westward route to the Indies. Columbus
seems to have seen both graphic sketch and letter in the early 1480s, and also a
chart sent to him by Toscanelli himself.[27] The correspondence between Toscanelli's estimate of the distance between Spain and Japan, that upon Behaim's
globe, and that claimed initially by Columbus is striking.[28]

The remaining surviving evidence for Columbus's cartographic knowledge is
slender, but it is still instructive. He speaks, for instance, of 'mappemondes' or
mappae mundi, in his journal of the first voyage.[29] There were maps of, and dia-
grams attached to, the *Imago mundi* of Pierre d'Ailly, but Columbus alludes here,
I am sure, to an older tradition of biblical, or T-O maps, a tradition to which
Behaim, for all his respect for Ptolemy, still clung. The old *mappae mundi* depicted, not physical, but Christian and biblical journeys towards the Jerusalem, and
towards the Terrestrial Paradise with its four rivers, described in such passages
from the Bible as Ezechiel 5:5 and Genesis 2:8–14. Memories of those who had
directed and made these journeys, such as King Solomon whose fleet plied to the
gold and treasures of Ophir, (I Kings 10:11,22, II Chronicles 9:22), or the Magi
of Matthew 2:1–12 and (to some) Psalm 71:10, or the prophets Elijah and Enoch
who awaited the Second Coming outside Paradise in accordance with interpretations of IV Kings 2:11–12 and Ecclesiasticus 44:16, or medieval pilgrims to
Paradise such as saints Brendan, or Macarius, were still preserved upon such
maps, together with remnants from an even older tradition such as sirens and
Amazons and Plinyian monsters.[30] Behaim shewed an interest in many of these

---

[24] Lev S. Bagrow (revised and enlarged by R. A. Skelton), *History of Cartography* (London,
1964), 107, 259.

[25] J. B. Harley, *Maps and the Columbian Encounter* (Milwaukee, 1990), 53–4.

[26] Adolf E. Nordenskiold, *Periplus. An Essay on the Early History of Charts and Sailing
Directions* (Stockholm, 1897), 87–8, 128. In his notes to the *Imago mundi*, Columbus is critical of
a certain 'pictura' which places Cathay, in his view, too far north; Buron (op. cit. n. 7), vol. iii, p.
747. Martellus so places Cathay.

[27] For the Toscanelli correspondence see, most conveniently, Morison, *Journals* ... (op. cit. n. 4),
pp. 13–4, and for the flawed reckoning of the degree Morison, *Admiral* ... (op. cit. n. 1), vol. i, p.
103.

[28] Ernest G. Ravenstein, *Martin Behaim, his Life and his Globe* ... (London, 1908), 64.

[29] Cecil Jane (tr.), *The Journal of Christopher Columbus*, revised and annotated by L. A. Vigneras,
with an appendix by R. A. Skelton (London, 1960), pp. 43, 60.

[30] One of the best examples of the biblical *mappae mundi* is the so-called Hereford World Map.
This is fully described in Gerald R. Crone, *The World Map by Richard of Haldingham in Hereford
Cathedral, circa A. D. 1285* (London, 1954).

mythical and scriptural countries and peoples[31]—and so did Columbus. We find the latter, in his *Journal* of the first voyage, actively looking out for sirens (and being a little disappointed by their actual appearance),[32] and he is certainly alerted to the discovery of monsters and tribes of female warriors.[33] He notes all Pope Pius II has to say about the Amazons, for instance; and the pontiff says a great deal.

The admiral's real and putative library of books and maps threatens to grow ever larger, and to pose problems we shall never be able finally to resolve; but even as it stands, it provides abundant mental food for our contemplation. We may make three points about it now. Firstly, it is very hard indeed to divide these books and maps into *our* categories of travel fact and travel fiction. We might initially be tempted to place the works of scholarly cardinals and popes, such as those of Pierre d'Ailly or Pius II, with their solemn accounts of world geography and history, into the factual category, together with the reports of established travellers like Marco Polo and John of Marignolli. And we might relegate seemingly obvious story books like Mandeville's, or medieval *mappae mundi* such as the Hereford Map (or the 1436 world map of Andreas Bianco with its depiction of Judas from the *Navigatio Sancti Brendani*), into that of fiction. But such attempted oppositions break down immediately. Much doubt has been recently cast, for instance, upon the veracity of Marco Polo's narrative as a factual travel account,[34] and an effort has been made to range it instead with 'encyclopaedic treatises' such as the *Imago mundi* or *Historia*. But these treatises, for all their claims to truth, were written, we should note, from the armchair. And there are some very strange stories abroad in, for example, the *Historia* of Pope Pius II. Pius speaks twice of the opposition between 'fabula' and 'historia', once in his preface and again in chapter XX. He reserves only to the latter the ability to speak 'verum'; but he can still report apparent fables, such as the story of the dogs of Rhodes who fawn upon Christians but bite Turks (LXXXVIII) (Columbus makes a special note of this).[35] John of Marignolli, a real traveller to the East, has some even stranger ones. He describes, for instance, the house of Adam (all made of marble slabs) still on the mountain outside Paradise to which Adam was expelled from the Garden of Eden, and he tells of Adam's great footprint in the rock, and of the lake made of the tears of Adam and Eve as they wept for their great loss—all, seemingly, with a straight face.[36] Cardinal Pierre d'Ailly may have drawn upon some of the tales of Mandeville, as we shall see below. And world maps filled with legends and 'fabulae' could coexist with the latest in Ptolemy and with portolan charts up to, and

---

[31] He has sirens and sea-monsters and tailed men, for instance, and marks Ophir and the island of St Brendan.

[32] Jane, *The Journal* ... (op. cit. n. 29), p. 143. He had most likely sighted the Manatee, or Sea-Cow.

[33] Jane, *The Journal* ... (op. cit. n. 29), pp. 68, 74, 140.

[34] See Jacques Heers, 'De Marco Polo a Christophe Colomb: Comment lire le *Devisement du monde*', *Journal of Medieval History*, x (1984), 125–43. The author here ranges Marco Polo's supposed account among 'encyclopaedic treatises', made at second hand.

[35] Since there is no modern edition of the *Historia*, I have used a copy printed in Paris in 1511.

[36] Emler (ed.) (op. cit. n. 14), pp. 499–500.

well beyond, the late fifteenth century. The most famous of these is the late
fifteenth century so-called Columbus map itself, with its world map filled with
allusions to the legend of St Brendan the Navigator and, as I think, Guillaume de
Deguileville, actually attached to such a chart;[37] but there are many more.

There are clearly factors different from our distinctions between travel fact and
travel fiction at work among the contents of Columbus's supposed library. If we
must choose between the two categories, then fiction seems to be the more
appropriate one. Yet, (and here is my second point), although the relevance to
travel appears more strikingly evident in some of the works the admiral read than
in others, there is nothing in this collection which is actually *irrelevant* to travel
and discovery. Put in another way, Columbus's known reading covers every aspect
of travel, from the geographically informative through the imaginatively
remarkable to the devotionally inspiring, sometimes in a single book. Even the
City of God may be claimed ultimately to be about travel, though travel primarily
of a spiritual nature, to be sure. In Columbus's known library, in short, fact,
'verum', has at least as much to do with the moral as with the physical landscape.
It appears, indeed, to have a moral dynamic built into its very foundations—that
which *tends*, or is conducive, to the truth; that is, to Christian truth. It may be no
accident that the *Geography* of the pre-Christian geographer, Ptolemy, impressive
as it was thought to be as a 'scientific' treatise, is the most lightly annotated of all
of Columbus's annotated books. Thirdly, and most importantly of all as I think,
this library in which our categories of fact and fiction are so jumbled, is, according
to another perspective, not jumbled at all. It is singularly well adapted to the
library of a cultivated Christian gentleman, or lady, ecclesiastical or lay. We do
not as yet know quite as much as we might about the libraries of the great noble
Spanish humanists, but the collection of, for example, Archbishop Alfonso de
Fonseca[38] might be allowed to be indicative, and so, above all, might that of
Queen Isabella of Castille.[39] Queen Isabella certainly had a concordance to the
Bible, and at least one copy of Plutarch's *Lives*, Seneca's *Tragedies* and John of
Genoa's *Catholicon*, as well as two of Mandeville's *Book*. She also had
Augustine's *City of God*, at least one book by Josephus and at least one (the *Vita
Christi*, in Latin) by Ludolf of Saxony.[40] The *Dialogus* written by her chaplain
for the instruction of her son, Don Juan, and in which the Queen herself is one of
the interlocutors, is filled with echoes of Columbus's known reading—and she had
no fewer than eight tapestries depicting the pilgrimage of Guillaume de Deguileville.[41]

---

[37] This world map and chart are fully described in Charles de la Roncière, *La Carte de Christophe
Colomb* (Paris, 1924). It is impossible definitively to prove that Columbus owned this map and
chart, but the argument is certainly suggestive.

[38] On this, see the suggestive pages in Jocelyn N. Hillgarth, *The Spanish Kingdoms, 1250–1516*,
2 vols. (Oxford, 1976–78), esp. vol. ii, pp. 175–82.

[39] Hillgarth (op. cit. n. 38), p. 352, and see especially Francisco J. Sanchez Canton, *Libros, tapices
y cuadros que coleccionó Isabel la Católica* (Madrid, 1950).

[40] Sanchez Canton (op. cit. n. 39), pp. 42–5, 54–5, 60, 67, 82.

[41] G. M. Bertini, 'Un dialogo humanistico sobre la educacion del principe Don Juan' in: *Fernando
. . .* (op. cit. n. 22), pp. 54–62.

Columbus's library may have little to do with our categories of science and imagination, then, but it fits seamlessly into that late fifteenth century outburst of enthusiasm for literary cultivation which was so materially assisted by the printing press. I would argue that it was deliberately crafted to be inserted in this way. As a result of this enthusiasm and this careful crafting, our distinctions are swept aside by a flood of writings whose principles of construction are wholly different from those upon which we incline to draw now. These travel writings were printed, and owned, rather because they were respectable and inspiriting to Christians than because they were true, or not true, in our sense. When we occupy ourselves with what we know of the admiral's reading, we occupy ourselves not with objective accounts as opposed to stories, but with received, even beloved, authorities. The distinctions between them which remain are distinctions of style, not status. The authorities upon which Columbus drew were crucially at one in the standing of their authors, in the moral direction of their message (perhaps in that order), and in the appeal of this standing and direction to great sovereigns and patrons, lay and ecclesiastical. Columbus's whole enterprise, we might remember, was itself dependent upon enthusiasm and appeal of this kind.

We may now turn to the second, and central, consideration I wish to address. How was this library actually employed in support of the admiral's proposed new routes to the wealth of the east?

It is, unfortunately, impossible to be quite certain of the order in which Columbus read and annotated his books, or to know whether he had put his library together as a whole before he secured the crucial attention of Queen Isabella in 1492. It is likely, however, that he at least possessed, and had made some notes upon, the *Imago mundi* of Pierre d'Ailly, and the *Historia* of Pope Pius II before he set out on the first voyage.[42] He certainly seemed to have the former under his eyes in 1491, in Spain.[43] The physician and astronomer, Paolo Toscanelli, had encouraged, as we saw, an exceedingly optimistic estimate of the distance over the Atlantic westwards from Spain towards land, and observations in both D'Ailly's *Imago mundi* and Pius II's *Historia* fortified this estimate by extending the known inhabited landmass eastwards, and bringing it close to Spain the other way. Columbus annotated all these observations carefully.[44] Marco Polo's accounts accorded with theirs, and Augustine's *City of God* helped too. The passage from it which Columbus appended to his copy of the *Historia* (XVII, xxiv) defends the authority of the prophet Ezra, and so of that prophet's encouraging declaration that the proportion of water to land on earth is small. Columbus again paid serious attention to the observations of the Prophet Ezra in his annotations to the *Imago mundi*, and it is highly probable that these annotations, so crucial to the undertaking as a whole, were made before he departed.[45] When the Talavera Commission delivered (as it thought) the definitive rejection of the admiral's plans in

---

[42] Buron (op. cit. n. 7), vol. i, pp. 28–9.

[43] Watts (op. cit. n. 3), pp. 85–6.

[44] Buron (op. cit. n. 7), vol. i, pp. 206–15, 224–7, 232–3, 262–3; De Lollis (op. cit. n. 6), p. 297.

[45] De Lollis (op. cit. n. 6), p. 366; Buron (op. cit. n. 7), vol. i, pp. 210–11.

1490, it did so, it said, because it could not support 'an affair ... which appeared uncertain and impossible to any educated person, however little learning he might have.'[46] Perhaps that stung Columbus into intellectual action.

When, on the first voyage, Columbus struck the coast of Cuba, after the first landfall at San Salvador, his first expressed thought was, when set against the background we have now reconstructed, a highly understandable one. He wrote in his *Journal* of that voyage, a journal intended for his sovereigns, that he thought it must be the Cipangu of Marco Polo, Toscanelli and Behaim.[47] As he went along what seemed to be a very long coast north-westwards, however, he felt compelled to abandon this idea, for the Cipangu of Behaim had only a short north-western coast. Thus he made the famous decision to turn back, missing the shores of Florida and forming his declaration that Cuba must in truth be mainland Cathay.[48] His reading served him to explain all this both to himself and to his supporters; and it served him further when, as he sailed south-eastwards again from Cuba / Cathay, he struck the present day Haiti. Perhaps this, then, was Cipangu / Japan? But it lacked the cities that Marco Polo and John of Marignolli had described. Thus, another solution was needed. I have mentioned Columbus's attachment of a passage from the *De antiquitatibus* of Josephus to the *Historia* of Pope Pius II, and how Columbus recalled this passage in his 'Lettera rarissima' to his sovereigns. This passage called upon one of Columbus's favourite biblical stories, the story of Hiram's fleet, bringing riches beyond all dreams of avarice to the Old Testament King Solomon, (I Kings 10: 11–12, II Chronicles 9: 22). Fleets from the Kings of Tarshish and the isles and the Kings of Sheba and Seba (Saba in the Vulgate) of Psalm 71: 10–11 sailed sometimes with this fleet (I Kings 10: 11), also bringing gifts to King Solomon as the Queen of Sheba herself did. If Haiti was not Cipangu, it might, then, be Sheba. The *Imago mundi* provided once again for this identification, for Pierre d'Ailly speaks (chapter XXIV) of Tarshish in connection with Cathay, and Columbus had added a long postil to this chapter, a postil in which he refers to Nicholas of Lyra, and to Ludolf of Saxony's statement that the rich Magi of Matthew came from these parts.[49] The Bible, biblical commentary and some of his other known books once more came all together to the admiral's assistance. John of Marignolli was particularly helpful. John claimed that he had himself sailed from the Malabar to an island called Saba, or Sheba; one, furthermore, still under the dominion of a queen.[50] Michael de Cuneo, a gentleman traveller on the second voyage, tells us that by then Columbus had firmly identified Hispaniola / Haiti with the biblical Sheba and its famous gold and spices and precious woods and ivories and rare creatures.[51] This identification, furthermore, explains the admiral's wish to explore Jamaica the moment it was cited, for Jamaica was presumably one of the other rich isles of Tarshish. It

---

[46] Morison, *Admiral of the Ocean Sea* (op. cit. n. 1), vol. i, p. 131.

[47] Jane, *The Journal* ... (op. cit. n. 29), p. 43.

[48] Jane, *The journal* ... (op. cit. n. 29), p. 51.

[49] Buron (op. cit. n. 7), vol. i, pp. 306–7.

[50] Emler (ed.) (op. cit. n. 14), pp. 497–502.

[51] Morison, *Journals* ... (op. cit. n. 4), pp. 224, 227–8.

might even be Pliny's gold-bearing island of Chrise. Queen Isabella, we might remark, had great tapestries (no longer, alas, surviving) which depicted the visit of the Queen of Sheba to King Solomon and the riches of the kings of Tarshish and the isles.[52]

So far, Columbus's library, mixed as it was from our point of view, had provided explanations of precisely the kind he needed; explanations which accounted for the decisions he took and for the discoveries he made, and explanations which were, above all, understandable to the noble and literary clientele he had perforce to address. The explanations it provided were, furthermore, encouraging enough to allow of hope for more than the somewhat meagre toll of gold and spices the first two voyages had so far yielded. There were wool-bearing trees on Hispaniola, after all, just as Sir John Mandeville had said there were on the islands beyond Cathay,[53] and the 'mainland', close to Jamaica, had two crop-bearing seasons a year, a characteristic Pliny had claimed for the lands close to India.[54] Amazons were to be found on Martinique.[55] The Bible, above all, might be expected to speak the truth. These accounts and correspondences did in fact serve their purpose, for they allowed of the eventual equipping of a third voyage.

I have said that this voyage was the most disastrous of them all for Columbus. It is also, and most interestingly for us, the one in whose reports travel fiction or, to use terms more appropriate to the period, appealing, enlivening and materially and morally encouraging stories seem to have played their greatest role; for it was on this voyage that Columbus made his famous—to some infamous—claim to have discovered the Terrestrial Paradise.

The fullest account of this claim is given in the letter to his sovereigns Columbus began, and perhaps completed, as he travelled back from Hispaniola to Spain in chains in October 1498. This letter is now known in two versions, one long printed, the other only very recently discovered in the early sixteenth century *Libro copiador de Cristobal Colon*.[56] In this letter, Columbus is explaining experiences we know from his *Journal* of the third voyage he had certainly had—the experience of the temperate climate off the coast of Venezuela, for example, and of the immense rush of sweet water from the Orinoco river into the Gulf of Paria—but he is explaining them in very special and, we must add, heightened terms.

The first part of the 1498 letter deals with Columbus's expressed conviction that

---

[52] Sanchez Canton (op. cit. n. 39), pp. 101, 124–5.

[53] Morison, *Journals . . .* (op. cit. n. 4), p. 242; Malcolm Letts (ed. and tr.), *Mandeville's Travels, Texts and Translations*, 2 vols., Works Issued by the Hakluyt Society, Sec. Ser., ci (London, 1953), see vol. ii, p. 186.

[54] Andreas Bernaldez reports on the two crop-bearing seasons, and Pierre d'Ailly gives this (from Pliny) as a characteristic of the region of India. Jane, *Select Documents . . .* (op. cit. n. 12), vol. i, pp. 120–1; Buron (op. cit. n. 7), vol. i, 260–1.

[55] Jane, *The Journal . . .* (op. cit. n. 29), p. 140.

[56] The *Libro copiador* is a copy-book of letters by Columbus himself. It may draw directly upon the admiral's own archives and is probably Italian in origin. See Antonio Rumeu de Armas, *Libro copiador de Cristobal Colon. Correspondencia inedita con los Reyes Catolicos sobre los viajes a America* (Madrid, 1989).

the seas, and so the surface of the earth, began to slope upwards at a point about 100 leagues west of the Azores, at which point the climate also changed, becoming temperate and mild.

> I have found such irregularities that I have come to the following conclusions concerning the shape of the world: that it is not round as they describe it, but the shape of a pear, which is round everywhere except at the stalk, where it juts out a long way.

The fact that the area appears to be raised up, the temperateness of its climate, its position at, as he believes, the very end of the east, the rush of sweet water from this great height into the Gulf of Paria, and the depth of the sweet water there; all of these, says the admiral, have convinced him that he has sailed to the very edges of the Earthly Paradise, and the outlet of its four rivers. But he could not try actually to attain this Paradise, he adds, for no-one may enter it but by God's leave. Columbus names a great host of impressive sources in his support; Isidore, Bede, John Damascene, Strabo, Peter Comestor, St Ambrose, John Scotus Eriugena.

The notion that the seas sloped upwards derived in the main from the taking of erroneous bearings upon the pole star when it was obscured by hazy weather, as Morison long ago explained.[57] But both it and the other notions were readily reconcilable with the admiral's reading, and with a wide range of that reading. Thus Pierre d'Ailly provided the impressive list of authorities Columbus offers, (*Imago mundi*, LV) with the small but significant exception of John Scotus. D'Ailly also provided material in support of the temperateness of the climate around Paradise (*Imago mundi*, VII and XI), on its four rivers and on its height above the surface of the earth (LV), a height unattainable by Noah's flood. Sir John Mandeville agrees on all these points. Indeed, we may find some echoes of Mandeville here in the respectable *Imago mundi* itself, and John adds observations about the inaccessibility of the Terrestrial Paradise which are very similar to those of Columbus.[58]

> And ye shall understand that no man living may go to Paradise ... Many great lords have assayed divers times to pass by those rivers of paradise, but they might not speed of their journey; for some of them died for weariness of rowing and over travailing, some waxed blind and some deaf for the noise of the waters, and some were drowned by the violence of the waves of the waters ...

I mentioned the small but significant exception of John Scotus among the sources Columbus drew from d'Ailly. John Scotus was the only source cited by John of Marignolli for the latter's own description of the Terrestrial Paradise. The admiral almost certainly had it from him. The variant version of this letter to be found in the *Libro copiador*, moreover, mentions Eli and Enoch sitting outside that Paradise Columbus claimed to have discovered.[59] This reinforces the suspicion that the *Chronicle* of the Friar-legate John of Marignolli may in fact have been the chief source upon which Columbus drew here,[60] followed closely by John

---

[57] Samuel Eliot Morison, 'Columbus and Polaris', *American Neptune*, i (1941), 124–37.

[58] XXXIII; Letts (op. cit. n. 53), pp. 214–7.

[59] Rumeu de Armas (op. cit. n. 56), vol. i, p. 360.

[60] Flint, 'Christopher Columbus ....' (op. cit. n. 15).

Mandeville. Columbus was filling the ears of his sovereigns, at this desperately low point in his career, with accounts which both pleased the ear, and placed him on a par with Franciscan Friar-legates (with one who was, in addition, servant to an Emperor) and their discoveries in the east.

The letter to his sovereigns, then, explaining the events of the third voyage, is as carefully dovetailed to that reading Columbus shared with his sovereigns and patrons as were the accounts of the earlier two. The only change is that this time the claims are larger. They are no less securely based than were the propositions advanced in explanation of the earlier voyages, but they have moved far further into that which we might perhaps describe as the devotional realm, and the moral dynamic in this letter is to that degree more powerful. True, there is a hint in his first *Journal* that Columbus had begun to think about the westerly position and temperate climate of the Earthly Paradise as he sailed back from the Azores on the first voyage,[61] but there is nothing to equal the outpourings of the letter from which I have just quoted until the deprivations of this third catastrophic expedition. This heightening of the emotional and religious temperature must, I am certain, be associated with these deprivations, and with the very real fear that the impetus for the whole enterprise might be lost, or at least removed from Columbus himself. When confronted with such threats, he extended his reach and played even more insistently upon chords attuned both to the literary ear (and John Mandeville is beautifully so attuned) and to the spiritual, this time with the special help of Friar John of Marignolli.

The matter of the spiritual, and of Columbus's association of his own efforts with those of a respected Franciscan brings me to one last, but I think important, perhaps *the* most important, book in the admiral's putative library. This book is the *Confessionale* of Antoninus Florentius, named earlier as one of the nine preserved books of Columbus. The *Confessionale* is interesting in a number of respects. It was the work of a Dominican Friar, Antoninus Florentius (1389–1459), a deeply respected pastor who, in his last years, became Archbishop of Florence; and it was a guide to the making of confession. Antoninus Florentius's *Confessionale* may have been meant originally for lay-persons, and it was extraordinarily popular, going into over 102 incunable editions in the late fifteenth and early sixteenth centuries.[62] It is highly likely, then, that both Columbus and his patrons knew of its contents;[63] and we may remark at once that this particular *Confessionale* was to a high degree critical of enterprises of the kind in which he and they were engaged.

Antoninus's *Confessionale* is especially critical of trade for excess profit. In a long chapter (chapter vii) to be found in the third section of the little book,[64] he dilates upon the almost inevitable sinfulness of such activities. A slightly larger

---

[61] Jane, *The Journal* ... (op. cit. n. 29), p. 176.

[62] On the popularity of the *Confessionale* see the *Catalogue of Books Printed in the Fifteenth Century now in the British Museum*, iv, (London, 1916), 226–7.

[63] Queen Isabella numbers confessionals among her books; Sanchez Canton (op. cit. n. 39), p. 63.

[64] There is no modern edition of the *Confessionale*. I have consulted a copy of the 1476 Venice edition, the version, that is, it seems Columbus had.

latitude might be allowed to persons who undergo great risks in the course of their trading, to those who cross wide expanses of land and sea in danger and so manifest the virtue of courage; but it is hard to find anything truly honest about such endeavours, the Archbishop avers. It may be that trade in support (though in modest, not excessive, support) of one's family might be described as a 'finem honestum'. It might be legitimate to trade for the care of the poor. But all such enterprises are dubious and fraught with temptations to the mortal sin of avarice. Columbus was, we must admit, peculiarly vulnerable to such accusations. His claims for his family were not modest, and it would be hard indeed to argue that his voyages were undertaken primarily in the interest of the poor. Also, though to varying degrees, these charges might with justice be levelled against Columbus's patrons and supporters. We can, then, add to the particular deprivations of the third voyage, an increasing need to emphasize the spiritual nature of at least some of the proposed rewards of the enterprise—a need which became perhaps all the greater as the search for these elusive rewards became ever more expensive, and moral excuses for their abandonment ever more tempting.

This need, the need to provide moral justifications and incentives, that is, especially for his sovereigns, may stand behind both the admiral's insistence upon the discovery of the Terrestrial Paradise and his frequent mention of the crusade against the infidel. Much has been made in recent literature of the admiral's messianism, and of his seeming involvement in the message of apocalyptic teaching, especially the apocalyptic teaching of the Franciscan friars.[65] The signs of this involvement are certainly there for all to see, but it may be that much of it sprang rather from the admiral's anxiety about the justification of his enterprises and about the provision of a 'finem honestum', than from a commitment to this message in all of its aspects. This search for justification may best explain, too, Columbus's frequent references to the Bible and to the Fathers, and his compilation of his *Book of Prophecies* towards the end of his active life. Take, once again, King Solomon and the treasure fleet, and that expressive passage from Josephus which Columbus both adds to the *Historia* of Pope Pius II and quotes in his 'Lettera rarissima' to the sovereigns after the fourth voyage. This was helpful, as we saw, in the matter of explaining the course of Columbus's first and second voyages and in his efforts to secure support for more travels. But it was helpful, too, in *justifying* that support, and especially in justifying it to his sovereigns. King Solomon had been a great and wise king, and he had been allowed access to tremendous treasure without its bringing him into immediate mortal sin. He had, indeed, used it to build the temple in Jerusalem. The kings of Tarshish and the isles, moreover, according to the passage from Ludolf of Saxony, had actually shewn the way in the matter of using such wealth appropriately, and in repressing the temptations to sin which might come with it.[66] Columbus's

---

[65] Watts (op. cit. n. 3), pp. 83–102; A. Milhou, *Colon y su Mentalidad Mesianica en el Ambiente Franciscana Espanol* (Valladolid, 1983).

[66] '(Munera) id est seipsos (offerent) quia se bene regendo devote domino serviunt et bona que operantur ei ascribunt (reges arabum et Saba) id est terrenas delectationes reprimunt.' ('In their offerings of gifts they offer themselves and their devoted service to the Lord by ruling well. The

sovereigns might also, then, be allowed such access safely. Great rulers and great causes do not, on this argument, merely allow the accumulation of the riches of the east; they might actually require it.

This, then, is the context within which Columbus built up his library of travel 'fact' and 'fiction', and this is the context within which he used it. His enterprises were perilous not merely in the physical, but in the financial and, above all, in the moral sense. He had to prepare himself, then, for every possible eventuality. He had to steer a course through the high seas of his patrons' tastes and consciences as well as through the perils of his dependence on their purses. He had to appeal to (and perhaps flatter them in) their actual knowledge, and appease their necessary anxieties. He had also, on such a voyage, occasionally to let go a little ballast. In the context of his insistence upon the reality of the Terrestrial Paradise and of the physical proximity of his ships to it on the third voyage, he called, as we have seen, upon a range of shared and highly respected resources; but he remained silent about one. Pope Pius II had expressed doubts, in his *Historia* (chapter V), about the reality of the existence of this eastern Terrestrial Paradise.[67] Columbus does not mark this doubt in his own annotated copy of the *Historia*, and he certainly gives no hint of it in his letter to his sovereigns. Thus, he edits the pontiff; and in a passage from the *Metamorphoses* he appends to the end of the *Historia,* moreover, he even edits Ovid. From a passage he quotes from Book I of the *Metamorphoses*, he omits lines 45–51, lines in which the poet speaks of an impenetrable torrid zone encircling the equator.[68] Columbus wants none of that—so he has none of it. He was well capable of using his library selectively—and manipulatively.

Columbus's need to justify his adventures dictated both his choice and his use of a remarkable collection of books. It underlay, in turn, his reports of his voyages to his sovereigns. These reports were as skilfully and carefully directed as was his reading. The great admiral displayed a great deal of literary cunning in pursuit of his purposes; far more than we have so far been inclined to attribute to him. When we look at how Columbus actually employed the intellectual resources he had accumulated, it appears, furthermore, that the morality of the cultivated Christian gentleman may have been perceived by him as the greatest of all of his threats. This, at least, is the morality he met with most vigour when times were most hard; and he met it with a moral fervour derived above all from works we might describe as at best loosely allied with the truth. Ambitions of the sort Columbus cherished were liable to arouse resistances easy to couch in moral terms, and objective fact, as we know, is of little or no use when faced with resistances of this order. The admiral may personally have shared the moral fervour he conveyed

---

Kings of Araby and Saba know they owe to Him all the goods of which they dispose, and they suffocate all earthly desires.') See also note 23.

[67] 'Nonnulli paradisum terrestrem sub ea coeli parte sitam crediderunt quibus sacrarum reluctatur autoritas literarum ...' ('Some believe that the earthly paradise is placed beneath that section of the heavens, but sacred learning does not support this ...'). See also note 35.

[68] De Lollis (op. cit. n. 6), p. 367. The omission is not remarked by De Lollis.

so energetically to his patrons; it is hard to know. We can say with firmness, however, that the carefully edited accounts of respected Christian authorities, fortified with beloved Christian travellers tales, were everything in such a situation, and that the admiral saw that they were everything. Columbus's mental journeys were, on one level, far more those of a medieval traveller than of a man of the Renaissance; but, on another, they economised with the truth in ways worthy of some of his most modern successors. Fiction as we might define it and, on occasion, the *suppression* of certain facts, were essential to the prosecution of the admiral's great purpose of discovery.

DIFFERENT READINGS OF HANNO'S VOYAGE FROM THE RENAISSANCE TO THE SEVENTEENTH CENTURY— FROM PURE ERUDITION TO IDEOLOGICAL DEBATE

MONIQUE MUND-DOPCHIE[*]

According to Raymond Mauny, the account of Hanno's voyage 'was providential to all those who approached the history of the countries of the West Coast of Africa: it came in the nick of time to lengthen the time span of a history which, without it, did not start until the arrival of the Arabs in the eighth century or even until that of the first caravels in the fifteenth century.'[1] Mauny's remark may have been inspired by the overwhelming profusion of writings devoted to the Carthaginian admiral's voyage that have come to light in the past hundred years, yet it might just as aptly apply to the number of works brought forth by Renaissance and seventeenth-century scholars on the subject. When confronted with an undatable and incomplete account which had been handed down to them by divergent traditions, which named places impossible to identify with certainty and contained accurate observations side by side with fabulous elements, these scholars were moved, as we are, to try and solve the riddles that abound in it. Yet they responded to these texts in ways that were not in all points quite similar to ours: some were more concerned with the problems of the ancient sources, while others were particularly influenced by the new context—political, economic and cultural—brought about by the Great Discoveries. How did they receive the account of a traveller who preceded by many centuries such explorers as Gil Eanes, Bartholomew Diaz and Vasco da Gama, at a time when the consequences of the expansion of the world were beginning to be felt? This is the question that the present paper will attempt to answer.

It should be pointed out to begin with that sixteenth- and seventeenth-century scholars could use the same texts and documents that are available to us today. In fact, the Greek translation of Hanno's short narrative engraved in the temple of Baal in Carthage was printed for the first time in Basel in 1533.[2] It was edited by Sigismundus Gelenius from the Palatinus Graecus 398 manuscript (Heidelberg)

---

[*] Department of Greek, Latin and Oriental Studies, Catholic University of Louvain, Belgium.

The author gratefully acknowledges Professor F. Corin's patient help in translating the French version of this paper into English.

[1] See p. 78 of R. Mauny, 'Le périple d'Hannon. Un faux célèbre concernant les navigations antiques', *Archeologia. Trésor des âges*, xxxvii (1970), 78–80.

[2] [Sigismundus Gelenius], Περίπλους Εὐξείνου Πόντου ... ῍Αννωνος περίπλους Λιβύης Πλουτάρχου περὶ ποταμῶν ... ᾿Επιτομὴ τῶν τοῦ Στράβωνος γεωγραφικῶν ... [= *Arriani et Hannonis periplus. Plutarchus de fluminibus et montibus. Strabonis epitome*] (Basel, 1533), 38–40.

and is, together with its apograph, the Vatopedinus 655 (Mount Athos), the only source available for the text.[3] It was translated into Italian as early as 1550 and was included with a commentary in the collection of travel accounts compiled by Giambattista Ramusio.[4] Both the Italian version and the commentary were then translated into French by Jean Temporal (1556) and were a direct source of inspiration for the English translation and commentary (1625) of Samuel Purchas, the author of *Hakluytus posthumus*.[5] Two Latin translations, one by Conrad Gesner and the other one by Joannes Jacobus Mueller, each with a new commentary, published in 1559 and 1661 respectively, owe nothing to others[6], whereas Abraham Berkelius's text, Latin version and commentary (1674) derive directly from the work of his predecessors.[7]

The indirect tradition concerning Hanno's voyage is no less well-known to our scholars and has always been available in its essential features. I am thinking mainly of the references to Pliny and Solinus that appear regularly in the medieval encyclopedias.[8] Well-known to the Humanists are also, among the most representative works:[9] Pomponius Mela's *Chorographia*, Arrian's *Indike*, the pseudo-Aristotle's treatise *De mirabilibus auscultationibus* and Athenaeus's *Deipnosophistae*.[10] For this reason they are confronted very early with the discrepancies between the different accounts. Thus, the island inhabited by the hairy people is described in the Heidelberg text as being located in the *Notu Keras* gulf, whereas Pliny and Solinus situate it near the *Hesperu Keras* promontory; in the former, Hanno is said to capture three hairy women, or *Gorillae*, whereas the latter speak of two Gorgons.[11] Similarly, the Heidelberg text makes a distinction between two islands: one in the *Hesperu Keras* gulf, from which Hanno stays away, the other one inhabited by hairy Gorillas, whereas Pomponius Mela peoples the former with Gorgons and the latter with hairy women who give birth to

---

[3] Aubrey Diller, *The Tradition of the Minor Greek Geographers*, Philological Monographies Published by the American Philological Association, 14 (New York, 1952), 3–14.

[4] [Giambattista Ramusio], *Primo volume delle navigationi et viaggi nel qual si contiene la descrittione dell'Africa* (Venice, 1550), fos. 121ᵛ–4ᵛ.

[5] [Jean Temporal], *Historiale Description de l'Afrique, tierce partie du monde … Tome premier* (Lyon, 1556), fos. **1ʳ–**6ʳ; Samuel Purchas, *Purchas his Pilgrimes in Five Bookes. The First* (London, 1625), 77–9.

[6] For Gesner's translation, see: *Ioannis Leonis Africani De totius Africae descriptione libri IX .. Ioanne Floriano interprete … His recens accedit Hannonis, Carthaginensium ducis navigatio, qua Libycam oram ultra Herculis columnas lustravuit, Conrado Gesnero interprete, cum scholiis* (Zurich, 1559); [Joannes Jacobus Mueller], *Hannonis periplus. Quem a se Latine conversum et annotatione quadam auctum in Inclyta Academia Argentoratensi … examinandum proponit Johann Jacobus Müller* (Strassburg, 1661).

[7] Abraham Berkelius, *Genuina Stephani Byzantini de urbibus et populis fragmenta … Accedit Hannonis Carthaginensis Regis periplus* (Leiden, 1674), 65–98.

[8] Pliny, *Historia naturalis*, ii. 169; v. 8; vi. 200; Solinus, *Collectanea rerum memorabilium*, 24, 56.

[9] Cf. Palaephatos, Περὶ ἀπίστων, xxxi; Aelius Aristides, *Orationes*, xxxvi.93, 94; Marcianus Heracleota, *Epitome peripli Menippei*, i.2.

[10] Pomponius Mela, *De chorographia*, iii.90, 93; Arrian, *Indike*, xliii.11–2; [Aristotle], *De mirabilibus auscultationibus*, 37; Athenaeus, *Deipnosophistae*, iii.83c.

[11] Hanno, *Periplus*, 18; Pliny, vi. 200; Solinus, 56.

children without having contact with men.[12] Finally, the importance of the expedition varies according to the sources. The Heidelberg text, Pomponius Mela and Arrian inform us that the navigation was interrupted on account of a shortage of victuals and of an increasingly hostile environment, whereas Pliny, on the contrary, gives credit to the admiral for achieving the circumnavigation of Africa from Gibraltar to the extreme confines of Arabia.[13] Because of these divergences, scholars assumed two opposite attitudes: some of them approached the different versions with a critical mind, whereas others selected the texts supporting their own presuppositions and ignored those contradicting them.

1. A TRADITIONAL APPROACH: HANNO'S VOYAGE IN THE LIGHT OF PHILOLOGY AND THE HISTORY OF ANTIQUITY

Many scholars have approached Hanno's voyage with serenity, and hardly depart from the attitude of the philologist or of the historian of Antiquity. Belonging to the academic and humanistic circles, so neatly described by François de Dainville and Numa Broc[14], they seek to discover the ancient world rather than the new worlds, and their aim is to recreate the life and labours of the Greek and Roman citizen in their usual surroundings. This is why they are mainly concerned with explaining the texts related to Hanno by resorting to other ancient texts, or, conversely, with commenting on an ancient author by referring to the Carthaginian explorer. This is the case, for example, with the excerpts from Pliny included in Solinus's comments, which were published by Joannes Camers (c. 1520) and by Claudius Salmasius (1629)[15], with the exegesis of Athenaeus by Isaac Casaubonus (1600) and that of Pomponius Mela by I. Vossius (1658).[16] It seems surprising, on the other hand, that Natalis Comes' treatise (first edition 1551) on mythology refers to Hanno's voyage, but the intention of corroborating one statement by means of another can again account for the fact:[17] the aim of Comes is to demonstrate that Lucian, in his *Verae historiae* (ii.12) gave a correct description of the inhabitants of the Islands of the Blest as disembodied souls. Hanno's report appears to him particularly suitable to confirm that of Lucian since

---

[12] *Periplus*, 14 and 18; Pomponius Mela, iii. 93.

[13] *Periplus*, 18; Arrian, *Indike*, xliii. 12; Pliny, ii. 169.

[14] See p. 135 of François de Dainville, 'L'enseignement de l'histoire et de la géographie et le "ratio studiorum"', *Analecta Gregoriana (cura Pontificiae Universitatis Gregorianae edita). LXX, Sectio A (n. 3): Studi sulla Chiesa antica e sull'Umanesimo. Studi presentati nella sezione di Storia Ecclesiastica del Congresso Internazionale per il IV Centenario della Pontificia Unversità Gregoriana. 13–17 ottobre 1953* (Rome, 1954), 123–56; Numa Broc, *La géographie de la Renaissance (1420–1620)* (Paris, 1980), 42.

[15] Joannes Camers, *In C. Iulii Solini polyhistora enarrationes ...* [Vienna, around 1520], 335; Claudius Salmasius, *Plinianae exercitationes in Caii Iulii Solini polyhistora ...* (Paris, 1629), 1296–7.

[16] Isaac Casaubonus, *Animadversionum in Athenaei Dipnosophistas libri XV. Opus nunc primum in lucem editum ...* (Lyons, 1600), 101; Isaac Vossius, *Observationes ad Pomponium Melam de situ orbis* (The Hague, 1658), 207–8, 302–3, 305.

[17] Natalis Comes, *Mythologiae sive explicationis fabularum libri decem ... Nuper ab ipso autore recogniti et locupletati ...* (Frankfurt, 1596), 274–82.

the admiral discovered, near *Hesperu Keras*, a mysterious island whose inhabitants remained invisible to his eyes and revealed their existence only by means of dreadful cries and the noise of flutes, cymbals and drums.

The method is not fundamentally different in the commentaries devoted to the Heidelberg text by Conrad Gesner (1559), Samuel Bochart (1646) and J. J. Mueller (1664). As a matter of fact these three scholars—each giving his preference to a particular aspect of the account—are especially interested in stating Hanno's identity, explaining the meaning of words considered difficult, bringing together the diverse occurrences of the names of the places visited by Hanno, and in confronting the direct and the indirect traditions. They may even happen to look at these with a critical eye. While Gesner relies entirely on the Heidelberg text and blames Pliny the Elder for departing from it[18], Samuel Bochart claims that the end of the account is not to be taken seriously and definitely relegates it to the sphere of the marvellous.[19] J. J. Mueller, for his part, follows Samuel Bochart closely, yet refuses to dismiss the end of the narrative and thinks he can trace small fragments of truth in it. More particularly, he maintains that the legend of the Gorgons, to which reference is made in both the Heidelberg text and in Pliny, rests on some real fact; yet, he never goes beyond the mere statement of it.[20]

Such analyses were bound to give rise sooner or later to a global vision of the voyage and its evaluation. This is the task to which Gerard Vossius, his son Isaac and the English scholar Henry Dodwell applied themselves. Gerard Vossius wrote an entry on Hanno in his treatise *De historicis Graecis libri quatuor* (1623) in which he brings up the information found in the ancient sources and points to the gaps in them and leaves us in doubt as to the reality of the voyage itself or at least as to the authenticity of the texts dealing with it.[21] Quite a different attitude is represented by Isaac Vossius in his *Observationes ad Pomponium Melam* (1658) and his *Variae observationes* (1685).[22] I. Vossius is so thoroughly convinced of the reality of Hanno's voyage that he sees in it the historical nucleus which gave birth to the legends of the Extreme West: Atlas, the Hesperides, the Gorgons, Perseus, etc. As for Henry Dodwell, he assembles, within the limits of the edition of *Geographi Graeci minores* prepared by John Hudson (1695), all the testimonies related to Hanno and demonstrates in a thorough analysis that the Heidelberg text is a forgery, a late compilation by a Greek from Sicily, and that there is at least one other narrative of the voyage, of which the indirect tradition gives an imperfect account.[23]

As appears from the above, the documents that we have just gone through do not

---

[18] Gesner (op. cit. n. 6), pp. 20–1.

[19] Samuel Bochartus, *Geographiae sacrae pars altera Chanaan seu de coloniis et sermone Phoenicum* (Caen, 1646), 710–5.

[20] Mueller (op. cit. n. 6), pp. 10 and 12.

[21] Gerardus Vossius, *De historicis Graecis libri quattuor* (Leiden, 1623), 415–6.

[22] Isaac Vossius (op. cit. n. 16), pp. 208, 302–3; Id., *Variarum observationum liber* (London, 1685), 51–3.

[23] Henry Dodwell, 'Dissertatio prima. De vero peripli, qui Hannonis nomine circumfertur, tempore', in John Hudson, *Geographiae veteris scriptores Graeci minores . . .*, vol. i (Oxford, 1698), 1–41.

differ greatly from the studies that today's philologists and historians have devoted to the Carthaginian admiral's navigation. However, if their authors are mainly interested in Antiquity, they are not totally impervious to the world in which they live or to the discoveries which contributed to its enormous expansion. Some of them can hardly refrain from identifying one particular place explored by Hanno with one discovered by the Portuguese and Spanish navigators. Thus Gesner believes the isle of *Cerne* to be Madeira and *Notu Keras* to be Cabo Hermoso, while J.J. Mueller identifies the isle of *Cerne* with Arguin, and *Hesperu Keras* with Cape Verde.[24] Others appear to be responsive to the great issues that stirred the minds of their contemporaries. Bochart may not be quite as neutral in the interest he takes in Hanno's voyage as he appears to be, for the Phoenician names scattered through the account add credit to the thesis of the learned pastor: Adam and Eve did speak Hebrew, an assertion which is supported by the Semitic roots attested by the toponyms of the whole world. Similarly, although Mueller restricts himself in his research to Antiquity, yet he also appends to his study a list of unanswered questions dealing with such controversial topics as the identification of America with an island that the pseudo-Aristotle and Diodorus of Sicily believe to have been discovered by the Carthaginians, or the identification of the Caribbean Islands with the Hesperides, of which Hanno had caught a glimpse. This shows that Mueller was not deaf to the controversies between the upholders and the opponents of the newness of America and of the radical heterogeneity of the Amerindians.[25] However, with the scholars of the first category, the concern with contemporary matters remains in the background and never becomes obtrusive.

2. A MIXED APPROACH: HANNO'S VOYAGE IN THE DOUBLE PERSPECTIVE OF ANTIQUITY AND THE GREAT DISCOVERIES

Other scholars, in opposition to those discussed so far, are systematic in confronting Hanno's voyage with the new geographical knowledge of the time. Ramusio's method is a particularly good illustration of this approach.[26] Ramusio loses no time in submitting his translation of the Heidelberg text to a Portuguese pilot who has just disembarked in Venice, with a cargo of sugar from São Tomé, and whose name he will keep secret. This unnamed sailor has no difficulty in locating the places on the African coast where Hanno stopped, from Thymiaterion, which he identifies with the city of Azomor, to the isle in the gulf of *Notu Keras*, in which he recognizes Fernando Póo. What is more, he manages to account for the presence of the marvellous in the Carthaginian narrative. The hairy women,

---

[24] Gesner (op. cit. n. 6), pp. 17 and 21; Mueller (op. cit. n. 6), pp. 8 and 11.

[25] On this topic, see, for instance, Margaret T. Hodgen, *Early Anthropology in the Sixteenth and the Seventeenth Centuries* (Philadelphia, 1964); L. E. Huddleston, *A Study of European Concepts of the Origins of the American Indians, 1492–1729* (Austin, 1966); Antonello Gerbi, *La natura delle Indie Nove. Da Cristoforo Colombo a Gonzalo Fernandez de Oviedo* (Milan & Naples 1976); Giuliano Gliozzi, *Adamo e il nuovo mondo. La nascita dell'antropologia come ideologia coloniale: dalle genealogie bibliche alle teorie razziale (1500–1700)* (Florence, 1977).

[26] [Ramusio] (op. cit. n. 4), fols. 122ʳ-4ᵛ.

who were mistaken for Pliny's Gorgons, are actually either monsters now extinct, or baboons.[27] Similarly, the area through which torrents of fire flow corresponds in reality to the equatorial region, which, according to ancient belief, was torrid and uninhabitable. If Hanno refused to admit that nature in this area was exuberant, the reason is that he simply wanted to avoid any controversy with the upholders of the traditional view.[28] As to Ramusio, he gives a personal bias to the commentary so as to show correspondences between the Carthaginian report and other ancient accounts and, on the other hand, he also comes up with problems of his own day. For example, he deplores the Portuguese opposition to further exploration, in particular the exploration of the Austral Continent. He points to Ptolemy's mistake which made the Indian Ocean into a landlocked sea, when the expedition of Hanno and those of the Portuguese had proved the contrary. Finally, he refers to the identification of the Hesperides with the Caribbean Islands, which was proposed, not without political afterthoughts, by Charles V's chronicler, Gonzalo Fernandez de Oviedo.

Such analyses by Ramusio and the Portuguese pilot did have a direct influence on the commentary that Samuel Purchas appended to his translation of the Heidelberg text; he borrowed from them most of the identifications of places as well as their interpretations of the marvellous, convinced of their basis in fact.[29]

The commentary of the German controversialist Bartold Nihus (first edition 1622), on the other hand, is in a quite different vein. First, it concerns the testimony of Pomponius Mela regarding the hairy women and demonstrates its inanity: of course there are other texts, both ancient and modern, mentioning cases of parthenogenesis or affirming the existence of hirsute beings; but Mela's text contradicts the Hanno tradition altogether. Second, Nihus dismisses all the localizations put forward for The Gods' Chariot Mountain (*Theon Ochema*) and the southerly island. He shows in this way how little credence should be given to Hanno's accounts, and he goes on straight away to condemn all the uses that have been made or will be made of the Carthaginian voyage.[30]

3. AN EXCLUSIVELY CONTEMPORARY APPROACH: HANNO'S VOYAGE IN THE LIGHT OF THE GREAT DISCOVERIES

A third category of scholars—for the most part geographers and chroniclers—far from concentrating on the substance of the texts, view the Carthaginian account in an exclusively contemporary perspective. Some do so in a rather innocuous manner: either they see in Hanno the remarkable predecessor of the Portuguese and other discoverers; or they resort to his report as a source of information on the

---

[27] See pp. 335–6 of Monique Mund-Dopchie, 'Les humanistes face aux "gorilles" d'Hannon', *Prose et prosateurs de la Renaissance (Mélanges offerts à M. le Professeur R. Aulotte)* (Paris, 1988), 331–41.

[28] Cf. pp. 170–1 of M. Mund-Dopchie, 'La survie du "Périple d'Hannon" au XVIe et au XVIIe siècle', *Humanistica Lovaniensia. Journal of Neo-Latin Studies*, xxxviii (1989), 163–75.

[29] Purchas (op. cit. n. 5), p. 79.

[30] Bartoldus Nihusius, *Epistola philologica ... excutiens narrationem Pomponii Melae de navigatione Hannonis ...* (second edition, Frankfurt, 1630).

ancient state of Africa. Nicolo Scillacio (1494), Sebastian Münster (1550) and J. A. Magini (1597), for instance, acclaim him as the first circumnavigator of Africa,[31] Luys del Marmol (1573) celebrates him as the inspirer of the grandiose schemes of Henry the Navigator,[32] Pierre Davity (1621) sees him as the originator of the torrid zone theory,[33] and André Thevet (1575), La Popelinière (1582), Cluverius (1621) and the Blaeu brothers (1649) as the illustrious forerunner whose legendary exploit will be repeated after him.[34] On the other hand, in Belleforest's treatise of cosmography (1575) and in Ortelius's and the Mercator-Hondius atlases, the admiral appears rather as one of the observers of the African reality from whom they borrow some information.[35]

A more committed reference to Hanno's voyage, however, is to be found in the *Lectiones antiquae* (1517) of Coelius Rhodiginus, who thinks that he can prove the significance of the biblical message in the profane field of natural science.[36] Thus, he discusses, for instance, the localization of the Earthly Paradise and he places it beyond the torrid zone, which, according to him, is symbolized in *Genesis* by the Cherub with the flaming sword guarding its gate. The fact is that the reality of this obstacle of the torrid zone is confirmed by the ancient tradition, according to which Hanno's southern navigation ends up in a fiery region made inaccessible by thunderstorms and excessive heat. This interpretation of the Carthaginian expedition in terms of a quest for Paradise is fortunately the only instance of its kind; La Popelinière was very sarcastic about it and he rightly ridiculed the primitive comparative method that brought it about.[37]

Finally, Hanno's navigation, just like other navigations which took place in Antiquity, was involved in the controversy that the colonization of America and of the African coast had aroused. For, if the admiral had actually accomplished the

---

[31] Nicolaus Scillacius, *De insulis Meridiani atque Indici maris nuper inventis* (s.l., [1494]), ep. praefatoria, in ed. G. Solimano, 'Il "De insulis" de Nicolò Scillacio', *Columbeis*, iv (1990), 43–119, see esp. p. 56; Sebastian Muenster, *Cosmographiae universalis libri VI ...* (Basle, 1550), 1114–5; Ioannes A. Maginus, *Geographiae universae tum veteris, tum novae absolutissimum opus duobus voluminibus distinctum. In quorum priore habentur Cl. Ptolemaei ... Geograpicae enarrationis libri octo ... In secundo volumine insunt Cl. Ptolemaei antiquae orbis tabulae XXVII ...* (Cologne, 1597), fo. 181[r].

[32] Luys del Marmol, *Primera parte de la Descripciòn general de Affrica ...* (Granada, 1573), fos. 45[v]–6[r].

[33] Pierre Davity, *Les Estats, empires, royaumes, seigneureries, duchez et principautez du monde* (St Omer, 1621), i, 254–5.

[34] André Thevet, *La cosmographie universelle. Tome I* (Paris, 1575), fo. â11[r–v]; Henri Lancelot Voisin de La Popelinière, *Les trois mondes* (Paris, 1582), fos. 6[v]–7[r]; Philippus Cluverius, *Introductionis in universam geographiam tam veterem quam novam libri VI* (Leiden, 1624), lib. I, cap. xiii, 1; Wilhelm & Joannes Blaeu, *Toonneel des Aerdriicx, ofte Nieuwe Atlas, dat is beschryving van alle landen, nu nieulyck uytgegeven* (Amsterdam, 1649), fo. 2[v].

[35] François de Belleforest, *La cosmographie universelle de tout le monde. Tome II* (Paris, 1575), col. 1788; Abraham Ortelius, *Theatrum orbis terrarum. Opus nunc denuo ab ipso auctore recognitum ... castigatum et ... auctum* (Antwerp, 1573), fo. 4; Gerardus Mercator & Judocus Hondius, *Atlas sive cosmographicae meditationes ...* (Duisburg, 1606), 38.

[36] Lodovicus Caelius Rhodiginus, *Lectionum antiquarum libri XVI ...* (Basle, [1517]), 22–3.

[37] Voisin de La Popelinière (op. cit. n. 34), fos. 6[v]–7[r].

circumnavigation of Africa, then the Portuguese could no longer claim their title of occupants. Moreover, Hanno could very well have reached America by chance, as Cabral did, for he had caught sight of the Hesperides lying at 40 days' sailing distance from *Hesperu Keras*, which takes us, according to Oviedo (1535), to the Caribbean Sea.[38] In this case, the Spaniards, in their turn, would be deprived of their title by occupancy. Small wonder then that the Portuguese geographer Gaspar Varrerius (1616) minimized the importance of the voyage and called attention to the many imperfections in the texts[39], and that, on the other hand, Hugo Grotius (1618), who was in his day the defender of the liberty of the seas, maintained that Hanno sailed before the Portuguese in the waters of the Cape of Good Hope where his compatriots had now settled down.[40] The supporters of Spain's taking possession of America did not renounce their claim. Charles V's official historian, Florian d'Ocampo (second edition 1553) and the Spanish Jesuit Mariana (1592) make Hanno leave Cadiz and give him Spanish crews[41]; in this way the occupant of the new worlds remains a Spaniard. Finally, Hanno was the first to land in countries to be colonized and since he failed to claim the privilege for himself or others, the discoverers considered themselves on terms of equality with him and enjoyed therefore the same right as he. This is also the position taken by the German jurist Christoph Besold (1619) in the interest of the Holy Roman Empire, as well as by Jan de Laet (1643), who championed the claims of the Batavians to reserve a part of the American territory for themselves, as other nations did.[42] Hanno's voyage, when seen only through Pliny's text, which interprets it in terms of a circumnavigation of Africa, can then be all things to all men and reveals above all the ingenuity of the leaders of the debate.

This inquiry has shown that two groups of scholars are particularly interested in Hanno's navigation. Those belonging to the first group study the texts with great attention and submit them to critical evaluation. They anticipate the debates on the authenticity of the Heidelberg text, and the discussions on the nature of the expedition, and propose a variety of solutions: these may concern the rare attestations of toponyms, the divergent sources, or the presence of marvellous elements borrowed from the Greco-Roman tradition. These scholars work in isolation, in the universities or in the shade of their cabinets; their universe is Antiquity. This explains why they comment on ancient texts by referring to other

---

[38] See vol. i, 14–8 of Gonzalo Fernandez de Oviedo y Valdés, *Historia general y natural de las Indias, islas y tierra-firme del Mar Océano*, ed. José Amador de Los Rios, 4 vols. (Madrid, 1851–54).

[39] Gasparus Varrerius, *Commentarius de Ophyra regione* (Rotterdam, 1616), fos. *5ʳ–*7ᵛ.

[40] Hugo Grotius, *Mare liberum sive de iure quod Batavis competit ad Indicana commercia dissertatio. Ultima editio* (Leiden, 1618), 58–61.

[41] Florian d'Ocampo, *Los cinco libros primeros de la Cronica general de España* (Medina del Campo, 1553), fos. 157ʳ–60ʳ; Joannes Mariana, *Historiae de rebus Hispaniae libri XXV* (Toledo, 1592), 38–44.

[42] Christophorus Besoldus, *De novo orbe conjectanea* [Tübingen, 1619], 12; Johannes de Laet, *Notae ad dissertationem Hugonis Grotii De origine gentium Americanarum et observationes aliquot ad meliorem indaginem difficillimae illius quaestionis* (Paris, 1643), 79–80.

ancient texts and why they hardly take into account progress brought about in the field of geography by the Great Discoveries.

Others, on the contrary, are not concerned with the authenticity of the texts and do not consider them in their totality. They are content with evoking a name, the emblematic figure of a great traveller like that of Jason or Ulysses, or they make a choice among the records and keep only those which will corroborate their presuppositions; above all they make use of Pliny's text, which suggests a circumnavigation of Africa. Hence, what exactly is stated in the account, its mode of description, the problematic identifications of the places of call, the discrepancies in the sources, all this actually matters very little to them. The only object of their passions and of their quibbles is the precursor of the Portuguese and Spanish explorers, for this second group of scholars are closely related to the political circles and the business world, both being involved in the colonial adventure and in unbridled competition.

Only a few attempt to reconcile the two tendencies by studying the Greek and Latin texts in the light of the progress made in African chorography. Besides, those who do venture to do so arrive at opposite conclusions: witness Ramusio and Purchas, on the one hand, who manage to draw the itinerary of the voyage, and B. Nihus, on the other, who throws in his hand and brings into discredit the tradition as it has come down to us.

Hanno's voyage fails then to arouse dreams in the Renaissance and seventeenth-century scholars; they have no poet proclaiming: 'Heureux qui comme Hannon a fait un long voyage ....'[43] But it bears witness in its own way, to the difficult confrontation between the old geography of Antiquity, haloed with the prestige of the *auctoritates*, and, on the other hand, the new geography, which was little by little to transform minds before the old one was relegated to the domain of the history of science.

---

[43] 'Blessed is he who like Hanno has made a long journey.' See Joachim du Bellay's sonnet: 'Heureux qui comme Ulysse a fait un long voyage ...'

WRITING IN EXILE:
JOACHIM DU BELLAY, ROME AND RENAISSANCE FRANCE

G. HUGO TUCKER*

INTRODUCTION: ANAMORPHOSIS—THE JOURNEY TO ROME

> La donq', Francoys, marchez couraigeusement vers cete superbe cité
> Romaine: & des serves depouilles d'elle (comme vous avez fait plus d'une
> fois) ornez voz temples & autelz.
>
> (Du Bellay, *Deffence*, 'Conclusion')

In his essay of 1872 on Joachim Du Bellay (*c.* 1523–60) the aesthetic critic, and Oxford Classics don Walter Pater wrote of the French Renaissance poet's journey to Rome and celebrated stay there (1553–57) in the service of his kinsman the Cardinal Jean Du Bellay:

> ... that journey to Italy, which he deplored as the greatest misfortune of his life, put him in full possession of his talent, and brought out all his originality.[1]

Pater's judgment here was at once both very right and very wrong. Wrong firstly, because Pater seems to have been thinking of Du Bellay more or less exclusively as the author of the Roman sonnet collection *Les Regrets* (January 1558), in order to ascribe to him, somewhat anachronistically, an originality derived directly from intense autobiographical experience and manifested artistically in an aesthetic of enhanced sincerity and spontaneity. No doubt he was encouraged, as the Parisian readership of 1558 might have been, by Du Bellay's ambiguous presentation of this elegiac and satirical sonnet sequence as a kind of disillusioned *journal de voyage* to Rome (and back) under the further guise of Ovidian exile. Yet this was also to underestimate the importance and diverse nature of Du Bellay's three other, generically very different, major Roman collections published in Paris on his return: in French, his *Divers Jeux rustiques* (January 1558) and grandiose *Antiqui-tez de Rome ... plus un Songe* (March 1558); in Latin, his four books of *Poemata* [*Elegia, Epigrammata, Amores, Tumuli*] (September 1558). Above all, Pater was wrong to imply an essential discontinuity between the artistic and philosophical preoccupations of the French poet's Roman productions, already mentioned, and those of the Parisian ones published prior to his departure in 1553—principally,

---

* Downing College, Cambridge, England.

Written during my stay as a Visiting Fellow (January-February 1992) at the University of Virginia (Charlottesville), to whose generous hospitality I am deeply indebted, as I am to the stimulating scholarly and intellectual exchanges I enjoyed there with Michael Brint, David Lee Rubin, Mary B. McKinley, Tibor Wlassics and Paul Barolsky—to all of whom this paper is dedicated.

[1] Walter Pater, *The Renaissance: Studies in Art and Poetry* (London, 1873; first pocket edition, 1924), 181.

the pioneering Petrarchist sonnet sequence *L'Olive* (1549; 1550) and the associated Horatian *Vers lyriques*, as well as the highly polemical literary manifesto *La Deffence et illustration de la langue francoyse* (1549) which prefaced them, and so also launched the Pléiade school of poets. Pater was very right, however, to see across Du Bellay's whole *oeuvre*, in the poet's abandonment of Paris for Rome, an enabling change, a radical shift of perspective that may aptly be described as a kind of cultural anamorphosis.

In fact, Du Bellay's fundamental journey to Rome begins well before he even leaves Paris physically—in the paradoxical pages of his assertively patriotic yet reverentially humanistic *Deffence*. In that famous tract he exhorts his compatriots to 'illustrate' the French vernacular and its literature through imitation, not of national writers and genres, but rather of the historically, linguistically and culturally distinct literatures of ancient Greece and Rome, or even of modern Italy.[2] Significantly, in his 'Conclusion', this enthusiasm for what is 'other' is envisaged metaphorically as an enthusiatic march on Rome and Greece, the profane pillage of antiquities being presented there as but a manifestation of the highest admiration and the precondition for triumphal return and embellishment of the French *patria*.[3]

A recent critic has rightly stressed that 'the voyage to Rome was both a rhetorical figure and a cultural paradigm for the French Renaissance', for we find an interplay between the literal, geographic journey thither and the literary, intellectual or imaginative one in several writers of the period—most notably, Michel de Montaigne.[4] Of the French *poets* who visited Rome and used their presence in the Eternal City as matter for their writing, Du Bellay was easily the foremost and probably the most subtle. Throughout his Roman collections we see reorganized and transformed the preoccupations, aspirations and fruitful tensions of his earlier Parisian poetry, literary *Deffence* and other prefatory texts. The perspective is no longer that of a French humanist poet of Paris exiled in time and space from the cultural *patria* of ancient Rome, as well as in time (alone) from the future ideal state of his nation's and of his own poetry and language. Rather, the perspective shifts to that of the French poet still searching through time for an idealized Rome of the past, but now located on the privileged yet ruined—even banalized—site of Rome itself, whilst he is geographically as well as temporally exiled from the now similarly idealized *patria* of France: the *patria* of his native Anjou, and of his former humanistic studies and innovative literary activities in Paris.

---

[2] On the *Deffence*'s significant contradictions and oscillations between France and Rome, see Margaret W. Ferguson, 'The Exile's Defense: Du Bellay's *La Deffence et illustration de la langue françoyse*', *Publications of the Modern Language Association of America*, 93 (1978), 275–89.

[3] See the epigraph above. For a study of Du Bellay's humanist ambivalence towards Rome, cf. Thomas M. Greene, *The Light in Troy: Imitation and Discovery in Renaissance Poetry* (New Haven & London, 1982), 220–41.

[4] Eric M. MacPhail, *The Voyage to Rome in French Renaissance Literature*, Stanford French and Italian Studies, 68 (Saratoga, California, 1990), 2 and *passim*.

In short, this new dual exile, now from the opposing perspective of Rome itself, creates a new space for *desiderium*—a liminary space for writing and for the creation of an autonomous poetic identity[5]—where the problems raised initially by the poet's *Deffence* and explored both implicitly and explicitly in his pre-Rome collections have been subjected to the trick of anamorphosis. The change affects not just the perception of the question of how to achieve an authentic cultural or poetic identity but also the underlying problematic of the relation of Art to Nature, of artifice to inspiration, and even of the immortalizing power ascribed to poetry itself.[6] Questions against which Rome, the supreme example of human transience, must form the supremely ironic backdrop, both unredeemed and unredeemable either by its own architectural and literary monuments, or by antiquarian scholarship, let alone by the vandalism of Renaissance (re)construction.

Du Bellay's humanistic voyage of 'return' towards the ever receding cultural *patria* of Rome is also a voyage of intellectual discovery and of poetic self-realization moving ever towards an as yet unrealized, unlocalized artistic *patria*. It is above all, then, a poet's odyssey—and one ambiguously caught, like that of Ulysses πολύτροπος,[7] between the movement of return and the movement of exploration, those twin poles of the single space of desire for homecoming, those dual manifestations of *patriae desiderium*.[8]

Du Bellay's ingenious confusion of autobiographical fact with poetic fiction and his concomitant dramatization of the radically changed humanist perspective from Rome itself are perhaps nowhere more manifest than in *Regrets* xxxii. There, with mimetic force, the humanist poet's initial expression (in the quatrains) of an excited, Faust-like, Odyssean anticipation of the acquisition of enhanced knowledge and skills on departing for Rome quickly transpires (in the tercets) to be but a memory and the speaker's true perspective to be, ironically, one of retrospection and disillusion after arrival:

EXAMPLE 1: *Regrets*, xxxii

> Je me feray sçavant en la philosophie,
> En la mathematique, & medicine aussi,
> Je me feray legiste, & d'un plus hault souci
> Apprendray les secrets de la theologie:

---

[5] Cf. (at least with respect to the *Regrets*) Jeffery C. Persels, 'Charting Poetic Identity in Exile: Entering Du Bellay's *Regrets*', *Romance Notes*, xxviii/3 (1988), 195–202; and Marie-Dominique Legrand, 'Exil et poésie: les *Tristes* et les *Pontiques* d'Ovide, les *Souspirs* d'O. de Magny, *Les Regrets* de J. Du Bellay', *Littératures*, 17 (1987), 33–47. Cf. below, n. 33.

[6] See G. Hugo Tucker, *The Poet's Odyssey: Joachim Du Bellay and the* Antiquitez de Rome (Oxford, 1990), *passim*.

[7] On the traditional ambiguity of the figure of Ulysses, cf. Gérard Defaux, *Le Curieux, le glorieux et la sagesse du monde dans la première moitié du XVIe siècle: l'exemple de Panurge (Ulysse, Démosthène, Empédocle)*, French Forum Monographs, 34 (Lexington, Kentucky, 1982), 52–68 (Ch. 3: 'Un héritage encombrant: Ulysse polytropon [*sic*]').

[8] Cf. Tucker, *The Poet's Odyssey* (op. cit. n. 6); id., 'Ulysses and Jason: a Problem of Allusion in Sonnet XXXI of *Les Regrets*', *French Studies*, xxxvi (1982), 385–96, on the rich Classical intertext with its ironic implication of folly and the impossibility of return.

> Du lut & du pinceau j'ebateray ma vie,
>> De l'escrime & du bal. Je discourois ainsi,
>> Et me vantois en moy d'apprendre tout cecy,
>> Quand je changeay la France au sejour d'Italie.
> O beaux discours humains! je suis venu si loing,
>> Pour m'enrichir d'ennuy, de vieillesse, & de soing,
>> Et perdre en voyageant le meilleur de mon aage.
> Ainsi le marinier souvent pour tout tresor
>> Rapporte des harencs en lieu de lingots d'or,
>> Aiant fait, comme moy, un malheureux voyage.

This rhetoric of personal disillusion with arrival in Rome implicitly undercuts the enthusiasms of the poet's own initial *Deffence*, with its fervid anticipation of the assimilation of Roman culture by France and its avid gaze towards the Eternal City. This ironic counterpoint is only amplified in the disappointed yet awestruck humanistic meditation of the *Antiquitez de Rome* upon the absence of Rome in Rome and upon the humanist's exile there from the ancient past, the perspective being broadened in that collection to the impersonal and universal. Yet in the *Regrets*, if the changed perspective is grounded in the literary pretence of personal confession, the seemingly personal element is itself also underpinned and authenticated there to the point of ambiguity by the semblance of autobiography, based on the patent fact of the poet's move to Rome. Indeed, the interpenetration of fact and fiction is such that the ambitious humanist program outlined by the speaker of *Regrets*, xxxii actually corresponds to the select library of books, inventoried as the contents of a travelling chest, which I have identified elsewhere as having accompanied Du Bellay to Rome and back.[9]

Conversely, in the dedicatory sonnet 'Au Roy' of the parallel *Antiquitez* a purely spatial retrospective gaze (in the quatrains) from the site of Rome back towards France is combined with a wishful anticipation (in the tercets), this time in the present, of the future cultural and military 'grandeur' and 'Monarchie' (World Dominion) of France as the new Rome: for the accomplishment of such a *translatio studii* and *translatio imperii* to France the poet's collection will be seen to have served as a 'bienheureux presage':

EXAMPLE 2: *Antiquitez*, 'Au Roy'

> Ne vous pouvant donner ces ouvrages antiques
>> Pour vostre Sainct-Germain, ou pour Fontainebleau,
>> Je les vous donne (Sire) en ce petit tableau
>> Peint, le mieux que j'ay peu, de couleurs poëtiques.
> Qui mis sous vostre nom devant les yeux publiques,
>> Si vous le daignez voir en son jour le plus beau,
>> Se pourra bien vanter d'avoir hors du tumbeau
>> Tiré des vieux Romains les poudreuses reliques.
> Que vous puissent les Dieux un jour donner tant d'heur,
>> De rebastir en France une telle grandeur
>> Que je la voudrois bien peindre en vostre langage:

---

[9] See Tucker, *The Poet's Odyssey* (op. cit. n. 6), pp. 239–40 (Appendix E: 'The Poems of Calcagnini and Other Contents of a Travelling-chest Belonging to the Du Bellays').

> Et peult estre, qu' alors vostre grand' Majesté
> Repensant à mes vers, diroit qu'ilz ont esté
> De vostre Monarchie un bienheureux presage.

Yet this Roman poetic 'presage' or portent of the as yet unrealized future of France is as 'malheureux' as the French poet's attempted voyage to the Roman past, being shot through with irony: the ultimate lesson of futility is provided by the 'poudreuses reliques' of ancient Rome's own 'grandeur' and 'Monarchie' on the very site from which the poet speaks and which serves as the thus questionable focus of France's emulative ambition. The imagined future will in fact be as corruptible and unfixable as the imagined past. The only certainty is the paradoxical exile of the poet's present, which is situated between the deaths (past and future) of both—just as indeed the present of the poet's and Henri II's shared living vernacular, French ('vostre langage'), was conceived of in the *Deffence* as caught between the exemplary past fate of the 'dead' Classical languages and its own inevitably similar future fate—'comme la Grecque & Latine pery & mis en reliquaire de livres' (I. xi).

I. IRONIC HENDIADYS

A. *French humanist pilgrim and Ovidian exile*

> At quoties studia antiqua antiquosque sodales,
> Et memini charam deseruisse domum, ...
> Quando erit ut notae fumantia culmina villae,
> Et videam regni iugera parva mei?
> (Du Bellay, 'Patriae desiderium' [*Poemata*, I. vii], 29–30, 49–50)

> Parve (nec invideo) sine me, liber, ibis in urbem
> Ei mihi, quod domino non licet ire tuo.
> (Ovid, *Tristia*, I. i. 1–2)

Such indeed is the consistent irony of Du Bellay's two-way vision across the temporal and geographical divide France-Rome / Rome-France, that in his Latin elegy 'Patriae desiderium' of the *Poemata* he even portrays himself as nostalgically regretting in Rome itself (and in the language of Rome)—on that privileged site and seat of all learning—the humanist intellectual companionship and classicizing enthusiasms ('studia antiqua antiquosque sodales') of the Collège de Coqueret in Paris, where he and other Pléiade poets such as Ronsard had studied under their Hellenist and Latinist mentor Jean Dorat.[10] The irony is subsequently underscored in the Latin elegy, as in *Regrets*, xxxi, by impersonation of Ovid's self-association in exile (*from* Rome) with Homeric Odysseus's longing for the smoke of his native hearth.[11]

The nostalgic hendiadys of 'studia antiqua antiquosque sodales', reinforced symmetrically by chiasmus, is in fact only part of a larger, heavily ironic and similarly chiastic hendiadys: that of the poet's dual stance towards Rome and France taken from opposing perspectives. The poetic *persona* is at once that of the

---

[10] For detailed discussion of this poem see Jozef IJsewijn, 'Joachim Du Bellay's *Patriae desiderium*', *Humanistica Lovaniensia. Journal of Neo-Latin Studies*, xl (1991), 244–61.

[11] See Tucker, 'Ulysses and Jason' (op. cit. n. 8), *passim* (comparing the Latin elegy with the French of *Regrets*, xxxi).

humanist *vates* drawing inspiration from the dead Roman poets, whose 'antique fureur' is invoked by him as latent beneath the sacred site of Rome's ruins, where these 'Divins Esprits' are entombed like the relics of Christian martyrs and felt to radiate a similarly forceful presence:

EXAMPLE 3: *Antiquitez*, i

> Divins Esprits, dont la poudreuse cendre
> > Gist sous le faix de tant de murs couvers,
> > Non vostre loz, qui vif par voz beaux vers
> Ne se verra sous la terre descendre,
> Si des humains la voix se peult estendre
> > Depuis icy jusqu'au fond des enfers,
> > Soient à mon cry les abysmes ouvers,
> Tant que d'abas vous me puissiez entendre.
> Trois fois cernant sous le voile des cieux
> > De voz tumbeaux le tour devotieux,
> > A haulte voix trois fois je vous appelle:
> J'invoque icy vostre antique fureur,
> > En ce pendant que d'une saincte horreur
> > Je vays chantant vostre gloire plus belle.

Yet at the same time the poet's *persona* is also that of an Ovidian exile cut off not just from France but implicitly also, like Ovid himself, from Rome.

In the *Regrets* (called *Tristia* by Du Bellay in Latin), the very first sonnet 'A son livre' re-enacts the exiled Ovid's opening address to his own elegiac *Tristia*. This striking literary association was readily noted by the contemporary French scholar Henri Estienne in his extensive marginalia here and in many other parts of Du Bellay's *oeuvre*:[12]

EXAMPLE 4: *Regrets*, 'A son livre'

> Mon livre (& je ne suis sur ton aise envieux)
> > Tu t'en iras sans moy voir la court de mon Prince.
> > He chetif que je suis, combien en gré je prinsse,
> > Qu'un heur pareil au tien fust permis à mes yeux!
> Là si quelqu'un vers toy se monstre gracieux,
> > Souhaitte luy qu'il vive heureux en sa province:
> > Mais si quelque malin obliquement te pince,
> > Souhaitte luy tes pleurs, & mon mal ennuieux.
> Souhaitte luy encor' qu'il face un long voyage,
> > Et bien qu'il ait de veüe elongné son mesnage,
> > Que son cueur, ou qu'il voise, y soit tousjours present:
> Souhaitte qu'il vieillisse en longue servitude,
> > Qu'il n'esprouve à la fin que toute ingratitude,
> > Et qu'on mange son bien pendant qu'il est absent.

This Ovidian address to the prospectively itinerant book also doubles as an ironic funeral epigram—as a *siste viator* poem such as Du Bellay's own opening *Tumulus* 'Romae veteris' of the *Poemata* (IV.i). It is as if the poetic speaker is himself now entombed—like ancient Rome itself—in the very site of Rome: dead, in exile from his *patria*, he must arrest the attention of the (apparently) living

---

[12] See Tucker, *The Poet's Odyssey* (op. cit. n. 6), pp. 20, 237 (Appendix C: '*Recueils factices* of Du Bellay, and their Annotators Henri Estienne and Panjas').

viator that is his book with the generically traditional wishes of safe return that paradoxically detain the traveller and yet transport him imaginatively home. Yet in this particular case the anticipated homecoming turns sour in the imagination, being ultimately envisaged as fraught with hostility and danger. Indeed, as distinct from Ovid's 'liber', which is exhorted to defend its author back in exile and incidentally itself, Du Bellay's 'livre' is envisaged as a more truly autonomous *viator*, advised to deal on arrival in France with its own inevitable assailants, the curse of its author's woes in Rome now merely serving as a weapon for it to use against others.

This intuition from the grave that is Rome of the perils of homecoming will later be confirmed ironically in *Regrets*, cxxx, where the disillusioned speaker himself—now returned to France, and extending the comparison with Ulysses to its logical conclusion—will dwell in hindsight on the divorce between past keen anticipation of homecoming and its present harsh reality: 'Mille souciz mordants je trouve en ma maison' (v. 10). The envisaged *patria* turns out in fact to be an alien land, and the alien land the *patria*—'Adieu donques (Dorat) je suis encor' Romain' (v. 12). The perspective has changed once more, and the humanist poet is again an exile.

B. Descriptio *and* contemplatio

> Vidimus et flavi contortas Tybridis undas,
>   Sparsaque per campos moenia Romulidum:
>   (Du Bellay, 'Romae descriptio' [*Poemata*, I. ii], 17–18)
>
> Ne sentez vous augmenter vostre peine,
> Quand quelquefois de ces costaux Romains
> Vous contemplez l'ouvrage de voz mains
> N'estre plus rien qu'une pouldreuse plaine?
>   (Du Bellay, *Antiquitez*, xv. 11–14)

With the exception of his Latin elegy 'Romae descriptio', Du Bellay's poetry is virtually never purely descriptive.[13] Any pretence at the concrete or the visual quickly yields to the abstract or the imaginative, for which it serves as a transparent disguise or a discreet vehicle; the object of the poet's contemplation tends to be as elusive and phantomatic as ancient Rome itself, and nowhere is this so true as in the visionary sonnets of the *Songe* appended to the *Antiquitez* as a kind of oneiric Apocalyptic commentary upon them. We find, therefore, another form of ironic hendiadys in Du Bellay's juxtaposition of the language of a physical viewing of Rome with that of mental vision and understanding—ironic because there is virtually nothing left to behold of ancient Rome, and a hendiadys because in Rome seeing is necessarily imagining, and intellectual *contemplatio* the only form of meaningful *descriptio*. Moreover, this holds true even before the impres-

---

[13] On the 'monumental' qualities of 'Romae descriptio' see MacPhail (op. cit. n. 4), pp. 41–5. On the contrasting nature of the poem, cf. also K. Lloyd-Jones, 'Du Bellay's Journey from *Roma Vetus* to *La Rome Neufve*', *Rome in the Renaissance: The City and the Myth. Papers of the Thirteenth Annual Conference of the Center for Medieval & Early Renaissance Studies*, ed. P. A. Ramsey, Medieval & Renaissance Texts and Studies, 18 (Binghampton, New York, 1982), 302–19, see esp. pp. 309–11.

sive yet equally thought-provoking spectacle of Rome's present architectural renaissance:

EXAMPLE 5: *Antiquitez*, xxvii

> Toy qui de Rome emerveillé contemples
>> L'antique orgueil, qui menassoit les cieux,
>> Ces vieux palais, ces monts audacieux,
>> Ces murs, ces arcz, ces thermes, & ces temples,
> Juge, en voyant ces ruines si amples,
>> Ce qu'a rongé le temps injurieux,
>> Puis qu'aux ouvriers les plus industrieux
>> Ces vieux fragmens encor servent d'exemples.
> Regarde apres, comme de jour en jour
>> Rome fouillant son antique sejour,
>> Se rebatist de tant d'oeuvres divines:
> Tu jugeras, que le demon Romain
>> S'efforce encor d'une fatale main
>> Ressusciter ces poudreuses ruines.

In *Antiquitez*, xxvii *regarder* and *juger* are twin facets of the same act, *contempler*—just as more generally the humanist poet's prospective and retrospective gazes are (as we have already noted) but twin facets of the same phenomenon, *patriae desiderium*.

C. Rome and Rome

> Nunc Romam in Roma quaerit reperitque Raphael,
>> Quaerere magni hominis sed reperire Dei est.
>>> (Celio Calcagnini, 'Raphaelis Vrbinatis industria', *Carmina*
>>> (Venice, 1553))

The ultimate form of ironic hendiadys only highlights further those of humanist pilgrim / Ovidian exile in, and *descriptio / contemplatio* of, Rome. It is to be found in the paradoxical juxtaposition of Rome's name with itself in *Antiquitez*, iii, where the speaker acts as a guide by turning his contemplative gaze and words upon an imagined naïve newcomer to the Eternal City, perhaps his former self, who is looking for Rome in Rome, bewildered at discovering but the absence of Rome in Rome. When later, in his *Journal de Voyage en Italie* (1580–81), Montaigne will become his own guide on the site of ancient Rome, his will be a similar reflection upon the unrecognizability, if not the absence, of Rome in Rome, knowledge of which could only be 'une science abstraite et contemplative, de laquelle il n'y avoit rien qui tumbast sous les sens':[14]

EXAMPLE 6: *Antiquitez*, iii

> Nouveau venu, qui cherches Rome en Rome,
>> Et rien de Rome en Rome n'apperçois,
>> Ces vieux palais, ces vieux arcz que tu vois,
>> Et ces vieux murs, c'est ce que Rome on nomme.

---

[14] Montaigne, *Journal de Voyage en Italie par la Suisse et l'Allemagne en 1580 et 1581*, ed. Maurice Rat (Paris, 1955), 103–4; cf. MacPhail (op. cit. n. 4), pp. 173–5.

Voy quel orgueil, quelle ruine: & comme
  Celle qui mist le monde sous ces loix
  Pour donter tout, se donta quelquefois,
  Et devint proye au temps, qui tout consomme.
Rome de Rome est le seul monument,
  Et Rome Rome a vaincu seulement.
  Le Tybre seul, qui vers la mer s'enfuit,
Reste de Rome. O mondaine inconstance!
  Ce qui est ferme, est par le temps destruit,
  Et ce qui fuit, au temps fait resistance.

Du Bellay's sonnet ironizes upon antiquarian confidence in the quest for Rome in Rome as expressed by Celio Calcagnini in his *Carmina* (1553), a work that travelled with Du Bellay in his travelling-chest. An epigram (quoted above) in that Ferrarese poet's collection boastfully asserted that 'Raphael now both seeks and finds Rome in Rome; to seek [it] is the mark of a great man, but to find [it] is the mark of God'. Du Bellay's negative reply in *Antiquitez*, iii to such humanistic hubris insists rather upon the problematic identity of a double Rome—disfigured yet alone able to resemble itself, divided against itself historically and architecturally yet one and the same, ostensibly resisting Time's tooth (at least in part) yet ever flowing with Time's flux, superficially recognizable by its name and its river yet essentially unknowable and ungraspable as identity itself or as any moment of being lost in Heraclitus's and Ovid's changing river of Time, which is ever 'consuming' and ever 'consummating' ('qui tout consomme'), but never still.[15]

In short, Du Bellay's poetic reply to Calcagnini problematizes the latter's positivistic juxtaposition of 'Rome in Rome' to make these two 'Romes' twin poles of the single, potentially infinite, dynamic process of humanistic searching—not static finding—in the flux of Time; as such it further underscores the dynamic ambivalence of the French poet's *patriae desiderium* as humanist in exile. Moreover, in all the aspects just mentioned that oppose it to Calcagnini's epigram on Raphael, Du Bellay's sonnet is itself a dynamic, creative reworking of its immediate neo-Latin literary model of 1553—a celebrated paradoxical epigram on Rome, published in Rome, by Janus Vitalis of Palermo.[16]

Antiquitez, iii is generated, then, not by direct physical vision of Rome in Rome, but, like the text of Montaigne's *Journal* later, through the cultural veil of literary mediation. In its recycling and reworking of previous literary matter through creative *imitatio* it itself participates in the dynamic generative-degenerative processes of Time 'qui tout consomme'. Indeed, like Time, the ambiguous artist

---

[15] See Tucker, *The Poet's Odyssey* (op. cit. n. 6), pp. 55, 103–4; and above, n. 9. For the River of Time and its associations in *Antiquitez*, iii, see Ovid, *Metamorphoses*, xv. 179–85 (tr. Du Bellay 1558), and Tucker (using Eric MacPhail) (op. cit.), p. 167 (and n. 132).

[16] See Tucker, *The Poet's Odyssey* (op. cit. n. 6), pp. 157–73; id., 'Sur les *Elogia* (1553) de Janus Vitalis et les *Antiquitez de Rome* de Joachim Du Bellay', *Bibliothèque d'Humanisme et Renaissance*, xlvii/1 (1985), 103–12. Prior to my discovery of the original 1553 text, G. W. Pigman III, 'Du Bellay's Ambivalence Towards Rome in the *Antiquitez*', in: *Rome in the Renaissance* (op. cit. n. 13), pp. 321–32, underestimates Du Bellay's debt to Vitalis's epigram, knowing only the far less subtle 1554 text.

both 'consumes' and 'consummates' the past in the production of his new text, whilst his meditative vision of Rome is caught between two other similarly anti-thetical visions of Time. The one is linear, and highlights the development, final death and present absence of Rome, the implied discontinuity with the past placing the humanist observer in historical exile. The other is circular, and posits the potential for regeneration—not through *translatio imperii*, but through a kind of artistic or architectural palingenesis *in situ*—the implied continuity of the 'demon Romain' offering the humanist poet the possibility of a return of sorts to Rome in Rome.[17]

II. POET AND *PERSONAE*: LITERARY RE-ENACTMENT

> non dubia est Ithaci prudentia, sed tamen optat
> fumum de patriis posse videre focis.
> (Ovid, *Ex Ponto*, I. iii. 33–4)

> adde quod illius pars maxima ficta laborum;
> ponitur in nostris fabula nulla malis.
> (Ovid, *Tristia*, I. v. 79–80)

The veil of literary mediation of experience is not of course peculiar just to Du Bellay or Montaigne's vision of the ruins of Rome; it inevitably interposes as well in both these self-referential yet allusive writers' visions and constitutions of themselves in their other texts—particularly in the *Regrets* of the one and in the *Essais* of the other. We have already noted how in Du Bellay's Latin 'Patriae desiderium' and in his parallel French sonnet xxxi of *Les Regrets*, the poet's *persona* is multi-layered—or rather, comprises a series of stratified *personae*, which correspond to the intertextual complexities of these poems in a kind of literary archaeology of the self. The poet re-enacts bilingually not just Homeric Ulysses's overriding desire to see the smoke rising above his native hearth, but also Ovid's own literary re-enactment and self-association with that literary archetype in his *Pontic Letters*.

Moreover, with each new layer, this intertextual *mise en abîme* serves to lend a spurious factuality to the latest literary impersonator's pretended true projection of himself in the text, just as the dramatic device of a play-within-a-play functions to suspend the audience's disbelief in the dramatic fiction of the external play itself.[18] If in the *Tristia* Ovid explicitly contrasts the reality ('nulla fabula') of his own 'woes' with the 'pars maxima ficta' of Ulysses's 'travails', so also, implicitly,

---

[17] On the philological ambivalence of *consommer*, see Tucker, *The Poet's Odyssey* (op. cit. n. 6), p. 63 (n. 16). The oscillation between a linear and a circular conception of Time and Eternity, is discussed in Deborah Lesko Baker, 'Du Bellay's Double Eternity: Two Sonnets from the *Antiquitez de Rome*', *Neophilologus. An International Journal of Modern and Medieval Language and Literature*, 73 (1989), 350–7.

[18] See Tucker, *The Poet's Odyssey* (op. cit. n. 6), pp. 14–21; id., 'Ulysses and Jason' (op. cit. n. 8), *passim*; cf. Italo Calvino, 'Levels of Reality in Literature', and 'The Odysseys Within the Odyssey', in his *The Uses of Literature: Essays*, tr. Patrick Creagh (San Diego, New York & London, 1986), 101–21, 135–45. For further comments on Latin Du Bellay's intertextuality here, see Dirk Sacré, 'Joachim Du Bellay poète latin: Notes de lecture', *Les Études Classiques*, 59 (1991), 275–8, see esp. pp. 277–8.

Du Bellay constitutes an apparently 'real' self set off in relief against a long, if not
infinite, series of receding literary echoes. The French poet's most famous
expression of *regret* for his ancestral countryside is far from being a simple,
spontaneous, expression of nostalgia:

EXAMPLE 7: *Regrets*, xxxi

> Heureux qui, comme Ulysse, a fait un beau voyage,
>   Ou comme cestuy là qui conquit la toison,
>   Et puis est retourné, plein d'usage & raison,
>   Vivre entre ses parents le reste de son aage!
> Quand revoiray-je, helas, de mon petit village
>   Fumer la cheminee, & en quelle saison,
>   Revoiray-je le clos de ma pauvre maison,
>   Qui m'est une province, & beaucoup d'avantage?
> Plus me plaist le sejour qu'ont basty mes ayeux,
>   Que des palais Romains le front audacieux,
>   Plus que le marbre dur me plaist l'ardoise fine:
> Plus mon Loyre Gaulois, que le Tybre Latin,
>   Plus mon petit Lyré, que le mont Palatin,
>   Et plus que l'air marin la doulceur Angevine.

In fact, the intertextual layering reaching back to Homer, both here and in the
'Patriae desiderium', involves further literary reminiscences of potentially ironic
significance: for example, Virgil's Meliboeus of the first *Eclogue*, driven from the
'patriae fines et dulcia ... arva' (vv. 3–4) in contrast with Tityrus the successful
suppliant visitor to Rome (vv. 19–35)—a Meliboeus as much pained as gratified
by the latter's hospitality and by the sight of smoking farm-house roofs that can
only remind him of all that he has lost. Above all, behind Du Bellay's Ovidian-
Homeric mask, we sense also that other elegiac impersonation of Ulysses-
Odysseus by Roman Tibullus (*Elegies*, I.iii.3, 5–10, 19–20)—a Tibullus stranded
and fearing death, like Odysseus, in a 'strange land' ('ignotis ... terris'), called
'Phaeacia' (in fact, Corfu), longing for his ancestral countryside and home, and
bitterly regretting the foolhardiness of having set out on a journey in the first
place, despite all the bad omens.[19] Indeed, as Henri Estienne noted in his copy
of *Les Regrets*, Du Bellay sets up his implicit impersonation of this Odysseus-like
Tibullus six sonnets earlier, with an explicit, rueful echo of his equally allusive,
Roman elegiac predecessor (*Regrets*, xxv.12–14):[20]

> N'estoit-ce pas assez pour rompre mon voyage,
>   Quand sur le seuil de l'huis, d'un sinistre presage,
>   Je me blessay le pied sortant de ma maison?

The 'presage' in the *Regrets* for Du Bellay's poetic odyssey from France to
Rome is as unfortunate as his Roman poetic 'presage' in the *Antiquitez* for
France's future 'grandeur' is treacherous. His is no 'beau voyage', but the
opposite, and the question of 'return' is implicitly as problematic for him as for
Ovid, Tibullus, Meliboeus, Ulysses, and, above all, as for 'cestuy là qui conquit
la toison'—Jason, that other epic voyager, whose homecoming 'entre ses parents'

---

[19] See Tucker, 'Ulysses and Jason' (op. cit. n. 8), pp. 388–9.
[20] See Tucker, *The Poet's Odyssey* (op. cit. n. 6), p. 21.

was the beginning of Medea's (second) 'exile', with all its tragic consequences for him, his betrothed and his children.[21]

III. BETWEEN ROME AND FRANCE
A. Dual Ulysses and the duplicities of travel

> dic mihi, Musa, virum captae post tempora Troiae
> qui mores hominum multorum vidit et urbes.
> (Horace, Ars poetica, 141–2)

> non huc Argoo contendit remige pinus,
>   neque impudica Colchis intulit pedem;
> non huc Sidonii torserunt cornua nautae,
>   laboriosa nec cohors Ulixei. ...
> Iuppiter illa piae secrevit litora genti,
>   ut inquinavit aere tempus aureum.
> (Horace, Epodon liber, xvi. 57–60, 63–4)

The figure of Ulysses which Du Bellay impersonates through a series of literary masks is essentially as ambivalent and as treacherous as the apparent benefits of travel—of 'beau voyage'—itself, the duplicities of the one matching the duplicities of the other. Horace, who commemorates Homer's 'resourceful', widely travelled, epic hero πολύτροπος in the Ars poetica, and as such makes him the exemplar of the power of 'virtus et ... sapientia' in the Epistles, does not hesitate in the Epodes to make him a figure of impiety: he and his 'laboriosa cohors' of men are excluded by Jupiter, along with all other such impious sea-farers—like Jason, Medea and the Phoenicians—from ever reaching the Islands of the Blest which are 'set apart' at the edge of the world. The example of 'virtuous' Ulysses 'proposed' in Horace's epistle is perhaps then not all that it seems:

EXAMPLE 8: Horace, Epistolae, I. ii. 17–22 [tr. Thomas Drant, 1567]

> rursus quid virtus et quid sapientia possit,
> utile proposuit nobis exemplar Ulixen,
> qui domitor Troiae multorum providus urbes
> et mores hominum inspexit latumque per aequor,
> dum sibi, dum sociis reditum parat, aspera multa
> pertulit, adversis rerum immersabilis undis.

> [Againe, how virtue, and a witte / at all assayes can ease
> The Poet made a mirror in / the wittie Vlixes.
> Who taminge Troye, the manors, and / the cities wyslye viewd
> Of manye men: (for him and his / whilste he through vaste sea rude,
> Did shape returne) who though he bore / ful manye a bitter shower,
> Yet had the adverse waves of him, / no soveraintie, or power.]

Indeed, the whole tradition of reflection upon Ulysses from Antiquity and through the Middle Ages to the Renaissance is split between admiration for his eloquence, astuteness, wisdom and pious determination to return home, on the one hand, and criticism of his guile, unscrupulousness and impious, restless curiosity, on the other hand.[22] Unsurprisingly, in works of Du Bellay's contemporaries we

---

[21] Cf. Euripides, Medea, vv. 1–13—translated by George Buchanan (Paris, 1544).

[22] See Defaux (op. cit. n. 7), chs 2–4; Dante, La Divina Commedia, eds. Emilio Pasquini &

also find ambiguous reflections of this dual tradition. The poetess Louise Labé begins her provocative, female love sonnets (*Euvres* (Lyon, 1555)) with an ironic evocation (in Italian) of the astuteness of 'Vlysse', whose (male) cunning would not be proof against the present (equally male) object of her hopeless female infatuation. Even more ambiguously, Estienne de la Boëtie (1530–63) opens his political 'Discours de la servitude volontaire'—written, according to his friend Montaigne (*Essais*, I.xxviii), 'contre les Tyrans' and 'bien proprement depuis rebaptisé *Le Contre Un*' by its Protestant publishers of 1576— with quotation of Odysseus's admirable defence in the *Iliad* (2.205–5) of Agamemnon's sole, supreme authority; yet it is a speech for which 'il faut excuser Ulysse ... conformant (je crois) son propos plus au temps, qu'à la vérité'. Indeed, as recent criticism has stressed, that other traveller to Rome and protégé of the Cardinal Du Bellay, François Rabelais associates the 'much travelled', 'versatile' Ulysses πολύτροπος with the 'cunning', 'knavish', 'treacherous' qualities of Panurge πανοῦργος.[23]

Nowhere was the meeting of the two contradictory traditions so enigmatically and profoundly apparent as in what Stanford has called the 'Janus-like figure' of Dante's Ulysses, and, more particularly, in his speech of exhortation to his small remaining 'cohort' of men—'quella compagna picciola' of 'compagni' 'vechi e tardi' (come to the 'West' of their travels and life)—on this their last voyage to (inevitable) shipwreck beyond the pillars of Hercules:[24]

EXAMPLE 9: Dante, *Divina Commedia: Inferno*, xxvi.90–142 [Ulysses's account of his last voyage], vv. 112–20

> 'O frati', dissi, 'che per cento milia
> perigli sieti giunti a l'occidente,
> a questa tanto picciola vigilia
>   de' nostri sensi ch'è del rimanente
> non vogliate negar l'esperïenza,
> di retro al sol, del mondo sanza gente.
>   Considerate la vostra semenza:
> fatti non foste a viver come bruti,
> ma per seguir virtute e canoscenza'.

Homer's archetypal epic figure of wise return to Ithaca is here set on a very different course, that of the ultimate folly of boundless curiosity and travel: for Dante, this is towards the forbidden Mount of Purgatory in the world 'sanza gente' (beyond the Straits of Gilbraltar), whilst for Horace this would have been, as we

---

Antonio Quaglio, 3 vols (Milan, 1988), see vol. i (*Inferno*), 288–94 ('Lettura del canto ventiseiesimo'), see esp. pp. 291–3; Ruggero Stefanini, 'Inferno xxvi', *Lectura Dantis, 6—Special Issue: Lectura Dantis Virginiana, I Dante's Inferno: Introductory Readings*, (1990), 332–50.

[23] See Terence C. Cave, 'Panurge and Odysseus', *Myth and Legend in French Literature: Essays in Honour of A.-J. Steele*, eds. Keith Aspley, David Bellos & Peter Sharratt, Publications of the Modern Humanities Research Association, 11 (London, 1982), 47–59, see esp. p. 59 and n. 16; cf. Defaux (op. cit. n. 7), *passim*, who further pinpoints (p. 61) the nuance of doubt in Clément Marot's *épître A la Royne de Navarre*, v. 157 ('Ulysse sage, au moins estimé tel').

[24] William B. Stanford, *The Ulysses Theme: A Study in the Adaptability of a Traditional Hero* (Oxford, 1954¹, 1963²; Michigan, 1968), 175–210 (Ch. 14: 'The Wanderer'), see esp. p. 178.

have noted, towards the forbidden Islands closed to impious sea-voyagers. Later, that enthusiastic traveller Montaigne will himself entertain a similar contradiction by making a critique of 'gloire' and 'curiosité', and thus implicitly of the curious traveller:

> Cette cy nous conduit à mettre le nez partout, et celle là nous defant de rien laisser irresolu et indecis. (*Essais*, I.xxvii)

This is perilously close to Horace's position in his epistle to his itinerant friend Bullatius, where he criticizes the supposed benefits of travel as illusory; 'ratio' and 'prudentia' (for Du Bellay, 'usage et raison') and thus freedom from care are to be found in the here and now at home, not in chasing after the imagined goals of travel. The best is never to have set out in the first place:

EXAMPLE 10: Horace, *Epistolae*, I.xi.25–30 [tr. Thomas Drant, 1567]

> ... nam si ratio et prudentia curas,
> non locus effusi late maris arbiter, aufert,
> caelum, non animum, mutant qui trans mare currunt.
> strenua nos exercet inertia; navibus atque
> quadrigis petimus bene vivere: quod petis hic est,
> est Ulubris, animus si te non deficit aequus.
>
> [If by wisedom, not well dight house / our cares are al undone,
> If those chaunge weather, not their wit, / which yont the sea do run.
> Our dilligence hath littell skill / we far and neare do skip,
> To purchase wealthe in every coaste / in wagon, and by ship.
> The worste place here as pleasaunte is / as that which thou wouldst
>   fynde,
> If thou hadst grace, to iudge a right, / and qualefie thy minde.]

The next best of course is to return as soon as possible whence we came. The Homeric epic of return lends itself ideally to neo-Platonic allegorization of the return of the soul to its heavenly Ithaca, such as we have, for example, from the Pléiade's mentor, Jean Dorat.[25] The worst is to drag out a long existence, in a linear trajectory, beneath the sun, until the release of the final shipwreck.

The contrast between the circular epic of Homer's Odysseus and the linear narrative of Dante's Ulysses has been illuminatingly explored by John Freccero, as indeed it was noted in the Renaissance by Dante's commentator, Christoforo Landino (1481).[26] It also mirrors geometrically and thematically that great *topos* of Greek pessimism, often alluded to by Du Bellay, that the best thing for man is never to have been born, and the next best to return as soon as possible whence he came, the worst being to drag out a long, but hopefully finite, (linear) existence under the sun.[27]

---

[25] In the form of notes from his lectures on Homer; see Tucker, *The Poet's Odyssey* (op. cit. n. 6), p. 50.

[26] John Freccero, 'Dante's Ulysses: from Epic to Novel', in: *Odysseus / Ulysses*, ed. Harold Bloom, Major Literary Characters (New York & Philadelphia, 1991), 189–202.

[27] Cf. principally Sophocles, *Oedipus Coloneus*, vv. 1224–7. On the ancient tradition of this pessimistic formula, its uses by Du Bellay and its subversion by Ronsard, see Tucker, *The Poet's Odyssey* (op. cit. n. 6), pp. 195–9.

Yet the exhortation of Dante's Ulysses can also be read as neither cynical, nor guileful, nor hubristic, but as true, noble, and wise—even though he does not strive to return home against all the odds like the 'exemplar' proposed by Horace, nor attempts to refound his home elsewhere like Virgil's Aeneas, upon whose exhortatory speech to his men his own is modelled (*Aeneid*, i. 198–207). For Landino, as for Cicero before him (*De finibus*, V.xviii.48–9), the figure of Ulysses can stand for man's natural, relentless pursuit of knowledge 'dearer than the *patria*' [Cicero], in an irresistible attraction towards perfection and the acquisition (through increase of knowledge and experience of the world) of 'il sommo bene' [Landino]. The equivalent for the poetic figure of Du Bellay, once embarked, is neither return to the idealized Ithaca of France (of the near past), nor return to the imagined Ithaca of the distant Roman past, nor recreation of that past Rome in future France, as if by a new Aeneas—all of which are understood to be ultimately impossible anyway; rather it is the continuing, linear voyage towards an infinitely distant, artistic *patria*, his poetic ideal, but also towards the inevitable shipwreck on the way, in the realization of his text.[28]

Du Bellay's Ulysses is no simple Homeric hero, then, but shares in the painful ambiguities and tensions of Dante's impious figure of self-exile without return. Above all, like Dante's Ulysses, he is no triumphant Columbus bursting through the pillars of Hercules actually to reach a new *patria* 'beyond the sun' and able also to return to the old one.[29]

B. Duplicitous Ovid and the dualities of exile

> ille [Ulixes] suam laetus patriam victorque petebat;
> a patria fugi victus et exul ego.
>   (Ovid, *Tristia*, I. v. 65–6)

> Fertile est mon sejour, sterile estoit le sien,
> Je ne suis des plus fins, sa finesse est cogneue,
>   (Du Bellay, *Regrets*, xl. 5–6)

> hi qui, quod nemo nescit, amare docent:
> hos tu vel fugias vel, si satis oris habebis,
> Oedipodas facito Telegonosque voces!
>   (Ovid, *Tristia*, I. i. 112–14)

We have already seen how the literary *persona* of Du Bellay as 'l'Ovide françois' in Rome is equally duplicitous, lending itself a spurious (and ironic) factuality by impersonating Ovid's clever factual self-contrast with the legendary figure of Ulysses. The effect is also to lend itself a heightened intensity; the extremity of the Bellayan-Ovidian exile is only reinforced by remembrance of the Homeric hero's triumphant return, whilst the proverbial sterility of his Ithaca serves as a foil to the intrinsically more attractive Ovidian-Bellayan *patria*.

---

[28] On the possible implication of this in the poetic exchanges between Du Bellay in Rome and his neo-Platonizing mentor Dorat in Paris, see Tucker, *The Poet's Odyssey* (op. cit. n. 6), pp. 48–51.

[29] Cf. p. 42 of Piero Boitani, 'Beyond the Sunset: Dante's Ulysses in Another World', *Lectura Dantis: A Forum for Dante Research and Interpretation*, 9 (1991), 34–53.

The parallel is also pursued at a deeper level. In the *Tristia* the authorial *persona* of Ovid issues paternal warning to his exile book to avoid contact with its controversial elder 'brothers'—the books of the *Ars amatoria*, left in Rome—or to call them, if encountered, 'Oedipuses' or 'Telegonuses', akin to those notorious parricides of Laius and (more notably) of Ulysses: 'Naso', their literary parent, has been the victim of their parricide, relegated as he is, through their fault, to the 'death' of exile. Likewise, in Du Bellay's projected authorial perception of his pre-Roman, Parisian literary production—including, most notably, the amatory *Olive*—there is a similar sense of the parricidal, the literary work having rapaciously consumed the parent poet's fortune, youth, health, resilience, creative powers and inspiration. In the lengthy, highly Ovidian, dedicatory poem 'A Monsieur d'Avanson' of *Les Regrets*, the Muses are understood, with the benefit of hindsight, to be but dangerous Sirens, to whose 'chant flatteur' he has foolishly succumbed (vv. 45–8). Indeed, in the pre-Roman Parisian collections themselves, the danger is presented as already apparent to their artistic parent: for example, in the pessimistic self-referential allegory of *L'Olive*, xlv (1549), or in the knowing 'Adieu aux Muses' (1552; adapted from the Latin of George Buchanan).[30]

As a result, the nostalgia later expressed in *Regrets*, vi for a privileged past relation to poetry and the Muses transpires, quite poignantly, to be but the idealizing self-delusion of an exile; the traditional, age-old interrogation of transience—*ubi sunt?*—may as much refer to what never was as to what was and has since passed away—whether the poet be thinking of France, or even of ancient Rome:

EXAMPLE 11: *Regrets*, vi

> Las où est maintenant ce mespris de Fortune?
>> Où est ce coeur vainqueur de toute adversité,
>> Cest honneste desir de l'immortalité,
>> Et ceste honneste flamme au peuple non commune?
> Où sont ces doulx plaisirs, qu'au soir soubs la nuict brune
>> Les Muses me donnoient, alors qu'en liberté
>> Dessus le verd tapy d'un rivage esquarté
>> Je les menois danser aux rayons de la Lune?
> Maintenant la Fortune est maistresse de moy,
>> Et mon coeur qui souloit estre maistre de soy,
>> Est serf de mille maulx & regrets qui m'ennuyent.
> De la posterité je n'ay plus de souci,
>> Ceste divine ardeur, je ne l'ay plus aussi,
>> Et les Muses de moy, comme estranges, s'enfuyent.

In this programmatic sonnet, the *regret* for a loss of self—for a death of self—as much as for a former state of poetic bliss, is of course very much a fiction of Ovidian exile, representing, quite spuriously, a stylistic change as a loss of identity. It is also coupled with an equally fictional *regret* for the very opposite

---

[30] Cf. Tucker, *The Poet's Odyssey* (op. cit. n. 6), pp. 20, 39–40, 43–5.

of the Ovidian, elegiac relation to misfortune and exile—for a Stoic capacity (previously possessed) to be indifferent to the vagaries of Fortune (now 'maistresse de moy'), and so to endure, and perhaps even to derive benefit from, the present so-called sufferings of exile.

This wishful, anti-Ovidian position, is in fact one advocated in another book from the Du Bellays' travelling-chest—the dialogue *Medices legatus de exsilio* (Venice, 1522) of the Venetian Greek scholar and Ciceronian Latinist Petrus Alcyonius (1487–1527?). This important work was the culmination of a whole series of consolatory letters, dialogues or treatises on exile in the Renaissance stemming from an older tradition of Platonic or Stoic writings on the subject, in which the particular significance of the human individual's exile was usually belittled or negated.[31] Either reference would be made to the larger neo-Platonic or Christian framework of humanity's exile in the 'prison' or 'island' of the world from the true heavenly *patria* (as we saw in Jean Dorat's allegorization of the *Odyssey*), or—as in Alcyonius's exile treatise—there might also be Stoic insistence upon the virtuous individual necessarily being, or constituting, his own *patria* anywhere in the world, exile being a contradiction in terms for the good man, and the accident of his birthplace an irrelevance.

The poetic *persona* of *Regrets* vi thus assumes not just an Ovidian pose of yearning for the lost *patria* and for the privileged poetic capacity associated with it, but also one of *regret* for a very un-Ovidian, equally idealized Stoic equanimity and consequent release from such yearning. This of course only highlights further the first form of *desiderium*, whilst amplifying a very realistic impression of the exile's ingenious capacity for self-delusion. In fact, Du Bellay's *persona* of French-poet-exiled-to-Rome is presented as caught imaginatively not just between exile and home but also, more fundamentally, between two contradictory conceptions of exile itself and so also of *patria*.

CONCLUSION: EXILE EXILED AND *PATRIAE DESIDERIUM* REDEFINED

> longa via est, propera! nobis habitabitur orbis
> ultimus, a terra terra remota mea.
> (Ovid, *Tristia*, I. i. 127–8)

> 'quo nos cumque feret melior Fortuna parente,
> ibimus, o socii comitesque.
> nil desperandum Teucro duce et auspice Teucro.
> certus enim promisit Apollo
> ambiguam tellure nova Salamina futuram.
> o fortes peioraque passi
> mecum saepe viri, nunc vino pellite curas:
> cras ingens iterabimus aequor'.
> (Horace, *Carmina*, I. vii. 25–32)

> Mais, ô bon Dieu, combien de mer nous reste encores, avant
> que soyons parvenuz au port! combien le terme de nostre
> course est encores loing! (Du Bellay, *Deffence*, II. xii)

---

[31] See Randolph Starn, *Contrary Commonwealth: The Theme of Exile in Medieval and Renaissance Italy* (Berkeley, Los Angeles & London, 1982), 136–47 and *passim*.

The Ovidian, partly Bellayan, dichotomy of the land of exile and the land of home, of the relegation of the author and the return home (in his place) of the epistolary text, is indeed a false one, despite the vast gulf that seems to separate the two. The extremes form a single axis of *desiderium*, delineate a single space of exile for the expression of loss and longing—whether for France or for ancient Rome, for poetic inspiration or for an ideal artistic *vita contemplativa*—and this space or axis is the very condition for new artistic activity, where, paradoxically, exile is exiled and a provisional *patria* ever renewed, and ever reconstituted.

This is the same fluid space as that of Alcyonius's virtuous Stoic exile, who is never an exile—or indeed, of Horace's Epicurean hero, Teucer (*Carmina*, I. vii), banishing banishment and his men's cares between the memory of the old Salamis and the promise of a new one beyond the sea, in an ode which itself, ironically, oscillates between rejection of the praise of foreign cities and celebration of the home in Tibur (Tivoli) near Rome. This is also the potentially infinite space suggested by Montaigne in 'De la vanité' (*Essais*, III. ix), through which, tortoise-like, he may continuously take his *patria* with him 'in the movable feast of travel and itinerant prose':[32]

> Qui ne voit que j'ay pris une route, par laquelle sans cesse et sans travail, j'iray autant qu'il y aura d'ancre et de papier au monde?

Above all, this is that infinite space of sea (first announced in Du Bellay's *Deffence*) which still remains to be traversed before that far off arrival at the ideal port of poetic self-realization and authenticity.[33]

The trajectory is a linear one towards the 'sommo bene' of the artistic ideal, towards the full realization of a poetic identity—of a poetic self—to which the poet is naturally drawn, like Landino's Dantean Ulysses (or Cicero's before him). For the individual mortal poet or essayist—as for mortal Rome itself—it is also necessarily a finite one, which will finish short of the ever distant ideal goal of an aesthetic (rather than ethical) *patria summi boni*. The true *patria*, the only *patria*, is in fact the inescapable, omnipresent *patria desiderii* of the here and now—of artistic activity and searching—located on the way. This is the *patria* of the poetic moment itself, celebrated and momentarily fixed in that fragile 'paper' 'monument' of the *Antiquitez*, and, in particular, in the closing sonnet of the collection.[34] Echoing Horace (*Carmina*, III. xxx), the poet's voice and the still vibrating strings of his 'luth' are presented as artistically unique and historically specific, situated not just between Rome and France, but also between the imagined ancient

---

[32] MacPhail (op. cit. n. 4), p. 199.

[33] The 'space' for 'writing' to 'forge' 'poetic identity', as defined in Tucker, *The Poet's Odyssey* (op. cit. n. 6), p. 30; also the 'intertextual space' illuminatingly analyzed by James S. Hirstein, 'La Rome de Virgile et celle du seizième siècle dans "Ad Ianum Avansonium apud summum pont. oratorem regium, Tyberis" de Joachim Du Bellay', *Acta Conventus Neo-Latini Sanctandreani: Proceedings of the Fifth International Congress of Neo-Latin Studies. St Andrews 24 August to 1 September 1982*, ed. Ian D. McFarlane, Medieval & Renaissance Texts and Studies (Binghamton, New York, 1986), 351–8.

[34] Cf. Tucker, *The Poet's Odyssey* (op. cit. n. 6), p. 226.

past and the as yet unrealized future moment of their own reading by posterity
(that is, for as long as Time should permit it):

EXAMPLE 12: *Antiquitez*, xxxii

>   Esperez vous que la posterité
>   Doive (mes vers) pour tout jamais vous lire?
>   Esperez vous que l'oeuvre d'une lyre
>   Puisse acquerir telle immortalité?
>   Si sous le ciel fust quelque eternité,
>   Les monuments que je vous ay fait dire,
>   Non en papier, mais en marbre & porphyre,
>   Eussent gardé leur vive antiquité.
>   Ne laisse pas toutefois de sonner
>   Luth, qu'Apollon m'a bien daigné donner:
>   Car si le temps ta gloire ne desrobbe,
>   Vanter te peux, quelque bas que tu sois,
>   D'avoir chanté le premier des François,
>   L'antique honneur du peuple à longue robbe.

In this way, in this implicit anti-*exegi monumentum*, the polarities of Rome and
France, past and present, *patria* and exile, are transcended, and it is in this more
fundamental sense too that Du Bellay, anticipating Montaigne, can declare
similarly, even in his 'Patriae desiderium':

>   Roma orbis patria est, quique altae moenia Romae
>   Incolit, in proprio degit et ille solo. (vv. 21–2)[35]

Like Walter Pater in 1872, some contemporaries or near-contemporaries of Du
Bellay almost certainly *did* fall into the trap of interpreting literally and
autobiographically 'l'Ovide françois''s ironic literary re-enactment of Ovidian exile
in Rome. No doubt they would have strongly empathized with the Pléiade poet's
apparent (Ovidian-Tibullan) *regret* for his native France.[36] For readers such as
these Montaigne also supplied an appropriately wry comment, tinged with
Stoicism, in 'De la vanité':

>   Si je craignois de mourir en autre lieu que celuy de ma naissance, si je pensois mourir
>   moins à mon aise esloingné des miens, à peine sortiroy-je hors de France; je ne sortirois pas
>   sans effroy hors de ma paroisse. (*Essais*, III.ix)

—humorous words, which seem to qualify Montaigne's own earlier critical
assessment of 'curiosité', and to celebrate implicitly the supreme vanity and
sublime folly of the writer and the traveller (as indeed also of Dante's Ulysses).[37]

For all of these manifestations, both geographical and literary, of *homo viator* the

---

[35] Cf. Montaigne's 'Romme ... seule ville commune et universelle' (*Essais*, III.ix); see MacPhail
(op. cit. n. 4), p. 179.

[36] Cf. the literal interpretation recorded in Jean Le Laboureur (1623–75), 'Histoire de la maison
Du Bellay', quoted in Tucker, *The Poet's Odyssey* (op. cit. n. 6), p. 7 (and n. 1).

[37] For extensive analysis of 'De la vanité' in this sense, see: MacPhail (op. cit. n. 4), pp. 161–205
(Ch. 5: 'Essaying Rome'); and Mary B. McKinley, 'Vanity's Bull: Montaigne's Itineraries in III,
ix', *Le Parcours des Essais: Montaigne 1588–1988. Colloque international: Duke University,
Université de la Caroline du Nord - Chapel Hill (7–9 avril 1988)*, eds. Marcel Tetel & G. Mallary
Masters (Paris, 1989), 195–208.

great voyage is one neither of *regret* nor of return, but of onward, ceaseless exploration and Stoic indifference to death, the only limit. The trajectory is ultimately linear, not circular, like that of Rome's destiny—indeed like that of world 'Monarchie' and History itself:

> ... ainsi parmy le monde
> Erra la Monarchie: & croissant tout ainsi
> Qu'un flot, qu'un vent, qu'un feu, sa course vagabonde
> Par un arrest fatal s'est venuë perdre icy.
> (*Antiquitez*, xvi. 11–14)

For the voyager this may be death in an alien land or sea, but for the poet Du Bellay or for the essayist Montaigne, as indeed for a whole culture, whether ancient Rome's or Renaissance France's, this is death in the alien domain of Art, in the 'book' itself, 'icy' in the text—'pery & mis en reliquaire de livres' (*Deffence*, I. xi).[38] A death like that of Dante's Ulysses—beyond the pillars of Hercules, perhaps, but still between the shores of one abandoned *patria* and the ideal shores of another.

---

[38] Cf. Terence C. Cave, *The Cornucopian Text: Problems of Writing in the French Renaissance* (Oxford, 1979), 69-76, on Du Bellay's initial preoccupation in the *Deffence* with the limitations and temporality of Art itself, in anticipation of the later Roman sonnet sequences, and on his recognition of the inevitable future death of the French vernacular itself (p. 69); cf. above, p. 5.

THE COLOURING EFFECT OF ATTIC STYLE AND STOICISM IN BUSBEQUIUS'S *TURKISH LETTERS*

ZWEDER VON MARTELS[*]

Until this century, letters formed the most immediate contact between travellers and their relatives and friends at home. Once letters arrived, they went from hand to hand, beloved because of their personal character and light style, and also as an authentic source of information. In the seventeenth century a growing quantity of such correspondence in the vernacular was published, and it soon became an accepted literary genre. Their authors took great liberty and chose to make their letters so lengthy that they almost equalled books or diaries; in some cases they were not addressed to a particular person but to an anonymous friend.[1]

The inspiration for this fashion may well have come from Busbequius's four long and unaddressed Latin *Turkish Letters*,[2] which describe his adventures and observations during his mission as ambassador of the Emperor Ferdinand I to the court of Sultan Süleyman the Magnificent between 1554 and 1562. They rapidly won favour with the public as is witnessed by the number of reprints in Latin, and soon also in English, French, German, and other languages.[3]

The *Letters* are to a certain extent to be considered as 'memoirs'. Not untypically for humanists, the author wished to emphasise his own role, without becoming boastful, or self-glorifying in an irritating manner. And, indeed, the many eulogies written over the centuries show that he succeeded in leaving an unforgettable impression of his achievements. Their autobiographical aspect is the key to the contents of these letters, the way these contents were represented and why the author concluded the work with a lengthy portrait of his Master, Emperor Ferdinand I, which stretches over 14 of the 335 pages in the first complete edition of

---

[*] Department of Greek and Latin, University of Groningen, The Netherlands.

[1] See F. Neubert, 'Die Entstehung der Französischen Epistolarliteratur', *Zeitschrift für Romanische Philologie*, 85 (1969), 56–92; C. D. van Strien, *British Travellers in Holland during the Stuart Period. Edward Browne and John Locke as Tourists in the United Provinces*, Studies in Intellectual History, 42 (Leiden, 1993), pp. 22–5, and *passim*.

[2] The title of the first complete edition of 1589 reads *Legationis Turcicae Epistolae Quatuor* ('Four letters about the mission to Turkey'). I refer to this edition as 'Ed. 1589'. Punctuation has been adapted to modern usage in accordance with the author's critical edition, which will be published together with a Dutch translation by M. Goldsteen in 1994 (Hilversum). The English translations are from vol. i of Charles Thornton Forster's & F. H. Blackburne Daniell's *The Life and Letters of Ogier Ghiselin de Busbecq, Seigneur of Bousbecque, Knight, Imperial Ambassador* (2 vols., Londen, 1881; repr. Geneva, 1971), to which I refer as 'FD'.

[3] See Z. R. W. M. von Martels, *Augerius Gislenius Busbequius. Leven en werk van de keizerlijke gezant aan het hof van Süleyman de Grote. Een biografische, literaire en historische studie met editie van onuitgegeven teksten* (Groningen 1989), 515–22 and *passim*.

1589. A short biographical section and a description of the circumstances in which the Turkish letters were written will lead to a discussion of the Attic style and stoic character of the letters under the influence of Lipsius's ideas. This will help us to understand the place of the *Turkish Letters* in the literature of the last part of the sixteenth century, and also explain their meaning.

The Life of Augerius Busbequius

Augerius Busbequius[4], born in Komen (Comines) in Flanders in about 1520–1521, studied law, literature, history and natural philosophy at the university of Louvain and several Italian universities. In 1552, following the example of some of his ancestors and friends, he entered the household of Ferdinand I, King of Austria, brother of the Emperor Charles V. Two years later, the king appointed him permanent ambassador to the court of Süleyman, the Ottoman sultan. It was only after some pressure from the king that he accepted this task, which many others had declined because of its danger.

Busbequius's hopes for a favourable treaty rested mainly on the turbulent situation within Süleyman's family. The history of these events forms one of the themes which links all four *Turkish Letters*. A brief explanation is in place as part of it will emerge later in this article. In the autumn of 1558, Bayezid, Süleyman's younger son revolted against what would be his inevitable fate after his father's death: after his elder brother Selim became the new sultan, he, together with all others who posed a threat to the throne, would be killed in accordance with the old customs. Collecting an army of loyal soldiers, bandits and drop-outs, Bayezid marched against his brother, but he was defeated by Selim's and his father's army near Konya at the beginning of June 1559. After his retreat to Amasya, he unexpectedly escaped to Persia in the summer of 1559. First the Shah pretended friendship and gave the fugitive prince a cordial reception; soon there were rumours about a future marriage between Bayezid's and the shah's family; but then, suddenly, Bayezid's soldiers were slaughtered in an ambush, he and his sons taken prisoner and kept as hostages. This tragedy which would inspire many European play writers ended in the summer of 1562, when the Shah gave his consent for the murder of Bayezid and his sons in exchange for a large sum paid by Süleyman and Selim. Busbequius, visiting the sultan on the very day that the news of this crime arrived, wrote to Ferdinand that the sultan seemed as happy as other parents would be after receiving news that their children had been rescued.

Eventually, in 1562, peace was concluded between Ferdinand and Süleyman and Busbequius left Constantinople. Already one of the emperor's counsellors, he was promoted to seneschal and chamberlain of the four younger sons of the new Emperor Maximilian II in 1567. At the same time, he became responsible for the imperial library, which, in 1576, was enriched with hundreds of Greek manuscripts he had bought in Constantinople. Though his correspondence shows a strong attachment to his fatherland, war in the Low Countries prevented his return. Moreover, the Habsburg emperors did not like to see him go.

---

[4] This biographical section is based on von Martels (op. cit. n. 3).

In August 1574, he was sent to Paris, where he became responsible for the property of Elizabeth, daughter of Maximilian and widow of the French king Charles VI. As agent of the Emperor, he wrote many letters about the political situation in France and the Low Countries. In these years, Busbequius increasingly played a role as patron for young and ambitious scholars, who admired his spirit, erudition, and broad interests, especially in history and literature.

When the civil war in France and general misery made life near Paris increasingly disagreeable and dangerous, he asked for permission to visit Flanders. But before he reached his fatherland, he died near Rouen on October 27 or 28, 1591.

THE GENESIS OF THE *TURKISH LETTERS*

Important scholarly discoveries are attached to Busbequius's name: the Monumentum Ancyranum, over 240 Greek manuscripts, plants such as the lilac and sweet flag, and a list of Crimean Gothic words. But no less precious a gift to posterity are his four *Turkish Letters*. Each of these is dated, the first September 1, 1554, the last on December 16, 1562, and each deals with a particular period of the embassy. At the beginning and end of each letter, and often in between, a friend in his native country is addressed in a lively, conversational style, but no name is given.

The author implies that they were written during his stay in Constantinople, and lets the reader participate in his uncertainties about future developments in Turkey, the negotiations, his despair about the uncompromising attitude of the Pasha, or in the promising events when Süleyman's son Bayezid revolted. Contemporary readers thought the *Letters* were genuine, and in fact Ludovicus Carrio[5] who published the first letter (together with a piece in which Busbequius exhorted Ferdinand to form a standing army that could equal the military power of the Turks) behind Busbequius's back in Antwerp in 1581,[6] explained in the dedicatory letter to Busbequius's old friend Nicolaus Micault[7] that he thought the letter was originally written to Micault, because he himself had often heard that both men had corresponded in the period of Busbequius's embassy. Busbequius carefully kept this myth alive, when the next three letters appeared one after the

---

[5] Ludovicus Carrio (1547–1595) frequented Busbequius's house since 1579 and was often seen in circles of other learned Parisian scholars. Yet he was not always liked as the gossiping correspondence of Lipsius and his friends show. For the questions about the role Carrio played in the publication of Busbequius's writings, see von Martels (op. cit. n. 3), pp. 80–6. Arnold van Buchell (who was a friend of Carrio) gives a description of the prosperous village of Saint-Cloud at this time *Description de Paris*, ed. A. Vidier & L. A. van Langeraad (Paris, 1900), 88. I do not know whether van Buchell visited Busbequius.

[6] The full title reads: *Itinera Constantinopolitanum et Amasianum ab Augerio Gislenio Busbequij, &c. D. ad Solimannum Turcarum Imperatorem C. M. Oratore confecta. Eiusdem Busbequij De Acie Contra Turcam Instruenda Consilium.* The latter writing is better known as *Exclamatio sive de re militari contra Turcam instituenda consilium.* It dates from 1576 and was reprinted almost forty times until the middle of the eighteenth century, but it was forgotten when the Ottoman empire lost its military superiority. See von Martels (op. cit. n. 3), pp. 91, 457 ff., 518 ff.

[7] Like Busbequius, Nicolaus Micault (1518–89) studied in Louvain and Italy. He was member of the Privy Council of Charles V and later of Philips II. See von Martels (op. cit. n. 3), pp. 57–9.

other in 1582 and 1589. Best proof for this is that, in later editions, he left the dedicatory letter unchanged, but corrected or altered many passages in the first letter as the printer's copy—a corrected copy of the first edition—shows.[8]

The gradual publication of the *Letters* between 1581 and 1589 points at their composition in that period. This is confirmed by several passages which contain evidence that they were written after the ambassador's return from Constantinople.[9] In the first letter dating from 1554 [*sic*], he refers to a book by Petrus Gyllius on the Bosphorus published in 1561. Another example is the passage about the famous inscription of Augustus's Achievements (the Monumentum Ancyranum). The author remarks that ' ... it is now agreed that *Ancyra* was dedicated to Augustus as the common gift of Asia.' Some years later Ludovicus Carrio confirmed that Josephus's *Antiquitates Judaeicae* was the source for this knowledge,[10] adding elsewhere that Justus Lipsius had shown it to Busbequius.[11] Lipsius must have given this information after the publication of the Monumentum Ancyranum by a friend of Busbequius, Andreas Schottus, in 1579, because the reference to Josephus does not occur between the names of classical authors mentioned in Schottus's commentary on the inscription.[12]

There is further evidence that the *Letters* were written around 1579 and after. Justus Lipsius's letter of August 23, 1584, for example, in which he asked Busbequius to send additions to his first two letters (a second, rather short letter had been published in 1582 attached to a reprint of the first letter and the *Exclamatio* as a loose gathering).[13] On August 23, 1584, Lipsius wrote to his friend that Plantin would certainly publish his Travel Descriptions ('Itineraria'), when he would receive them: 'We are looking forward to whatever addition' ('qualecumque augmentum'.)[14] Time passed uneventfully, but two years before the work was finally published by Gilles Beys in Paris in 1589, Plantin wrote Busbequius a letter stating that he had received the third *Turkish Letter*, which he thought worthy to be printed, preferably with the fourth *Letter*, which Busbequius

---

[8] This edition is preserved in the Museum Plantin-Moretus in Antwerp (classmark: R.19.6).

[9] Fr. Marcks, 'Zur Chronologie von Busbeeks Legationis Turcicae Epistolae IV', *Jahresbericht über das königlige Pädagogium zu Putbus* (Putbus, 1909), 3-11. See also Z. R. W. M. von Martels, 'The Discovery of the Res Gestae Divi Augusti'. *Res publica litterarum*, 14 (1991), 147-56.

[10] See Carrio's letter to Lipsius of May 15, 1581 (München ,Bayerische Staatsbibliothek, Cod. Lat. 10365, fo. 105): 'Dum hic Antverpiae sum, beneficio oratoris Redenaei nanciscor exemplar indicis illius Ancyrani multo diligentius et exactius descriptum. Quod Busbequio gratissimum futurum certe scio, eo magis quod iam locum veteris scriptoris illi indicas ubi co<mmun>itas Asiae Augusto eum locum D<e>D<icauit>, i<dem> q<uod> exemplar ipsius Augusti. Vale mi Lipsi.'

[11] See L. Carrio, *Emendationum et observatonum liber secundus* (Paris, 1583), fo. 51ʳ.

[12] Andreas Schottus, *De vita et moribus Romanorum. Excerpta ex libris Sexti Aurelii Victoris a Caesare usque ad Theodosium Imperatorem* ... (Antwerp, 1579), 69–77.

[13] Compare its title: *Itinera Constantinopolitanum et Amasianum ab Augerio Gislenio Busbequio ad Solimannum Turcarum Imperatorem C. M. Oratore confecta. Eiusdem Busbequii de re militari contra Turcam instituenda consilium. Altera editio.* On the *Exclamatio*, see n. 6.

[14] *Justi Lipsi epistolae (pars II: 1584-1587)*, eds. M. A. Nauwelaerts & S. Sué (Brussels, 1983), 140/1: Lipsius to Busbequius, letter of August 23, 1584. Lipsius held the chair of Latin in Leiden, where Plantin had opened a printing office.

had also 'found back' ('retrouvée').[15] What Busbequius meant by 'found back' is puzzling, unless we assume that he wanted Plantin to believe that the *Letters* were authentic. On the other hand, it is questionable whether Lipsius and Plantin did not see through it that Busbequius was preparing them during these years. Lipsius's words 'whatever addition' ('qualecumque augmentum') in his letter from 1584, are perhaps an allusion to Busbequius's writing in the intervening years.

Besides these arguments two others—the Attic style and the stoic character of the *Letters*—prove that they date from the last ten or fifteen years of Busbequius's life. Before I discuss them, some attention must be paid to the place of the genre of the letter in the humanist tradition.

THE ART OF LETTER WRITING

In the Renaissance, the genre of letter writing was expanded to fields and subjects unknown in classical antiquity. This tradition began with Petrarch's discovery of Cicero's letters to Atticus and Quintus in the middle of the fourteenth century. The collections of Petrarch's own correspondence were at first much admired and imitated, but replaced by contemporary models as soon as later humanists had improved their style and language through constant study of classical authors. In Erasmus's time Latin had reached a high level of maturity and the same was true of the theory of letter writing.

Humanists were very much aware of the possibilities and limits of each genre. Busbequius often uses phrases like: 'Now you have got a book not a letter', 'there is the same unrestrained liberty in a letter as in conversation'. Elsewhere he compared the letter to conversation between friends.[16]

When we consider the structure of the *Turkish Letters*, their length, colloquial style, and even the choice by the author of this genre as the most appropriate for a collection of varied stories, we are reminded of Erasmus's words in his *De epistolis conscribendis*, an influential manual on the art of letter writing. A short summary[17] of his ideas might not only give an impression of how a letter should be, but also of the *Turkish Letters*, which, I think, Erasmus would have appreciated enormously.

Erasmus sticks to the traditional division of letters into the deliberative, the demonstrative and judicial types; but he adds a fourth, the 'genus familiare', a type of mixed letter, often private, which does not fit into the usual rhetorical divisions, but which occurs frequently, for example letters with a narrative, or instructions,

---

[15] *Correspondance de Chr. Plantin*, eds. M. Rooses & J. Denucé (Antwerp, 1883-1918), see vols. viii-ix, p. 211 (1248): Plantin to Busbequius, letter of May 25, 1587. The edition of 1589 was entitled: *Augerii Gislenii Busbequii D. Legationis Turcicae Epistolae quatuor. Quarum priores duae ante aliquot annos in lucem prodierunt sub nomine Itinerum Constantinopolitani & Amasiani. Adiectae sunt duae alterae. Eiusdem de re militari contra Turcam instituenda consilium.*

[16] Ed. 1589, fo. 116ʳ; FD, pp. 313–4.

[17] Erasmus, *Collected Works. Literary and Educational Writings. 3: De conscribendis epistolis / Formula / De civilitate*, ed. J. K. Sowards (Toronto, 1985), esp. pp. 12 ff. See also the studies mentioned in n. 23.

letters of thanks or congratulations. It is, in a phrase of Erasmus, 'as rich as the world itself'.

In search for a definition of the letter he says that, if there is something that can be said to characterize this genre, it can hardly be defined more concisely than by saying that the wording of a letter should resemble a conversation between friends, neither unpolished, rough, nor artificial, nor confined to a single topic, nor tediously long. Thus the epistolary form favours simplicity, frankness, humour and wit.

As to the form of the letter, he believes that letters should not be required to conform to a single type: this is to impose a narrow and inflexible definition on what is by nature diverse and capable of almost infinite variation.

Erasmus contests the opinion of those who require a specific style, language or length of letter. How can a single style be devised for such an infinitely varied range of topics, since no subject can be excluded from the letter? The letter should consist of carefully considered thoughts and well-chosen words. Quintilian considers the best style to be that which is most suited to the topic, place, the occasion, and the character of the listeners; when dealing with great matters the letter should be dignified; in matters of less importance, unpretentious; in matters of little importance, elegant and amusing; in pleasantries it should give delight with subtlety and wit; in eulogies it should have a degree of pomp, in descriptions, clarity.

Erasmus also mentions brevity, which he defines as the ability to concentrate a great amount of material into the fewest words possible, not merely to write few words, but in such way that is suitable to the topic, place and recipient. The truly brief letter is that from which nothing can be subtracted without detriment to the content, and which is so well written that even after several readings it does not cloy; at the same time, even a letter kept within the prescribed limit of twelve lines may be so lacking in brevity that it seems longer than the *Iliad*.[18]

THE TRANSITION FROM THE CICERONIAN STYLE TO THE ATTIC STYLE. LIPSIUS AND BUSBEQUIUS

Readers of the *Turkish Letters* will acknowledge that the author was trained in applying the rules for the art of letter writing as found in Erasmus's *De conscribendis epistolis*, either through Erasmus, or directly through the reading of classical authors. But Erasmus's instructions do not explain the contrast between Busbequius's earlier and later writings, especially noticeable in his *Turkish Letters*. For this, we have to direct our attention to his friendship with Lipsius, which began during Lipsius's short stay in Vienna in 1572. Busbequius was then about 50 years old, Lipsius about 25. In a letter, Lipsius wrote that he visited Busbequius—'his hero' as he called him—and that, as usual, they had talked at length about literature.[19] Later Lipsius mentions his name several times with great

---

[18] After Busbequius's death, Justus Lipsius developed Erasmus's ideas on letter writing in his *Epistolica Institutio* (1591).

[19] *Justi Lipsi epistolae (pars I: 1564-1583)*, eds. A. Gerlo & M. A. Nauwelaerts & H. D. L. Vervliet (Brussels, 1978), pp. 75: Lipsius to Pighius, letter of June 13, 1572.

respect for his erudition. This veneration was balanced by Busbequius's respect for Lipsius's merits as a Latinist.[20] Shortly after the publication of the first *Turkish Letter* in 1581, Lipsius dedicated his *Saturnalia* to Busbequius. In his dedicatory letter he remarks:[21]

> Vidimus nuper libellum duplicem Itineris et Consilii tui; libellum, sed qui meo animo scholas dissertationesque superat multorum sapientum. Brevia omnia, fateor, et eo placent magis, quia inclusa prudentia, non ostensa. Quin genus ipsum dictionis (etsi id minime inter tuas curas) priscum adstrictumque, sententiis occultum; et quod vere invideo, subtilis brevitas innata tibi, nobis adfectata.

> Recently we saw your bipartite little book containing the description of your journey and your plan for a strategy against the Turks;[22] yes, a little book, but one which in my view surpasses the lectures and discourses of many wise men. Everything is short, I discover, and it is even more pleasing because practical judgment is included, not displayed. Really your style (though it is not a thing which troubles you very much) is true to the old usages and concise and full of hidden thoughts; and—something I truly envy—a subtle brevity comes naturally to you, whereas I strive for it artificially.

In order to understand the importance of this section, a brief digression on Lipsius's ideas about style is needed.[23] Lipsius's earliest writings before 1570 were in a Ciceronian style, the dominant style of the century, notwithstanding Erasmus's violent attacks in his *Ciceronianus*. But probably after his visit in 1568 to Antonius Muretus, professor of Latin in Rome, a champion of the Ciceronian style, but at the same time one of the very first to shift his interest towards the style of later Latin authors, Lipsius became deeply interested in authors of the silver Latin period like Tacitus and Seneca, but also in Plautus. His edition of Tacitus dates from 1575. When, in 1577, he published his *Epistolicarum quaestionum libri V*, a book of textual criticism, he stated that to him Plautus's antiquated style had more savour than Cicero's. At the same time he wrote to a friend that his own style was now aimed less at splendour ('nitor'), extravagance ('luxuria'), and artificial oratorical ornament as used by Cicero ('cincinni Tulliani'); it was now more concise ('pressa'), but he did not know whether of too-studied a brevity.[24]

---

[20] See von Martels (op. cit. n. 3), pp. 358–60.

[21] *Justi Lipsi epistolae (pars I: 1564-1583)* (op. cit. n. 19), pp. 325–6: Lipsius to Busbequius, letter of January ?, 1582.

[22] Lipsius was thinking of the *Exclamatio* (see n. 6).

[23] For this Attic style, the genre of letter writing and stoicism, see: *Style, Rhetoric, and Rhytm. Essays by Morris W. Croll*, eds. J. M. Patrick et. al. (Princeton, 1966); E. Catherine Dunn, 'Lipsius and the Art of Letter-Writing', *Studies in the Renaissance*, iii (1956), 145–56; W. Trimpi, *Ben Jonson's Poems. A Study of the Plain Style* (Stanford, 1962); Erasmus, 'Opus de Epistolis Conscribendis', in: *Opera omnia I-2*, ed. J.-C. Margolin (Amsterdam, 1971); J. L. Vives, *De conscribendis epistolis. Critical Edition with Introduction and Annotations*, ed. Ch. Fantazzi, Selected Works of J. L. Vives, ii (Leiden, 1989)), esp. pp. 1–17 (= General Introduction); G. Abel, *Stoizismus und frühe Neuzeit* (Berlin, 1978); J. Lipsius, *Over standvastigheid bij algemene rampspoed*, tr. and introd. P. H. Schrijvers (Baarn, 1983); David Halsted, 'Distance, Dissolution and Neo-Stoic Ideals: History and Self-Definition in Lipsius', *Humanistica Lovaniensia*, xl (1991), 262–74.

[24] *Justi Lipsi epistolae (pars I: 1564-1583)* (op. cit. n. 19), pp. 187–90: Lipsius to Janus Lernutius, letter of 13 June 1577. See also *Style, Rhetoric, and Rhytm. Essays by Morris W. Croll* (op. cit. n. 23), p. 17 (n. 11).

Such remarks remind us of Lipsius's above-mentioned letter in which he praised Busbequius style. Before discussing this style, we must discard Lipsius's words 'style is not a thing which troubles you very much' as purely rhetorical; they were clearly in response to the end of the first *Turkish Letter* where Busbequius argues that his friend 'cannot require elegant writing from a man who is hurried and overwhelmed with business' [Ed. 1589, fo. 48ᵛ; FD, pp. 172–3]. The wording of the examples from Busbequius's *Letters* quoted in this article are sufficient proof that the author was interested in the style of his writings.

And what are we to think of Lipsius's implicit denial of any change in Busbequius's style, when he wrote that brevity was inborn to Busbequius, not studied as by himself? Was he sincere, or was he flattering?

Busbequius's early writings are characterized by balanced periods, and vocabulary taken from Cicero and his contemporaries. This is true both for his diplomatic letters and other writings. But a change from the Ciceronian towards an Attic Latin style, in which expressiveness rather than formal beauty was the aim, can be noticed in his diplomatic correspondence with Emperor Rudolph II, in the last decade of Busbequius's life, between 1581 and 1589.[25] This style resembles that of his *Turkish Letters*, but—as is to be expected—the typical features of the Attic style occur less frequently in these diplomatic letters than in the *Turkish Letters*. This is not surprising: the latter were literary letters, polished with the utmost care; the less pretentious diplomatic letters, however, were often written in great haste and for practical purposes.

Though we are aware of the different character of the Turkish and diplomatic letters, this should not prevent us from comparing the style of two strikingly similar passages. The first derived from a diplomatic letter of June 31, 1559; the corresponding one is in the third *Turkish Letter*. They show that the diplomatic letters were source material for the composition of his *Turkish Letters*, especially those parts dealing with Bayezid's revolt mentioned above.

BUSBEQUIUS TO FERDINAND	THIRD *TURKISH LETTER*
(Letter from June 31, 1559; Vienna, Österr. Staatsarchiv, Turc., I, 14 (2) fos. 122b–dʳ)	[Ed. 1589, fos. 96ᵛ–97ʳ; compare FD, pp. 271–3]
§ 1. Ipse Princeps Turcarum, quo magis (ut opinor) suorum animos in Paiazethem filium accenderet atque ipsum perterrefaceret, suum Muffti consuluit (is est supremus apud istos sacrorum antistes unde in rebus dubiis oracula petuntur),	§ 1. Quae postquam ad Suleimannum perlata sunt, ad suum Mufti (quem supremum Turcarum sacris antistitem haud dubie memineris), a quo in rebus dubiis tanquam a quercu Dodonea responsa petuntur, refert,
§ 2. quid de eo sentiendum esset, qui se uiuo atque incolume pecunias populis imperaret, manus cogeret, loca expugnaret, exercitum duceret, quo item supplicio dignus esset, qui talia conanti opem aut fauorem praestaret aut ei militaret;	§ 2. quomodo habendus sit, qui se vivo pecunias et manus cogat, oppida expugnet, imperii quietem turbet. Quid item de iis censeat, qui castra eius sequantur, et talia conanti auxilio sint;

---

[25] For this correspondence, see Busbequius, *Epistolarum legationis Gallicae libri II. Ad Maximilianum II et ad Rudolphum II* (Brussels, 1632).

§ 3. postremo, quid de eo iudicandum, qui huiusmodi hominem nihil peccare defenderet et contra ipsum duci {exercitum} aut gladium stringere detrectaret.
§ 4. Muffti ita rescripsit, ut, qui huiusmodi hominem quacumque ratione iuuarent, graui supplicio dignos significaret;
§ 5. qui uero contra eum arma ferre nollent, ueluti prophanos ac fidei suae desertores execraretur.
§ 6. Rescriptum postmodum in uulgus dissipatum et per Chiauss Bassy ad Baiazethem (ut putant) missum.
§ 7. Sed nudiustertius rediit huc Chiaussius quidam, quem ad Soltanum Selinum cum literis a patre missum Paiazethis milites interceperant.

§ 8. Is huiusmodi mandata Paiazethis referebat ad Principem: nihil sibi cum eo esse rei, neque contra ipsum hoc bellum suscepisse, neque eius dicto cum fratre sibi negotium esse et de uita certamen, cuius gladio aut sibi cadendum sit aut illi suo pereundum.
§ 9. Cum enim utrumque superstitem esse non liceat, sibi statum esse non expectare diutius, sed hanc rem uiuo patre uelle definire.
§ 10. Proinde recte facturum patrem, si se huic ipsorum contentioni non immisceat;

§ 11. alioqui statim ut eum contra se traiecisse audierit, se totam Asiam caedibus atque incendiis repleturum, tantam stragem editurum, quantam nec Tamerlanes edidisset, nec quisquam fidei ipsorum infestissimus hostis edere posset;
§ 12. neque esse, quod pater speret se eum in potestatem redigere posse:
§ 13. sibi fugam exploratam esse et de certo loco, quo se recipiat, prouisum esse.

§ 14. His ille non leuem curam istis iniecisse uidetur.
§ 15. Allatum est etiam his diebus Paiazethem oppidum, cui pro Sanziacho filius Selini praefuerat, maximis exactis pecuniis grauiter uexasse ac paene hostili more diripuisse.

§ 3. ac postremo de iis qui arma capere recusent, et nihil eum peccare defendant.
§ 4. Respondit Mufti eum hominem et qui eius sectam sequantur, videri quovis supplicio dignos;
§ 5. qui vero contra eum arma ferre detrectarent, tanquam profanos et religionius desertores pro intestabilibus habendos.
§ 6. Hoc responsum in vulgus effertur atque opera praefecti Chiaussorum ad Baiazetum mittitur.
§ 7. Paucis post diebus rediit Constantinopolim quidam de corpore Chiaussorum, quem a Suleimanno ad Selimum ablegatum Baiazetes interceperat.

§ 8. Per quem patri nunciabat sibi cum eo cuncta pietatis officia constare; nulla contra eum arma mota, neque recusare, quin ei in rebus omnibus dicto audiens sit. Cum fratre sibi negotium et de vita certamen, cuius ferro sibi necessario cadendum sit aut illi suo.
§ 9. Nefas superesse utrumque. Hoc dissidium eo vivo finire sibi certum esse:

§ 10. proinde ipsum rectius facturum, si se certamini eorum non interponat, neque alterutri auxilio sit.
§ 11. Quod si (ut ferebatur) mare traiiciat, ut Selimo suppetias eat, ne speret se facile in potestatem redactum iri.

§ 12. Exploratum habere perfugium,

§ 13. sed eum non prius transiturum in Asiam quam ipse incendiis, caedibus, ruinis totam deformasset, nihilo mitius quam aut Tamerlanes aut alius quivis hostis importunissimus.
§ 14. Haec ita renunciata haud mediocrem Suleimanno curam attulerunt.
§ 15. Simul audiebatur Axuar oppidum, cui filius Selimi pro Singiacco praefuerat, a Baiazete captum, exactaque magna pecunia foedum in modum direptum.

In both versions the arguments are almost identical, though the later one is more concise, counting only 271 against 308 words in the earlier one. I will concentrate on some stylistic differences in paragraph 11 to 15 of both columns, but need first to summarize the contents of the preceding parts and give the translation of the following paragraphs.

In the first two paragraphs, Süleyman asks the mufti how he should treat his son

Bayezid, who had raised money and gathered an army, attacked and captured towns, and troubled the peace of the empire? In § 4 the Mufti replied that such a man merited the severest punishment. The following paragraphs 5 to 11 narrate that a message was sent by Bayezid to his father. Bayezid called on his father not to interfere in the contest with his brother. Then Busbequius continues as follows:

§ 11. Otherwise as soon as he heard that he had crossed the sea, he would fill Asia with death and fire, he would cause confusion such as Tamerlan had caused and as could not be caused by any of the greatest enemies of their belief

§ 12. And there was no reason for his father to hope that he could bring him under control for a second time.

§ 13. His way of escape was ascertained and a sure place to which he could retreat, was provided for.

§ 14. With these words Bayezid seems to have caused them much anxiety.

§ 15. During these days, too, a message arrived that Bayezid had maltreated a town governed by a son of Selim, exacting great amounts of money, and that he had plundered the town in an almost hostile manner.

§ 11. But if, as was rumoured, he should cross the sea to go to Selim's assistance, he warned him not to hope that he would find it an easy task to get him into his power.

§ 12. He had secured for himself a refuge in case of defeat.

§ 13. The moment Süleyman set foot on the soil of Asia, he would lay the country waste with fire and the sword as mercilessly as Tamerlan.

§ 14. Such a message caused Süleyman no small anxiety.

§ 15. At the same time news arrived that the town of Akscherh, which was governed by Selim's son as Sanjak-bey, had been taken by Bayezid and, after a large sum of money had been exacted, had been ruthlessly sacked.

In the right-hand column (= R.) of these five paragraphs, the order of the arguments used by Bayezid in his answer to his father is inverted: § 11 left (= L.) corresponds with § 13 R.; § 12 L. with § 11 R., and § 13 L. with § 12 R. It is obvious why the author made these changes in the *Turkish Letters*: Bayezid's words are now more frightening to Süleyman: first the arrest of Bayezid by his father or his murder is precluded; secondly the threat of a terrible war all over the country acts as a climax. The concluding § 14 R. leaves little doubt about the effect on the sultan; but the reader of the diplomatic letter § 14 L. is still uncertain about the impact of Bayezid's words on the party of the sultan.

Not only has the order of the arguments been changed, vocabulary and figures of speech have been altered as well. A shorter expression than 'Exploratum habere perfugium' § 12 R., corresponding to § 13 L., would be hard to find. An antithesis in § 13 R., where Süleyman's future initiative (expressed by 'eum non prius transiturum in Asiam') is opposed by the terrible actions which Bayezid himself might take (expressed by 'ipse incendiis ... '). On the other hand the fragment in § 11 L. produces a balanced sentence characteristic of classical Latin.

'Nec quisquam fidei ipsorum infestissimus hostis edere posset' in § 11 L. is replaced by the much shorter and stronger rhythmic sentence: 'aut alius quivis hostis importunissimus', an expression derived from Cicero's *Catalinarii*. Similarly an expression by Aulus Hirtius in his *Bellum Alexandrinum*, xxiv.3: 'patriam turpissimis incendiis et ruinis deformare', was probably used in § 13 R. for 'incendiis, caedibus, ruinis totam deformasset'; here 'caedibus' is added, but Busbequius likes a division into three items and, moreover, the asyndeton.

Another important feature of the *Turkish Letters* in particular is that the whole story is represented as if it were a tragedy with three main figures: Süleyman,

Selim and Bayezid. In the diplomatic letters, too, Busbequius was aware of the dramatic character of the events, writing at the end of 1558, just at the very beginning of Bayezid's revolt: such hatred as existed between Bayezid and his brother Selim is material for a tragedy and there, as well, such feelings cannot easily be composed. But elsewhere in the diplomatic correspondence, the events are certainly not represented in this manner consistently, as we can see, for instance, in § 14 L., where 'istis' refers to the whole of Süleyman's party; in § 14 R., by contrast, Süleyman's personal anxiety is emphasised.

There are references to drama in more places in the *Turkish Letters*.[26] Its origin may be the prominent role theatre played in humanistic education, but it may also be the influence of the edition of Tacitus published by Lipsius in 1575.

These short passages do not give a complete idea of the difference between Busbequius's style at the time of his embassy and twenty or more years later. Moreover, it would be wrong to suggest that the same style is applied everywhere in the four *Letters*. But they do demonstrate an evolution of his style: the style and vocabulary of earlier writings were influenced by figures of speech and vocabulary belonging to the Ciceronian period. The *Turkish Letters*, however, show a significant change: the style is now more concise, and the vocabulary is rich, precise and chosen from ancient literature as a whole. The author does not hesitate to introduce younger words like: 'alcoranus', 'moschea', 'jughurta'. There are even some examples of Turkish language, Notable are some quotations derived from Tacitus, and more generally the aim at brevity could be his influence as well. Busbequius's language is coloured by many poetic expressions, often from Virgil, but from several other poets as well. Characteristic for this period and style in which Cicero was no longer the exclusive model are references to Plautus's verses and vocabulary, sometimes in significant positions. Variation in figures of speech is also sought, with frequent antitheses, parentheses, ellipses, assonance, repetition, asyndeton. Important, too, are the *sententiae*, or proverbial expressions, already noticed by Lipsius in his reaction to the publication of the first of the *Turkish Letters*. An example is the following almost Tacitean statement on the Turks:

> Tantos longinqui temporis felicitas huic genti spiritus fecit, ut nihil iniquum putet quod velit, nihil aequum quod nolit [Ed. 1589, fo. 50ʳ]

> A long career of success has made the Turks so arrogant, that they consider their pleasure to be the sole rule of what is right and what is wrong. [FD, p. 176]

These characteristics show that Busbequius was following the fashion for Attic style, and a remark in a letter to Lipsius quoted below shows that he regarded his friend Justus Lipsius as its principal advocate. The significance of this friendship cannot, therefore, be underestimated. Although the two men did not meet after 1572, Lipsius's students and friends, almost all fellow countrymen, were constant visitors at Busbequius's house near Paris, and it is no coincidence that they worked on authors like Plautus, Apuleius, Aulus Gellius and Silius Italicus.[27]

---

[26] Compare, for instance, the dramatic description of Mustafa's murder by eunuchs of his father, Süleyman [Ed. 1589, fo. 22ᵛ; FD, p. 117–8].

[27] Compare I. Gulielmius, *Plautinarum quaestionum commentarius* (Paris, 1583); Apuleius, *Opera omnia*, ed. P. Colvius (Leiden, 1588); Aulus Gellus, *Noctes Atticae*, ed. L. Carrio (Paris 1585). See

In many respects the *Turkish Letters* call to mind the letters of the younger Pliny. But it would be a mistake to forget the influence of Cicero's letters, so different in style from his other works, shocking Petrarch when he first read them. Paradoxically, Erasmus and Lipsius recommended Cicero's letters as models for letter writing.

THE REEMERGENCE OF STOICISM[28]

The fashion for Attic style was accompanied by a vigorous revival of stoicism provoked by political upheaval and fierce wars raging both in the Low Countries and in France during the last decades of the sixteenth centuries. Lipsius became its strongest defender through his *De constantia*, published in 1584. It was his conviction that of all philosophies stoicism cared most for the general benefit.

Busbequius's reaction to this philosophy is known from his letter of 12 July 1584, to Lipsius, who had presented him with a copy of his *De constantia*. He first praised Lipsius for having widened the boundaries of the Latin language, and increased the territory of Roman eloquence; then he added: ' ... you taught us [*here he also meant 'me'*] to speak according to the custom of the ancients ...'—a remark of central importance, as it corroborates my observation that Busbequius's style changed during these years. With this remark on style and language, the author interweaves a second, not less interesting one, in which he approves wholeheartedly of Lipsius's attempt to reintroduce stoicism as the dominant philosophy. He comments that after what Lipsius had done for the Latin Language, one thing is left: that he adopt the task of moral censorship, that he lead errant souls back to gravity as it existed in old times, and correct their inconstancy, foolishness and wickedness. In Latin the whole passage reads as follows:[29]

> ... Linguae Latinae pomeria magna cum laude protulisti, aucti per te fines Romanae eloquentiae, triumphasti de barbarie, restat ut morum censuram, quam tibi omnis eruditorum populus, veluti consulari et triumphali, summo consensu defert, libens suscipias. Rege nunc errantes animos, revoca ad pristinam severitatem, castiga levitatem, stultitiam, improbitatem; docuisti nos more veterum loqui, doce etiam vivere; nihil est te dignius, nullum maius operae precium facere potes; illo tibi debemus multum, isto debebimus omnia ...

But the question arises whether Busbequius's sympathy for stoicism is interwoven expressly in the *Turkish Letters*? The key to an answer lies in the autobiographical content of this work.

What is so intriguing in the *Letters*, is paradoxically the information that is left out. Busbequius is particularly reticent about men who would have detracted from

---

also W.-H. Ehlers, 'Silius Italicus, *Punica*', *Göttingische Gelehrte Anzeigen*, 243 (1991), 102–1; this article deals both with Carrio and Franciscus Modius, whose *Novantique lectiones ... in quibus .. Silius, Censorinus ... alii supplentur, emendantur ...* appeared in 1584, and who was an old acquaintance of Carrio and a correspondent of Lipsius, but he probably never met Busbequius.

[28] See also Zweder von Martels, 'A Stoic Interpretation of the Past: Augerius Busbequius's Description of His Experiences at the Court of Suleiman the Magnificent (1554-1562)', *Journal of the Institute of Romance Studies*, 2 (1993), 165-79.

[29] *Justi Lipsi epistolae (pars II: 1584-1587)*, eds. M. A. Nauwelaerts & S. Sué (Brussels, 1983), 134–5: Busbequius to Lipsius, letter of July 12, 1584.

his own merits. For instance, in the first *Turkish Letter* dealing with the long journey to Amasya, his two older and more experienced colleagues, the influential Hungarian humanist Antal Verantius and his colleague Franciscus Zay,[30] are hardly mentioned. Then, in the short second *Letter* dating from the Summer of 1556, Busbequius explained what had happened in Turkey during his journey from Amasya to Vienna and back to Constantinople and he briefly described the cold reception of Ferdinand's reply to the Sultan by the Pashas after his return at the beginning of 1556. The long period between his arrival and the Summer of 1557, in which he lived together with his colleagues in the caravansary, is passed over in silence. This is hardly noticed, because the third and fourth *Letters* are dated to 1560 and 1562 respectively; they only describe his personal experiences and observations, starting with the departure of Verantius and Zay, and ending with the successful completion of his negotiations in 1562 and his return to the court of the Emperor.

Another example is Albert de Wijs who stayed in the same embassy from 1559 onwards. When Busbequius returned home in 1562, De Wijs reluctantly accepted the appointment as permanent ambassador, after the promise had been given that a successor would be found. But these words were soon forgotten, and he died in Constantinople many years later. Busbequius's comments about this man with whom he had lived for over three years are surprisingly terse:

> Venit ad me in ea castra Albertus de VViis, vir honestus et bonis literis non leuiter imbutus, patria ni fallor Amersfordiensis. [Ed. 1589, fo. 108ᵛ]

> During my stay at Süleyman's army camp [in the summer of 1559], Albert de Wijs, a gentleman and a good scholar arrived. If I am not mistaken, he is a native of Amersfoort. [FD, p. 297]

That is all. Elaborate accounts of the deeds of Verantius, Zay and De Wijs would have diminished the importance of the role played by the author. His rhetoric becomes even more clear, if we observe how he interspersed his stories with complimentary accounts of his own deeds, so as to leave a good impression of his personality: how he dealt with the Turks in the most difficult situations, and managed to overcome their intimidation and attempts to deceive him; the way he took advantage of Bayezid's revolt, his care for his servants and the Christian community in Constantinople, and last but not least, his broad interest in culture and literature. In this he often followed Aristotle's advice that one should not sing one's own praise, but a third person should fulfil this task.[31]

---

[30] The humanist Antal Verantius (1503–1573) was appointed bishop of Fünfkirchen in 1553 and bishop of Erlau in 1557, after his return from Constantinople. Franciscus Zay, born in 1503, studied probably in Padua. He fought with King Louis of Hungary at Mohács and later entered the service of King Ferdinand. Hij headed the Nassades, ships which formed the Habsburg fleet on the Donau. See von Martels (op. cit. n. 3), pp. 157–8; M. D. Birnbaum, *Humanists in a Shattered World. Croation and Hungarian Latinity in the Sixteenth Century*, UCLA Slavic Studies, 15 (Columbus, Ohio, 1985), pp. 213–41 (Verantius), 68–9 (Zay).

[31] Baldesar Castiglione's influential *Il cortigiano* (1528) has an interesting passage in which the remark is made that self-glorification is natural, and a number of useful advices is given. See Baldesar Castiglione, *The book of the Courtier*, tr. G. Bull (first ed. 1967, Harmondsworth, 1980), 59-60.

For instance, through his portrait of his physician William Quackelbeen, a humanist of great literary and scientific learning, Busbequius gains much sympathy, but only indirectly. By praising him highly and adding that he thought his friend worthy to become his successor, had he not died of the plague, Busbequius could show his own generosity and much of his praise fell back upon himself.[32]

Most flattering, too, was the portrait of the generous and peace-loving Ali Pasha, with whom he had negotiated successfully since the summer of 1561 and who had not hesitated to show his feelings of friendship through many personal gifts when Busbequius left Constantinople. It is placed in strong contrast with that of Rüstem Pasha, Ali Pasha's predecessor, who was depicted as avaricious, sour, and unwilling to compromise, and with whom one clearly feels Busbequius had little in common.[33] Yet the most interesting example of this rhetorical technique aimed at self-praise is the portrait of Ferdinand.

THE PORTRAIT OF FERDINAND

The portrait of Ferdinand follows the description of Busbequius's return to the court of the emperor, and forms an unexpected and long epilogue to the last letter. It inspired biographers and eulogists of Ferdinand, but its place in the entire framework of the *Letters* has never been explained. I will unravel its meaning in four steps.

1. The portrait is in the first place an historic account of the emperor's life, as the author remarks in the second half of his portrait: 'Putas me laudare, ad historiae fidem epistolam scribo' ('You may think it is a panegyric I am composing, but I am writing my letter with strict historical accuracy') [Ed. 1589, fo. 160^r/2].

2. But its flattering character makes it hard to deny that it is plainly also an ideal portrait, or panegyric of a sovereign. Ferdinand is depicted as the most virtuous of all kings and emperors of history. In fact, the best virtues of stoicism can be discovered in Ferdinand's character and deeds. He is an emperor who measures all his actions by God's law, who makes his personal interests subordinate to his subjects' welfare. He lays down the law most uprightly and as strictly for himself as for others, and he keeps his passions under control. Then Busbequius states—and this passage reminds us of his letter to Lipsius after the publication of the *De constantia*[34]:

> Romani suos censores moribus praefectos habuerunt, qui populum in officio et vetere disciplina retinerent. Hic nullo censore opus. Vita principis pro censura est. Is omnibus praelucet, exemploque est, quid fugiant, quid sequantur. [Ed. 1589, fo. 158^v]

> The Romans had their censors appointed to regulate morals, and to keep the nation firm in the path of duty and the customs of their sires, but among us no censor is required, as the life of our sovereign supplies his place. His bright example shows us what to avoid and what to follow. [FD, p. 403]

---

[32] See Ed. 1589, fos. 125v–6v; FD, pp. 335–6.
[33] See especially Ed. 1589, fo. 129^v; FD, pp. 345–6.
[34] See page 151.

3. The third and fourth steps of our interpretation relate the portrait to its wider context. It is interesting how he first introduces Ferdinand to the reader. Almost at the end of his last letter, Busbequius writes that he was longing to return home, because life at court was not to his liking: deceit abounds there and sincerity is rare.

> Optabile est sibi posse vivere et musis, et cum paucis et non fallacibus amicis in agelli angulo consenescere. Aut nulla est in hoc terrestri exilio, aut ea demum vera vita est. Nimium quantum saepe pluris fiat in aula nobilis scurra quam vir bonus, ut non absurde boni viri inter aulicos speciem oculis subiecisse videantur, qui asinum pinxerunt inter simias. De communibus aulis loquor. Nam me non fugit multas atque hanc praecipue viris in omni laudis genere praestantibus tanquam rarissimis luminibus illustrari. Ut ut sit, mihi solitudo et studiorum nutrix quies turba et strepitu aulico potior. Sed discedere cupientem, vereor, ne Princeps optimus retineat, aut certe domo iam abditum retrahat. [Ed. 1589, fo. 156ᵛ]

> To be able to live for oneself and literature and to grow old in some quiet country nook, with a few honest friends, is indeed an enviable lot. If there is any true life to be found in this earthly pilgrimage, surely it must be this. Far too often in a court is a buffoon of rank valued more highly than a man of merit; indeed a picture of an ass among monkeys gives an excellent notion of the position of an honest man among courtiers. For I freely admit that many courts, and especially this one, derive lustre from the presence of men of distinction in every walk of life, who shed around them a glorious light. Be this as it may, I prefer solitude and rest, nurse of studies to the throng and tumult of a court. But though I long to depart, I am afraid my most gracious Sovereign may detain me, or at any rate summon me back, when I have reached my retirement at home. [FD, p. 400]

So far this may all seem rather commonplace, unless it is understood that this wish to live in some quiet country retreat, with a few honest friends, and this longing for solitude and study are familiar stoic ideals, shortly before exemplified by Lipsius through the garden of his friend Carolus Langius in the *De constantia*.[35] The next passage reinforces this idea. Busbequius continues that if the Emperor recalls him:

> ... tum vero unum relinquetur solatium in quo conquiescam, quod mihi sanctissimi Imperatoris faciem, vel (ut melius dicam) spirantem verae virtutis imaginem assidue spectare et contemplari dabitur. Nam cave putes solem hoc Principe quicquam illuxisse melius, neque cui iustius rerum arbitrium delatum sit. [Ed. 1589, fo. 156ᵛ]

> ... then one consolation will be left me, namely, that it will be granted me to gaze upon the most sacred person of my Emperor continuously, or to express it better upon the living image of real virtue. For I assure you my master is the noblest prince on whom the sun ever shone. His character and his virtue give him a claim to empire such as few have ever possessed. [FD, pp. 400–1]

After this he continues his eulogy from which some significant passages have already been quoted.

In other words, to Busbequius there is not much difference between continuous contact with the Emperor, the personification of stoic virtues, model of wise statesmanship and behaviour—and on the other hand, a life of solitude and study. Here we should think of the study of books in order to acquire stoic ideals like virtue and practical wisdom.

---

[35] Cf. L. Forster, 'Meditation in a Garden', *German Life and Letters*, N.S. 31 (1977), 23–35; Schrijvers (op. cit. n. 23), pp. 24, 87–92.

4. The last step in my interpretation looks at the function of Ferdinand's portrait within the context of the four letters. Although these letters were not printed simultaneously, but after each other, and although they are different in length and structure, no-one has ever doubted that they belong together on grounds of their genre, themes and subject. It fits the humanistic theory, that a poem, letter, or book should form an artistic and rhetorical unity. If this is true, Ferdinand's portrait—lengthy and very different from the other parts of the four letters—has a special function within the context of these four letters.

Busbequius wanted to give an exemplary picture of his own role during his embassy. He preferred not to elaborate on the life and work of colleagues like Verantius, Zay and De Wijs, but added portraits of those men, whose words or deeds were testimony to his own virtues. This is one of the functions of Ferdinand's portrait as well. Busbequius writes:

> Viros bonos et eruditos iisque artibus excultos, quibus bona opera Reipublicae navari potest, praecipua benevolentia complectitur. His se dat, positaque maiestate veluti cum paribus mutua amicitiae officia exercet ... Nullo dilectu, an illi vetere et credita maiorum, an sua et praesenti laude clari sint. Cum his tempus ..., quod negotiis superest, libenter ponit. Hi sunt apud eum in pretio, ut qui publice multum interesse iudicet suum virtuti locum et honorem restitui. [Ed. 1589, fo. 158ʳ]

> Ferdinand is extremely kind towards men of worth and learning, who are trained in the pursuits which do the State good service. In dealing with men of this description he lays aside his royalty and treats them, not as a master, but as an intimate friend on a footing of perfect equality ... making no distinction between those who owe their high position to the credit they derive from the glory of their ancestors, and those who have been elevated by their own merits and have proved their worth ... These are the men he values, holding, as he does, that it is of great public importance that merit should occupy the position which is its due. [FD, pp. 403–4]

The author is clearly hinting at himself: the natural son of a noble, certainly not aristocratic family, he had risen to a position of distinction close to the Emperor. Deeply aware of his personal relation to the Emperor, he concludes the passage with the following seemingly modest words:

> Quum reliqua tibi narrassem, ne hoc quidem te ignorare volui, sub cuiusmodi Imperatore militarem. [Ed. 1589, fo. 161ʳ]

> ... as I have narrated my other adventures to you, I wished that you should not remain in ignorance of the character of the Emperor I serve. [FD, p. 414]

It is important to realize that the virtues admired in Ferdinand are very similar to those upheld by Busbequius as ambassador: self-restraint, perseverance and, if needed, self-sacrifice for the general good; care for one's servants and love for literature as far as it is useful to other people. This means that Ferdinand's portrait parallels Busbequius's own experiences as ambassador, and his virtues are to be seen reflected in Ferdinand's portrait as in a mirror.

Stoic influences can be detected in earlier parts of the four letters as well, especially at the beginning of the fourth. There we read how Busbequius lent money to a number of prisoners of war to pay his ransom. But it soon appeared that many were not going to return the money, as a result of which he got into deep financial trouble.[36] The author of the *Turkish Letters* dwells rather long on these events, and the passage is clearly meant as a justification of his own imprudence. Interesting are the deliberate stoic undertones of his defense. One of these is almost at the end, where the writer concludes his defence with the following stoic expression taken word for word from the stoic poet Silius Italicus (*Punica*, xiii. 663): 'Ipsa sibi virtus semper pulcherrima merces' [Ed. 1589, fo. 123ʳ]: 'Virtue is its own reward'. [FD, p. 329] Silius Italicus was one of the authors studied by Busbequius's friends,[37] and that the poet's words were deliberately quoted can be deduced from what follows. After the description of his help to prisoners in various ways, Busbequius writes:

> Ego vero laetor non modo me re posuisse, verum etiam exemplo. Quo prouocati plerique et ipsi bonam operam nauarunt. [Ed. 1589, fo. 123ʳ]

> I am glad to say that I not only did my part in contributing, but also by my example was the means of inducing many others to come forward and give valuable assistance. [FD, p. 330]

And he illustrates these words with the story of a contemptible Italian-Greek who could not be induced to give any money at all to the prisoners, seeing their imprisonment as the will of God, which he did not wish to oppose.

Here we are confronted with the important stoic principle that one should set an edifying example,[38] the same idea which returns in Ferdinand's portrait! But in addition we have Busbequius's response to one of the most debatable matters in the discussions about stoicism since Lipsius's publication of the *De constantia*. It is the discussion about man's free will, destiny and God's will.[39] Busbequius's private view becomes clear through this story: he attached importance to the idea of free will, condemning the idea that one should await one's fate.

The history of Bayezid's hopeless revolt provides other examples of Busbequius's interest in this discussion about destiny (*Fatum*).[40] He recalls an interesting discussion with his guard during a picnic on an island near Constantinople. It was about Bayezid, who was then a prisoner of the Persian shah. The ambassador pitied Bayezid's fate, because—as he said—the prince had no choice except to take up arms or submit to certain death. But the Turkish guard condemned him strongly. Then Busbequius replied: 'You are making Bayezid guilty of a monstrous atrocity, but you do not charge Selim, the father of the present Sultan, with any crime though he took up arms not merely to resist his father's will, but against his very person'. The other replied: 'With good reason, for the issue of his enterprise showed clearly enough that he did what he did by prompting from above, and that it was preordained'. Busbequius answered: 'On this principle you will interpret whatever has been undertaken, although from the

---

[36] See von Martels (op. cit. n. 3), pp. 300–4.
[37] For the lively interest in Silius Italicus, compare note 27.
[38] Compare Halsted (op. cit. n. 23).
[39] Schrijvers (op. cit. n. 23), pp. 19 ff.
[40] See Ed. 1589, fos. 147ᵛ–8ᵛ; FD, pp. 382–4.

most wicked motives, if it proves successful to be done rightly, and you will ascribe it to God's will; and will thus make God the author of evil, nor will you reckon anything to have been done well or the contrary, except by the result'.

Living in Paris, Busbequius made up his mind to write an account of the most fruitful years of his life. His choice was either to rearrange the old diplomatic and private correspondence, or to select the best parts from his old letters and notes, and to rewrite them. The latter was, of course, the greatest challenge. Inspired by Lipsius's new teaching in style and stoicism, he gradually developed the scheme in which his own actions were emphasised. The personal letter, whose use proliferated in the Neo-Latin tradition, was suitable for this purpose. Though the *Turkish Letters* were not published together, they eventually made an artistic and rhetorical unity and each part—including Ferdinand's portrait—has a function within the whole work, allowing more than one interpretation, rich as it is in experiences, observations, thoughts and allusions.

In giving his *Letters* an autobiographical dimension, Busbequius was not alone. Antonius Muretus published a volume of his own correspondence in 1580. Here the letters were presented neither chronologically, nor according to addressee, but their arrangement was so organised that they gave a positive picture of the humanist himself.[41]

At the end of his first letter Busbequius claims that his narrative is written in a spirit of honesty and truth.[42] The partial rediscovery of his diplomatic correspondence from the years of his embassy and some personal letters to friends and scholars has made it possible to investigate the value of this promise to the reader. In general, he followed his diplomatic correspondence closely, although the picture of what had happened was in a few places somewhat distorted partly by his understandable lapses of memory, partly by the fictional structure of his *Letters*.[43] It is clear that the different style and the more dramatic form of the *Turkish Letters* infringe the validity of particular stories, as does Busbequius's desire to emphasize his own achievements and to give them a stronger stoic appearance. Yet, these small disadvantages could not persuade him to abandon his plan. On the contrary, he rightly recognised, through long acquaintance with the best authors, that truth does not consist in minute detail, but rather in conveying a right impression. And indeed, in doing so he successfully convinced contemporary and later generations of readers, so that the *Letters* are now not only an important witness of the period of his embassy itself, but also an interesting source for the intellectual history of the end of the sixteenth century and after.

---

[41] See J. IJsewijn, 'Marcus Antonius Muretus epistolographus', *La correspondance d' Erasme et l'epistolographie humaniste. Colloque international tenu en novembre 1983*, Travaux de l'Institut Interuniversitaire pour l'Étude de la Renaissance et de l'Humanisme, viii (Brussels, 1985).

[42] Ed. 1589, fo. 48v: 'Me quidem in hac mea infantia consolabitur nullius mendacii sibi conscius animus. Quod est in huiusmodi narrationibus praecipue spectandum'; FD, p. 173.

[43] See von Martels (op. cit. n. 3), p. 79, and *passim*.

BARLAEUS'S DESCRIPTION
OF THE DUTCH COLONY IN BRAZIL

A. J. E. HARMSEN[*]

In 1941, the naval historian M. G. de Boer described several misconceptions about the battle of the Downs (1639), where a Dutch fleet of small ships cornered a Spanish Armada and subsequently vanquished it. 'I think I can show how these stories came into the world', he continues. 'When shortly after the battle, on the thirteenth of November, Caspar van Baerle held his Oration on the victory, the professor, who probably knew himself to be more at home in classical antiquity than in a naval battle, and who does, in fact, repeatedly lose track in his description, declared that one should not examine his utterances too closely: "If somewhere in the names of the ships, I err or go astray, remember then, that I too, together with our sailors, am befogged and blinded by the smoke and the fog, so it is hardly possible for me to recognize and distinguish friend from foe and one ship from the other."'[1]

De Boer was mainly interested in the factual contents of Barlaeus's oration, but he neglected to consider the question of what seventeenth-century readers would expect from such historical descriptions. This article, which focuses on Barlaeus's *History of Johan Maurits's Achievements in Brazil*, will explain this issue on the basis of Vossius's rules for historiographers. It deals also with the structure, contents, sources and style of Barlaeus's *History*. But first we must introduce the reader to the background of Johan Maurits's expedition to Brazil, and answer the question why Barlaeus was the most suitable person to accomplish the task of describing its history.

THE EXPEDITION OF JOHAN MAURITS OF NASSAU TO BRAZIL
The traditional world view of Dutch merchants, strongly influenced by humanism, was thoroughly upset by the colonisation of America. They gradually distanced themselves from the classical perception of the world, in which Athens and Rome were the centres, Gibraltar and the Ganges the utmost limits. At the same time, the

---

[*] University of Leiden, The Netherlands.
I wish to thank Ms I. C. Grunnill for the English translation of this article.
The punctuation of the Latin passages has been adapted to modern usage.
[1] M. G. de Boer, *Tromp en de Armada van 1639*, Nederlandsche Akademie van Wetenschappen, Werken uitgegeven door de Commissie voor Zeegeschiedenis, vi (Amsterdam, 1941), 58. See C. van Baerle, *Oratie over de zee-strijdt met de Spaensche vloodt in Duyns ...* (Amsterdam, 1639), 20: 'Indien ik erghens inde namen der Schepen misse of dwael, ghedenckt, dat ik met onze Maetroozen ook van den roock en smook benevelt en verblind word, dat het my qualijk mogelijk is vyanden en vrienden en 't een schip van 't andere te erkennen en t'onderscheyden.'

discoveries of the New World seemed a realisation of predictions, for instance, by Seneca that 'there will come an age in the far-off years where Ocean shall loose the bonds of things, when the whole broad earth shall be revealed, when Tethys shall disclose new worlds and *Thule* not be the limit of the lands'.[2] There was little agreement about how Indians were to be treated. Allied to revulsion from the inhuman treatment of the Indians by Spaniards and Portuguese was the wish to christianize and educate those savages. But others were full of contempt for the godless barbarians, and shamelessly supported their own government's pursuit of riches at the cost of the natives.

Such was the world in which Johan Maurits of Nassau operated as Governor-General of Brazil. He was appointed by the States General in The Hague and the West India Company in Amsterdam in 1637, and served until 1644. His appointment offered the great-nephew of William the Silent the opportunity to fulfil his administerial and military ambitions. It enabled him to build the grandiose Mauritshuis in The Hague and, in Brazil, beautiful and imposing buildings like the palace of Vrijburg and the country house Boa Vista. Essential to Johan Maurits, advocate of humanist culture, was the establishment of an enlightened government, which, as he hoped, would bring prosperity and happiness to natives and colonists alike.

In this context, he regarded it his duty to have his new land and people, and its flora and fauna described systematically. Several learned men assisted him. Best known are Gulielmus Piso (1611-78) and George Marcgraf (1610–43). Piso had studied medicine in Leiden and Caen, and, afterwards, started a practice as physician in Amsterdam, which he resumed after his return from Brazil.[3] His colleague Marcgraf, who had read mathematics, medicine and botany, was less fortunate, because after his stint in Brazil, he was sent to Angola as an official of the West India Company, where he died soon after. Both men left extensive records of their researches in Brazil. Their most important publications were included in the *Historia naturalis Brasiliae* of 1648. We also possess a large map of Brazil which is attributed to George Marcgraf.[4]

Among the artists working for Johan Maurits were the painters Albert E(e)ckhout, and Frans Post, who was also an architect of buildings and fortresses. The great number of paintings and drawings brought back from this Brazilian expedition form a rich source of information, and were the inspiration for many murals, tapestries, paintings and book illustrations.[5]

---

[2] Seneca, *Medea*, vs. 375–9 (Loeb; tr. F. J. Miller). See T. van Hout, 'Amerika en de Oudheid. Een beschouwing over Lipsius', *Hermeneus. Tijdschrift voor antieke cultuur*, lxiv (1992), 243–51.

[3] E. Pies, *Willem Piso (1611–1678). Begründer der kolonialen Medizin und Leibartz des Grafen Johann Moritz von Nassau-Siegen in Brasilien. Eine Biographie* (Düsseldorf, 1981).

[4] The *Historia naturalis Brasiliae* comprises: G. Piso, *De medicina Brasiliensi libri quatuor* and G. Marcgravius, *Historia rerum naturalium Brasiliae libri octo* (Leiden & Amsterdam, 1648). See the contributions of J. D. North, P. J. P. Whitehead & F. Guerra in: E. van den Boogaart, H. R. Hoetink & P. J. P. Whitehead, *Johan Maurits van Nassau-Siegen, 1604–1679. A humanist Prince in Europe and Brazil. Essays on the Occasion of the Tercentenary of his Death* (The Hague, 1979).

[5] On the illustrations see the exhibition catalogues *Maurits de Braziliaan*, eds. J. de Sousa Leão et al. (The Hague, 1953); *Zo wijd de wereld strekt. Exhibition Catalogue, 21 December 1979– 1*

Another interesting member of Johan Maurits's court in Brazil was his private chaplain, the erudite poet Franciscus Plante, author of several Neo-Latin poems, of which his *Mauritias* (1647)[6] was the most important. This epic, in the manner of Virgil, is an account, in twelve books, of Johan Maurits's achievements in Brazil. It was sumptuously produced and lavishly illustrated.[7]

It was not just because of his humanist conception of princehood that Johan Maurits valued this homage. His dismissal in 1644 was preceded by a series of conflicts with the governors of the West India Company, who in his opinion were not sufficiently disposed to invest money in the infrastructure of Brazil and consequently missed the chance of structural prosperity and economic affluence for the country.

CASPAR BARLAEUS (1584–1648)

But Caspar Barlaeus himself, the author of the great 'History of Count Johan Maurits of Nassau's recent achievements during eight years in Brazil and elsewhere'[8], had not taken part in the expedition to Brazil. Actually, he never left the Low Countries, except once, in 1620, to Caen to obtain (like George Marcgraf) his doctorate in medicine. Barlaeus did not practise as a physician, but was regent of the States College and Professor of Philosophy in Leyden until 1621, when he was dismissed because of his support of the Arminians, the losing party in a religious controversy with the Gomarists. After 1632, he and G. J. Vossius became the first professors of the Athenaeum Illustre in Amsterdam.

Barlaeus's acquaintance with Brazil went back as far as 1622, when he published a Latin adaptation of a history of the West Indies by Antonio de Herrera, entitled *Novus orbis*. A description of Brazil by Petrus Bertius, first printed in 1600,[9] was

---

March 1980, Mauritshuis, Den Haag, eds. E. van den Boogaart et al. (The Hague, 1979); and especially P. J. P. Whitehead & M. Boeseman, *A Portrait of Dutch 17th Century Brazil. Animals, Plants and People by the Artists of Johan Maurits of Nassau*, Koninklijke Nederlandse Akademie van Wetenschappen. Verhandelingen Afdeling Natuurkunde, II/87 (Amsterdam etc., 1989).

[6] *Mauritiados libri XII. Hoc est: rerum ab heroe Ioanne Mauritio Comite Nassaviae &c. in Occidentali India gestarum descriptio poetica* (Leiden, 1647).

[7] See W. A. P. Smit, *Kalliope in de Nederlanden* (Assen, 1975), 238–41 and R. A. Eekhout, 'The *Mauritias*. A Neo-Latin Epic by Franciscus Plante', in: Van den Boogaart, *Johan Maurits ...* (op. cit. n. 4), pp. 377–93. Eekhout is rather negative about Plante's qualities as a poet and a latinist, but this does not detract from the prince's desire for epic glorification.

[8] *Rerum per octennium in Brasilia et alibi nuper gestarum, sub praefectura Illustrissimi Comitis I. Mauritii, Nassoviae, &tc. Comitis ... historia* (Amsterdam 1647). The book was published as a large folio volume with full-page illustrations by Joannes Blaeu. For a facsimile translation, see: C. Barlaeus, *Nederlandsch Brazilië onder het bewind van Johan Maurits Grave van Nassau 1637–1644. Historisch, geographisch, ethnographisch*, tr. S. P. l'Honoré Naber (The Hague, 1923). For an abridged translation in Portuguese, see *História dos feitos recentemente praticados durante oito anos no Brazil*, tr. Cl. Brandão, pref. M. G. Ferri (Coleção Reconquista do Brazil, São Paulo, 1974). J. A. Worp published a biography of Barlaeus in *Oud Holland*, iii (1885), 241–65; iv (1886), 24–40, 172–89; v (1887), 93–125; vi (1888), 87–102, 241–76; vii (1889), 89–128.

[9] In: P. Bertius, *Tabularum geographicarum contractarum libri quatuor* (Amsterdam, 1600), 604–11. For the full title of Herrera's *Novus orbis*, see n. 17.

appended to this publication. Petrus Bertius was Barlaeus's teacher and also his predecessor as regent of the *Staten College*, and Professor of Ethics in Leiden.

Amongst the throng of encomiasts of the stadtholder Frederik Hendrik, Barlaeus had distinguished himself, perhaps in the first place through his one-book, epic poem *Sylvae Ducis obsidio* (1629), on the conquest of 's-Hertogenbosch by Frederik Hendrik, celebrated elsewhere by over forty poets. Through its language, versification, and treatment of the subject, the poem radiates a grandeur that was new in the Netherlands. Among earlier subjects of his poems were the conquest of the Spanish 'silver-fleet' by Piet Heyn (*Argo Batava*), the battle of the Downs (*Auriacus triumphans*; 1639), and many martial panegyrics, of which the most recent one was the *Laurus Flandrica* (1644).[10] In these descriptive panegyrics, Barlaeus imitated late Latin examples (mainly by Claudius Claudianus, Statius, Silius Italicus and Rutilius Namatianus). The poems are strongly mythological, full of hyperbole, and always very lively in style. Introductory words like 'Sed vide' bring the reader right into the action.

Barlaeus was also a respected editor of both prose and poetry. Apart from an extensive description of Italy (*Nova et accurata Italiae hodiernae descriptio*; Amsterdam, 1626), he edited the Dutch and Latin poems of Constantyn Huygens (*Momenta desultoria*).[11] When Maria de' Medici visited Amsterdam in 1638, he described the festive spectacle in a large work containing both poetry and prose, the *Medicea Hospes*[12], which was translated into Dutch by Vondel.

Barlaeus's knowledge of shipping and colonial history first became apparent in a long eulogy on Elias Herckmans' learned poem *Der zee-vaert lof*,[13] printed in the preliminary pages of that poem in 1634 (one of the illustrations of this prestigious publication is an etching by Rembrandt). Herckmans' work became an important source of information for Barlaeus. In Brazil, he had been a member of the High Council in Pernambuco, and, afterwards, governor of Tamarica and Rio Grande. In 1643, he was vice-admiral on Brouwer's voyage to Chile and took over command when Brouwer died. A year later he died in Recife. In his *History*, Barlaeus incorporated parts of Herckmans' official reports (such as the 'Beschryving van Parayba'[14]) in a Latin adaptation.

---

[10] Full titles of these works are: *Argo Batava, inscripta virtuti, ac fortunae, fortissimi, felicissimique herois Petri Heinii* (Leiden, 1629); *Auriacus Triumphans, sive in victam potentissimi Hispaniarum regis, in Freto Britannico, classem poemation. Ad Celsissimum Auransiorum* [sic] *Principem, Fredericum Hendricum* (Amsterdam, 1639); *Laurus Flandrica. Sive in expugnationem validissimi Flandriae Propugnaculi, quod Cataractam (vulgo Sassam) Gandavensem vocant, auspiciis potentissimorum Federati Belgii, ordd. ductu armisque celsissimi Principis Frederici Henrici, Arausionensium Principis, Comitis Nassaviae, &c.* (Amsterdam, 1644).

[11] *Momenta desultoria. Poëmatum libri XII* (Leiden, 1644).

[12] *Medicea Hospes, sive descriptio publicae gratulationis, qua serenissimam augustissimamque reginam, Mariam de Medicis, excepit Senatus populusque Amstelodamensis* (Amsterdam, 1638).

[13] *Der zee-vaert lof. Handelende vande gedenckwaerdighste zeevaerden met de daeraanklevende op en onderganghen der voornaemste heerschappijen der gantscher wereld. Zedert haere beginselen tot op den dagh van huyden. In VI Boeken beschreven* (Amsterdam, 1634).

[14] MS Algemeen Rijksarchief, The Hague, Inv. Oude West-Indische Compagnie, Kamer Zeeland bundel 46.

V. MAP OF A PART OF BRAZIL AND THE CARIBBEAN SEA
Engraving by Theodorus de Bry (1592) (see page vii of this book)

'FAMAE NASSOVIORUM STUDIOSUS'

In 1644, Barlaeus wrote a poem for Johan Maurits who returned to the Netherlands after seven years in Brazil (*Mauritius redux*).[15] Johan Maurits's expedition to Brazil is pictured as part of the national struggle against Philip IV, King of Spain. The poem is full of vivid descriptions of the great distance, the blazing sun, the savage natives, and the coveted sugar. It ends with an exhortation to the Dutch authorities to fulfil their obligations to this colony.

Within the circle of Johan Maurits, Barlaeus already had many friends, including Constantyn Huygens, secretary of the stadtholder Frederik Hendrik, and personal friend of Johan Maurits. Their extensive correspondence and exchange of poems are witness to this. Piso thanked Barlaeus in a letter of September 1645 for his help in securing a job, and in a postscript, he conveys the greetings of Johan Maurits and Huygens. Plante wrote two laudatory poems when Barlaeus suddenly died in 1648.[16]

Barlaeus expressed his opinion about the Dutch policy in South America for the first time in his preface of Herrera's *Novus orbis* (1622), where he says that the conquest of South America would be no less profitable than honourable.[17] And in his letter of September 1, 1633, to Godefridus van Haestrecht we read:

> Divinator non sum, sed is mihi videtur esse astrorum aspectus: nisi pacem nobis largiatur Hispanus, carebit intra triennium Brasilia sua & suavissimis cannis.[18]

> I cannot tell the future, but I think this is written in the stars: if the Spaniards do not offer us peace, they will lose their Brazil and their sweetest sugar within three years.

Such ideas must have had Johan Maurits's sympathy. Barlaeus, in his turn, must have been attracted by the vigorous humanism and tolerance of the circle of Johan Maurits, who (if only because of the trading interest) respected the feelings of the Indians, Catholics and even the Jews in Brazil. In a letter of December 1639, in which Barlaeus presented a copy of his poem on the battle of the Downs to the Count, he compares the military successes of the Dutch in their war against Spain to those of Johan Maurits against the same enemy in the New World.

A few years later, when Barlaeus started work on his *History*, Johan Maurits and even the authorities of the West India Company gave him every support, placing documents at his disposal and allowing him to interview various people. We have, however, no proof dat Johan Maurits commissioned the *History*. The following letter, in which Johan Maurits asked Barlaeus to *bargain* with the publisher for copies for his friends, suggests that Johan Maurits did not finance the publication,

---

[15] *Mauritius redux. Sive gratulatio ad excellentissimum & illustrissimum Comitem, I. Mauritium, Comitem Nassaviae, Cattimeliboci ac Dietziae, Bilsteinii Dominum, Brasiliae terra marique praefectum, &c. Cum ex orbe Americano in Europaeum sospes appulisset* (Amsterdam, 1644).

[16] MS Leiden University Library, Pap. 2; reproduced in Pies (op. cit. n. 3), pp. 154–5.

[17] Antonio de Herrera (Tordesillas), *Novus orbis, sive descriptio Indiae Occidentalis, auctore Antonio de Herrera ... Metaphraste C. Barlaeo ... Accesserunt & aliorum Indiae Occidentalis descriptiones ...* (Amsterdam, 1622), fo. *3: '... [Indiae Occidentalis terrae] quibus imperare non minus utile quam gloriosum foret.'

[18] C. Barlaeus, *Epistolarum liber ...* (Amsterdam, 1667), Ep. 212, p. 450.

but that the initiative came from the printer, Joannes Blaeu.[19]

> Mijn Heer. Ick sende U. Ed. mits desen weer het gedeelte van de Brasiliaense Historie,
> dewelcke een ijeder een, voornamentlick die geene, so desen staeltjes gesien hebben, met
> groot verlangen verwachten: twijfele oock niet U. Ed. sal sorge dragen, dat het geheele
> werck metten eersten moge aen 't licht comen, en voor de goede vrienden, soo veel
> exemplaren bedongen worden, als mogelick is. Waertoe mij verlatende, sal U. Ed. in de
> goddelicke protectie bevelen en altoos verblijven. Mijn Heer U. Ed. gantz dienstwillige
> Diener J. Maurice Conte de Nassau. Haeg den 18 april 1647.

> Dear Sir, I return to you the part of the history of Brazil, which book everyone, especially
> those who have seen these samples, awaits with great expectation. I do not doubt that you
> will make certain that the entire work will be published at the first opportunity, and that as
> many copies for our good friends will be bargained for as is possible. I put my trust in you
> and I will commend you to the divine protection and always remain your obedient servant,
> Johan Maurits, Count of Nassau. The Hague, the 18th of April 1647.

AIM AND STRUCTURE OF THE *HISTORY*

Now we come to discuss the structure of the *History*. After the dedication to Johan
Maurits, Barlaeus sets out his aims: against the background of the Dutch war of
liberation against Spain, he wants to describe the history of Brazil, restricting
himself to the period of Johan Maurits's governorship (1637–44); his second aim
is the praise of that great patriot and the preservation of his name for posterity.
Dealing with the previous history of Brazil, the author gives a concise description
of the country. After Johan Maurits's departure to Brazil, his first actions are
reported: the battle at Porto Calvo, and other events in 1637. Barlaeus then
discusses the interior affairs, and Johan Maurits's official journey to Parayba and
Rio Grande. These regions are treated extensively. Then several setbacks are
mentioned: the failed assault on the Bahía de Todos os Santos, and admiral Jol's
unsuccessful attack on the Spanish treasure-fleet, followed by an account of
internal affairs. The historian shows his objectivity in describing the conflict
between Johan Maurits and the Polish general Artichewsky, who led the Dutch
army, portraying Johan Maurits as a honourable man, without failing to do justice
to Artichewsky. Barlaeus is one of the few Dutch historians to value Artichewsky's contribution.[20] The next subject of the *History* is the adapted version of A.
van der Dussen's report on Brazil to the West India Company, the 'Rapport van
den staet der geconquesteerde landen in Brasijl, gedaen door d'Heer Adriaen van
der Dussen aen de vergaderinghe der XIX ter Camer Amsterdam, den 4 april
1640.'[21] What follows is a description of Vrijburg, Olinda, Mauritsstad and Boa
Vista; and next of the Spanish preparations of 1639, which led to the four-day

---

[19] MS Leiden University Library, Pap. 1b.

[20] See J. C. M. Warnsinck's preface on Artichewsky in Joannes de Laet, *Iaerlyck verhael van de
verrichtinghen der geoctroyeerde West-Indische Compagnie in derthien boecken*, 4 vols., eds. S. P.
l' Honoré Naber & J. C. M. Warnsinck, Werken uitgegeven door de Linschoten-vereniging, 34, 35,
37, 40 (The Hague, 1931–37), see vol. iv, p. lxviii. In his opinion Barlaeus's objectivity is all the
more praiseworthy for his writing the book on Johan Maurits's commission; it can however not be
proved that Johan Maurits commissioned the *Historia* (op. cit. n. 8).

[21] MS Algemeen Rijksarchief, The Hague, Inv. Oude West-Indische Compagnie, Kamer Zeeland
bundel 46.

naval battle off the coast of Brazil (12, 13, 14 and 17 January 1640), and a comparison with the battle of the Downs (21 October 1639). Then comes the history of Jol's and Lichthart's failed undertaking against the Spanish treasure-fleet, and also the description of an eclipse of the sun. After this, Barlaeus relates how the Portuguese in Portugal threw off the Spanish yoke, and how they made overtures to the Dutch in Brazil. The adapted version of a report on the Tapuyans by Johan Rab van Waldeck follows. Finally the author discusses Johan Maurits's honourable discharge, and evaluates the measures taken by Johan Maurits during his governorship. The entire story of 333 pages is written without any division into chapters or sections. A reprint of the poem *Mauritius redux* is added as bonus.

VOSSIUS'S RULES FOR SEVENTEENTH-CENTURY HISTORIOGRAPHERS

De Boer's rebuke to Barlaeus because of the lack of factual precision in his speech on the battle of the Downs, can easily be applied to the *History*. Indeed, to a modern historian, it may not seem particularly useful, as facts and praise easily succeed each other, and many passages show subjectivity and are full of superstition.

But if we look for Barlaeus's motivation in writing his *History* as it is, we will find that seventeenth-century historians had different ideas about the aims of historiography. Here our best guide is Gerardus J. Vossius, Barlaeus's *collega proximus*. In his *Ars historica*, Vossius defined history as the knowledge of facts of which it is meet to preserve the memory, if one is to live well and happily.[22] And to achieve this aim, one should not just set down factual information about people. Description of comets and the animal behaviour that seem to predict the future are also considered to be suitable. The same is true for praise of heroic figures. Vossius also quotes Pliny: 'It seems to me a particularly splendid achievement not to allow those who deserve immortality to sink into oblivion.'[23] The main purpose of historiography is to demonstrate the significance of divine rule, and in this context, it is the task of the historian to encourage virtue: 'Here one is principally taught virtue and exhorted to virtue.'[24] Therefore, to Vossius it is no drawback when panegyric and historical facts are combined together in a historical work, even though Aristotle had clearly laid down the division between poetry and history in his *Poetics*.[25]

DESCRIPTION OF BRAZIL: THE COUNTRY AND ITS INHABITANTS

Barlaeus's hand as historian and editor can be seen in a long passage at the beginning of the *History*, in which he describes the country and its inhabitants (pp.

---

[22] Gerardus J. Vossius, *Ars historica, sive de historia, & historices natura, historiaeque scribendae praeceptis, commentatio . . . Editio secunda . . . locupletata* (first edition, 1623; Leiden, 1653), p. 15.

[23] Pliny, *Epistulae*, v. 8; quoted by Vossius (op. cit. n. 22), p. 24.

[24] Vossius (op. cit. n. 22), p. 25.

[25] See C. S. M. Rademaker, *Gerardus Vossius, Geschiedenis als Wetenschap*, Geschiedenis van de Wijsbegeerte in Nederland, ix (Baarn, 1992)), 25 en 31; and about the theoretical and practical works on history by Vossius, see: Nicholas Wickenden, *G. J. Vossius and the Humanist Concept of History*, Respublica literaria Neerlandica, viii (Assen, 1993).

20–3). It is largely based on Petrus Bertius's text from 1600, which Barlaeus had appended to his 1622 Latin adaptation of Herrera's description of the West Indies. By cutting parts and adding new elements from recent travel accounts, by stylistic embellishment and a carefully thought-out structure, an entirely new text was born. Barlaeus's followed the method of ancient geographers, as he had done before in his *Italiae descriptio*.[26] In this description of various Italian towns, as a rule, twelve descriptive features can be distinguished: the etymology of the name of the town or region; the location and shape of the town; its foundation; praise by ancient writers; its history in antiquity; its history in modern times; agriculture and industry; buildings, with special interest in inscriptions; monasteries; famous persons; nearby villages; and, finally, demographical particulars.

Since there were fewer sources available about the New World than there were on Italy, which had been often described in Antiquity and the Renaissance, Barlaeus was unable to incorporate all the twelve descriptive features in his *History of Johan Maurits's Achievements in Brazil*. However, borrowing from Spanish geographers and using his own common sense, he managed to give his work historical dimension. This can be seen in the discussion of the introductory passages below.

Barlaeus first sketches the geographical location of Brazil (p. 20): 'On the western side, Brazil faces at considerable distances the wild coast of the Caribbean, Peru, which is the most noble of the provinces of the New World, and high mountain ranges. To the south there are unknown regions, islands, seas and straits. The eastern shore is washed by the Atlantic Ocean, the northern by the Northern Ocean. The Portuguese define Brazil as the country between the river Maranhaõ and the estuary of the Silver River or Rio de la Plata.' Then Barlaeus goes on to describe the shape of the country: it looks like an inverted triangle, with its base straddling the equator and the north, and its tip pointing to the south. For this information he quotes the Spanish geographer Nicolaus de Oliveira. 'It is wrong to believe that these people or that all Americans are aboriginal, because we are assured that all mankind has sprung from Asian ancestors. Who the first inhabitants were, and how they got here from the Old World, whether through the Anian [Bering] Strait, or an overland route from Europe over the North Pole, or crossing the islands in the north, or by way of Atlantis (which lay near and opposite the Strait of Gibraltar, and which some people on the basis of what Plato writes in the *Critias* and *Timaeus* take to be America), or whether they were driven there by a storm, is not certain.' Barlaeus does not wish to voice an opinion on this subject himself. Vincent Pinson and Diego Lopez discovered this country for Ferdinand and Isabella of Spain; Pedro Alvarez Cabral and Amerigo Vespucci for the king of Portugal. The territory is very pleasant and healthy because of its moderate climate. The proof of this is the longevity of the people: some become a hundred years old. There is only a moderate variation in temperature, but the difference in rainfall and the general stability of the weather is substantial. Barlaeus illustrates Brazil's location in the manner of contemporary geographers, describing the country in relation to the position of other continents:

---

[26] Full title: *Nova et accurata Italiae hodiernae descriptio* (Amsterdam, 1626).

Incolae Antoeci sunt Hispanis, Mauris, Aethiopibus; Perioeci Afrorum extremis & Iavensibus; Antipodes Aureae Chersonesi populis.

The inhabitants of Brazil are 'antoeci' [i.e. they live opposite] to the Spaniards, the Mauretanians and the Ethiopians; they are 'perioeci' to the South African people and the Javanese [i.e. they live on the same latitude]; they are antipodes[27] of the people of Chersonesus Aurea [= Malaysia.][28]

(p.21:) The most important products of Brazil are sugar and red dye-wood. (...) Here, too, the historian seizes upon the opportunity to make a comparison with ancient Greece: 'Nature there has concealed that sugar in long canes, from which the sweetest and tastiest juice, stronger than Attic honey, is expressed, then boiled in metal vats and quickly moulded into cone or pyramid-shaped loaves, or once the thickest syrup has been extracted it is left to be made into granular sugar.' He then describes the Portuguese sugar factories, the *ingenhos*. (...) His description of the language of the Indians is rather naive. Like Petrus Bertius before him, he repeats Maffeius's conjecture that the Indian language did not have the letters *F*, *L* and *R*, because they did not possess the concepts of *fides*, *lex* and *rex*.[29] After this, the inhabitants are described: Some are uncouth, some are gentle. Some are white, some are dark. Men and women go around naked, except in the region of San Vincente, where the people are more sophisticated and wear wild (p. 22:) animal skins. Their strong bodies, they paint with colours, or smear with the black sap of the *Genipapus* apple. And they ornament themselves with birds' feathers of various colours. (...) They have no religion, although they venerate thunder and lightning. (...) They are polygamous and often divorce.

Barlaeus had mixed feelings: on the one hand, he depicts the Indians as powerful children of nature; on the other, as an uncivilized people, useless for trade and industry. Statements about their customs are sometimes put in perspective by a comparison with the situation at home:

They do not treat their wives badly, but look after them, except when they are drunk, which among the Dutchmen is not infrequent either.

Uxores non malè habent, sed curant, nisi potu alienata mente, quod & Belgis non infre-quens.[30]

MIRACULOUS SIGNS

It is interesting (and in line with Vossius's rules) that Barlaeus mentions omens, although he clearly does not share the general belief in them. In the following passage about the eclipse of the sun, he gives a further explanation for this.

Incidit in finem Anni quadragesimi supra millesimum & sexcentesimum Eclipsis Solaris, quae totum penè Solem Brasiliensium oculis eripuit. Quod noto, non tanquam rem miram his seculis, quibus rerum istarum caussae innotuere, verùm quia in omen conveniens à

---

[27] On the terms 'antoeci', 'perioeci' and 'antipodes', see J. B. Harley & D. Woodward, *The history of cartography*, vol. i (Chicago, 1987), 163.

[28] See the world map and the eleventh map of Asia in Cl. Ptolemaeus, *Geographiae libri octo*, ed. P. Bertius (Leyden, 1618).

[29] Ioannes P. Maffeius S.J., *Historiarum Indicarum libri XVI ... Accessit Ignatii Loiolae vita* (Cologne, 1590); see p. 76 on the letters of the Brazilian alphabet.

[30] Barlaeus, *Historia* (op. cit. n. 8), p. 22.

benevolis civibus accepta fuit. Illis puta, qui Principibus coelestem favorem & Numinis indulgentiam ex siderum observatione promittere amant. Hi vota sua sperantis erigebant & hanc aetherei luminis privationem, Hispanici fulgoris in his terris occasum defectumque interpretabantur.[31]

At the end of the year 1640 an eclipse of the sun occurred in Brazil in which the sun was almost completely obscured from the gaze of the Brazilians. I record this not so much because this is remarkable in these times, when we have learned the causes of these phenomena, but because it was interpreted by well-wishing citizens as a favourable omen. Namely by them who love to predict celestial favour and divine indulgence for princes on the basis of observation of the stars. They expressed their best wishes and interpreted this darkness as predicting the downfall and defeat of the Spanish overlords.

BARLAEUS'S STYLE AND HIS PRAISE OF JOHAN MAURITS

In his description of Brazil as discussed above, Barlaeus's style is sober and to the point. Elsewhere, when the author tries to influence his reader, he often uses tripartitions and ciceronian periods. This is especially true when Johan Maurits's merits are praised. The style is accommodated to this lofty aim. Short and long sentences alternate. The involved grammatical structure sometimes adopted is clear from the following example:

> Latuere haec loca Veteres, ut ne quidem famam sui ad nos tot seculis transmiserint. Quae Plato in Critia & Timaeo ex Solonis, hic ex relatu Sacerdotum Aegyptiorum perhibet de Atlantica Insula extra Fretum Herculeum posita, in quam paucorum ex Hispania dierum sit trajectus, quae Europae Asiaeque par magnitudine, Africam Aegyptum usque, Europam ad Tyrrhenum mare armis possederit, auri argentique sit ferax, utpote fabulis & ubere falso permixta, Americam segniter, Utopiae aliquod regnum & luxuriantis in Platone ingenii commenta certius monstrant.[32]

> To the Ancients these regions were hidden, so that they were unknown to us, too, for many centuries. What Plato says in his *Critias* and *Timaeus*, on Solon's authority, which the latter gets from the sacred books of the Egyptians, about the island of Atlantis lying outside the Strait of Gibraltar, that it could be reached in a few days from Spain, rivals Europe and Asia in size, possessed Africa up to Egypt, and Europe up to the Tyrrhenian sea by force of arms, and is rich in gold and silver—all this has become so interwoven with fables and the rich fruits of fancy, that it shows at the most a resemblance to America, while it certainly is an Utopia, or something sprung from Plato's rich imagination.

Another characteristic of Barlaeus's style is the sudden shift from classical to contemporary history, and from the events in Brazil to the hostilities in Europe. Here, for example, is the conclusion of his account of Johan Maurits's four sea battles before the coast of Brazil:

> Sic dissipatâ & fugata validissima Classe, fidem fecit Nassovius nondum cum Scipionibus, Regulis, Cimonibus, Duilliisque ac Pompejis exstinctam esse fortitudinem. Et ut recentia memorem, post victum mari nostro interno Bossusium, Britannico Sidoniae Ducem, Flandrico Spinolam & nuper sub Dunis Brittannicis Ocquendum, haec gloriae Foederatorum accessit illustris victoria. Qua Hispanorum in Orbe occiduo vim fregimus, tot navium stupendum apparatum elusimus, spem recuperandi has terras labefactavimus & potentiae Belgarum illudere parantibus justae defensionis instrumenta ostendimus.[33]

---

[31] Barlaeus, *Historia* (op. cit. n. 8), p. 196.
[32] Barlaeus, *Historia* (op. cit. n. 8), pp. 12–13.
[33] Barlaeus, *Historia* (op. cit. n. 8). p. 171.

By routing and dispersing this mighty fleet, Johan Maurits has proved that bravery was not lost with heroes like the Scipios, Regulus, Cimo, Duillius and Pompeius. And to remind you of what has happened more recently, after vanquishing Bossu in our own waters, the Duke of Medina Sidonia on the English coast, Aytona on the Slaak and only recently d'Oquendo near the English Downs, this illustrious victory adds to the glory of the country. With this we have broken Spain's power in the West, eluded the armada, shattered their hope of regaining these territories, and we have shown the power of a just defence to those who tried to mock the power of the Netherlands.

Such praise for Johan Maurits is maintained till the end of the book. All criticism is dismissed,[34] and significantly the work ends with a sentence in which the author summarizes his appreciation for Johan Maurits's character and achievements:

Mauritius horum securus, consilio suo & suorum grandibusque exemplis nixus, non opinione plebeja aut absentium vaga & inconsulta meditatione in Barbaro orbe, pacis bellique temporibus, inter apertos occultosque hostes, terra ac mari eas res gessit, quae seculo dignissimae, Foederatis, Nassoviis, ipsi gloriosae, Societati utiles fuerunt. Ut, si verè aestimare volumus, non Comiti Praefectura, sed Praefecturae Comes datus fuerit, nec administratae ab ipso Brasiliae ullos, praeterquam hostes, poenitere possit.[35]

Johan Maurits, not bothered about this, keeping his own counsel and that of his men, and following great examples, but not popular opinion or the vague and irresponsible considerations of those who were not present, has accomplished in a barbarous world, in times of peace and war, in the midst of declared and secret enemies, on land and sea, what has been an ornament to the century, glorious to the country, the Nassaus and himself, and useful to the Company. So we can say in truth that the territory was not given to the governor, but the governor to the territory, and that nobody except the enemy could complain about his administration of Brazil.

It is with sentences like these that Barlaeus proves himself to be a true historiographer in the tradition advocated by Vossius. Alternating panegyric with historical objectivity, he preserves for posterity the memory of a great man.

---

[34] For instance, the criticism from the Governors of the West India Company. See Barlaeus, *Historia* (op. cit. n. 8), p. 333.

[35] Barlaeus, *Historia* (op. cit. n. 8), p. 333.

GRYPHIUS IN ITALY

PETER SKRINE*

At the beginning of June 1644 a small party left The Hague on the first stage of a journey that was to last over three years and prove to be of great importance in the artistic development of one of its members, the German poet and dramatist Andreas Gryphius. The party consisted of two or three young noblemen, all probably of Pomeranian extraction, including the poet's somewhat younger friend Wolfgang von Popschitz, the poet himself, and a certain Wilhelm or Guilhelm Schlegel, son of a prosperous Pomeranian merchant from the port of Stettin. Schlegel had been put in touch with Gryphius by a physician called Origanus, who was a colleague of the poet at the University of Leyden and a friend of the doctor-poet Paul Fleming, one of his major German contemporaries. Schlegel needed a suitable travelling companion for the tour he was planning, and Gryphius seized the opportunity thus offered him to visit distant countries and thereby enhance what his obituarist and first biographer Baltzer Siegmund von Stosch[1] calls his 'civilische prudentz', a term which might be best understood to mean social polish and *savoir-vivre*, as well as an understanding of government and political institutions. An agreement was drawn up between the merchant's son and the scholar poet. The bargain struck, the peregrination could begin.

No doubt Gryphius was ready for a change. He was twenty-seven years old, intensely gifted, erudite and introspective, yet observant, too, and interested in what went on around him. The lyric poet was already formed before he set out—witness the publication of his first collection of sonnets at Lissa in Poland in 1637—but not the man of the world and his literary projection, the comic dramatist. The three comedies he was later to write, and which make him one of Germany's finest if least appreciated comic writers, needed first-hand exposure to the frets and foibles of humankind which, like any observant traveller, he was bound to experience *en route* and which probably proved a more fertile source of inspiration than any of the plays he may or may not have seen in the playhouses of the cities through which he passed.

On 3 July Gryphius and his party reached Paris. As was then the practice, they probably travelled by barge and boat as much as by coach, but it is not known

---

* Department of German, University of Bristol, England.
[1] Stosch's funeral oration and obituary, entitled *Dank= und Denck=Seule des Andreae Gryphii*, was published in 1665, the year after the poet's death. It is reprinted in *Text und Kritik. Zeitschrift für Literatur. 7/8: Andreas Gryphius*, ed. Heinz Ludwig Arnold (Munich, 1980), together with a German translation of Johannes Theodor Leubscher's Latin life (1702) and Christian Stieff's brief German biography (1737). Both later accounts owe much to Stosch.

what route they took, only that on the way they visited 'viel herrliche Orte', a remark which suggests that they passed through the great cities of what was then the Spanish Netherlands.[2] Our information about what they saw when they got to Paris is almost equally scant and speculation has tended to fill the picture out.[3] What is recorded is that Gryphius, who was to accept the post of *syndicus* or chief legal adviser to the principality of Glogau on his return to Silesia, made a point of visiting the city's civic sights, no doubt with a view to gaining an insight into the way Europe's major metropolis was run. Stosch tells us that he visited the 'Rath und Zeughaus', that is the Hôtel de Ville in what was then known as the Place de la Grève, a building begun in 1533 to plans by Domenico Bernabei, known as 'Boccadoro', and burnt down during the Commune of 1871, and the Arsenal, which had been converted for safety's sake under Louis XIII and since 1631 housed a court established by Richelieu to try special cases such as that of Fouquet in 1664, the year of Gryphius's death. He also visited the palace (no doubt the Louvre) and royal gardens, and other 'raritäten', but these drew his attention less than the rare editions in the library of Cardinal Mazarin. This had opened its doors to scholars as recently as 1643,[4] and news of this fact had doubtless reached Gryphius in Leyden. Indeed the prospect of seeing 'des Herrn Cardinals herrliche und überglauben zugeputzte Bibliothec' may well have prompted him to accept Schlegel's offer. Stosch observes that it was open to the public in the middle of the day, so that he was able to enjoy it to the full.

At this point Stosch also tantalisingly mentions the fact that Gryphius kept a diary of his journey. Like his other personal and posthumous papers it has not survived, and this has left room for speculation where the hard facts would be so much more interesting. But already a keynote of his peregrination has been touched upon: his love of books. After five years of intense academic study, the invitation to leave academe behind and set off with Wilhelm Schlegel and his four charges may well have seemed to Gryphius an almost Faustian release. But unlike Goethe's Faust, surfeited with learning and hungry for real life, Gryphius remained as curious and scholarly as ever. The love of books had drawn him to his patron Georg Schönborner and, six months after his death, to the new university of Leyden. In the summer of 1638 he had accompanied Schönborner's sons to that

---

[2] See E. S. Bates, *Touring in 1600: A Study in the Development of Travel as a Means of Education* (London, 1911, repr. London, 1987), 182–7, for an account of means of communication and transport in the Netherlands, France and Italy. 'No one who knew his business as a sight-seer omitted Antwerp', Bates observes on p. 122.

[3] This is particularly true of Willi Flemming's treatment of Gryphius's visits to France and Italy in his biographical study of the poet, *Andreas Gryphius. Eine Monographie*, Sprache und Literatur, 26 (Stuttgart, 1965). For more circumspect accounts see Marian Szyrocki, *Andreas Gryphius. Sein Leben und Werk* (Tübingen, 1964), 31–7 and Eberhard Mannack, *Andreas Gryphius*, Sammlung Metzler, 76 (Stuttgart, 1968), 14–15.

[4] Christan Stieff, writing in 1737, identifies the library visited by Gryphius in Paris as that of the Cardinal and Duke of Richelieu, a detail that has been taken over into subsequent accounts. For the Mazarin library see Emile Leroy, *Guide pratique des bibliothèques de France* (Paris: Editions des bibliothèques nationales, 1937), p. 101, and Alfred Franklin, *Histoire de la bibliothèque Mazarine depuis sa fondation jusqu'à nos jours* (second revised edition, Paris, 1901).

new Mecca of European learning, where he was soon immersed in the study of
zoology and anatomy as well as law; from 1639 to 1644 he supervised, conducted
classes and lectured in a wide variety of subjects ranging from mathematics,
metaphysics, natural philosophy and astronomy to chiromancy, and, more
appropriate here, the antiquities of Rome. In 1643 he gave a public lecture on the
vanity of all things and a class on practical anatomy. One could easily picture him
in a Rembrandt painting. By 1644 his erudition, as his obituarist says, had become
incomparable. Book collections were to draw him throughout his travels.

When the party left Paris is uncertain, but it must have been by late July 1644,
for it took six days to travel from Paris to Angers. They were certainly there in
August, for a sonnet (no. 16 of Book 2) dated 14 August records his impression
of Queen Henrietta Maria on the occasion of her entry into that city on that day,
its tone of reverential admiration culminating in three lines that convey the public
presence and private grief of King Charles's consort with a nobility worthy of Van
Dyke:

> Schaw' an die Majestät die in den Augen spielt
> Das Antlitz das entdeckt / die sorgen die es fühlt /
> Und lerne / das was hoch / auch schmacht' in höher grawen.

How long the party lingered in Angers and its largely Protestant vicinity and why
they did so is a mystery: they did not reach the next recorded stage of their
journey until November 1645, when they moved on southwards to Marseilles. No
doubt his four aristocratic charges were happily contained at the famous Academy
of Equitation at Angers, which in those days was a magnet for Germans, Poles,
Danes and Flemings, as well as Scots and Englishmen.[5] He for his part is much
more likely to have been attracted to the congenial ambiance of Saumur, where
Protestants and Catholics co-existed on good terms and talked of higher things.
Yet the Angers year 1644–1645—this missing year in Gryphius's relatively well-
documented life—gives pause for thought. Could Gryphius have been engaged in
activities of a confidential nature to which he never alluded later? And if so, what
might they have been? There is evidence that in Leyden he was acquainted with
Princess Elizabeth, the daughter of the Winter King and Queen, grand-daughter
of James I and dedicatee in 1644 of Descartes' *Principia Philosophiae*. A sonnet
he later addressed to her conveys more, perhaps, than just respectful familiarity:

> Wie offt hab ich verhofft / Durchlauchtes Licht der Welt /
> Und Wunder aller Zeit / zu knien vor ihren Füßen /
> Und Sie / wiewol vorhin / in tieffster Pflicht zu grüßen.
> Umsonst! weil Land und Stand mich als in Bande stellt[6]

This respectful tone is present again in the dedication to her of the second

---

[5] An informative account of life and conditions for foreign students in Angers in the 1650s is
provided by Duncan Thomson, *A Virtuous & Noble Education* (Edinburgh: The Board of Trustees
of the National Galleries of Scotland, 1971). This describes the travels and education of the sons
of the third Earl of Lothian in Holland and France during the years 1651 to 1657.

[6] Posthumous sonnets, no. 46. See Hugh Powell, 'Gryphius and the culture of his time', in
Gryphius, *Cardenio und Celinde*, ed. H. Powell (Leicester, 1961), pp. xx–xxiv. Quotations are taken
from Andreas Gryphius, *Gesamtausgabe der deutschsprachigen Werke*, ed. H. Powell (Tübingen,
1963–), here Volume iii, pp. 117–18.

edition of *Olivetum*, his Latin epic on the subject of Christ's agony (Lissa, 1648).
Now, in Angers, he had set eyes on the exiled Queen of Charles I, the later hero
of his *Carolus Stuardus*, a topical political tragedy that is singularly well
informed, as Günter Berghaus has demonstrated.[7] It is therefore tempting to
speculate whether its future author was in some way involved in covert dealings
connected with the House of Stuart, in the affairs of which France, Germany and
the Netherlands were all caught up. Might Angers have been the base for a secret
mission to Holland or even England? It has certainly been claimed that in 1646
he was the bearer of some message to Venice, where Elizabeth's brother Philip
was negotiating the provision of reinforcements to help against the Turks, a
mission understandably close to the heart of a descendant of the author of
Lepanto.[8] We should not overlook the fact that it was no exception for people of
his kind and station to be entrusted with confidential messages and missions.

On leaving Angers, Gryphius and his party progressed to Marseilles where they
embarked for Florence. The exact time the voyage took is not known, but they had
landed in Italy by 19 December 1645, for on that day the poet was viewing the
art collection of the Grand Duke of Tuscany, Ferdinand II of Medici. Then, early
in 1646, they reached Rome. Significantly it was here, and not in Florence, that
the most important cultural encounters of his peregrination were to take place. No
wonder then that here poetry takes over. It can provide deeper insights than the
bald accounts the obituarists provide.

Five sonnets record Gryphius's encounter with Rome (nos. 17 and 39–42 in
Book II, 1650), backed up by five epigrams (nos. 79, 80 and 83–85 in Book III of
the *Epigrams*, 1663) and two further epigrams in Book I (nos. 55 and 73). The
first sonnet explicitly to mention Rome is no. 17. Addressed to Wilhelm Schlegel,
it takes up and adapts to the specific case of their impending journey themes and
images which Gryphius had already deployed to perfection in sonnet 6 of the so-
called Lissa collection under the title 'Vanitas, vanitatum, omnia vanitas'. This
poem and particularly its later revised version as no. 8 of Book II is the first word-
painting of its kind to have been created in German in the seventeenth century.
Gryphius evokes a landscape that is visual, almost tangible, yet at the same time
the complex metaphor for an insight that transcends locality and time. In this
symbolic landscape the frail promise of young life embodied in the shepherd boy
and the wild flower takes on an intense and lasting quality although, or perhaps
because, they are implicitly threatened by the oncoming storm or indeed the
clumsy boot of the poet onlooker anxious to find the flower again before it is too
late, and well aware that eternal values are of no consequence to most people. Out
of the landscape of this extraordinary poem , which seems to echo favourite
images of Poussin, who had reached Rome in 1624, the remains of ancient Rome
seem to rise up, verbal counterparts of the crumbling yet majestic ruins in so many

---

[7] Günter Berghaus, *Die Quellen zu Andreas Gryphius' Trauerspiel 'Carolus Stuardus': Studien
zur Entstehung eines historisch-politischen Märtyrerdramas der Barockzeit*, Studien zur deutschen
Literatur, 79 (Tübingen, 1984).

[8] See Peter Skrine, 'James VI & I and German Literature', *Daphnis. Zeitschrift für Mittlere
Deutsche Literatur*, xviii (1989), 1–57.

paintings of the time: one thinks of Paul Brill and his disciples, and particularly of Claude Lorrain's 'Pastoral Landscape with the Arch of Titus', with its close visual similarities to the poem.[9] Yet the vestiges of past grandeur are not even described in its lines. Their presence is conveyed by poetic statements of a wisdom inherited from antiquity, subtly presented in such a way that what we see first in our imaginations are thriving cities, then a piece of broken marble round which a flock of sheep are grazing, and finally a shattered inscription in praise of vanished glory.

Such was the Rome Gryphius no doubt expected to see, prepared as he was by the paintings and especially the engravings he had already seen of it which dwelt for preference on scenes such as his sonnet evoked. Sonnet 17 makes this clear. Offered to Schlegel on his name-day in lieu of a bunch of flowers, the circum- stances of its composition and the identity of its addressee make it a love poem, though not a homosexual one. Its opening and closing lines are a *jeu d'esprit* in which fidelity serves as the ribbon binding Schlegel's heart to his. But the centre of the poem is quite different in tone. As if stimulated by the opening flower image, Gryphius's old preoccupation with vulnerability and transience surfaces again in close conjunction with his favourite image of the millennial empire destroyed in a matter of hours. But now the impending journey leaves its traces in the text, for the ruins in the landscape are given an identity: Pergamus first, consumed in flames, then Rome itself, reduced to dust borne on the Tiber or blown by a wanton wind.

As Gryphius approached Rome in 1646, images of imperial decline and fall were uppermost in his mind. The sequence of four sonnets (Book ii. 39–42) may seem a meagre record of what then occurred. But the sonnet is a remarkable form in the hands of such a poet. Instead of pouring forth his thoughts on first beholding the Eternal City in a conventional manner—let alone in Latin—his sequence of Roman sonnets begins indirectly, obliquely almost, as if the subject were too imposing to be addressed head on. Instead, sonnet 39, entitled 'Auf einen ungeschickten Römer', gives vent to his exasperation with another tourist—maybe one of his four young aristrocratic charges—who claims that Rome has nothing to offer him, when he, the poet, sees relevance in everything around him. It is the portrait of a man fundamentally unsuited to any meaningful Roman holiday, a foil as it were to the poet himself, for whom every sight and stone had interest and meaning. The first line introduces a theme—the acquisition of wisdom—that is integral to Gryphius's Roman experience. The sonnet's obtuse tourist is surrounded by wisdom embedded in all that has survived the ravages of time and manifesting itself in everyday life as 'Scharfsinnigkeit', that 'acutezza' so prized by the baroque era: yet anyone looking at him would be unable to refrain from bursting into laughter at his 'Grobheit', his crass ignorance and dull stupidity.

The second sonnet in this 'Roman' sequence may seem almost equally oblique, but it is in fact much more specific. We sense that the cherished destination has

---

[9] Unlike Gryphius's poetry, Lorrain's painting figures in Walther Rehm's classic study, *Der Untergang Roms im abendländischen Denken. Ein Beitrag zur Geschichtsschreibung und zum Dekadenzproblem* (Leipzig, 1930; repr. Darmstadt, 1966).

been reached and that the poet is adapting to his new environment. It is addressed to 'Cleander' and in facetious mood sets out to answer his question:

Du fragst wie Bibulus die Zeit zu Rom vertreibe?

Bibulus, like the subject of the previous sonnet, is a direct antithesis of Cleander and by implication of the poet. He is characterized so vividly that it is hard, even in that age of convention in poetry, to think of him as not being based on a real-life model. Bibulus is uninterested in ancient inscriptions, books or statues and is equally indifferent to what is going on at the papal court: he is as closed to the cultural significance of the past as he is to current affairs. The Vatican, which amazes the poet, Bibulus ignores, as he does Rome's churches. Such touches are telling: they reveal that Gryphius, a staunchly Lutheran poet acutely conscious of the less attractive aspects of counter-Reformation activity in Silesia and elsewhere, was, like Milton seven years before him, able to draw a distinction between the Church of Rome (i.e. 'popery') and the Church in Rome, a divine and eternal institution. Milton had been there in 1638–39 at the height of the pontificate of Urban VIII: Gryphius saw the Rome of Innocent X, whose portrait by Velasquez, painted in 1650, is the quintessential icon of seventeenth-century papacy. But the contemporary politico-religious dimension escapes Bibulus; he also leaves scholars in peace, a touch from which we may deduce that Gryphius, always eager to add to his already copious knowledge, made a point of seeking them out.

In his life of the poet, Stieff tells us that in Rome he made the acquaintance of the Chevalier Borrhi, whom he calls the well-known chemist. But this is a retrospective view: when Gryphius met Giuseppe Francesco Bórri, he was only nineteen years old and still a pupil, albeit a precocious one, of Athanasius Kircher and Théophile Raynaud at the Collegio Romano, and had not yet turned into the quack and charlatan who criss-crossed seventeenth-century Europe, attaching himself to hypochondriac princes and potentates addicted to the practices of alchemy. Was Gryphius caught by the gaze of those green eyes? And was he trying to break their spell and exorcise memories of this experience when, in Amsterdam, on his way home to Germany, he plunged into the macabre gloom and emotional confusion of his drama *Cardenio und Celinde*? He also met Bórri's teacher, Kircher, the German Jesuit polymath, who had shown 'many singular courtesies' to John Evelyn when the latter visited Rome shortly before.[10] Evelyn's sojourn in Rome had lasted from 4 November 1644 to 18 May 1645, and it is therefore revealing to read his detailed impressions of the city as a background to Gryphius's own sparsely documented experience of it during the first four months of 1646. We may assume that a good deal of what Evelyn saw Gryphius saw, too. Both men were dependent on guide-books such as J.H. von Pflaumern's *Mercurius Italicus* (1628), which has been described as the best of the seventeenth-century guide-books to Italy, and Fioravante Martinelli's more specialized and up-to-date *Roma ricercata nel suo sito* (Rome, 1644), with fine illustrations by Dominique Barrière, which was actually published during Evelyn's residence in the city. Like other foreign visitors up until the twentieth century,

---

[10] *The Diary of John Evelyn*, ed. E. S. de Beer, 6 vols. (Oxford, 1955), vol. ii, pp. 212–405.

they were also very much dependent on the guides who catered for a cultured clientèle, such as the renowned Giovanni Alto, alias Hans Gross of Lucerne (*c.* 1577–1660), a member of the Swiss Guard, with whom Gryphius and his companions would have been able to converse without great difficulty. Gryphius's command of Latin made communication easy, especially with other scholars, but in the sonnet Bibulus not only disdains scholarship; unfortunately he also finds no 'Schauplatz' to his liking and is even deaf to song. This must surely be a reference to the remarkable flowering of dramatic and vocal music in seventeenth-century Rome that reached its perfection in the oratorios of Carissimi, the already illustrious and famous teacher of music at the German College in Rome, and which made such a lasting impression on contemporary visitors such as Francis Mortoft and Evelyn himself.[11]

> Wee heard here such sweete Musicke, that a man could not thinke his paines il spent, if he should come two thousand mile, if he were sure to be recompensed with nothing else, but to heare such melodious voyces,

Mortoft enthused. But Bibulus in Gryphius's sonnet is incapable of being ravished by such entertainment; indeed he is even capable of sleeping through the firework displays put on for the common people—a rare mention in the poetry of the time to the baroque delight in pyrotechnics. The only thing that keeps Bibulus in Rome is 'Albaner Wein', that wine better known today as Frascati.

Gryphius loved the gardens. One of the few personal details we know about his Roman sojourn is that on 1 March 1646 he visited Tusculum in the Alban Hills, the birthplace of the elder Cato and the favourite residence of Cicero, which must have been a recommendation in itself. On the way from Frascati to Tusculum, his guide would have pointed out the so-called ruins of Cicero's school and villa. But the greatest delight this excursion afforded him was the opportunity to set eyes on the Villa Aldobrandini and its already legendary gardens. Designed by Giovanni della Porta between 1598 and 1603 for Cardinal Pietro Aldobrandini, the nephew of Clement VIII, they were intended to be a modern counterpart of the best that Antiquity had enjoyed. Stosch tells us that Gryphius visited both the house and its 'delikatesten Gärte [*sic*]', gardens which, so he tells us, vied with those of the Hesperides—a comment in which we can for a moment perhaps hear the poet's own voice speaking. Their dramatic effect cannot have been lost on the emergent baroque playwright as he beheld the water theatre cut into the hillside at the rear of the villa, with its five niches filled with statuary and the fountains rising in front of them, their water-jets blending with the great cascade precipitating itself downwards to create a perfect rainbow when the sun shines out. Perhaps the classical associations of the location made the gardens of the Villa Aldobrandini all the more appealing, and perhaps it was of them that he was thinking when in

---

[11] *The Diary of Evelyn* (op. cit. n. 10), p. 233, and Francis Mortoft, *His Book, Being his Travels through France and Italy, 1658–1659*, ed. Malcolm Letts, Works issued by the Hakluyt Society, Sec. Series, lvii (London, 1925; repr. London, 1987). See also Howard E. Smither, *A History of Oratorio. Vol. i: The Oratorio in the Baroque Era: Italy, Vienna, Paris* (Chapel Hill, 1977), vol. i, pp. 118–19 and 145.

his third Roman sonnet, at the climax of his valedictory survey of the city, he singles out its gardens alongside its books and catacombs.

Sonnet 41, entitled 'Als Er aus Rom geschieden', is the finest of the Roman sonnets. Poetically it marks the summation of his Roman experience as well as a leave-taking, and it therefore deserves to be quoted in full:

> Ade! begriff der welt' Stadt der nichts gleich gewesen /
> Und nichts zu gleichen ist / In der man alles siht
> Was zwischen Ost vnd West / vnd Nord vnd Suden blüht,
> Was die Natur erdacht / was je ein Mensch gelesen.
> Du / derer Aschen man / nur nicht vorhin mit Bäsen
> Auff einen hauffen kährt / in der man sich bemüht
> Zu suchen wo dein grauß (fliht trüben Jahre! fliht /)
> Bist nach dem Fall erhöht / nach langem Ach / genäsen.
> Ihr Wunder der gemäld / jhr prächigen Palläst /
> Ob den die kunst erstarrt / du starck bewehrte Fest /
> Du Herrlichs Vatican / dem man nichts gleich kan bawen;
> Ihr Bücher, Gärten / grüfft'; Ihr Bilder / Nadeln / Stein /
> Ihr / die diß vnd noch mehr schliß't in die Sinnen eyn /
> Ade! Man kan euch nicht satt mit zwey Augen schawen.

Its complex text is imbued with the restrained grief of parting, yet perhaps surprisingly, it is no melancholy elegy even though its second quatrain does revert to the image of dust and its abstract connotation, transience ('fliht trüben Jahre! fliht!'). At the centre of the poem—the final line of the octet rather than the start of the sestet in conventional Petrarchan fashion—a new and different theme emerges, and the contemplative gloom of the words 'Fall' and 'Ach' gives way to a jubilant 'erhöht' and 'genesen' as the tonality modulates to the major key. Gryphius's Rome is a Rome resuscitated, its artistic life in the present a triumph over decadence and decay. In a burst of gratitude and enthusiasm the poet recalls the wonders he has seen, and we realize that the verbs 'sehen' and 'schauen' encapsulate Rome as fully and truly as the word 'adieu'. The momentous significance of this poem in the context of Gryphius's Roman experience and his philosophy of life cannot be emphasized enough. It is also clear that it breaks with the mood of Du Bellay's *Les Regrets* and *Les Antiquités de Rome*, written and published almost a century before. Whereas Du Bellay had lamented:

> Nouveau venu, qui cherches Rome en Rome
> Et rien de Rome en Rome n'aperçois,[12]

Gryphius takes his leave of a city that is still the 'epitome of the world', a city that not only was but still is incomparable and in which may be seen all a human being could ever wish to see. In the same sonnet (no. 3 in *Les Antiquités*) Du Bellay had gone on to write:

> Et ces vieux palais, ces vieux arcz que tu vois,
> Et ces vieux murs, c'est ce que Rome on nomme,

---

[12] Joachim Du Bellay, *Les Antiquités de Rome*, no. 3. The French poet's responses to Rome are described in K. Lloyd-Jones, 'Du Bellay's journey from *Roma Vetus* to *La Rome Neufve*', in: *Rome in the Renaissance, The City and the Myth: Papers of the Thirteenth Annual Conference of the Center for Medieval and Renaissance Studies*, ed. P. A. Ramsey, Medieval & Renaissance Texts and Studies, 18 (Binghampton, New York, 1982), pp. 301–19.

and this was no doubt what Gryphius had expected. But in his own sonnet the dust and ashes are swept to one side. Far from being just the heap of ruins for which he had mentally prepared himself, Gryphius's Rome was rising from its ashes and he, darkest of German poets, can only marvel at its new-found glories—its paintings and its palaces, its massive fortifications, its Vatican, incomparable in its splendour, its libraries and its gardens, its obelisks and statues, stones and catacombs. To these and everything else that has made a lasting impression on his senses he bids farewell:

> Ade! Man kan euch nicht satt mit zwey Augen schawen.

Two eyes are not enough to see Rome to the full. Gryphius has seldom if ever been compared to Goethe, but here his poetry is imbued with a sensuous quality that almost anticipates that great German visitor to Rome in the 1780s.

So far, so good. But that is not the end. Placed no doubt deliberately after his farewell to the City, the fourth and last of Gryphius's Roman sonnets opens up a very different dimension of his experience of Rome, and one which affected his sensibility deeply. Of all the sightseeing he undertook, it was his visit to *Roma subterranea* that made the most lasting impact on his creative imagination. Nowhere does he contrast more strikingly with Du Bellay before him or with Goethe after him than in this sonnet describing a visit to the catacombs. Neither the late-eighteenth-century Goethe nor the renaissance Du Bellay could conceivably have retained this as their most persistent and stimulating memory of the Eternal City, for neither of them had Gryphius's baroque need to respond to the challenge of the new Rome that was rising during the Counter-Reformation period on the dual foundations of its imperial past and the recently rediscovered heritage of the persecuted but divinely chosen early Christians. The rediscovery of the catacombs by Antonio Bosio (1575–1629) had begun in 1593, when his first expeditions took place.[13] But the findings of the Columbus of this subterranean world were not recorded in print until the posthumous publication of his *Roma sotterranea* in 1632 and the augmented Latin edition by Paolo Aringhi that followed it in 1651. For Gryphius, therefore, as for Evelyn, a visit to the catacombs was a novel experience; indeed for the German poet the descent into the netherworld where the early Christians had worshipped and been buried was an experience of the utmost personal importance. This is evident at once in the way he conveys the reality of the place and the actuality of his personal response. Yet his sonnet is in no way self-indulgently autobiographical or even descriptive: it is too short for that. Instead it seems more intent on articulating ideas. In the opening line the poet descends into the claustrophobic narrowness of the catacombs, and as he does so, his understanding of the early Christians grows. As the darkness closes in on him, and he ponders on their sufferings and on their deaths, an unexpected lightening of mood occurs, culminating in an eighth line whose jubilant praise of self-sacrifice possesses a distinct similarity to the sentiments of Corneille's exultant martyr-hero, Polyeucte, in the tragedy which had

---

[13] See James Stevenson, *The Catacombs. Rediscovered Monuments of Early Christianity*, Ancient Peoples and Places, 91 (London, 1978), 50–1.

been first performed and published shortly before Gryphius arrived in Paris. These vaults, the poet realises, contain the remains of countless men and women who rushed, metaphorically speaking, out of the darkness in which they hid from persecution into the bright light of death. This central line is followed by a sequence of paradoxes that could almost be called conceits and which border on the sublime cleverness of the metaphysicals, his English contemporaries: into these subterranean caverns the Church had to put down its roots and in their darkness its light had to be kindled; founded upon a rock—the divine pun that gave St Peter his name—the Church had to live and develop underground. Such symbolism had its own deep relevance for seventeenth-century Germany.

These images and ideas are taken up and explored further in an epigram (Book I. 73), which is a brilliant 12-line variation on the sonnet. It, too, takes us down into the subterranean vaults of the 'living dead', but it then culminates with three lines that raise a question mark over the building activity which Gryphius could see all around him in the Rome of his own day:

> Wir gehn mit Menschen umb: Drumb hört uns keine Leichen.
> Sie wohnten / schaw / wie tieff! Doch stig ihr Geist hinauff.
> Wir bawen hoch! Ach! Ach! Wohin sinckt unser Lauff.

Such lines capture the tension any sensitive visitor to Rome must feel between the here-and-now and the almost miraculous capacity of the past to regenerate itself and of the spirit to work its wonders. Was Gryphius perhaps thinking of Innocent X's grandiose project to make the Piazza Navona a memorial to his pontificate? He had begun to put his ideas into action the year before their arrival, and he was shortly to call in Borromini to advise him. Soon Borromini's St Agnes the Martyr would rise above the vestiges of Domitian's stadium, with Bernini's Fountain of the Four Rivers standing in front of it. Though Gryphius does not mention the Pope's ambitious undertaking, it must have left a profound impression on him, for nowhere was there a bolder attempt to recreate in the present the grandeur of the past.

The ideas germinating in Gryphius's mind during his descent into the catacombs fused with others which are expressed *in nuce* in some of the epigrams he composed at much the same time. For instance one on the ruins of the Coliseum (Book III. 80) presents them not as the scene of martyrdom, as one might expect, but as a place of entertainment; in a manner that anticipates Lohenstein the epigram turns on the word 'Spiel' as the poet muses that here where the famous Roman games used to take place, what he sees being played out are the tragedies ('die Traur=Spil') staged by Time itself. This epigram makes the link between his Roman experience and his own creative writing particularly clear. His own first martyr-tragedy, *Catharina von Georgien*, must have been taking shape in his mind as he toured the sights of Christian Rome. In it he dramatizes a near-contemporary subject—the subjugation of Christian Georgia by the Persia of Shah Abbas—drawn from the *Histoires tragiques de notre temps* by Claude Malingre, alias Sieur de Saint Lazare, published in Paris in 1635. But unlike his first play, *Leo Armenius*, or indeed Corneille's martyr masterpiece, *Polyeucte*, its central figure is a woman. But why should he have turned to a heroine of this kind? His Roman experience provides the answer. In his first book of *Epigrams*, which he no doubt arranged in careful order, the juxtaposition of two epigrams makes the connection clear. Epigram 55 is on the discovery made in 1599 that the body of St Cecilia in her church of Trastevere was still incorrupt—an event commemorated in visual terms by Stefano Maderno's statue of the saint as she looked when the sarcophagus was opened:

Jung; doch verständig / schön / doch züchtig / reich / doch rein.

This gracefully modelled line introduces a 6-line poem which recalls the martyr's death, the threefold attempt to decapitate her, and her 1200-year entombment.[14] It culminates in a rhetorical question that turns on its head its author's characteristic preoccupation with the mutability of all earthly things:

Kan was nicht irdisch ist wol Erd und Asche werden[?]

It is surely significant that this paean in praise of the triumph of spiritual beauty over time and corruption is immediately followed by an epigram on the sufferings and death of Catherine of Georgia, his own dramatic heroine, who was able through faith and sheer effort of will to ignore her torment and triumph over her own human frailty. There is something grandly Roman about the prologue of the tragedy he was about to commit to paper: Eternity, an allegorical figure, descends on to a stage strewn with corpses and the discarded insignia of earthly glory, and in majestically portentous lines proclaims to the awe-struck audience that the stage is her domain. From now on, the exaltation of martyrdom on the borderline between the present and eternity was to become his favourite theme. Counter-reformation Rome confirmed the poet in the direction he was taking.

Gryphius and his party left Rome on 5 April 1646. They were not entirely sorry, or at least they were glad to say good-bye to the lice and nits, as a epigram (no. 79 in Book III) entitled 'Roma Caput rerum' sardonically records.

Rom ist das Haupt der Welt / voll Witz wie ich befinde /
Voll Weißheit / voll Verstand / doch auch voll Läuß und Grinde.

They travelled up the Italian peninsula, pausing again in Florence, though there is no record of what they saw on their second visit. Indeed one of the most striking features of Gryphius's visit to France and Italy as recorded by his biographers and captured in his own poetry is the apparent disregard for the cultural and, more particularly, the literary achievements of both countries. It is understandable that for Gryphius, as for many another academically trained Protestant visitor, the claims of classical antiquity loomed larger, and the sights associated with it made a dominant impression. This was particularly the case in Italy. Yet was he really as blind to the modern achievements of Italy as his biographers would have us believe? Or could it be that their own ignorance of Italian and French culture made them select what they themselves knew and recognized from the records, such as Gryphius's diary, to which they, or at least Stosch, the first of them, may have had access? His last tragedy *Aemilius Paulus*

---

[14] It is interesting to note that Bosio also wrote a history of the martyrdom of St Cecilia which was translated into German and published at Graz in 1604 under the title *Histori vom Leyden der heiligen Jungfrawen vnd Martyrin Caeciliae, vnd jhrer heiligen Mitgesellen vnnd Martyrer, Valeriani, Tiburtii vnd Maximi.*

Papinianus, published in 1659, is the most 'Roman' of all his works, and offers an analysis of the collision between one man's personal integrity and the corruption and arbitrary violence of tyranny. Yet the author takes the opportunity of a reference to the underworld in one of its choruses to bring to his readers' attention the unexpected fact that he was familiar with Dante's *Inferno*. Not only does he quote six lines from Canto XII in the original Italian; he also provides his own eight-line German rendition of the description of Phlegethon, the boiling river of blood in which those violent against themselves or others suffer their appropriate torment:

> [Ma] ficca li occhi a valle, chè s'approccia
> la riviera del sangue in la qual bolle
> qual che per vïolenza in altrui noccia,

lines which he translates 'nur überhin' as follows:

> Schlag dein Gesicht auff dises tiffe Thal
> Es rauscht daher / der Blutt=Fluß / darinn kocht
> Der mit Gewalt geschadet und gepocht /
> Und nun die Straff erträgt in diser Qual.

The canto's climax comes when the great centaur, Nesso, points out the tyrants whose violence and cupidity caused such suffering—which is of course precisely the theme of the tragedy and its depiction of the nascent monster Caracalla. References to Dante are rare indeed in seventeenth-century German literature, and quotations from him unusual in the extreme. Does this footnote therefore provide a hint that there had been a meeting of minds between the great Italian and the German baroque poet whose second book of sonnets (the one that includes the 'Roman' sequence) comes to its climax with the Last Judgment, Hell, and the eternal bliss of the elect? Or is it just a souvenir of Florence—a quotation copied into a commonplace book or taken from a copy of the *Divina Commedia* bought with every intention of one day reading it as thoroughly as it deserved? Perhaps the answer lies midway between these two alternatives. Like Dante, Gryphius had an imagination compounded of deep spirituality, sharp satire and a propensity for sombre rumination; of all the Germans of his period he alone had the intellectual equipment to respond to Dante and the linguistic range to render him in German. But his mind worked in different categories and systems. There was fleeting recognition across a gulf of four hundred years, but their ships passed in the night.

On 15 April the party left Florence for Bologna, a city which was later to be the setting for his most personal play *Cardenio und Celinde* (1650). They then moved on to Ferrara, where the poet had the opportunity to pay his respects to the memory of three great men of letters, Ariosto, Tasso and Guarini, who had done much to shape the imagination of his period and whose popularity in Germany was considerable. From Ferrara they travelled via Francolino to Polesella, where they embarked, sailed down the Po and, despite contrary winds, reached Venice safely. In fact their journey was remarkably fast: by 22 April Gryphius was being shown round the Treasury of St Mark's. They must have stayed in Venice several weeks, but the only event reported of it is the ceremony on 9 May at which he presented a hurriedly produced copy of his *Olivetum*, printed in Florence, to a distinguished company of Venetians. The epic's dedication to the Venetian Senate suggests that he was proud of it and well aware that Latin verse was still an international currency of inestimable value on the European cultural market. In this respect his journey had paid off quite as well as Milton's.

The remainder of the peregrination back to Germany remains vague in the extreme. After leaving Venice they seem to have passed through Padua before heading northwards. The crossing of the Alps left no discernible mark on Gryphius's poetry: Germany had to wait almost another century before their grandeur was revealed in 1736 by Albrecht von Haller in his poem *Die Alpen*. His seventeenth-century precursor had no eye for the sublime in Nature: what roused his admiration were the works of man and the workings of the spirit. In due course—the date remains uncertain—they reached Strasburg, where Gryphius broke his homeward journey, completed his tragedy *Leo Armenius* and began work on *Catharina von Georgien*. The party may well have split up at this point, leaving Gryphius and Schlegel to continue on their own down the Rhine, visiting Frankfurt and the *Reichskammergericht* or Imperial Court of Appeal at Mainz on the way. From Cologne they proceeded to Amsterdam and thence by ship to Schlegel's home town, Stettin. There Gryphius completed his second tragedy, took his leave of his travelling companion, and on 8 November 1647 headed back to war-torn Silesia. The last of the five 'Roman' sonnets, no. 43, gives expression to the almost unbearable contrast between what he had seen and what he now could see. He had seen the great sights of his cultural world; he had found his vocation as a dramatist, and his fame as a scholar was spreading far and wide. Yet he felt as though he had come back from the land of the living to the land of the dead. Perhaps he sensed a deep affinity between himself and the petrified man he had seen and marvelled at in the Palazzo Ludovisi in Rome, a now vanished villa which housed the collection of sculpture begun by Cardinal Ludovico Ludovisi, the nephew of Pope Gregory XV (1621–23). The curious scientist spoke with the voice of the questioning poet in the two epigrams which record this encounter (Book III. 83 and 84). In the first, Gryphius conveys his sense of the precariousness of existence and his own physical and mental vulnerability:

> Ists möglich daß ein Ort dich unvergänglich macht /
> In welchem / was man ehrt und schätzt und wünscht / verschmacht?
> Sprecht mehr / daß sterbend wir in Staub und nichts vergehn /
> Du kontest lebend nicht / todt wirst du stets bestehn.

Death and life, stone and flesh, past and present merge as the poet gazes in wonder at the man of stone:

> Last ander' Ertz und Erd und Stein zu Gräbern haben:
> Die Glider / die du schawst / sind in sich selbst begraben.

What was the profoundest insight he had gained from his Italian journey? Addressing Cleander—his *alter ego* or his friend Schlegel?—in epigram 81, his answer to the latter's leading question goes right to the heart of his position as a writer and thinker on the borderline between Latin and the German vernacular, Antiquity and the modern age. It shows that his encounter with France, Rome and Italy made him face the uncertain future despite the values and attractions of a past he rightly cherished:

> Du fragst warumb ich nicht zu Rom will Bürger werden:
> Weil Rom / von dem du sagst / nicht mehr auff dieser Erden.

THE TRAVELLER-AUTHOR AND HIS ROLE
IN SEVENTEENTH-CENTURY GERMAN TRAVEL ACCOUNTS

JILL BEPLER*

According to contemporaries, travel literature was among the most popular vernacular reading matter in the seventeenth century in Germany. As yet there is no short-title catalogue of German seventeenth-century imprints which would allow an exact quantification of the production and distribution of travel literature, nor are there specialized bibliographies of the genre. A look at the catalogues of the Frankfurt and Leipzig book fairs during the seventeenth century, despite their notorious unreliablity, gives a fair indication of the enormous interest in literature of this kind. Travel descriptions are generally found under the heading 'libri historici', clearly indicating their character as historical narrative. Auction catalogues also provide evidence of the popularity of the genre with readers and book collectors, as do the surviving library catalogues and collections of the period. Over the past decade there has been a great surge of scholarly interest in late medieval and early modern German travel and travel literature.[1]

Recent studies on early modern travel have demonstrated the central importance of apodemic literature, works providing systematic rules useful for travel and observation.[2] This genre emerged in the German-speaking lands in the late

---

* Herzog August Bibliothek, Wolfenbüttel, Germany.

[1] The most recent studies are: *Reiseberichte als Quellen europäischer Kulturgeschichte. Aufgaben und Möglichkeiten der historischen Reiseforschung*, eds. Antoni Maczak & Hans Jürgen Teuteberg, Wolfenbütteler Forschungen, 21 (Wolfenbüttel, 1982); Jill Bepler, *Ferdinand Albrecht, Duke of Braunschweig-Lüneburg (1636-1687). A Traveller and his Travelogue*, Wolfenbütteler Arbeiten zur Barockforschung, 16 (Wiesbaden, 1988); Jörg Jochen Berns, 'Peregrinatio academica und Kavalierstour. Bildungsreisen junger Deutscher in der Frühen Neuzeit', in: *Rom—Paris—London. Erfahrung und Selbsterfahrung deutscher Schriftsteller und Künstler in den fremden Metropolen. Ein Symposion*, ed. Conrad Wiedemann, Germanische Symposien Berichtsbände, 8 (Stuttgart, 1988), pp. 155-81; *Der Reisebericht. Die Entwicklung einer Gattung in der deutschen Literatur*, ed. Peter J. Brenner (Frankfurt am Main, 1989); Wolfgang Neuber, *Fremde Welt im europäischen Horizont. Zur Topik der deutschen Amerika-Reiseberichte der Frühen Neuzeit*, Philologische Studien und Quellen, 121 (Berlin, 1991); *Reisekultur. Von der Pilgerfahrt zum modernen Tourismus*, eds. Hermann Bausinger et al. (Munich, 1991); *Reisen und Reiseliteratur im Mittelalter und in der Frühen Neuzeit*, eds. Xenja von Ertzdorff & Dieter Neukirch, Chloe, Beihefte zum Daphnis, 13 (Amsterdam, 1992).

[2] Justin Stagl, 'Die Apodemik oder "Reisekunst" als Methodik der Sozialforschung vom Humanismus bis zur Aufklärung', in: *Statistik und Staatsbeschreibung in der Neuzeit*, eds. M. Rassem & J. Stagl (Paderborn, 1980), pp. 131-202; Justin Stagl, 'Die Methodisierug des Reisens im 16. Jahrhundert', in: *Der Reisebericht*, ed. P. J. Brenner (Frankfurt am Main, 1989), pp. 140-77; Justin Stagl, 'Der Reisende ist dem Philosophen, was der Arzt dem Apotheker—Über Apodemiken und Reisehandbücher', in: *Reisekultur. Von der Pilgerfahrt zum modernen Tourismus*, eds. H.

sixteenth century, and was based on the logical method of the philosopher Petrus Ramus. Published in handbooks, dissertations or appended to topographical works and guide books, apodemic theories determined modes of observation and description throughout the seventeenth century. The traveller was given advice on how to prepare himself for his journey, which rules to observe while travelling and how exactly to plan his study of each region and town in order to extract the maximum information on its topography and administration. Rules for note-taking are most impressively documented in the charts provided in some apodemic works, showing the orders in which the buildings of any town can be categorised, proceeding from general divisions (eg. buildings ecclesiastical / civic) to the most specific. These categories operated in forming not only the nature of the enquiries made by travellers but also the character of the diaries they wrote *en route*, thus already prejudicing the structure of a travelogue which might later be prepared from original notes. However much the mode of enquiry might have been determined by such handbooks, contemporaries remained convinced that there was scope for individual observation and a justification for printing travel accounts.

Like all prose narrative of the sixteenth and seventeenth centuries in Germany, the ideal travelogue was expected to provide both instruction and moral improvement. The instruction was intertwined with the factual information on the countries portrayed, heavily indebted to the structuring of apodemic literature. Moral improvement was to be found among other things in the identification of the reader with the traveller, whose safe return from the spiritual and physical dangers of his journey were attributed to the hand of providence. This projection of the traveller as an exemplary figure, rather than as a critically and emotionally responsive individual, determined the process of selection by which personal and subjective experience and anecdote entered the text. Travel itself was seen as a test of moral rectitude and a lesson in the vanity of human affairs, ultimately governed by the hand of providence, to which the traveller testified in his travelogue in the religious sense of *Zeugnis ablegen*. Wolfgang Neuber rightly points out that it is this element which paves the way to the reception of travel literature as devotional literature.[3] The topos of the traveller's testimony to the power of providence continues throughout the seventeenth century, indeed it becomes a narrative convention. 'Providentialism' waned towards the end of the century, gradually displaced by Baconian principles of 'new science' in what has been described as a process of secularisation of knowledge.[4] As Kaspar von Greyertz has shown, the individual began to seek signs of providence in his or her inner life rather than

---

Bausinger et al. (Munich, 1991), pp. 38-47; Justin Stagl, 'Ars Apodemica: Bildungsreise und Reisemethodik von 1560 bis 1600', in: *Reisen und Reiseliteratur im Mittelalter und in der Frühen Neuzeit*, eds. Xenja von Ertzdorff & Dieter Neukirch (Amsterdam, 1992), pp. 141-89.

[3] Wolfgang Neuber, 'Zur Gattungspoetik des Reiseberichts. Skizze einer historischen Grundlegung im Horizont von Rhetorik und Topik', in: *Der Reisebericht*, ed. Peter J. Brenner (Frankfurt am Main, 1989), pp. 50-67, here p. 57.

[4] Udo Krolzik, *Säkularisierung der Natur. Providentia-Dei-Lehre und Naturverständnis der Frühaufklärung* (Neukirchen-Vluyn, 1988).

in external manifestations and in this connection the self-searching autobiographical texts of the Pietists marked a new beginning.[5]

The 'providentialism' of travel literature ties it in with the vast devotional literature of the early modern period and, perhaps unexpectedly, with another species of biographical publication in Germany, the *curriculum vitae* of the funeral sermon. The description of a life, like that of a journey, invites meditation on the authentic experiences of an individual which can be interpreted in retrospect as proof of divine intervention and guidance. The journey and its safe and successful conclusion provides the ultimate metaphor for the various stages and the end of a fulfilled life.

The printing of Protestant funeral sermons in Germany flourished between 1550 and 1750. An integral component of these publications, which often contained secular orations, occasional poetry and even music, was the *curriculum vitae* of the deceased. This biographical section was often culled from personal papers and diaries, and was sometimes even an autobiographical account written especially for the occasion. Although it is impossible to know exactly how many funeral sermons were actually published, it is estimated that approximately 250.000 such imprints from the German-speaking territories have survived.[6] From the way in which these texts were collected and collated it is clear that they were read both as devotional literature and as biography. In the early stages of the development of the printed funeral sermon, the *curriculum vitae* of the deceased played only a minor role as a didactic element in the text. There was initial controversy among Lutherans as to whether the life of the deceased should be mentioned from the pulpit at all. Its acceptance varied regionally, but by the late sixteenth century it had been generally established and was universally justified as providing the congregation with exemplary models of how to lead a Christian life and make timely preparations for death.

Although there has been much recent research on German funeral sermons, their potential contribution to a study of attitudes towards early modern travel has yet to be exploited. In the context of the *curriculum vitae*, the travels of the deceased occur mainly in connection with education, but they can also include travels on behalf of an employer and journeys made for private reasons. The concept of travel for enjoyment figures as little here as it does in the travel handbooks of the day. Travel was only morally justified if it could be shown to serve a legitimate purpose.

To go on a journey signified a departure from the framework of God-given order and the estate and community into which one had been born in order to expose oneself to unknown dangers and hardship. If all this was undertaken for curiosity's sake, it was presumptuous and thus sinful. The journey itself and its hardships

---

[5] Kaspar von Greyertz, *Vorsehungsglaube und Kosmologie. Studien zu englischen Selbstzeugnissen des 17. Jahrhunderts*, Veröffentlichungen des Deutschen Historischen Instituts London, XXV (Göttingen, 1990).

[6] Rudolf Lenz, *De mortuis nil nisi bene? Leichenpredigten als multidisziplinäre Quelle unter besonderer Berücksichtigung der Historischen Familienforschung, der Bildungsgeschichte und der Literaturgeschichte*, Marburger Personalschriften-Forschungen, 1990 (Sigmaringen, 1990).

could be interpreted in retrospect as punishment, the safe return of the traveller as a sign of forgiveness and purification. With the teachings of Luther a new concept of profession emerged which imbued work and everything associated with the pursuit of a profession with religious significance and dignity. Thus a journey undertaken for secular professional reasons by a merchant, courtier, diplomat or student, could assume metaphorical significance and demonstrate the divine protection enjoyed by the traveller. Peril and exposure to mortal danger were seen as tests of the religious steadfastness of the traveller who is saved only by an act of faith. The moment of crisis and danger in a journey becomes a metaphor for the traveller's rebirth as the better Christian he is when he returns home.

The justification of travel in travel handbooks and of travel literature in prefaces and treatises operates within the biblical-allegorical framework of life as a pilgrimage and the traveller as the reader of the book of nature, whose greatest wisdom is the insight into the vanity of human affairs and the inconstancy of fortune. Thus James Howell, writing in 1642, defined the ultimate purpose of travel in the following terms:

> Language is the greatest outward testimony of Travell: yet it is a vain and verball Knowledge that rests only in the Tongue; nor are the observations of the Eye any thing profitable, unlesse the Mind draw something from the Externe object to enrich the Soule withall, to informe, to build up, and unbeguile the Inward man, that by the sight of so various objects of Art and Nature, that by the perlustration of such famous Cities, Castles, Amphitheaters, and Palaces, some glorious and new, some mouldred away, and beaten by the Iron Teeth of Time, he come to discerne the best of all earthly things to be but fraile and transitory. That this world at best is but a huge Inne, and we but wayfaring men, but Pilgrimes, and a company of rambling Passengers.[7]

In addition to experiencing the vanity of the material world, the traveller also exposes himself to danger and physical hardship and thus learns to appreciate the transitoriness of his physical self. The experience of hardship and privation was seen to be a means of learning the Christian virtue of humility. In 1664 Christoph Eißlingen published a new edition of Salomon Schweigger's description of his journey to Constantinople and the Holy Land which had first appeared in 1610.[8] In his preface 'An den vielgünstigen und Reißbegierigen Leser', Eißlingen elaborates on travel as the school of Christian stoicism for the traveller himself:

> man lernet wie Paulus vermahnet / sich in die Zeit schicken / hoch und nidrig seyn / gnug haben und Mangel leiden / dienen und bedient werden / Insonderheit lernet man die große Kunst / in Widerwertigkeit gedultig seyn / wann es wol gehet / daß man dem Glaß-schwachen Glück nicht zuviel traue / Item / daß man durch widerwertig Glück nicht desperat und verzagt / sondern behertzt und freudig seyn ...[9]

These are the ideas taken up and developed by Philipp Han, preacher in Magdeburg, in his funeral sermon for Johann von Arnim published in 1610 under

---

[7] James Howell, *Instructions for Forreine Travell 1642 (Collated with the second edition of 1650)*, ed. Edward Arber (London, 1869), p. 106.

[8] Salomon Schweigger, *Gezweyte neue nutzliche und anmuthige Reiß-Beschreibung / Die Erste nach Constantinopel und Jerusalem ... Nebens einen kurtz verfasten richtigen Wegweiser / durch Teutschland in Italien* (Nuremberg, 1664).

[9] Schweigger (op. cit. n. 8), unfol.

the title *Christliche Betrachtung Aller Gottes Heiligen und Gleubigen Pilgram- und Bürgerschafft.*[10]

The biblical text on which Han preached was Psalm 39, 'Herr Ich bin beyde dein Pilgrim und dein Bürger / wie alle meine Väter'. The sermon explains why David uses the image of the traveller / pilgrim to denote the harshness of human existence. In the 'applicatio ad personam defuncti' which follows, the travels of Johann von Arnim, the hardships he endured and his Christian steadfastness are recorded:

> Was aber hierneben der selige Herr / auff solcher ferner Reiß und in der Frembd / für molestias, Beschwerung und Ungemach außgestanden / ist theils leicht zu erachten / theils aus seinem Itinerario zu ersehen / und nicht alles zu erzehlen: Da er offt mit Jesuitern und München / Griechen und Türcken / und dergleichen Abgöttischen und Barbarischen Leuten / in einem Schiff und über einem Tisch sich behelffen müssen / zu zeiten wegen grawsamer Sturmwinde und Ungewitter / in höchster Leibsgefahr gewesen / auch wol in mangelung Proviantz / Hunger und Durst / ja manches unsanfftes Lager versuchen und außstehen müssen. Daraus ihm doch Gott gnediglich geholffen / und gesund wider zu den seinen kommen lassen / weil er sich ihm / als sein Pilgrim / mit täglichem Gebet befohlen / und in aller Noth und Gefahr / all sein vetrawen auff ihn gesetzet.[11]

The reason for the traveller's safe return is seen to be his total submission to the power of providence.

Han himself was, as the quotation shows, familiar with von Arnim's travel diaries, which he had obviously read in connection with the composition of the funeral sermon. His dedicatory preface to the family encourages the publication of the diaries:

> Denn mir nicht zweiffelt / solches werde nicht allein dem seligen Herrn von Arnim / zu fernerm lobwürdigen Ruhm und Ehren / sondern auch vielen Reisenden / Gelehrten und Adelspersonen / zu angenehmen gefallen / guter Anreitzung / und mercklichen Nutzen gereichen.[12]

The publication of the travel diaries would thus benefit future travellers and also confront the reader with exemplary behaviour ('guter Anreitzung') and a demonstration of the power of providence.

The recording of instances of a divine presence at work in one's own biography, shown by Kaspar von Greyertz to have been central to autobiographical writings of the seventeenth century in England, is a central aspect of the subjective element in early modern travel accounts. Henry Newcome's justification for writing his autobiography in the mid-seventeenth century—'that to record divine providences is not the least portion of God's praise, of our duty, and of posterity's patrimony'[13]—is an argument with which most travellers justify the publication of their

---

[10] Philip Han, *Christliche Betrachtung Aller Gottes Heiligen und Gleubigen Pilgram- und Bürgerschafft... Bey der Ansehnlichen und sehr Volckreichen Sepultur... Herrn Johan von Arnims / Der Primat Ertzbischofflichen Kirchen zu Magdeburg Domherrn / etc. und zeit seines Lebens / in vielen abgelegenen / zufförderst auch im gewesenen gelobten Lande und irrdischen Hierusalem / wolerfahrnen Pilgrims: numehr aber ewig seligen Bürgers im newen Himlischen Hierusalem* (Magdeburg, 1610).

[11] Han (op. cit. n. 10), fo. Eii(r).

[12] Han (op. cit. n. 10), unfol.

[13] Greyertz (op. cit. n. 5), p. 68.

travel descriptions. Johann Michael Heberer, in the first chapter of his *Aegyptiaca servitus* (1616)[14] refers in just this context ('zu welchem ende ich mir fürnemblich vorgenommen nachfolgende reisen zu beschreiben') to his Christian duty to give bear witness and give thanks to God:

> So erkenne ich mich auch vor andern desto mehr schuldig / Gott dem allmechtigen / für solche seine unausprechliche güte / gnad / und barmhertzigkeit / die zeit meines lebens danckbar zu sein / und solche an mir armen und verlornen menschen erwiesene güte und wunder / bey der Gemeine zu preisen / und bey den alten und jungen ohn underlaß zu rühmen.[15]

In undertaking a journey, the traveller of the early modern period voluntarily left the safe framework of established order provided for him by his home, family and civic identity in order to pursue a greater good, usually in the sense of further qualification or service to the state, and thus exposing himself to danger in the wider sense for the common good. While giving thanks to providence for a safe return, the writer / traveller also encouraged the reader to identify with his fate.

In descriptions of moments of crisis and danger, most travel writers assume an overtly didactic stance towards the reader. Heberer's travel account, *Aegyptiaca servitus*, depicts the ultimate hazards to which the traveller could be exposed. In 1585, on his passage from Malta, he was captured by Turkish pirates and sold into slavery in Egypt. After three years imprisonment and service in the galleys, Heberer returned to his native Palatinate in 1592. His travelogue is divided into four books, describing his journey up to the point of his capture, his years of slavery, his return to Heidelberg and his later diplomatic journeys on behalf of the court there. Having described the dramatic scenes of his capture, Heberer addresses the reader directly, inviting reflection on the inconstancy of human fortune:

> Allhier gebe ich dem günstigen Leser / und einem jeden Christen Menschen zu bedencken / die unbestendigkeit des Glücks / die wunderbar und unversehliche zufäll deß Menschlichen Lebens.[16]

Intensifying the impression of the speed with which fortunes could be reversed, and appearances shown to be totally unreliable, Heberer recapitulates the last scene of danger he had depicted, his narrow escape from religious persecution by the Catholics in Marseilles:

> Und daß ich von mir selber sage / der ich erst vor Sieben oder Acht wochen noch in Franckreich / lustig / freudig / frey eigen und ledig / vermeinte zu Marsilien der Christen Gefengnüs zuentgehen / Wie solt ich mir haben traumen lassen / daß ich in so kurtzer zeit / nicht allein uber die 2000 Meil / uff dem Wilden Meer solte verworffen werden / Sondern auch in Egypten / da ich die Tag meines Lebens / keine gedancken hin gehabt / in Heidnische Dienstbarkeit gerahten / und mit dem Wasser der Trübsal auß dem Paradieß / des Fluß Nili / getrencket werde?[17]

---

[14] Johann Michael Heberer von Bretten, *Aegyptiaca servitus: Das ist / Warhafte Beschreibung einer Dreyjährigen Dienstbarkeit / So zu Alexandrien in Aegypten ihren Anfang / und zu Constantinopel ihr Endschafft genommen. Gott zu Ehren und dem Nechsten zur Nachrichtung … (1616),* ed. Karl Teply (Graz, 1967).

[15] Heberer von Bretten (op. cit. n. 14), p. 3.

[16] Heberer von Bretten (op. cit. n. 14), p. 102.

[17] Heberer von Bretten (op. cit. n. 14), p. 103.

Few travellers of the seventeenth century had experiences to recount which could vie with the dangers encountered by the pilgrims and voyagers of the fifteenth and sixteenth centuries. The tension between the two central elements of the travelogue in the early modern period, the outer journey and the 'providentialism' of its exemplary revelations remained constitutive, however, and is well demonstrated in a text from the mid-seventeenth century. *Wahrhafftige Reiß-Beschreibung / Aus eigner Erfahrung* ... is a travelogue first published by the Stuttgart chancery official Hieronymus Welsch in 1658, which enjoyed a modest success with the contemporary reading public. It was reissued in 1659 and 1664, printed by the Stuttgart printer Rößlin and distributed by the famous Endter publishing house in Nuremberg, the most important book centre in southern Germany.[18] The sparse critical attention the work has since received concentrates on the passages in which Welsch describes the havoc he witnessed during and after the eruption of Vesuvius in 1631, while he was in staying in Naples. Both this description and his comments on Mount Etna seem to have caused Viktor Hantzsch, the nineteenth-century geographer, to write an entry for Welsch in the *Allgemeine Deutsche Biographie*. In Ludwig Schudt's standard work on German travellers to Italy in the seventeenth and eighteenth centuries, Welsch's travelogue is again cited in this context and then dismissed as containing, at least for Italy, no observations which would raise it above the ordinary.[19] It is this alleged averageness which suggested the text as a case study of the tenaciousness of the conventional nature of 'providentialism' in seventeenth-century travel writing.

Little is known about Hieronymus Welsch beyond what we glean from his travelogue, not even his exact dates. He was born in Nördlingen in Württemberg in about 1610, and can still be traced as living in Stuttgart in 1664. After an education which must have included attendance at a Latin school, he left home in 1630 at the age of twenty with the express intention of acquiring a knowledge of the world and foreign languages (Howell's 'outward testimony of Travell') in order to qualify for a position of responsibility on his return. After eleven years of travel throughout Europe, during which time he served both as a clerk and as a soldier, Welsch returned to his native Württemberg and entered the service of the court at Stuttgart. His travelogue, published seventeen years after his return, appears to be his only printed work.

Welsch clearly sees the value of his travelogue in the depiction of two realms, the countries which formed the stations of his journey and his experiences of extreme danger, in particular during his hazardous sea voyages and his military service. This dual interest is elaborated on in the dedicatory epistle to Eberhard Duke of Württemberg, which prefaces the work. Welsch shows himself aware that there is no shortage of travel descriptions written by people from all levels of society, but claims that his own experience, especially of danger, makes his travel description of unique value:

---

[18] Reinhard Wittmann, *Geschichte des deutschen Buchhandels. Ein Überblick*, (Munich, 1991), p. 87.

[19] Ludwig Schudt, *Italienreisen im 17. und 18. Jahrhundert*, Römische Forschungen der Biblioteca Hertziana—Max-Planckinstut in Rome, 15 (Vienna, 1959).

mir solche Sachen selbst mit Augen anzusehen / und würcklichen zu erfahren / auffgestossen / daß dergleichen eigne Begnussen in andern gemeinen Reiß-Büchern nicht vil zu lesen.[20]

In his preface to the reader Welsch again stresses his particular fate in having survived over thirty situations in which his life had been in peril, 'hin und wider auff dem Lande / als auch auff dem Meer und Wasser'. The main purpose of the publication of his description is to testify to the power of providence and give thanks to God for his preservation:

ermeldte meine Reise ... von mir darumben beschrieben worden / förderist gegen dem getrewen Gott mich dardurch danckbarlichen zubezeigen / daß er mich von seinen allmächtigen Geschöpffen und Wunderwercken dieser Welt / so viel hat sehen und erfahren lassen ...[21]

In keeping with the dual purpose of the narrative, the imparting of factual information and the autobiographical account of the journey itself, Welsch uses a device standard to the vernacular travelogue. He continually interrupts his own personal chronological narrative by inserting chapters dedicated to historical, political and topographical information about the countries being described.[22] These chapters are of course heavily indebted to Welsch's own reading. Despite his claims to veracity Welsch does in fact also describe towns and countries he had actually never seen, albeit always with a caveat that proximity had allowed him to glean the necessary information. This leads him to devote several pages to Venice, described because he had 'fast so vil Nachricht erlangt / als ob ich wurcklich alldorten gewesen wäre.'[23] The same is obviously true of Portugal, which Welsch judges he can write on because he had visited Spain. Having reached Malta and thus being only a day's sailing away from Africa, as he says, Welsch feels justified in giving an account of North Africa and Palestine based on his reading and his personal enquiries. For the same reason he includes chapters on the Holy Land, referring the reader to more detailed information, 'in etlichen Hierusalomitanischen Reiß-Büchern außführlichen zu lesen.'[24] In the sections which deal with the actual stations of his journey, Welsch goes to great pains to stress that his descriptions are based on his own personal observation, repeatedly declining to comment on places he had only passed through quickly. He does indeed provide lively accounts of many of the cities he visited, especially in Spain, a country little visited by Protestant German travellers, where he was greatly impressed by the theatrical spectacles and Catholic processions and horrified by the practice of bull-fighting.

Personal experiences, the details of his various employments, lodgings, travelling companions, are only touched on in moments of crisis, or if they have exemplary value. Thus Welsch justifies relating the story of a German who had robbed his employer and compatriot, a knight templar in Malta. The knight avoided making the crime public and allowed the man to leave the island in order to avoid

---

[20] Welsch, *Wahrhafftige Reiß-Beschreibung*, fo.)(2r.

[21] Welsch (op. cit. n. 20), fo.)(2r.

[22] This technique is noted by Neuber (op. cit. n. 1) in many of the texts he examined.

[23] Welsch (op. cit. n. 20), p. 21.

[24] Welsch (op. cit. n. 20), p. 168.

dishonouring the German nation. Welsch comments:

> solches gedencke ich vornemlich darumb / weilen mir diser Gesell hernach zu Palermo (wie daselbsten zu lesen) wunderbahrlich aufgestossen.[25]

Fifty pages later this delinquent is recorded as having met his just reward in Palermo, where Welsch sees him in prison and is able to point the moral for the reader. Within Welsch's text there is a recurrent narrative pattern for examples of the inconstancy of fortune, such as the above.

On his travels in Italy and Malta Welsch is moved to pity by the fate of the galley slaves, object lessons in the reversals of fortune and presented to the reader in antithetical terms:

> Weilen dann auff einer Galeern allerley Volck / als Türcken und Christen / hohe und geringe Stands-Personen / Geist- und Weltliche / Gesunde und Krancke / Grosse und Kleine / Listige und Einfältige / Fröliche und Trawrige zusammen kommen / mit Ketten aneinander geschlossen werden / und in grossem Elend / vil ärger als die Hund beyeinander hausen und leben müssen / so hab ich solches ohne hertzliches Mitleiden nicht betrachten mögen.[26]

It is, however, in the depiction of his own perils and sufferings that Welsch most often has recourse to images of the inconstancy of fortune and it is his own rescue that provides proof of providence at work. In his preface, Welsch quantifies his total exposure to danger as thirty situations in all. Sea travel was of course particularly hazardous, and in Welsch's account, each voyage is especially numbered in the marginalia to the text. A trip from Naples to Reggio by ship, provides three perilous situations, all related with the standard coupling of the hand of providence and narration as a vote of thanks: 'also / daß wir nahend alle darüber zu Grund gegangen / wo Gott (dem sey Lob dafür) solches nicht gnädig verhütet hätte.'[27] In 1633 he undertook his eighth voyage, from Palermo to Sardinia, during which the boat was hit by a terrible storm, which Welsch describes in terms of his utter surrender to Providence:

> in Summa / es war mir als halb todt / dirmisch / endlich müd / schläfferig / Gott und dem Sterben nunmehr gantz ergeben / nicht mehr als wann ich in der Welt lebte / sondern als wann die Galeern zwischen trüben Wolcken und einem ungestümmen Wasser (massen mir dann seithero ein solches offt und vil mal im Schlaf und Traum vorkommen) unter dem Himmel in der Lufft schwebte.[28]

Parallel to these situations of immediate physical danger, Welsch also interprets the progress of his journeys and personal fortunes in terms of providentialism and as exemplifying inconstancy. Having been offered a position in the service of a Spanish commander of a sea port near Naples, Welsch decides to defer acceptance until he has visited Malta, commenting significantly: 'so doch bey mir allein ein curiosität gewesen'. This journey is thus given the stigma of curiosity, travel without real purpose, and the misfortune it involves him in is implicitly seen as divine punishment. From the start Welsch's attempt to reach Malta is ill-starred. Unable to afford a decent berth on a direct route, he decides to travel via Syracuse and sails first to Agosta, where he is tricked out of money by a travelling

---

[25] Welsch (op. cit. n. 20), p. 142.
[26] Welsch (op. cit. n. 20), p. 113.
[27] Welsch (op. cit. n. 20), p. 98.
[28] Welsch (op. cit. n. 20), p. 199.

companion. Having finally reached Syracuse, he finds he has missed the ship and incurs great expense waiting for the next. A storm on the crossing to Malta means that the boat has to seek shelter on an uninhabited stretch of coast, where the passengers are trapped for twelve days without provisions. In Malta Welsch's luck changes slightly for the better in that he gains the protection of the German knight. On his return to Messina, however, he finds that the Spanish commander has employed someone else because he had failed to return. As all his hopes had been pinned on the prospect of employment, Welsch has to pawn some of his possessions in order to pay for a crossing to Palermo, where he hopes to be taken on at the court of the viceroy. A high sea make it impossible for the boat to sail into the harbour, so the passengers are put ashore on the coast and walk to the next town to await the arrival of the boat. Three days pass without the ship being sighted. Welsch is destitute, all his belongings are on board, he has no resources. In a scene reminiscent of the hermit / withdrawal from the world scenario of Grimmelshausen's *Simplicissimus*, Welsch recounts how, as he watched alone from the coast he had meditated on his own foolhardiness and misfortune: 'als bin ich endlich in ein recht hertzliche Trawrigkeit gefallen / sehr zaghafft worden / und hab solches alles zu betrauren nicht verhindern mögen.'[29] Seeing a cave nearby, he enters and surrenders himself to the power of prayer:

> darinnen ich auff die Knie nidergefallen / und Gott umb Hülff und Rettung sehr inniglich angeruffen. Nun darff ich mit Warheit sagen / daß ich in disem Gebett nicht nur ein trefflichen Mut und hertzhafftes Vertrawen zu Gott erlanget / sondern als ich auch gantz getrost wider auß der Höle heraußgegangen / so bin ich alsobald eines Schiffs / noch weit von dannen / auff dem Meer ansichtig / und darmit bey mir selbsten unsers Schiffs gewiß vertröstet worden.[30]

On reaching Palermo, Welsch is hired by a Spanish nobleman as part of the retinue to accompany an embassy to Germany. The providential nature of the whole episode is presented to the reader:

> da hab ich eigentlich erfahren / ob es wol das Ansehen gehabt / als wann die versaumung deß Schiffs zu Syracusa / und alle andere Widerwärtigkeit zu meinem grösten Verderben wolten außschlagen / daß solches (als ein rechtmässige Ursach diser Reise nach Palermo) mir hingegen zu meinem guten zeitlichen Glück gereicht.[31]

The second half of Welsch's travel description contains an account of his years as a soldier with the French army between 1634 and 1641. In a pivotal chapter Welsch prepares the reader with an interpretation of what is to follow and its exemplary character:

> Sehr wol und weißlich wird gesagt / daß es mit einem Menschen / in diser unbeständigen Welt / nicht anderst als mit einem Rechenpfennig beschaffen / dann derselbe vil / wenig / vil oder gar nichts gelten kan / alles nachdem er von dem Rechenmeister oben auff die Linien der tausenden / oder auff die geringere gelegt / oder gar wider auffgehoben wird: Gleiches Exempel hat sich mit mir selbst begeben / als in der währender Zeit / so ich in Franckreich war / in Glück und Unglück / in Armut und Reichthum / in geringem und gutem Ansehen gewesen / wie solches hernach zu vernehmen ist.[32]

---

[29] Welsch (op. cit. n. 20), p. 191.
[30] Welsch (op. cit. n. 20), p. 191.
[31] Welsch (op. cit. n. 20), p. 196.
[32] Welsch (op. cit. n. 20), p. 326.

The chapter concludes:

> Hierauß ist zu sehen / wie Gott die / die von der Welt manchmalen verschmächteste / gar bald kan befördern / auch wider ihr selbst und allermännigliches Verhoffen / erhalten.[33]

The self-stylisation of the traveller / author as an exemplary figure associates the seventeenth-century travel description very closely with the novel of its day, the prime example being Grimmelshausen's *Simplicissimus*. Towards the end of the century, the satirist Christian Reuter selected the autobiographical travel account as a vehicle for demasking bourgeois pretensions. His novel *Schelmuffskys Wahrhafftige Curiöse und sehr gefährliche Reisebeschreibung Zu Wasser und Lande ... eigenhändig und sehr artig an den Tag gegeben ...* (1696)[34] parodies the providentialism of travel descriptions such as that by Welsch.[35] The work is dedicated to the Great Mogul and it is to a heathen, and not to God, that Schelmuffsky proves his gratitude by publishing his travels. The preface to the reader, 'An den Curiösen Leser', plays on the *topoi* of the genre, the exposure to risk and danger, the authenticity of the account, the uniqueness of the traveller's experiences:

> Es hat der Tebel hohlmer mancher kaum eine Stadt oder Land nennen hören / so setzt er sich stracks hin / und macht eine Reise-Beschreibung zehen Ellen lang davon her / wenn man denn nun solch Zeug lieset / (zumahl wer nun brav gereiset ist / als wie ich) so kan einer denn gleich sehen / daß er niemahls vor die Stuben-Thüre gekommen ist / geschweige / daß er fremden und garstigen Wind sich solte haben lassen unter die Nase gehen / als wie ich gethan habe.[36]

Throughout the work the narrator refers to his text as 'meine sehr gefährliche Reise-Beschreibung' and recounts the ridiculous 'dangers' to which he has been exposed. The standard vote of thanks found in Welsch's text, whenever he records delivery from a critical situation, is parodied in Reuter's novel by the narrator's constant blasphemous phrase 'der Tebel hohlmer'. The narrator / traveller aims not at the moral improvement of the reader, but, in keeping with his role as a braggart, at the arousal of horror, amazement and wonder, as in the parodied description of a sea voyage: 'Wie es uns aber dasselbe mahl auf der See erbärmlich gieng / werden einen die Haare zu Berge stehen / wer folgendes Capitel lesen wird.'[37]

By the end of the seventeenth century the providentialism traced here with its origins in the pilgrimage reports of the early sixteenth century had degenerated into an empty formula and become the subject of satire.

---

[33] Welsch (op. cit. n. 20), p. 329.

[34] Christian Reuter, *Schelmuffsky. Zweite, verbesserte Auflage. Abdruck der Erstausgaben (1696-1697) im Parallel-Druck*, ed. Wolfgang Hecht (Halle ad der Saale, 1956).

[35] On Reuter see: Wolfgang Hecht, *Christian Reuter*, Sammlung Metzler, 46 (Stuttgart, 1966). On Reuter's use of travel literature see: Jörg-Ulrich Fechner, 'Schelmuffskys Masken und Metamorphosen. Neue Forschungsapekte zu Christian Reuter', *Euphorion. Zeitschrift für Literaturgeschichte*, 76 (1982), 1-26.

[36] Hecht (op. cit. n. 35), p. 5.

[37] Hecht (op. cit. n. 35), p. 42.

THOMAS PENSON:
PRECURSOR OF THE SENTIMENTAL TRAVELLER

C. D. VAN STRIEN[*]

INTRODUCTION

In the seventeenth century, travelling and writing about it was very much an occupation associated with the upper classes. One of the few surviving travel accounts of this period written by a working-class person is *Penson's Short Progress into Holland, Flanders and France.* Between 1691 and 1698 a calligraphed copy of the journal was lent out to more than 80 different people.[1] If we want to know what made it so popular with Penson's friends and acquaintances, it may be helpful to study the journal not only against the background of contemporary travel accounts, but also against that of later eighteenth-century travelogues. But first a little more about Penson himself.

The author of the manuscript was born in 1652 and educated at Christ's Church Hospital (1655–66) before he was apprenticed for eight years to a writing master. In 1676 a son, Jonathan, was born to him and his wife Mary. At the time of his journey he was a member of the Society of Arms Painters, a group of craftsmen operating with the consent of the College of Arms. A business card dating from the 1680s details his professional activities: 'Thomas Penson, Arms Painter at the sign of the King's Arms on Ludgate Hill, where you may have pedigrees, curiously written, and painted Arms, Funeral Escutcheons, Ensigns, Cornets, Drums, Trumpet Banners, or anything drawn according to Heraldry, also palls of velvet. Honni Soit Qui Mal y Pense.'[2]

From the journal's preface it would appear that at the time he set out for Holland he was 'full freight with trouble', presumably because his wife had died or had left him, for there is also an outburst against the 'pernicious ... Doctors Commons', the society of ecclesiastical lawyers who also had jurisdiction over the affairs of laymen relating to marriage, legitimacy and wills. In 1694 he remarried and the next year he is mentioned as living in the parish of St Martin Ludgate, with his wife Deborah (King) and a son John.[3]

---

[*] Vlietland College, Leiden, The Netherlands.

[1] Rough copy with names of people who borrowed the book, BL, MS Harl. 3516; fair copies (1690), Edinburgh, Nat. Lib. of Scotland, MS 3003; Leeds University Brotherton Lib., MS Trv d2 (1697). An edition is in preparation by the author.

[2] Guildhall Library MS 12,818/3 (Christ's Hospital Children's Registers, 1635-1657), fo. 216. Baptism son, MS 6540/2, Paarish Register, St Bride's. Arms painters, BL, MS Harl. 1454; card, BL MS Add. 38,140, fo. 165.

[3] Cf. George D. Squibb, *Doctors' Commons: A History of the College of Advocates and Doctors of Law* (Oxford, 1977), pp. 1–3. For his marriage, see *A True Register of all the Christenings,*

Penson may have undertaken the tour to recover from the strain he must have suffered at the breaking up of his family, possibly combining therapy and pleasure with business; in any case he very carefully noted down matters to do with his profession. On 30 June 1687 Old Style, he embarked on a ship bound for Rotterdam. His itinerary was that taken by the majority of tourists in Holland: after a brief stay in Rotterdam he moved on to Amsterdam, passing through Delft, The Hague and Leyden. He remained in Amsterdam for two months, longer than most others, and then travelled to Antwerp by way of Utrecht, Gouda and Rotterdam. Via Gent, Lille and Péronne he reached Paris, and after having made a trip to Versailles and run out of money, he arrived back in London on 22 November. He had spent roughly three months in Holland, a week in Flanders and seven weeks in France.

SEVENTEENTH-CENTURY TRAVEL JOURNALS

Before going into a more detailed analysis of Penson's journal, one or two remarks about seventeenth-century tourism and the practice of keeping a travel journal may be in order. The travelogues of this period very strongly reflect the educational background of travel. Young members of the upper classes wrote them to show their parents and patrons they had travelled with profit. Those which got published were mostly written by scholars, many of whom as 'governors' accompanied the young noblemen on their journeys. Their accounts, just as those kept by people who toured mainly for pleasure, were written according to a set pattern derived from geographical descriptions found in atlases and guidebooks.[4] The emphasis is on the descriptions of the various towns, their history, the sights and the customs of the people, elements which were linked together by a succinct narrative of the journey. After the description of the last city of a particular country, we usually find general observations. This approach already occurs in accounts of travels dating from the beginning of the century such as Thomas Coryat's *Crudities* (1611; second edition, 1776), William Lithgow's *Rare Adventures* (1614; tenth edition in 1692) and George Sandys' *A Relation* (1615; seventh edition in 1673).[5] Thus the travelogue offered authors a loose framework into which they

Marriages and Burialles in the Parishe of St James, Clarkenwell, vol. iii Marriages 1551 to 1754, *Harleian Society*, vol. 53 (London, 1887), p. 215. D. V. Glass, *London Inhabitants Within the Walls, 1695*, London Record Society Publications, vol. ii for the year 1966 (London, 1966), p. 229.

[4] Cf. C. D. van Strien, *British Travellers in Holland during the Stuart Period. Edward Browne and John Locke as Tourists in the United Provinces*, Studies in Intellectual History, 42 (Leiden, 1993), especially chapter 1; travel journals with an emphasis on descriptions followed by general observations were still written at the end of the eighteenth century, cf. M. M. G. van Strien-Chardonneau, *'Le Voyage de Hollande', récits de voyageurs français dans les Provinces-Unies, 1748–1795* (doctoral dissertation) (Groningen, 1992), to be published in *Studies on Voltaire and the Eighteenth Century* (1994).

[5] Titles of these works: Th. Coryat, *Crudities Hastily Gobled up in Five Moneths Travells in France, Savoy, Italy, Rhetica ...* (London, 1611); W. Lithgow, *The Totall Discourse of the Rare Adventures and Painefull Peregrinations of the Long Nineteen Yeares Travayles from Scotland to the Most Famous Kingdomes in Europe, Asia, and Africa* (London 1614); G. Sandys, *A Relation of a Journey Begun An. Dom. 1610. Foure Bookes. Containing a Description of the Turkish Empire,*

could introduce material which particularly interested them, for example descriptions of public buildings or all sorts of collections of art and natural 'rarities'. Authors very critically read works previously published, pointing out and correcting any mistakes,[6] and although some refrained from including material already printed by a predecessor, overlaps were frequent, if only because the various travellers, who relied on the same guidebooks, could not avoid mentioning the principal sights. A brief survey of the best known English scholarly travelogues dealing with the United Provinces may serve as an illustration of the genre.

The great naturalist John Ray in his *Observations* (1673; in Holland in 1663)[7] particularly emphasized Latin inscriptions, including the printed *Series lectionum* of the universities of Louvain, Leyden and Utrecht. According to a critic, his book might 'well serve as a pattern for travelling, with that improvement and advantage, as ought to be aimed at by all discreet travellers'. Much of Ray's material came from the manuscript travel journal of Sir Philip Skippon, his travelling companion and former student, who had financed the journey. Ray's general observations on the customs of the United Provinces were provided by another friend, Francis Barnham Esq.[8] In Dr. Edward Browne's *An Account of Several Travels through a Great Part of Germany* (1677; in Holland in 1668), the emphasis in the section on Holland was also mainly historical. He borrowed much from the then popular travel guide *Les délices de la Hollande* by Jean de Parival. His descriptions of the cities are occasionally enlivened by anecdotes found there, such as the story of Jacob van Heemskerk's spending the winter of 1596–97 on Novaya Zemlya and that of the Anabaptists' revolt in Amsterdam in 1535. His general observations are limited to a brief *laudatio* of Holland, inspired by Sir William Temple's *Observations*.

Another doctor of medicine, Ellis Veryard, in his *An Account of Divers Choice Remarks in a Journey through the Low Countries, France, Italy and Part of Spain* (1701; in Holland 1682), drew extensively on previous authors, particularly Guicciardini's classic *Description of the Low Countries* (1567), and although he stressed his interest in 'new discoveries tending to the improvement and perfection of arts and sciences' (the book contains an 'index of natural and other more curious remarks'), the emphasis in the section on Holland is historical as in the previous publications. There is once more the story of Nova Zembla (more extensive this time), that of the siege of Haarlem by the Spaniards and that of the anabaptist John of Leyden, who proclaimed himself 'king of Münster in the year

---

of Aegypt, of the Holy Land, of the Remote Parts of Italy and Islands Adjoyning (London, 1615).

[6] Mr de Blainville, *Travels through Holland, Germany, Switzerland, and Other Parts of Europe, but especially Italy*, tr. G. Turnbull *et al.*, 3 vols. (London, 1743–45). Blainville was tutor to the sons of secretary Blathwayt (1705–07), and criticized M. Misson's *A New Voyage to Italy* (*passim*), Browne (p. 2 and p. 28) and Veryard (p. 18).

[7] Title: *Observations, Topographical, Moral, & Physiological; Made in a Journey through Part of the Low-Countries, Germany, Italy and France* ... (London, 1673). Philip Skippon, *An Account of a Journey Made thro' a Part of the Low Countries, Germany, Italy, and France*, published in 1732 in Churchill (op. cit. n. 11), vol. vi, pp. 359-736.

[8] Review in *Royal Society of London. Philosophical Transactions*, vii (1673), p. 5170.

1534; having driven off the bishop and taken the government into his own hands'.[9] The most recent historical event referred to was the murder of the De Witt brothers at The Hague in 1672. Among the numerous Latin inscriptions there are those on the memorials of Admiral Tromp and Prince William of Orange in Delft, and several others already printed by Ray. The extensive general observations deal with the history of Holland, its geographical situation and natural produce, its people, government, religion and customs. They are quite conventional but formed part of Veryard's educational concept as advertised in his preface: 'There is hardly any nation from which, by carefully observing their laws and customs, their methods of civil government and the wise management of their ministers, a prudent man may not reap some benefit. By seeing their different manners and humours he may learn to form his own.'

A good illustration of the encyclopedic character of these books is the full title of Dr John Northleigh's *Topographical Descriptions with Historico-Political and Medico-Physical Observations, made in Two Several Voyages through Most Parts of Europe* (1702; in Holland 1686). In this text, which occasionally mentions the names of Ray and Guicciardini, more space is devoted to matters of natural history than in Veryard. It is true, there are the usual inscriptions and references to historical events, and the general observations once again deal with government, manners and customs, but Northleigh also did his best to introduce material not yet mentioned in travelogues previously published, as, for instance, descriptions of the palaces of the Prince of Orange in the surroundings of The Hague, or that of the shallows of Pampus in the Zuiderzee off Amsterdam. The passage on music houses may be worth quoting, not only because it is one of his rare points of criticism on Holland but also for its relevance to Penson's account: 'What is most blamable in the government of this city is the public licence they give to *Musick-houses*, where women and men enter in the face of the world to make their bargains for lewdness and debauchery, in which point they exceed all whatever I saw of this kind in all my travels, not excepting even Rome itself'.

These books of travels were written for a scholarly public and reviewed in learned journals.[10] They were looked upon as encyclopedic works of reference in which there was no place for anecdotes of a personal nature such as those found in Coryat, Sandys and more particularly in Lithgow.[11] Variety was provided by all sorts of scientific and topical information and appropriate historical anecdotes. Browne's account of his crossing to Holland is very impersonal. After giving the names of some shallows off the Norfolk coast, including one that had only recently been formed, he calls attention to a natural phenomenon: the burning of

---

[9] Quotation from preface; in the section on Holland there is relatively little on the more modern sciences. For John of Leyden, see p. 9.

[10] *Royal Society of London. Philosophical Transactions*, published from 1665–66 onwards; for French journals, cf. ed. J. Sgard, *Dictionnaire des journaux. Dictionnaire de la presse, 1600–1789* (Paris, 1991).

[11] Cf. John Locke's criticism of the Travels of B. de Monconys (1666): 'it is in some measure imperfect, and has many particulars of no use to any but himself', in: A. and J. Churchill, *A Collection of Voyages and Travels*, 4 vols. (London, 1704); 6 vols., second edition (London 1732), vol. i, p. 170.

the sea, 'but the moon rising there appeared nothing but froth'. He next dwells on
the obligation of ship's captains to take a pilot before sailing up the river and
concludes the passage by mentioning all the towns on the river Maas starting at
its source. We do not learn whether he enjoyed himself on board, what people he
met and how he occupied his time during the passage. Coryat on the other hand
occasionally treated his readers to passages like the following: 'I arrived in Calais
... after I had varnished the exterior parts of the ship with the excremental
abullitions of my tumultuous stomach, as desiring to satiate the gormandizing
paunches of the hungry haddocks.'[12] Around 1700, authors who introduced this
sort of personal digressions or trivialities were duly criticized, witness the
treatment dealt out to Martin Lister M.D., whose otherwise informative account
A Journey to Paris in the Year 1698 (1698; third edition, 1699; much on scholarly
collections) was soon followed by a parody. Joseph Addison's *Remarks on Several
Parts of Italy* (1705) was also made fun of by the ironical *A Table of All the
Accurate Remarks and New Discoveries, in ... Mr Addison's Book of Travels*
(1706). Daniel Defoe, the author of *Tour through the Whole Island of Great
Britain* (1724–27) believed that a traveller should not weary 'his reader's patience
in observing trifles'[13] and the explorer William Dampier affirmed he had taken
pains not to dish up 'a polite and rhetorical narrative' but had given 'a plain and
just account of the true nature and state of the things described'.[14] By the end of
the seventeenth century readers expected travelogues to contain useful information
of a reliable nature, which should be presented in a plain style.[15]

Other travellers of this period, even if they never intended to publish their
accounts, presumably modelled their journals on these publications, although a
young tourist such as eighteen-year-old Justinian Isham (travelled 1704–07), whose
work was supervised by a 'governor', must have done so more closely than older
travellers who were under no strict obligation to write. Isham, for whom keeping
a travel account must have constituted part of his educational programme, included
much more historical information than is found in the journals of an anonymous
London merchant who toured Holland and France in 1695–99 or the merchant
John Farrington (1710), both probably in their forties or fifties. They seem to have
felt at liberty to introduce more of their personal experiences, combining them
with the more traditional descriptions of cities and public buildings. Thus the

---

[12] Coryat, *Crudities* (op. cit. n. 5; reprint Glasgow, 1905), vol. i, p. 152.

[13] Martin Lister, *A Journey to Paris in the Year 1698*, ed. by R. P. Stearns (Urbana, Chicago &
London, 1967), pp. xii–xiii. Lister did not conform to the traditional arrangement of the travel
account, having written 'to satisfy my own curiosity' (p. 1). 'I could never have forgiven myself
if I had transcribed the many fine inscriptions I met with ... , you may read them in the *Description
of Paris*' (p. 195). Cf. *Nouvelles de la République des Lettres*, 1699, vol. i, p. 352: 'Cet auteur
méritait un peu cette critique parce que son livre est écrit fort négligemment et qu'il y a bien des
bagatelles.' For Addison, see Charles L. Batten, *Pleasurable Instruction: Form and Convention in
Eighteenth-Century Travel Literature* (Berkeley & London, 1978), p. 12. For Defoe, see Batten (op.
cit.), p. 48.

[14] Preface of *A Voyage to New-Holland*, 1703, as quoted in R. W. Frantz, *The English Traveler
and the Movement of Ideas, 1660–1732* (New York, 1968), pp. 60–1.

[15] Cf. Frantz (op. cit. n. 14), pp. 59–61.

London merchant's friends and other readers of his journal were given a picture of the various Dutch towns and sights, but also of the traveller himself, who left his sons at schools in Overschie and Dordrecht, heard the news of the bombardment of Brussels and met lots of people. For all we know, this merchant and Farrington may also have been in the habit of writing private diaries, such as the one kept by Samuel Pepys during his brief stay in The Hague in 1660. If Pepys had kept a travel journal he would certainly have paid more attention to the sights and possibly have left out some of the comments on the people he met. In private diaries the author himself is the main character, something amply illustrated by the diaries of James Yonge, a ship's surgeon, who arrived in Amsterdam as a prisoner of war (1666–67) and Jeremy Roch, a sailor who was shipwrecked on the Dutch coast (1678). These diaries are very personal and emphasize the hardships their authors suffered and the way in which the Dutch took advantage of their plight. In the travel journals of this period the tourist himself never becomes the centre of attention, the emphasis is always on the description of the country.[16]

PENSON'S SHORT PROGRESS INTO HOLLAND, FLANDERS AND FRANCE

When Thomas Penson started to work out his notes, he must have known what a finished travel account was supposed to look like. However, being an inexperienced author he found writing a laborious business and, working from various notebooks, the composition of his book occupied him until 1690. His statement in the preface, asking his readers not to expect 'a lofty style of florid language' or 'a plentiful crop from a hungry soil, but ... kindly pass over the many errors', was not merely polite rhetoric, for he admitted he had never tried anything like this before. However, judging by the 'panegyric verses' written by grateful readers and included at the back of the volume, Penson had made a good job of it. There were no complaints about his naivety, on the contrary. A Mr Hurst dwelt on Penson's most important scenes: the rarities at Leyden, the Long Cellar at Amsterdam and the nunnery at Antwerp. His friend Edward Hatton was of the opinion that the English gentry should follow Penson's example and produce 'choice diaries' like his. Francis Hancock said with hyperbolic praise that Penson's style surpassed that of 'all English authors', and the Cambridge scholar Joshua Barnes, comparing him to Ulysses, wrote that the manuscript merited publication.

---

[16] Justinian Isham, Account of a Tour on the Continent, Northamptonshire Record Office, Isham Lamport, 5274, 5275; An Account of my Two Voyages beyond Sea, 1695 and 1699, Yale Univ. Libr. MS Osborn b 155; An Account of a Journey through Holland ... in several letters to Mr N. H., BL, MS Add. 15570, passage on Friesland publ. by C. D. van Strien & Ph. H. Breuker, 'Friesland in de reisverslagen van Britse reizigers omstreeks 1700', It Beaken, lii, 4 (1990), pp. 194–216; The Diary of Samuel Pepys. A New and Complete Transcription, eds. R. Latham & W. Matthews, 11 vols. (London, 1970–83); ed. Frederick N. L. Poynter, The Journal of James Yonge, 1647–1721, Plymouth Surgeon (London, 1963); Three Sea Journals of Stuart Times; Being, First, The diary of D. Cooper ... Secondly, The Journals of J. Roch ... Thirdly, The Diary of F. Rogers, ed. B. S. Ingram (London, 1936).

In trying to bring out what it was that readers liked in Penson's work, its apparently unusual, possibly innovative character, we shall look in detail at some important aspects: the descriptions, the narrative and the way opinions and feelings are expressed, quoting as much as seems necessary to give the reader an impression of the text.[17]

DESCRIPTIONS

From the very beginning, it is clear that this journal provides little in the way of learned interests, apart from a long list of 'rarities' seen in the anatomical collection at Leyden, probably copied from the official guidebook. Penson did not—and was not able to—supply information of a scholarly and scientific nature. Nor was he interested in the Latin inscriptions academic tourists were so fond of. Penson must have omitted them on purpose and instead inserted some inscriptions in Dutch he had seen on public buildings. Penson, who clearly wrote for friends and colleagues, gives ample evidence of his professional interest in funereal ceremonies, gravestones and coats of arms. His description of Amsterdam starts with some criticism of its armorial shield which contains a serious heraldic imperfection ('a pale sable on a field gules, it being directly against the rules of good armoury to lay colour upon colour or metal upon metal. But, it being the gift of an emperor, let it pass.') As a painter-stainer he was also interested in the famous stained glass windows of the church at Gouda of which he gives a detailed enumeration. However, far more space is devoted to what is usually the main ingredient of travel journals: descriptions of the principal public buildings.

Much more than the average writer of travel journals, Penson seems to have realized how easily a long succession of descriptions can weary readers. From time to time he introduces his descriptions with reassuring remarks. That of the Town Hall of Amsterdam opens with the promise that he will only mention a few of its curiosities 'because I would not make the perusal of these my *Short Travels* too tedious', and in any case a full description was beyond his powers.[18] This is followed by an account of his visit: we see him going up the stairs into the Great Hall and down again into the 'dire place where sentence of death is given to such malefactors as forfeit their lives to the law'. Here 'I beheld four lofty pillars, the upper part of which were with great art formed for naked women (only so far as modesty permits) with drooping heads and kerchers [handkerchiefs] in their hands in such apt postures for weeping, that I could almost imagine they cried aloud'. The description ends with a much less solemn account of the bells which made 'extraordinary pleasant music'.

Penson rarely gives a static, encyclopedic description of a building with the exact measurements and the correct number of pillars if it is in a church, but while stressing his own presence he usually concentrates on what is going on inside. Thus when dealing with the 'Kerck oft Plaats van Godts-dienst' in Rotterdam, he

---

[17] Contemporaries also distinguished these aspects, cf. Batten (op. cit. n. 13), pp. 82–3, 110–11.

[18] Cf. Mary Wortley Montagu: 'I will not tease you with descriptions' (*The Complete Letters of Lady Mary Wortley Montagu*, ed. R. Halsband, 3 vols. (Oxford 1965–67), see vol. i, p. 8; first ed. (1763); (in Holland 1716).

describes a scene in which people are being catechised by their minister. In his comments on the Exchange he also describes the action: It

> is daily very full of merchants, who are obliged to come on at the ring of the bell, which holds till about a quarter of an hour after twelve. Then the doors are shut up and an officer placed at each, with a money-box in his hand, and whosoever will then come in must pay six stuyvers, or also stay out. About the middle of exchange time there comes a person whose place it is who gives notice first with a tinkling brass and afterwards by a loud outcry of what sort of merchandise are in the city to be sold and where they may be seen.

Many of these descriptions are in fact sketches of the customs of the people. A good example is the one in which he describes a visit to the kermis at Gouda, slightly reminiscent of a Dutch genre painting:

> I went into one of the chiefest houses in the fair, where was a boor with a short cloak (so plentifully patched that it was hard to find which was the first colour) and under it a cymbal; also another with a violin. There I saw excellent sport by the dancing of the Mannekin and his Vrow, the Fryer and the Freyster, some singing, some dancing, some drunk and few sober.

NARRATIVE

While Penson's descriptions are much more colourful than those found in most other travel journals of this period, his treatment of the narrative is even more unusual, if only for the amount of space it takes up: as much as all the descriptions taken together. Right at the start there are 'stories', whose main subject, with one exception (on the queen of Portugal who passed through Rotterdam on her way to Lisbon), is Thomas Penson, who presents himself in situations and settings typical of the places he is visiting.

Thus we learn how at Queenborough, a tiny village in Kent which retained its ancient priviledges as a borough, the travellers went to church accompanied by the mayor and six of his aldermen, walking stiffly 'as if they had their fishing boots on' and afterwards 'had the honour to kiss Mrs Mayoress'. This is followed by an account of a storm, which Penson did his best to make sound dramatic: 'the mighty waves rolling over us and sometimes lifting us up as it were to the very heavens.' For more effect Penson even introduced dialogue in which the captain says to the seamen: 'Come boys, we will try once more to save our anchor, if it be possible; else the next thing will be to cut our cable.' A lengthy passage deals with his visit to the Long Cellar, a 'music house' in Amsterdam, which he claims he only wanted to visit because he was 'curious to know the customs of the place'. After an initial conversation with one woman ('Sir, you shall sleep with me tonight') he beckoned another 'much handsomer':

> This also was very free in her embraces and offered me all the kind things I could desire, inviting me home to her lodging, whither I went with her. Where so soon as I came in, her maid filled a large rummer of wine and set by me on the table. We tippled that off and was very merry with singing etc. and had another filled. Nor could I ask anything of her that she did not freely impart to me. And intreated me to stay all night, which I as decently refused as I could, with a promise to come to her on the morrow, which visit I ever after omitted. Thus my curiosity led me to tread the serpent's path, but was not stung, which I must own as a blessing from Heaven since neither importunity nor opportunity was then wanting.[19]

---

[19] The description of the Long Cellar reminds one of Coryat's remarks on the courtesans in

A complication of a different nature arose when much later during the passage from Rotterdam to Antwerp the boat ran aground:

> it was resolved that some of the ship's crew should go before us and we would endeavour to make to land on foot over the sands and through the shallow waters, which in many places proved almost up to our middles. Thus having stripped our lower parts, set forward with bag and bagage, both men, women and children and travelled the compass of three English miles (which with the difficulty of picking our way to avoid being caught by the toes by the great crabfish, which lay on the sands) and were sadly tired with carrying ourselves and bagage after this unaccustomed way of travelling. And at last when we were hardly able to creep, had a high bank to climb, but by helping one another (God be thanked) we got on shore about three of the clock in the afternoon. We congratulated each other with a hearty welcome and lay down on the ground to rest a little while.

A farmer finally took the travellers in a cart covered with fresh straw ('a triumphal chariot') to Lillo, from which, the next day, Antwerp was reached. The section on Flanders also contains quite a few stories but there are hardly any in the chapters devoted to France. One senses that Penson had reached the limits of his creativity and could not find the energy to intersperse the descriptions of the principal sights with an account of his adventures. A final anecdote concerns one of his fellow–passengers, who, throughout the journey in the coach from Paris to Calais, had been occupied reading her massbook. As soon as she was on board the packet boat, she proclaimed herself to be a Huguenot refugee. 'She caught hold of my hand saying out aloud: "Englishman, Englishman, no Papist, no Papist!"' and to the indignation of three Jesuits who travelled with them she threw her book and rosary into a fire.

With his descriptions Penson showed his friends what he had seen, but since he did not primarily aim at instruction, he took care not to make these as all-important as in the travel accounts published by scholars. Similarly the narrative was transformed from a thin story line giving some unity to the whole into something like the real backbone of the story. By placing much emphasis on events that had happened to him personally Penson provided his text with human interest and gave his readers a central character with whom they could to a certain extent identify.

FEELINGS AND OPINIONS

The reader's involvement in the journey, which is primarily due to the lively descriptions and pleasant stories, is enhanced by Penson's feelings and opinions. In his preface and in the description of the storm, he briefly shows his personal feelings of grief and bitterness towards the Doctors Commons, but he does not allow these emotions to get the upper hand. During the storm, when everybody panicks, even some sailors, Penson remains calm:

> I was generally above deck and did silently view and admire the works of our great Creator. And certainly the Royal Psalmist spoke great truth when he said: 'Those that go down to the sea in ships and occupy their business in great waters, they behold the wonderful works

---

Venice, with a print showing him 'saluting' one of them; he told his readers he had tried to make her give up her profession (i, pp. 401–8).

of God, etc.' To whose good pleasure and disposal I had cheerfully committed myself (and that little I had remaining out of the ruins of a desolate family), when first I resolved to travel.

Similar feelings of awe and resignation appear in the passage on the anatomic collection of the university at Leyden:

Here I beheld the wonderful works of our Great Creator, composed and set together by the art of man. At my first approach I was struck with an awful admiration, almost questioning within myself whether I should dare to go in or no. For as in a wood we behold trees in great numbers stand confusedly together, so here appeared (as it were) an army of the bones of dead men, women and children, which seemed so to stare and grin at us, as if they would instantly make us such as themselves.

After a long enumeration of the exhibits, Penson concludes the account of his visit with a reflection on the transience of life:

But certainly none can be spectators of these admirable works of the Great God, without a holy reverence and fear as well as mortified thoughts and apprehensions. I am sure the memory of them did not soon depart from me and even now at the writing hereof make some fresh impressions of that which indeed every one of us ought at all times to keep in remembrance, viz. that we must certainly die etc.

However, as Penson proceeds on his journey, more down-to-earth feelings are much more in evidence. Again and again he underlines how he enjoys the trip, singing together with other travellers, cracking jokes and trying to make himself understood in a mixture of languages. During the journey from Lille to Paris, Penson even made a picture dictionary showing a pigeon, a fish, a sheep and a few eggs, to ensure that at the inns he would get the meals he wanted.

Penson takes us through a wide range of human emotions. First there is his reaction when he came ashore at Rotterdam: 'A strange world it seemed to me when I first landed to see people of another dress and hear another language and the houses seemed to threaten to fall on our heads, they are built so much leaning forwards.' Later we learn about his feelings of pity for the inmates of the madhouse in Amsterdam: 'Although their several actions and antic postures may afford diversion to the beholders, yet as a thoughtful man cannot but pity their misery, so also ought he to be touched with a thankfulness to God that he is not cast in the same mould.' Then there is Penson's indignation when he sees that priests make a lot of money out of people's belief in miracles, and the pleasure he takes in the company of an English father who was his guide at Gent. While drinking healths with tourists, the priest even drank 'prosperity to the Protestant religion', cautiously adding: 'If it be of God it will stand, if not it must fall.' Finally there are the sentiments Penson felt in the English nunnery at Antwerp, nicely contrasting with his more profane occupation in the Long Cellar in Amsterdam. He was admitted into a parlour and through an iron grate conversed with an elderly nun who, when he was about to leave, made the suggestion he should talk to a novice:

There soon appeared (as an angel of light) a delicate, proper, young, beautiful lady, all in white garments and barefaced, whose graceful presence was delightful to behold and yet struck an awful reverence, considering she was devout and religious. And having paid my respects and fed my greedy eye a short moment on this lovely creature', they discussed the advantages and disadvantages of monastic life. 'Taking my leave they assured me that at the altar they would recommend me to God Almighty in their prayers, that he would preserve

me in my travels and restore me safe to my friends and relations; so we parted. Thus I have
faithfully set down what materially passed between us.[20]

Penson is fully alive. He is not an absent traveller like Ray, Browne and the
other scholars. In underlining that his life is in God's hands, he shows personal
religious feelings, which it is true remain rather superficial. Far more emphasis is
given to his interest in his fellow human beings in whose company he feels happy.
He leaves us in no doubt about his susceptibility to female charms, although his
moral code (and literary convention) prevents him from fully yielding to the
temptations of the flesh. Penson is very much the hero of his own story and, not
always taking himself seriously, he seems to invite the reader to do the same.

LATER DEVELOPMENTS IN THE TRAVEL GENRE

At the end of the seventeenth century, Penson was not the only one who felt that
entertainment should receive more attention in travelogues: lots of adventurous
anecdotes appeared in the many accounts of voyages to remote countries.[21] But
the more personal approach was also taken by travellers who remained nearer
home. A bestseller of 1686 was *Some Letters*, an account of a journey in France,
Switzerland and Italy by Gilbert Burnet D.D. Much of the appeal of the book
(which abounds with descriptions of the traditional kind) lay in the personal way
in which Burnet reflected on what he saw, distributing praise and blame
(especially of religious superstition) as he thought fit.[22] The success of Madame
d'Aulnoy's *Travels into Spain* (1692), which included many anecdotes about her
experiences on the road, was mainly due to its chatty style. A reviewer wrote:
'Tout ce qui peut instruire est si adroitement mêlé et égayé par des bagatelles
agréablement racontés que cette relation divertit infailliblement ceux qui ne
cherchent que cela dans la lecture.' The final remark testified to the critic's view
that the book was not written for scholars: 'C'est un badinage presque continuel.'
However, this did not prevent it from being included in John Harris' *Navigantium
atque Itinerantium Bibliotheca: or a Compleat Collection of Voyages and Travels*
(1705), which comprised many far more serious works e.g. those by Browne, Ray
and Northleigh.[23] The same anecdotical spirit emerges from two guidebooks,

---

[20] This is what 36-year-old Thornhill (*Sir James Thornhill's Sketch-book Travel Journal of 1711;
a Visit to East Anglia and the Low Countries*, ed. Katherine Fremantle, 2 vols. (Utrecht, 1975), see
vol. ii, p. 70) wrote about the nuns at Gent: 'I stole privately close to a grate through which I
peeped and saw several nuns on their knees—telling their beads etc. amongst which was a most
beautiful creature whose neat white dress and innocent countenance added not a little to her
advantage'; cf. also C. D. van Strien, 'Recusant Houses in the Southern Netherlands as seen by
British Tourists, c. 1650–1720', *Recusant History*, 21 (1991), pp. 495–511.

[21] Cf. James Sutherland, *English Literature of the Late Seventeenth Century*, Oxford History of
English Literature (Oxford, 1969), p. 292.

[22] Title: *Some Letters Containing an Account of what seemed Most Remarkable in Travelling
through Switzerland, Italy and Parts of Germany* ... Reviews in e.g. *Bibliothèque Universelle et
Historique*, v (1688), pp. 538–44 and *Nouvelles de la République des Lettres*, mars 1687, pp. 280
ff.

[23] Full title: Madame d' Aulnoy, *Letters of the Lady's Travels into Spain, with a Great Variety
of Modern Adventures*, 1692, 14th English ed. 1774; French ed. 1691; 1692; reviewed in *Histoire*

William Mountague's *The Delights of Holland* (1696; in Holland in 1695) and
Joseph Shaw's *Letters to a Nobleman* (1709; in Holland, 1700).[24] The authors'
main business was to provide information, but the occasional anecdotes in the
narrative of their journeys through Holland, give the books a personal touch. The
former opens with 'a pleasant adventure' relating how some of Mountague's
countrymen on arrival at their inn at Helvoetsluis 'immediately fell to kissing and
feeling the maids, which is not so customary here as at home'. Mountague tells
his readers he thoroughly enjoyed his trip although it took him some time to get
used to the Dutch. Shaw remains closer to his scholarly predecessors, but he too
included anecdotes in which he exhibited his personal views, feelings and a sense
of humour.

Readers who in ever increasing numbers toured Europe for pleasure must have
appreciated these books which did not overemphasize the relation between travel
abroad and education. In the course of the eighteenth century, more and more
authors when considering publication of their scholarly travels realized they should
also pay serious attention to making the book pleasant reading. Arthur Young,
who had considered expurgating trivial and personal information from *Travels in
France* (1792), a book mainly concerned with agriculture, decided against it since
these inconsequential details 'would best please the mass of common readers'.[25]
Penson, who probably belonged to this social class, understood that the average
reader would only pick up his book if it also provided entertainment, and that is
why he introduced himself as the central character, thus becoming a crucial
element of the reader's experience. As Dr Johnson later said, readers were not
interested in the work of a traveller who took them 'through wet and dry, over
rough and smooth, without incidents, without reflection'. Whatever the public may
have thought of Penson's work as a whole, they certainly appreciated the scenes
in which he humorously cast himself in the role of a moral guide, enabling his
readers to compare 'their own state' with that of their hero.[26] By dwelling on his
own feelings Penson plays on the feelings of the reader, who is often inclined to
laugh at this preposterous arms-painter who pretends he is able to give a
description of Holland, Flanders and France. At the same time, through shared
experiences, we take a personal interest in him and continually wonder what
situation our hero will find himself in next. As far as can be verified Penson's
account is that of a real journey in which the fictional element is limited, still he

---

des ouvrages des savants (VII), juillet 1691; J. Harris, *Navigantium atque Itinerantium Bibliotheca:
or a Compleat Collection of Voyages and Travels*, vol. ii, pp. 733–62. J. M. Diez Borque (*La
sociedad española y los viajeros del siglo XVII* (Madrid, 1975), pp. 48–51).

[24] Titles: William Mountague, *The Delights of Holland, or a Three Months Travel about that and
the other provinces, with Observations and Reflections on their Trade, Wealth, Strength Beauty
Policy ...* ; Joseph Shaw, *Letters to a Nobleman, from a Gentleman Travelling through Holland,
Flanders and France ...*

[25] A. Young, *Travels*, Introduction, as quoted in Batten (op. cit. n. 13), p. 34.

[26] *The Idler*, no. 97, 23 February 1760; Ibid.: 'He that instructs must offer to the mind something
to be imitated or something to be avoided; he that pleases must offer new images to his reader, and
enable him to form a tacit comparison of his own state with that of others.'

described his experiences in a way not unlike that found in the creative writing we usually associate with fiction.

In Thomas Penson the travel journal seems to have arrived at a point more than halfway between that written by the scholarly historian Thomas Coryat in 1611 and the work of eighteenth-century authors such as Smollett and Sterne, whose travels provided them with inspiration, not for documentaries, but for novels in which fact becomes indistinguishable from fiction. Smollett's picaresque novel, *Peregrine Pickle* (1751) records the hero's stay in Holland in chapters 64 and 65. The usual sights are only mentioned, not described, and far more attention is paid to Peregrine's diverting adventures, which are slightly reminiscent of Penson's anecdotes. And in spite of all the differences, Penson's tender feelings, too, seem to find an echo in those of the Sternian tourists from *Tristam Shandy* (vol. vii, 1765), *A Sentimental Journey* (1768), or from Coriat Junior's *Another Traveller* (1767), written in imitation of the former.[27] These books, in which the description of the country has become immaterial and whose narrative is hardly coherent, constitute a parody of the travel genre, and present us in many short sketches with all sorts of personal impressions and feelings that occur to the main characters in the course of the journey. Coriat Junior fittingly characterizes this development of the literary travelogue by his motto, which comes from Montaigne: 'Ce sont mes fantaisies, par lesquelles je ne tâche point à donner à connaitre les choses, mais moi.' Penson's readers must have appreciated the variety of tones the narrator adopted towards his central character, particularly the mixture of solemnity and irony. It must have been the combination of this novel tone and the largely traditional form that made this travelogue an attractive reading experience for Penson's contemporaries. Three centuries after Penson recorded his journey it still is, not in the least since we may, in the light of what happened to the travelogue in the second half of the eighteenth century, perceive him as a very early 'sentimental' traveller.

---

[27] Among Sterne's followers who travelled in the Netherlands are Coriat Junior (= Samuel Paterson), *Another Traveller! or Cursory Remarks and Tritical Observations Made upon a Journey through Part of the Netherlands in the Latter End of ... 1766*, 2 vols. (London, 1767; second edition, 1769; third edition, 1782) as *An Entertaining Journey to the Netherlands*); [A. Becket], *A Trip to Holland* (London, 1786); James Douglas, *Travelling Anecdotes through Various Parts of Europe* (London, 1782); *A Tour Sentimental and Descriptive through the United Provinces, Austrian Netherlands and France, Interspersed with Parisian and Other Anecdotes* (London, 1788); cf. the title of a contemporary guidebook: *An Entertaining Tour Containing a Variety of Incidents and Adventures, in a Journey through Part of Flanders, Germany and Holland, Historical, Political and Entertaining; Describing with Incidents and Anecdotes Amsterdam, Bruges ...* , by an English gentleman (London, 1791).

GOETHE'S AND STOLBERG'S ITALIAN JOURNEYS AND THE ROMANTIC IDEOLOGY OF ART

ROGER PAULIN*

In the eighteenth century, travel literature assumes a virtually unassailed authority. It forms an indispensable section of any well-ordained library. Thus, the earliest accessions book of the new library of my own Cambridge College, Trinity, has an entry 'Itinerum Script.'[1] and a mid-eighteenth-century shelf list[2] indicates that there was already a special class assigned for authors like Montfaucon, Addison (the author of *Remarks on Several Parts of Italy*), Misson, or Samuel Sharpe. The eighteenth century brings us those great collections and digests of travel literature that look so well in country-house libraries: Prévost, Pinkerton, or Clarke. Just into the nineteenth century, the Germans (who else?) will produce compendia of the literature on travel. One such is Johann Beckmann, *Litteratur der älteren Reisebeschreibungen*, in two volumes, published at Göttingen in 1807-09, based on the collection of that university library. But this work, contemporary with, say, Humboldt's *Vue des Cordillères*, still quotes as its motto the old seventeenth-century polymath Morhof on the subject of travel literature: *Eorum usus potest esse maximus ad res varias.*[3]

Few travel accounts written between, say, 1775 and 1825, would dispute that honoured truth. And indeed, it was because of those very 'res variae' that readers seeking information about Italy, the subject of my paper, would turn. For how much more convenient to have your information supplied in progressive stages, through different landscapes and climates, with interspersed accounts of useful arts and *moeurs*, and how much easier than reading Vitruvius, or Vasari, or Alberti and the many other authorities whom the real travellers (including Goethe) lugged along with them in their valises and saddlebags. But in the eighteenth century, travel literature, like every other literary genre, was being subjected to redefinitions, restrictions, and subversions. It is a reaction away from it that produces Laurence Sterne's *Sentimental Journey*; a narrowing down of its scope, away from those 'res variae', produces Goethe's account of Italy, one that many are agreed to call an 'aesthetic journey'.

Let us remind ourselves in the most basic fashion, of the facts surrounding Goethe's *Italienische Reise*. Fulfilling a lifelong burning wish and desire, Goethe

---

* Department of German, University of Cambridge, England.
[1] Accessions book, first half of eighteenth century, Trinity College, Cambridge, Add. MS a. 114.
[2] Shelf list, 1760, Trinity College, Cambridge, Add. MS a. 130.
[3] Johann Beckmann, *Litteratur der älteren Reisebeschreibungen. Nachrichten von ihren Verfassern, von ihrem Inhalte, von ihren Ausgaben und Uebersetzungen. Nebst eingestreueten Anmerkungen über mancherley gelehrte Gegenstände*, 2 vols. (Göttingen, 1807–09), [ii].

set off from Carlsbad in September 1786, travelling over the Brenner, across Northern Italy to Venice, then down via Bologna and Perugia to Rome, later to Naples
and Sicily, and back to Rome. He kept a considerable number of rough notes,[4]
and wrote numerous letters back home. In 1789 appeared *Das Römische Carneval*,
the first published reference to his Italian journey. In 1795-96, Goethe planned a
second full-scale journey to Italy, with the intention of producing a major account
of the character of the Italian people, culture, and nations. The Revolutionary Wars
put paid to this, although there are extensive preparatory notes.[5] From 1813-14
onwards, in the process of writing his autobiography, *Dichtung und Wahrheit*,
Goethe turned to his Italian experience, bringing out the first two volumes (up to
and including Sicily) in 1816-17; the final volume (*Zweiter Römischer Aufenthalt*)
finally appeared in 1829. Goethe used his existing notes quite extensively, but to
the horror of succeeding generations, he cut up the letters from the period and
pasted them on to sheets of paper, with more regard to convenience than to the
living memory of their recipients.[6]

The *Italienische Reise* is one of those works by Goethe that has always elicited
superlatives or a hushed, deferential tone. And there is every good reason for this.
But whereas this travel account is remarkable for its achievement of harmony, its
unity of purpose, its sense of the integrity of man and nature, its bringing alive of
past culture without descent into antiquarianism, its superb landscapes, its
over-arching aesthetic awareness, but also its elegiac motto 'Et ego in Arcadia';
whereas it undoubtedly and triumphantly achieves all of these things, we do well
to remember that Goethe's position as a writer, scientist, and minister of state, was
in 1816 not immune to the critical attentions of his fellows. A younger generation
in particular, the Romantics, who had once seen Goethe as the living proof of a
regeneration of their national literature, were now more inclined to see him as a
light that had failed.

The reasons for this reaction are as complex as they are difficult to summarize.
Let us therefore begin with a letter written in 1818 by Friedrich Schlegel, a major
older representative of German Romanticism, to his wife Dorothea:

> Goethe hat selbst bey seinen entschiedensten Anbetern mit seinem Angriff gegen die neue
> Kunst gar kein Glück gemacht. Endlich habe ich denn nun diese sämtlichen Kunst- und
> Druck hefte auch gelesen und kann nicht genug erstaunen über den über, oder beßer zu

---

[4] These are found in Erich Schmidt, *Tagebücher und Briefe Goethes aus Italien an Frau von Stein
und Herder,* Schriften der Goethe-Gesellschaft, 2 (Weimar, 1886), and *Goethes Werke,* herausgegeben im Auftrage der Großherzogin Sophie von Sachsen-Weimar, 143 vols. (Weimar, 1887–1919),
see Abt. 3, vol. 1 (Weimar, 1887), and Abt. 4, vol. 8 (Weimar, 1890).

[5] *Goethes Werke* (op. cit. n. 4), vol. 34, p. ii.

[6] Cf. Melitta Gerhard, 'Die Redaktion der ''Italienischen Reise'' im Lichte von Goethes
autobiographischem Gesamtwerk', in: *Jahrbuch des Freien Deutschen Hochstifts* (Frankfurt am
Main, 1930), 131-50; ed. Albert Meier, *Ein unsäglich schönes Land. Goethes 'Italienische Reise'
und der Mythos Siziliens / Un paese indicibilmente bello. Il 'Viaggio in Italia' di Goethe e il mito
della Sicilia* (Palermo, 1987); Gerhard Schulz, 'Goethe's *Italienische Reise*', in: *Goethe in Italy,
1786-1986: A Bi-Centennial Symposium November 14-16, 1986, University of California, Santa
Barbara: Proceedings Volume,* ed. Gerhart Hoffmeister, Amsterdamer Publikationen zur Sprache
und Literatur, 76 (Amsterdam, 1988), 5-19.

sagen unter aller Erwartung miserablen Mischmasch und Quark. In der That laßen sich doch die Deutschen alles bieten, wenn sie einmal einen Narren an einem gefressen haben. Dagegen lese ich seine erste italiänische Reise von 86 mit vielem Vergnügen. Das ist doch frisch und unbefangen beschrieben und sehr viel Schönes darin, obgleich auch schon viel Feindliches und Schlechtgesinntes daneben. Besonders sieht man aber aus mehrern äußerst naiven Bekenntnissen, wie er eigentlich damals (wie auch noch jetzt) gar nichts von der Kunst verstanden. Von den unbedeutendsten oder gemeinsten Sachen macht er einen großen Lärm und das Größte läßt er unbemerkt vorübergehn.[7]

The tone is disrespectful and disdainful; the greatest disdain is reserved for a recent polemic, *Neudeutsche religios-patriotische Kunst*, not by Goethe himself, but by Heinrich Meyer, and published in 1817 with Goethe's blessing. It had condemned the efforts of the young school of German painters in Rome, known as the Nazarenes. These, it was averred, in their Catholicizing religious zeal, their enthusiasm for the pre-Raphaelite primitives Giotto and Masaccio, their concern for a truly national style of German art based on earlier models, had in Goethe's eyes forgotten that art is based on timeless principles, laid down by the Greeks, but still valid for us now. It is concerned not with the propagation of doctrine and the depiction of the, often tasteless, manifestations of religious rite and superstition, it is not a 'repristinisation' of early styles, but it has to do with the innate qualities common to all mankind, for which, again, Greek art is exemplary.[8] In Goethe's essay, *Antik und modern*, published in 1818, the Romantics could read that all the great Renaissance artists, down to their beloved Raphael, had, even when treating Christian or biblical subjects, instinctively followed these Greek principles; the Romantics could remark those words, 'Jeder sei auf seine Art ein Grieche! Aber er sei's',[9] in which Goethe extends the invitation to be inclusive, not narrowly national, sectarian, or exclusive. These, and other such statements, had merely brought him the accusation of paganism and anti-national, cosmopolitan thinking.[10] We need not take too seriously the zealotry of the Catholic convert Dorothea Schlegel, writing to her two sons, the painters Johannes and Philipp Veit, adjuring them to avoid the 'heathenish' Faust illustrations done by the Nazarene, Peter Cornelius;[11] advising them to shun Goethe's anti-Christian stance and that of his 'Mephistopheles', the art historian Heinrich Meyer.[12] For, they argue, when Goethe does actually write about medieval Christian art, as in his periodical *Kunst und Altertum*, he fails to acknowledge that it was the Romantics who first drew attention to this style, following the lead that the young Goethe himself had given in his enthusiastic essay on the Strasbourg minster of 1773.

---

[7] Friedrich Schlegel, *Kritische Ausgabe*, eds. Ernst Behler et al. (Paderborn etc., 1958– in progress), see vol. xxx: *Die Epoche der Zeitschrift Concordia*, ed. Eugène Susini (Paderborn etc., 1980), 211.

[8] Richard Benz, *Goethe und die romantische Kunst* (Munich, 1940), 210-54.

[9] Goethe, *Sämtliche Werke, Artemis-Gedenkausgabe*, 17 vols. (Zurich, 1977), see vol. xiii, p. 846 (all further references to Goethe's works from this edition, as SW in text).

[10] Cf. Friedrich Schlegel, *Kritische Ausgabe. xxviiii: Vom Wiener Kongreß zum Frankfurter Bundestag*, eds. Jean-Jacques Anstett & Ursula Behler (Paderborn etc., 1980), 200.

[11] Schlegel (op. cit. n. 10), p. 278.

[12] Schlegel (op. cit. n. 10), pp. 200 f.

VI. 'EIN FELSENTHAL BEY SORENTO'

Engraving by Philipp Hackert. From Friedrich Leopold Graf zu Stolberg, *Reise in Deutschland, der Schweiz, Italien und Sicilien* (Königsberg & Leipzig, 1794), vol. iii, pp. 140-1

That was now a long way back in the past, subject to major changes in emphasis and overlaid with views of art that had seemingly less appreciation for a style that was northern and nationally German. Goethe's desertion of this standpoint could be recorded in a whole series of statements, over a period of at least twenty years, in which his avowed neo-classicism seems to have hardened. This appeared to be true, despite his admiration for individual Romantic artists like Runge or Cornelius, or his friendship with the young collector Sulpiz Boisserée, a protégé of Friedrich Schlegel's, whose collection of Rhenish medieval art is today the pride of Munich's Alte Pinakothek. Friedrich Schlegel, as the passage quoted above indicates, could not withhold praise from Goethe's *Italienische Reise*, despite the gulf between their respective ideologies. Ludwig Tieck, one of several Romantics to have followed Goethe's example in going to Italy, was more severe, but it was the severity of the jilted admirer:

> Goethes Buch über Italien hat mich angezogen und mir äußerst wohlgetan. Nicht, daß ich seiner Meinung immer wäre, daß ich dieselben Dinge zum Teil nicht ganz anders gesehen hätte; sondern diese Erscheinung hat mich nun endlich nach vielen Jahren von dem Zauber erlöst (ich kann es nicht anders nennen), in welchem ich mich zu Goethe verhielt: ... Ist es Ihnen nicht auch aufgefallen, wie dieses herrliche Gemüt eigentlich aus Verstimmung, Überdruß sich einseitig in das Altertum wirft und recht vorsätzlich nicht rechts und nicht links sieht? Und nun: ergreift er denn nicht auch so oft den Schein des Wirklichen statt des Wirklichen? ... Er vergißt um so mehr, daß unsere reine Sehnsucht nach dem Untergegange-nen, wo keine Gegenwart uns mehr stören kann, diese Reliquien und Fragmente verklärt und in jene reine Region der Kunst hinüberzieht. Diese ist aber auch niemals so auf Erden gewesen, daß wir unsere Sitte, Vaterland und Religion deshalb geringschätzen dürften ... Ich hatte auch die Antike gesehen, Sankt Peter, und konnte den Straßburger Münster nur um so mehr bewundern. Nach dem auswendig gelernten Raffael verstand ich erst die Lie-blichkeit und Würde altdeutscher Kunst—und dies wäre Oberflächlichkeit, Einseitigkeit etc. in mir gewesen? Ich liebe die Italiener und ihr leichtes Wesen, bin aber in Italien erst recht zum Deutschen geworden.
>
> Und nun! Ist Goethe als Greis nicht gewissermaßen von neuem irre geworden? Und etwa durch neue Entdeckungen?—Durch dasselbe, was auch in seiner Jugend da war, was er zum Teil kannte, durch Gedanken, die er zuerst ausgesprochen. Ohne Vaterland kein Dichter! Sich von diesem losreißen wollen, heißt die Musen verleugnen.[13]

For, Tieck protests, can one national style not open our eyes to another? Can one not be drawn to the ageless qualities of art, where time, school, private circum-stances count for nothing, by the very awareness of nation and fatherland? These are hard words. When, therefore, Tieck in 1823 published his cycle of poems on his Italian journey, *Reisegedichte eines Kranken*, there were certain 'correctives' to Goethe's view of Italy: in Verona, he recalled Shakespeare's Juliet, and Dietrich von Bern from the *Nibelungenlied*; in Florence, he would remember Boccaccio; arma would give rise to the insight that a person failing to take in Correggio would never enter into the true secret of art.[14]

The question that arises from these Romantic reactions to the *Italienische Reise*

---

[13] Tieck to Solger, 16 December 1816. *Goethe in vertraulichen Briefen seiner Zeitgenossen*, ed. Wilhelm Bode, 3 vols. (Weimar, 1979), see vol. ii, pp. 667 f.

[14] In the poems, 'Verona', 'Juliens Grab', 'Boccaz', 'Parma'; Ludwig Tieck, *Gedichte*, 3 vols. (Dresden, 1821-23, repr. Heidelberg 1967), see vol. iii, pp. 114 f., 118 f., 143, 279 f.

is: could Goethe deliberately have constructed his account of Italy in such a way, perhaps not to cause direct offence, but certainly to make his position unmistakably distinct from others? Goethe did actually say to Sulpiz Boisserée in 1815 that he was planning his revenge on Tieck and the brothers Schlegel—once his Italian journey was completed.[15] One can, of course, if one so wishes (but it has not been a major preoccupation of Goethe scholarship), see Goethe's works from about 1800 onwards responding to the Romantic challenge to his authority, some subliminally, some directly.

The real answer lies elsewhere. Whatever case for anti-Romantic polemics that might be made, it must rest more on circumstantial than direct evidence. A comparison with another, near-contemporary, Italian Journey can give us more secure indications as to Goethe's position. This other account of Italy is, however, in its turn ultimately linked with the Romantic movement. It was mentioned earlier that Goethe in 1795-96 had planned a second full-scale Italian Journey, with the intention of producing a compendious work on all aspects of Italy, its history, art, people, fauna and flora, geology, etc. One of the sources to which he refers occasionally in his notes is 'Stolberg'. This is not altogether surprising, as it was the most recent travel account of Italy written in German: *Reise in Deutschland, der Schweiz, Italien und Sicilien in den Jahren 1791-92.*[16] Furthermore, the author, Friedrich Leopold von Stolberg, was an old acquaintance and friend of Goethe's, indeed his companion on the first Swiss Journey of 1775. Stolberg is a major author in his own right who stands rather too much in the shadow of his mighty contemporary Goethe. There are clear reasons for this: the Stolberg family is rooted in the whole sentimental culture of the eighteenth century that we identify in Germany with the name of Klopstock (one of the Stolberg brothers was actually a godson of Edward Young, of the *Night Thoughts*,[17] the *Urtext* of this culture). Stolberg is noted for his conflation of this culture, with its emphasis on feeling, its equation of religion and art, its cult of the absent departed—the culture of *Werther*, if you will—and a lively awareness of Greek classical culture, as evidenced by his poetry and dramas in the stanzaic and verse forms of the ancients, and his translations of the *Iliad* and of Plato. Far from seeing classical antiquity and its culture as being incompatible with Christianity, Stolberg (like Klopstock) is convinced that Socrates's teaching may be easily reconciled with Christ's;[18] for him the Christian art of Raphael and Klopstock represents the further unfolding of the doctrines of Plato (GW XVII, v, xv). This commodiousness does not extend to the Greek pantheon as such; Schiller's famous poem, *Die Götter Griechenlands*, in its regret for the sensuous ever-presence of the Greek gods, had elicited from Stolberg a charge of atheism and idolatry and a timely

---

[15] Sulpiz Boisserée, *Tagebücher. i: 1808-1823*, ed. Hans-J. Weitz (Darmstadt, 1978), 228.

[16] All references to this work and to others by Stolberg in: *Gesammelte Werke der Brüder Christian und Friedrich Leopold Grafen zu Stolberg*, 20 vols. (Hamburg, 1820-25, repr. Hildesheim & New York, 1974) (referred to subsequently in text as GW with volume number).

[17] *The Correspondence of Edward Young 1683-1765*, ed. Henry Pettit (Oxford, 1971), 539.

[18] Socrates appears among the precursors of Christ in Friedrich Gottlieb Klopstock, *Der Messias*, vii. 398 ff.

Xenion or two from Schiller by way of response.[19] Thus there was a certain logic in the step Stolberg and his family took in 1800, in embracing Catholicism. In a sense, this is the first of that wave of Romantic conversions that included so many writers and painters, a statement of intent and belief that only within the Church of Rome could be found that union of the spiritual and the temporal, art and religion, that would overarch all human activities, but by the same token ward off the godless workings of the *Zeitgeist*. Stolberg is a correspondent of Romantic converts like Friedrich Schlegel, Adam Müller or Christian Schlosser, and of patriotic zealots like Fouqué; but he also remains on good terms with Goethe. The reissue of his and his brother's collected works in 1820-25, in a superbly produced edition, was a reminder that his contribution the arts and letters was far from negligible. Volumes six to nine of that edition comprise the Italian journey, lavishly furnished with plates, including engravings of the Stanze of Raphael.

In an important letter to Wieland dated 30 January 1794, Stolberg sets out the main thrust and emphasis of his forthcoming account of Italy:

> Elisische Schönheit der Natur, Milde u: Ergiebigkeit des Klima, Charakter des Volks, Flüchtiger Blick auf die Geschichte der Länder u: Städte, besonders in Großgriechenland u: Sicilien; Vergegenwärtigung der alten Schriftsteller, vorzügl: der Dichter u: Geschichtschreiber, durch Darstellung des Localen u: der Sitten; Wercke der alten u: der neuen Kunst, in sofern ein Dilettante der hierin Leie ist, u: nur seine Empfindung reden läßt, [davon sprechen kann,] das sind meine vorzüglichsten Gesichtspuncte. Daß während eines volljährigen Aufenthalts in Italien u: Sicilien, unter dem lebhaftesten Volk Europens, einem Volck dessen Geisteslanlage sehr ausgezeichnet ist, dessen Liebenswürdigkeit von vielen verkannt wird, manche kleine Charakterzüge mir auffallen mußten, stellen Sie sich leicht vor. Unter dem liebenswürdigen Landvolk der paradisischen Insel Ischia, u: im hohen Felsenthal am Meer bey Sorento, habe ich die glücklichsten Monate der Reise zugebracht. Ich habe zwey Eruptionen des Vesuv, eine glühende Lavakatarakte des Aetna, u: vom Gipfel des Aetna ganz Sicilien gesehen. Die meisten Reisenden gehen nur bis Neapel. Wenn sie nur die ganze Küste des Neapler Meerbusens u: dessen Inseln besuchen, u: Vietri u: Cava besuchen wolten, so sähen sie schon Paradiese, aber die wenigsten thun einmal das.[20]

Is this radically different from statements made by Goethe in his *Italienische Reise* or in connection with it? To a certain extent it is not, although Goethe's main interest does not lie in history, and Stolberg's account of the historical background is anything but 'flüchtig; nor could one say, with the notable exception of his evocation of Homer's land of Alcinous in Sicily, that Goethe's summoning up of 'klassischer Boden' means following in the footsteps of the Latin poets, one of Stolberg's less endearing characteristics. And yet there is superficially a great deal in common between Stolberg and Goethe. Nor need this surprise us, given that accounts of Italy at this time feed quite substantially on the patterns established by their predecessors. Both Goethe and Stolberg stand firmly on the antiquarian knowledge provided by Winckelmann, augmented by their companions Hirt (Stolberg) or Moritz (Goethe); their sense of landscape and artifact will be enhanced by the artists whom they encounter or who actually accompany them:

---

[19] See pp. 89f. of Friedrich Sengle, 'Die "Xenien" Goethes und Schillers als Dokument eines Generationskampfes', *Neues zu Goethe. Essays und Vorträge* (Stuttgart, 1989), 86-111.

[20] Friedrich Leopold Graf zu Stolberg, *Briefe*, ed. Jürgen Behrens, Kieler Studien zur deutschen Literaturgeschichte, 5 (Neumünster, 1966), p. 304.

Nicolovius (Stolberg), Tischbein and Kniep (Goethe), Hackert and Angelika
Kaufmann (these, for both Stolberg and Goethe, pointing to the continuing
development of the classical style). Where Stolberg employs Bartels' or Brydone's
accounts of Italy, Goethe uses Riedesel or Volkmann.

These, very superficial, similarities, may be extended: both Goethe and Stolberg
are interested in botany and integrate the plants of Italy into their landscape
descriptions; both indulge in set-piece nature depictions (such as the eruptions of
Vesuvius and Etna) that underlie the century's preoccupation with both the
picturesque and the sublime; both record conversations with people at all social
levels, and many an *abbate* opens up his antiquarian cabinet for the distinguished
pittore (Goethe's incognito) or the noble *conte*. Both are indifferent to medieval
art, notably in Sicily; both detest such deviations from the norm of classical
decorum as the palace of the mad prince of Pallagonia. Both seek to evoke a
living past, one (Stolberg) rather through compendiousness and comprehensive-
ness, through large tracts of Tacitus, Livy, and Diodorus, or endless quotations
from Homer and Virgil; the other is not content merely to stand on the hallowed
ground of classical antiquity, but employs the real sense of topography and field
observation to counterbalance the imperiousness of the imagination and the
emotions.

Our list of differences could be equally long, but two only need suffice. Goethe's
journey was selective, not all-inclusive. His published account, while manipulating
the raw material of the actual journey, does not in fact leave out any significant
station of his journey that might have been deemed unsuitable for inclusion. It is
well to remember that Goethe spent little time in Florence, and bypassed Syracuse
altogether: both of these cities contained too many of the things for which he had
but limited tolerance—Christian iconography, and ruins, respectively. Goethe's
account has no place for the great cities of northern Italy, Genoa, Turin, and
Milan, that are so important in Stolberg's scheme of things, little on the Italian
mainland south of Naples, whereas Stolberg has much to say on Calabria. But
these are not the main differences. They are religious or ideological. When Stolberg stands on the Alpine pass that leads over to Italy, his eye is directed inwards,
then heavenwards, not out to the landscape that will systematically unfold as he
traverses it:

> Es ist ein großer Anblick, wenn man diese Alpen hinter sich sieht. Sie trennen nicht nur
> Italien von Savoyen, sie trennen unsere neuere Welt von jener ehrwürdigen, älteren, von
> welcher wir alles, was gesittete Menschen von Barbaren unterscheidet, Künste, das Licht der
> Wissenschaften, ja das heilige Feuer der Religion erhalten haben. Italien war genau mit
> Griechenland verbunden, dessen Pflanzstädte dem untern Theile dieses Landes den Namen
> Groß-Griechenland gaben. Andre griechische Völker wohnten in Klein-Asien; ihre
> Pflanzstädte waren auf der Küste von Afrika und von Asien zerstreut, in Egypten saßen
> griechische Könige auf dem alten Thron der Pharaone, ehe es eine römische Provinz ward.
> Die Herrschaft Roms vereinigte alle Völker, die das mittelländische Meer umwohnen. Bald
> hoffe ich am Gestade dieses Meers zu stehen, dessen Wogen Italien und Sicilien, die
> Trümmer von Karthago, Griechenlands Vesten in Europa und Asien, wo jeder Strom und
> jedes Vorgebürge durch Fabel und Geschichte berühmt ward, seine besungenen Inseln, das
> mystische Egypten, und Israels geweihtes Erbe anspülen, wo die durch lange Morgenröthe
> ihrer Geschichte, und durch das Hahnengeschrei der Propheten angekündigte Sonne der
> Wahrheit und der Liebe aufgog, welche bald über Alpen und Meere, vom Ganges bis zum
> Eisgestade strahlend, die Völker leuchtend erwärmte; zwar durch aufsteigende Erddünste oft

verdunkelt wird, aber an ihrem Himmel auch am Ende der Tage nicht untergehen soll! (GW VI, 311)

The passage is interesting in that it makes the Mediterranean and its littoral the cradle of all civilisation and religion, with significant pointers eastward. In that sense, Stolberg is aligning himself with so many predecessors and contemporaries; it will also be the burden of his later multi-volumed *Geschichte der Religion Jesu Christi*. Out of comparative mythology emerges the true 'mythology', the only acceptable religion. Goethe's first encounter with Italy, by contrast, is through a variety of sense impressions and awarenesses:

> Nach Mitternacht bläst der Wind von Norden nach Süden, wer also den See hinab will, muß zu dieser Zeit fahren; denn schon einige Stunden vor Sonnenaufgang wendet sich der Luftstrom und zieht nordwärts. Jetzo nachmittag wehet er stark gegen mich und kühlt die heiße Sonne gar lieblich. Zugleich lehrt mich Volkmann, daß dieser See ehemals Benacus geheißen, und bringt einen Vers des Virgil, worin dessen gedacht wird:
>
> > Fluctibus et fremitu resonans Benace marino.
>
> Der erste lateinische Vers, dessen Inhalt lebendig vor mir steht, und der in dem Augenblicke, da der Wind immer stärker wächst und der See höhere Wellen gegen die Anfahrt wirft, noch heute so wahr ist als vor vielen Jahrhunderten. So manches hat sich verändert, noch aber stürmt der Wind in dem See, dessen Anblick eine Zeile Virgils noch immer veredelt. (SW XI, 31 f.)

Classical antiquity is clearly one factor, but religion is not. Stolberg's mottos, from Plato and Petrarch, in their insistence on a progression to higher reality and higher sources of (moral) beauty, stand in contrast to Goethe's 'Et in Arcadia ego' that underlines both the joy of achievement and fulfilment, but also the sense of its fragility and evanescence.

The question of the Romantic ideology of art as a possible foil to Goethe's account of Italy, is not difficult to solve pragmatically. Goethe had not substantially altered his views on Christianity or Christian art or on the pre-eminence of classical culture, since first setting foot in Italy in 1786. He had remained true to a position from which he had no cause to veer. The original diary jottings do not suggest that there was any substantial editing for the *Italienische Reise* of 1816-17, that indicated a change of stance. We might learn for instance that Goethe had actually seen much more religious art in Venice than he later admits, but the account of Venice would still be remarkable for what it does not choose to record. Goethe might suppress the occasional anticlerical remark, but the cause of organised religion will nevertheless suffer some indignities—although not in all its aspects. Goethe's dislike of what his disciple Heinrich Meyer later calls 'widerstrebende Gegenstände'[21]—crucifixions, martyrdoms and the like—could not be more clearly enunciated. The *Italienische Reise* thus reflects no substantial shift in Goethe's stated emphasis; only it committed, for the Romantics, the sacrilege of stating the unacceptable in the sacred precincts of Italy, especially of Rome, the place of so many Romantic conversions and near-conversions. And yet comparison with Stolberg's account will bring out more subtle underlying

---

[21] See p. 22 of [Heinrich Meyer], 'Ueber die Gegenstände der bildenden Kunst. I', in: *Propyläen. Eine periodische Schrifft herausgegeben von Goethe*, 1. Bd., 1. Stück (Tübingen, 1798), 20-54.

differences that show both Goethe and Stolberg to be writing 'ideological' travel accounts of Italy.

The first example may not seem to be the obvious contrast that it is: the respective accounts of the temple ruins at Agrigentum (Girgenti). For Goethe, this archeological site, like that at Segesta, was not a comforting spectacle. The sheer hugeness of the Greek temple was difficult to reconcile with notions of classical architecture nurtured on Vitruvius or Palladio: the disordered and misshapen heaps were disharmonious:

> Der Tempel des Herkules hingegen ließ noch Spuren vormaliger Symmetrie entdecken. Die zwei Säulenreihen, die den Tempel hüben und drüben begleiteten, lagen in gleicher Richtung wie auf einmal zusammen hingelegt, von Norden nach Süden; jene einen Hügel hinaufwärts, diese hinabwärts. Der Hügel mochte aus der zerfallenen Zelle entstanden sein. Die Säulen, wahrscheinlich durch das Gebälk zusammengehalten, stürzten auf einmal, vielleicht durch Sturmwut niedergestreckt, und sie liegen noch regelmäßig, in die Stücke, aus denen sie zusammengesetzt waren, zerfallen. Dieses merkwürdige Vorkommen genau zu zeichnen, spitzte Kniep schon in Gedanken seine Stifte. (SW XI, 302)

Note that Goethe is unwilling to admit the most likely cause for this disruption and collapse in a volcanic area: an earthquake.[22] Art—Kniep the artist—is, however, to hand to render the disorder orderly, to make the ruinous into the picturesque. Stolberg is different:

> Ich bin versichert, daß diese Tempel, so wie auch die von Selinus, durch ein fürchterliches Erdbeben, vielleicht durch verschiedene, in solche Steinhaufen verwandelt worden. Zerstörende Menschenhand wirft alles flach über einander; nur der Natur gewaltiger Arm vermochte diese ungeheuern Massen so durch einander zu schleudern.
>
> Siegend lächelt sie jetzt, diese immer junge Natur, unter den Trümmern der stolzen gegen sie ohnmächtigen Kunst. Mitten unter den Steinhaufen entgrünet dem Boden ein Hain von Feigen- und Mandelbäumen. Im Tempel des olympischen Zeus sah ich zum erstenmal einen Pistazienbaum. Er war schon bedeckt mit vielen noch kleinen röthlichen Nüssen, und blühete zugleich. (GW VIII, 464)

He has few qualms in allowing for an earthquake as cause, for this is merely one manifestation of nature, the other and destructive side of the regenerating force that is now causing the ruins to be re-integrated into beneficent mother nature. In his account of Segesta, Goethe too had described the vegetation out of which the temple is seen to soar, yet his discomfort at the aspect of the ruins and their loneliness, is almost palpable. For Stolberg, the wrecks of time can be seen as part of the process of history that has brought us through change and decay and destruction to a religious faith not subject to these vicissitudes. Goethe could find no certitude in the contemplation of these processes where they detracted from an organic view of man and nature.

The second example makes Goethe's and Stolberg's positions plainer:

> Von der Schönheit, im vollen Mondschein Rom zu durchgehen, hat man, ohne es gesehen zu haben, keinen Begriff. Alles Einzelne wird von den großen Massen des Lichts und Schattens verschlungen, und nur die größten, allgemeinsten Bilder stellen sich dem Auge

---

[22] Cf. p. 442 of Wilhelm Erich Mühlmann, 'Goethe, Sizilien und wir', *Germanisch-Romanische Monatschrift*, NF. 26 (1976), 440-51; Ernst Osterkamp (ed.), *Sizilien. Reisebilder aus drei Jahrhunderten* (Munich, 1986), 370 ff.

dar. Seit drei Tagen haben wir die hellsten und herrlichsten Nächte wohl und vollständig genossen. Einen vorzüglich schönen Anblick gewährt das Coliseo. Es wird nachts zugeschlossen, ein Eremit wohnt darin an einem Kirchelchen und Bettler nisten in den verfallenen Gewölben. Sie hatten auf flachem Boden ein Feuer angelegt, und eine stille Luft trieb den Rauch erst auf der Arena hin, daß der untere Teil der Ruinen bedeckt war und die ungeheuern Mauern oben drüber finster herausragten; wir standen am Gitter und sahen dem Phänomen zu, der Mond stand hoch und heiter. Nach und nach zog sich der Rauch durch die Wände, Lücken und Öffungen, ihn beleuchtete der Mond wie einen Nebel. Der Anblick war köstlich. So muß man das Pantheon, das Kapitol beleuchtet sehn, den Vorhof der Peterskirche und andere große Straßen und Plätze. Und so haben Sonne und Mond, eben wie der Menschengeist, hier ein ganz anderes Geschäft als anderer Orten, hier, wo ihrem Blick ungeheure und doch gebildete Massen entgegenstehn. (SW XI, 182 f.)

Goethe is fascinated by the thought of the Roman buildings, the Colosseum and the Pantheon, in the moonlight (or bright midday sun), the effect of such effulgence in breaking down surface line and detail and creating mass; the way of seeing has to change, in order to appreciate fully the essence of the object contemplated. Stolberg, too, has a vision of bright light in the Pantheon:

Ein großes Gefühl ergreift einen, wenn man mitten in der Rotunda steht, umfangen vom Eindruck der hohen Einfalt, die von allen Seiten auf das Auge, tief auf die Empfindung wirkt. Die Reihe der Jahrhunderte, welche seit der Gründung dieses Tempels entflohen sind, schwebet mit ihren in Staub gesunknen Menschengeschlechtern vor dir vorüber. Die Erde war mit Götzenaltären bedeckt, als Agrippa dieses Denkmaal von der Macht des Augustus erhub.

Es wehete die Morgenröthe der Sonne, welche den Erdkreis erhellen sollte. Dem lebendigen Gotte ist nun der Götzentempel gewidmet. Ich empfand es mit frohem Schauer, sah auf, und da strahlte über der offnen Wölbung die Bläue des unendlichen Himmels. Wolken umhüllen ihn dann und wann, aber sie weichen dem Strahl der allerleuchtenden Sonne. (GW VII, 274)

For him, however, notions of light are immediately transferred over into the metaphorical sphere. Sunlight, sky, and temple are reintegrated into the Platonic-Christian sun image, the ray descending from the source of all light to the newly-reconsecrated place of worship. Interestingly enough, Stolberg employs in the preface to his translation of Plato the same image of light shining down through the rotunda of the Pantheon, to describe the harmony of Socrates' life, teaching and death (GW XVII, x). What for Goethe has visual concreteness and even extends the contours of seeing, becomes for Stolberg an allegory of existence.

Thirdly, we have accounts by Goethe and Stolberg of a painting by Raphael. Raphael and Michelangelo, as we know, whether from Sir Joshua Reynolds' discourses, or Winckelmann, or Mengs, and as all *cognoscenti* and *dilettanti* at the time knew, represent for the eighteenth century the twin peaks of human achievement in art. As the century proceeds, however, we notice Raphael moving ahead in esteem, until he becomes almost the sole icon, 'Der Göttliche Raphael', with which the young Romantics, Wackenroder and Tieck, invested their religion of art. Stolberg's account of Raphael in his *Reise* may be seen as an important stage in that awareness. The painting concerned is a St Agatha in the Palazzo Ranuzzi in Bologna, attributed at the time to Raphael (even bad art history has its rightful place in the history of taste!). St Agatha is, of course, revered as an

example of virtuous fortitude, preferring death to union with an unbeliever.
Neither Goethe nor Stolberg is seemingly interested in the legend, only in the
figure:

> Trifft man denn gar wieder einmal auf eine Arbeit von Raffael, oder die ihm wenigstens mit
> einiger Wahrscheinlichkeit zugeschrieben wird, so ist man gleich vollkommen geheilt und
> froh. So habe ich eine heilige Agathe gefunden, ein kostbares, obgleich nicht ganz wohl
> erhaltenes Bild. Der Künstler hat ihr eine gesunde, sichere Jungfräulichkeit gegeben, doch
> ohne Kälte und Roheit. Ich habe mir die Gestalt wohl gemerkt und werde ihr im Geist
> meine 'Iphigenie' vorlesen und meine Heldin nichts sagen lassen, was diese Heilige nicht
> aussprechen möchte. (SW XI, 116)
>   Im Pallaste Ranuzzi ist eine heilige Agatha von Rafael, welche mir lieber ist, als die viel
> berühmtere Cecilia. Jene hat den vollen Ausdruck erhabner Ruhe, mit weiblicher Anmuth
> verbunden, welche kein Maler so wie Rafael darzustellen weiß.(GW VII, 42f.)

Both are using the critical language handed down to them from the French via
Winckelmann, Stolberg in almost unaltered form, with 'erhabene Ruhe' and
'weibliche Anmuth', key terms in Winckelmann's notions of classical art, here
applied, without any special accentuation or qualification, to Raphael. His art may
be subject to the historical process of change, yet the critical language suggests a
timelessness, in its enshrinement of the universal truths of Christianity. Goethe,
too, conjoins Raphael and classical art, not by subjecting them to an ascending
scale of values, but by equating the human and appealing ('gesunde, sichere
Jungfräulichkeit') with the Euripidean heroine who was the subject of his
classicizing adaptation. Thus, as the secularized language of Christian charity and
forgiveness may permeate the expression of that Greek-sounding drama, so the
purely Christian associations of St Agatha (and accompanying martyrdom) may
be subsumed under general, universal notions of chastity, purity, and forbearance.
Raphael, as that essay *Antik und modern* of 1818 puts it, becomes a Greek in his
ability to abstract essential human qualities from a particular context. Stolberg's
laconic 'welche kein Maler so wie Rafael darzustellen weiß', is echoed by a
number of further superlatives (like the interspersed poem, *Rafael*, GW VII,
217-221) in the course of his Italian journey that place Raphael beyond criticism
(GW VII, 242f.), that make him painter, poet, and philosopher in one (GW VII,
258, a point echoed in the preface to the Plato translation, GW XVII, v), that
equate him with Homer (GW, IX, 382), and, interesting enough, link his name
with that of Albrecht Dürer (GW IX, 366). For Raphael and Dürer, in the
Romantic ideology of art, are the twin representatives of South and North, linked
in their piety, their love of their native land, their simplicity, and their perceived
placing of the heart over mere technique.

In that respect, Stolberg's account of 1794, republished in 1822, can be seen as
an important document of a pre-Romanticism that soon allies itself with the
movement proper. Yet, no less than Goethe, Stolberg would not want to jettison
the view of art, poetry and religion that he had brought with him from the
eighteenth century which had nurtured him. What the Romantics failed to
appreciate, was that Goethe, far from losing any sense of proportion and decorum,
had not changed. The remembrance of Italy, rekindled during the work on his
autobiography, served to remind him of insights won twenty-five years earlier, in
front of works of art no longer physically present. Stolberg's insights, by contrast,
while indebted to a culture of sentimentality that by 1816 had taken on different

contours and emphases,[23] now formed part of the notions of Christian art that his Romantic contemporaries were using in their ideological confrontation with Goethe. That, I believe, is the relationship of these two Italian journeys to each other.

---

[23] Cf. *Briefe aus dem Stolberg- und Novalis- Kreis. Nebst Lebensbild und ungedruckten Briefen von Tiecks Schwägerin, der Malerin und Ordensoberin Maria Alberti*, ed. Heinz Jansen, Veröffentlichungen der Historischen Kommission Westfalens, xix: Westfälische Briefwechsel Bd. 2 (Münster, 1932), repr. ed. Siegfried Sudhof (1969).

'THE WHEEL OF TIME IS ROLLING FOR AN END'

JAN H. A. LOKIN[*]

And[1] let us not remember Italy the less regardfully, because, in every fragment of her fallen Temples, and every stone of her deserted palaces and prisons, she helps to inculcate the lesson that the wheel of Time is rolling for an end, and that the world is, in all great essentials, better, gentler, more forbearing, and more hopeful, as it rolls!'[2]

These are the words with which Dickens ended his account of a journey through Italy in 1844/5, which was published in the *Daily News* under the title *Travelling Letters, Written on the Road*. Two years earlier, in 1842, Dickens had visited America and had recorded his impressions in a book called *American Notes*. The titles were deliberately different in order to draw attention to the different forms of travel reporting he used. His American experiences were written in the form of sharp analytical observations, which today are still surprisingly up-to-date; these analyses he called *Notes*. They caused a storm of protest in America because they were full of the sort of observations which Americans certainly did not want to read, and definitely not when written by someone whom they had treated and *fêted* as if he were one of their own writers. They had viewed the author as an enlightened person who was ruthlessly exposing all the rotten institutions in the old country, and now suddenly they were reading sharp commentaries on the American penal system, the prevalence of pigs on Broadway, corruption in the House of Representatives, the universal habit of spitting, the hypocrisy on copyright, and the appalling conditions suffered by slaves. Dickens's descriptions of Italy, on the other hand, were more a collection of images and sketches, in short, *Pictures*. The quotation above shows him to be an optimistic man. Full of confidence in the outcome, he saw the history of man as a journey through time to a final destination, a better world for a chastened humanity. Many writers of the nineteenth and twentieth centuries have cherished this belief in progress. They see proof of it in industrialization, technical advances and legitimization of it in Enlightenment and in rational thought. In this sense, Dickens was a child of his time. Nevertheless he could also have intended his last sentence simply to provide a neat literary peroration, without any double meaning. In Italy more than anywhere else, he was surrounded by evidence of a past that was a great deal more glorious than the present. Decay and destruction were all around him, side by side with the blue sky, the pine trees, and the magnificent architecture and

---

[*] University of Groningen, The Netherlands.
[1] The quotations from Dickens's works I have taken from *The Oxford Illustrated Dickens*. As for the events in Dickens's life, I refer to the great Dickens biography by Peter Ackroyd, London 1990.
[2] *Pictures from Italy* (London, 1966), 433.

ruins. In the middle of his story he writes: 'Everything is in extremes. It seemed as if one reached the end of all things.' A very different *end*, indeed, to the conclusion of the account of his Italian journey quoted above. An end, moreover, that did not satisify him. Dickens expressed his hope for a better world when he wrote:

> Years of neglect, oppression and misrule, have been at work, to change their nature and reduce their spirit; miserable jealousies, fomented by petty Princes to whom union was destruction and division strength, have been a canker at their root of nationality, and have barbarized their language; but the good that was in them ever, is in them yet, and a noble people may be, one day, raised up from these ashes. Let us entertain that hope![3]

Dickens continued to cherish this hope, even in the face of contrary evidence. His far too clear an insight into human nature withheld him from believing that technical advances would automatically result in better human beings. He lacked that blind faith of many of his contemporaries in progress, and saw clearly the various misuses to which technical inventions could lead. In addition, he had a sharp eye for the many useful things that were being sacrificed to the so-called advancement. I will illustrate this with Dickens's literary reaction to what was probably the most momentous event during the industrialization of England, that is, the coming of the train and the relentless laying of the iron road, which would completely change the appearance of towns and countryside. Here, I shall confine myself to fiction, and not discuss the countless journalistic descriptions published in *Household Words*, and *All the Year Round*. From the latter paper—both owned and edited by Dickens himself—comes a collection of individual stories which also appeared together as *The Uncommercial Traveller*. These stories can hardly be regarded as travel reports; they are rather musings and descriptions of atmosphere, jotted down by 'a traveller for the great house of Human Interest Brothers having rather a large connection in the fancy goods way'.[4] Their subjects are a shipwreck, the Chatham dockyard, the City of London churches, birthday celebrations, and other such topics.

Nor do I wish to dwell too long upon Dickens's own lust for travel. In the years 1832-33, when Dickens was a reporter for the *True Sun* and the *Morning Chronicle*, he travelled a great deal. He had to cover election campaigns, dinners, and public meetings all over the country. Then, as now it was a race to come with the earliest and most accurate report of an event. Since there were no telephones, reports had to be brought to the paper overnight by stage coach. Dickens had memories of these chases 'through the dead of night':

> I have often transcribed for the printer from my shorthand reports, important public speeches in which the strictest accuracy was required ... writing on the palm of my hand, by the light of a dark lantern, in a post chaise and four, galloping through a wild country, all through the dead of night.[5]

This hectic existence was what Dickens loved, not so much for pleasure but rather because it was an ideal outlet for his restlessness. Any form of indolence

---

[3] *Pictures from Italy* (London, 1966), 433.
[4] *The Uncommercial Traveller* (London, 1973), 1.
[5] Cf. Peter Ackroyd, *Dickens* (London, 1990), 155.

or leisure was completely alien to him. It was the journey itself, not the landscape or the tourist attractions which appealed to him, or in Ackroyd's words: 'It was the rush and the speed which entranced him, the rush of the wind and whirling roads, it was working against time and above all, the desperate need for speed.'[6] In company, and later in the circle of his family and friends, Dickens was never tired of telling his experiences as a roving reporter in the old coaching days.

In Dickens's youth, travel was what it had been for centuries: a difficult undertaking seldom indulged in for pleasure. Most people travelled on foot. The amount of walking they did seems quite extraordinary to us. Dickens himself used to walk for miles as relaxation after having eaten, or between sessions of writing. In *The Pickwick Papers* we read: 'At dinner they met again, after a five-and-twenty mile walk, undertaken by the males at Wardle's recommendation, to get rid of the effects of the wine at breakfast.' This has often been considered an exaggeration. When Sam Weller visited his stepmother at The Marquis of Granby in Dorking, he walked back to London, also a distance of some twenty-five miles. Little Nell wandered all over England with her grandfather and met many other travellers walking everywhere. Horses and carriages were using the same road as travellers on foot, and in summer there were always groups of people sleeping and eating on the verges of the highways. The safest way to travel was in a group. So a traveller often joined up with one of the numerous travelling players' groups, such as that of Vincent Crummles in *Nicholas Nickleby*, Sleary's Circus in *Hard Times*, and Jarley's Wax Works in *The Old Curiosity Shop*.

The main roads were always crowded. The most crowded route was the one between London and Dover. It is this route that David Copperfield took when he ran away from the firm of Murdstone and Grinby in search for his aunt, Betsy Trotwood. The scene is typical Dickensian: a helpless child of ten, on his way to an unknown destination in a strange and hostile world. He covered twenty-three miles on the first day, but was robbed of all his money before he had travelled any distance. The following day, he was forced to sell his jacket for a pittance. At night he slept in haystacks. No-one paid the slightest attention to him, proof that such stray children were a quite normal occurrence, as today in the large cities of South America and Asia. The road swarmed with riff-raff, and the brutality of the tramps, especially, scared David stiff: 'The trampers were worse than ever and inspired me with a dread that is yet quite fresh in my mind. Some of them were most ferocious-looking ruffians who called after me to come back and speak to them and, when I took to my heels, stoned me.'[7] A tinker, accompanied by a woman with a black eye, stopped the boy and demanded his money, threatening: 'or I 'll knock your brains out'. But as David prepared to give him his last penny, he saw the woman's lips forming the word 'no'. Then the tinker stole his handkerchief, and, again soundlessly, the woman said: 'Go.' As David made himself scarce, he saw how the man 'turned' upon the woman with an oath and knocked her down: 'I never shall forget seeing her fall backward on the hard road, her hair

---

[6] Cf. Peter Ackroyd, *Dickens* (London, 1990), 156.
[7] *David Copperfield* (London, 1966), 186.

all whitened in the dust, wiping the blood from her face with a corner of her shawl.' David was so scared that he hid whenever he came across such people, 'which happened so often that I was very seriously delayed.' It made a deep impression on the ten-year-old boy, and although Dickens wrote this episode when he was 38, it was, without doubt, based on similar scenes witnessed as a twelve-year-old, when at night he roamed through London.

Travelling by stage was not less dangerous. Alongside the bodily discomforts of the cold, the stench, and the bone-rattling shaking of the coach, one had to get out and walk when the coach could not make it up a hill. On top of all that, the intentions of fellow passengers were not clear, and no-one could trust the other an inch. At the beginning of his novel about the French Revolution, *A Tale of Two Cities*, Dickens describes the journey of the Dover mail coach in 1775. This description forms also a literary introduction: the deliberately evoked atmosphere of discomfort and distrust immediately draws the reader into the story and sets the tone for the whole book.

> There was a steaming mist in all the hollows, and it had roamed in its forlornness up the hill, like an evil spirit, seeking rest and finding none. A clammy and intensely cold mist, it made its slow way through the air in ripples that visibly followed and overspread one another, as the waves of an unwholesome sea might do. It was dense enough to shut out everything from the light of the coach-lamps but these its own workings, and a few yards of the road; and the reek of the labouring horses steamed into it, as if they had made it all.
>
> Two other passengers, besides the one, were plodding up the hill by the side of the mail. All three were wrapped to the cheek-bones and over the ears, and wore jack-boots. ... In those days, travellers were very shy of being confidential on a short notice, for anybody on the road might be a robber or in league with robbers ...
>
> If any one of the three had had the hardihood to propose to another to walk on a little ahead into the mist and darkness, he would have put himself in a fair way of getting shot instantly as a highwayman.[8]

When a rider comes out of the mist at full speed and approaches the coach to deliver a secretive message, 'Recalled to life', to one of the passengers, the mystery is complete. The reader is gripped by a curiosity which holds him fast.

How different is this from the mail coaches in his first book, *The Pickwick Papers*, which Dickens wrote when he was 24 years old, and made him famous overnight. *The Pickwick Papers* is a travel book—in The Netherlands, Mensing[9] translated it as: *Samuel Pickwick en zijn reisgenoten* ('Samuel Pickwick and his fellow-travellers')—set in pre-industrial England. Although it was written in monthly instalments, like all of Dickens's works, there is, especially in the first half, a certain momentum, (figuratively speaking), which he never achieved again. It is the momentum of youth, enthusiasm and happiness: the year 1836, in which the first instalments of *The Pickwick Papers* appeared, was also the year of his marriage. The publishers Chapman and Hall originally intended to surround some illustrations of an unsuccessful sportsman with a few amusing anecdotes. But the

---

[8] *A Tale of two Cities* (London, 1967), 4.
[9] C. M. Mensing, first translator of Dickens's collected works, which appeared in the edition of A. C. Kruseman and E. and M. Cohen.

writer they commissioned, the relatively unknown Boz—the pseudonym behind which Dickens lurked—demanded that he be allowed to set the tone of the stories and that the artist, the well-known Robert Seymour, should follow his lead. The sportsman eventually only played a minor role as the clumsy Nathaniel Winkle, 'the sporting Winkle, communicating additional lustre to a new green shooting coat'. No, the hero became the immortal Pickwick, whom Dickens introduced in the minutes of the Pickwick Club as follows:

> A casual observer might possibly have remarked nothing extraordinary in the bald head, and circular spectacles, which were intently turned towards his (the secretary's) face, during the reading of the above resolutions: to those who knew that the gigantic brain of Pickwick was working beneath that forehead, and that the beaming eyes of Pickwick were twinkling behind those glasses, the sight was indeed an interesting one. There sat the man who had traced to their source the mighty ponds of Hampstead, and agitated the scientific world with his Theory of Tittlebats, as calm and unmoved as the deep waters of the one on a frosty day, or as a solitary specimen of the other in the inmost recesses of an earthen jar.[10]

When Seymour committed suicide shortly after the first instalment, and Dickens was allowed to choose his own illustrator—Hablôt K. Browne, with the pseudonym Phiz—success was assured. Pickwick and his companions travelled through England by mail coach, and the descriptions of these trips are all that later generations remember about a method of travel which has completely disappeared. Likewise, the Dutch derive their knowledge of the tow-barge from the sketches of Hildebrand.[11] Thus *The Pickwick Papers* is a book which overflows with a love of life, projecting the image of a coach packed with warmly-wrapped passengers—the very picture one finds on Dutch Pickwick tea-bag labels. Its passengers continually fortify themselves with stimulating beverages in the inns. After changing horses, the coachman—old Tony Weller 'with a face like an underdone beef' —enthusiastically cracks his whip and blows some clear notes on the posthorn which echoes in the fresh cold air.

Winter seems to dominate in Dickens's early stories, not a damp, cold and uncomfortable winter, rather one of roaring fires, drinking songs, laden tables, with Christmas as apex—Christmas, the celebration which has been virtually designed by Dickens. (If he had lived in the Netherlands, the feast of 'Sinterklaas'[12] would probably have become even cosier—or, if you prefer, snugger—than it already is. No wonder that the Dutch Dickens expert Godfried Bomans[13] had such a soft spot for Sinterklaas.)

The Pickwick Papers contains a number of separate stories, connected by the coach journeys. These travel descriptions are not only the glue which holds the stories together, they also determine the mood of the book, which is itself different

---

[10] *The Posthumous Papers of the Pickwick Club* (London, 1967), 2.

[11] Hildebrand is the pseudonym of the protestant minister Nicolaas Beets (1814–1903)—the author of many books, poems and articles. His fame rests entirely on his first book, the *Camera obscura*.

[12] Sinterklaas (St Nicolas) is the only saint who survived the reformation in the Netherlands. On St Nicolas eve (December 5) the Dutch give each other presents, adding self-made poems.

[13] Godfried Bomans (1913-71) was the most popular Dutch writer of his time. He was a great Dickens lover and cofounded the Haarlem Branch of the Dickens Fellowship.

from the one evoked in the introduction to *A Tale of Two Cities*. Here is an example: the description of the journey to Wardle's Manor Farm in Dingley Dell, where—how could it be anything else?—the Pickwickians are going to celebrate Christmas:

> They have rumbled through the streets, and jolted over the stones, and at length reach the wide and open country. The wheels skim over the hard and frosty ground: and the horses, bursting into a canter at a smart crack of the whip, step along the road as if the load behind them—coach, passengers, cod-fish, oyster barrels, and all—were but a feather at their heels. They have descended a gentle slope, and enter upon a level, as compact and dry as a solid block of marble, two miles long. Another crack of the whip and on they speed, at a smart gallop ... The lively notes of the guard's key-bugle vibrate in the cold air... At last they pull up at the inn yard where the fresh horses, with cloths on, are already waiting and the passengers look with longing eyes and red noses, at the bright fire in the inn bar, and the sprigs of holly with red berries which ornament the window. After having refreshed themselves they are all ready for starting, except the 'two stout gentlemen', whom the coachman inquires after with some impatience. Hereupon the coachman, and the guard, and Sam Weller, and Mr Winkle, and Mr Snodgrass, and all the hostlers and every one of the idlers, who are more in number than all the others put together, shout for the missing gentlemen as loud as they can bawl. A distant response is heard from the yard, and Mr Pickwick and Mr Tupman come running down it, quite out of breath, for they have been having a glass of ale a-piece, and Mr. Pickwick's fingers are so cold that he has been full five minutes before he could find the sixpence to pay for it. The coachman shouts an admonitory 'Now then, gen'l'm'n!' the guard re-echoes it; Mr. Pickwick struggles up on one side, Mr. Tupman on the other; Mr Winkle cries 'All right'; and off they start. Shawls are pulled up, coat collars are re-adjusted, the pavement ceases, the houses disappear, and they are once again dashing along the open road, with the fresh clear air blowing in their faces, and gladdening their very hearts within them.[14]

So far, we have shown how Dickens used the journey as a literary introduction in *A Tale of Two Cities*, and as a welding device for the separate adventures in *The Pickwick Papers*. As a last example of a journey by coach I want to examine that to Little Nell's hiding place in the *Old Curiosity Shop*. Here, the function of the travel description is different, this time symbolic. The journey is a last trip in more ways than one, and transcends what is actually described. No other literary character made such an impression on Dickens's contemporaries as the frail figure of Little Nell, who roamed through England with her thieving grandfather; a child who had to look after an old man in both material and moral respects. Little Nell dies at the end of the story, but neither Dickens nor the public were able to accept this death. In a letter, he wrote: 'All night I have been pursued by the child and this morning I am unrefreshed and miserable'; and in another to his friend, the actor Macready: 'I am slowly murdering that poor child and grow wretched over it. It wrings my heart. Yet it must be.'[15]

When it finally ended, the whole of England went into mourning 'and on the New York harbour front crowds gathered and asked the incoming trans-Atlantic passengers: "Is Little Nell dead"?' Today, Little Nell's death is seen as the ultimate in sentimental vulgarity. For Dickens's contemporaries, public lamentations and crying sessions were signs of sincerity and ways of purging their

---

[14] *The Posthumous Papers of the Pickwick Club* (London, 1967), 376.
[15] Cf. Peter Ackroyd, *Dickens* (London, 1990), 318.

feelings. 'Who will not weep at the death of Little Nell?', exclaimed a newspaper. Oscar Wilde maliciously modified this exclamation in: 'Who will not laugh at the death of Little Nell?' Times had changed by then.

When Little Nell's hiding place is eventually discovered, the single gentleman, Mr Garland, Kit and the postboy set off for the village. Once again it is winter, and as the journey progresses, the reader becomes more certain that Nell will not be found alive. Dickens conveys this through the description of the journey—a masterly description. The trip is cold and hard from the start: 'It was a bitter day. A keen wind was blowing, and rushed against them fiercely, bleaching the hard ground, shaking the white frost from the trees and hedges and whirling it away like dust.' While they travel, 'all day long it blew without cessation. The night was clear and starlit but the wind had not fallen and the cold was piercing.' And the travellers, of course, say to each other 'A dismal night indeed. Hark how the wind is howling.' Dickens masterfully describes a completely different kind of journey on the second day: now there is no cutting wind, only the deathly silence of the falling snow:

> As on the second day it grew dusk, the wind fell; its distant moanings were more low and mournful. By degrees it lulled and died away and then it came on to snow. The flakes fell fast and thick, soon covering the ground some inches deep and spreading abroad a solemn stillness. The rolling wheels were noiseless and the sharp ring and clatter of the horses' hoofs became a dull, muffled tramp. The life of their progress seemed to be slowly hushed and something death-like to usurp its place.[16]

The travellers lose their way, and the last stretch is covered at a walking pace:

> As each was thinking within himself that the driver must have lost his way, a church bell, close at hand, struck the hour of midnight [*of course midnight, the hour of the waking of the dead*], and the carriage stopped. It had moved softly enough, but when it ceased to crunch the snow, the silence was as startling as if some great noise had been replaced by perfect stillness.[17]

Through these words, we are prepared for Little Nell's death, a story, which will not be continued here. But like other great authors, Dickens is here creating a different reality from a journey through wind and snow; he hints at the end of all things.

A completely different description of the course of human life is given by Mr Pecksniff from *Martin Chuzzlewit*: 'Mr. Pecksniff was a most exemplary man, fuller of virtuous precepts than a copy-book. Some people likened him to a direction-post, which is always telling the way to a place, and never goes there.'[18] When Mr. Pecksniff warmed his hands before the fire, he warmed them 'as benevolently as if they were somebody else's, not his.' This is his description of mankind and its destiny:

> 'What are we', said Mr. Pecksniff, 'but coaches? Some of us are slow coaches'
> 'Goodness, Pa!' cried Charity.

---

[16] *The Old Curiosity Shop* (London, 1967), 527.
[17] *The Old Curiosity Shop* (London, 1967), 528.
[18] *Martin Chuzzlewit* (London, 1968), 12.

VII. CARTOON INSPIRED BY DICKENS'S *ALL THE YEAR ROUND*
From W. Mankowitz, *Dickens of London* (London 1976), p. 189.
By courtesy of Weidenfeld and Nicolson Publishers.

'Some of us, I say,' resumed her parent with increased emphasis, 'are slow coaches; some of us are fast coaches. Our passions are the horses; and rampant animals too!'
'Really, Pa!' cried both the daughters at once. 'How very unpleasant.'
'And rampant animals too!' repeated Mr. Pecksniff, with so much determination, that he may be said to have exhibited, at the moment, a sort of moral rampancy himself: 'and Virtue is the drag. We start from The Mother's Arms, and we run to The Dust Shovel'[19]

Martin Chuzzlewit appeared in 1843, a year after Dickens's American trip. As is well-known, Martin Chuzzlewit also travels to America. Dickens inserted this journey in an attempt to push up the sales figures, which were lower than expected. Dickens was always looking for ways of improving them. His usual method was to introduce new characters until one caught the public's imagination. At one point, but without success, he even brought Mr Pickwick out of his retirement in Dulwich. Martin Chuzzlewit sets sail for America without any of the usual preparatory scenes. With hindsight, we should be grateful that the public forced this 'flight' on him, because in the descriptions of Martin's American adventures, Dickens surpasses his *American Notes*. Here follows what he writes about the increasing tension on board as the ship—*The Screw*—approaches the promised land:

And now a general excitement began to prevail on board; and various predictions relative to the precise day, and even the precise hour at which they would reach New York, were freely broached. There was infinitely more crowding on deck and looking over the ship's side than there had been before; and an eruption broke out for packing up things every morning, which required unpacking again every night ... Those who had been ill all along, got well now, and those who had been well, got better. An American gentleman in the after-cabin, who had been wrapped up in fur and oilskin the whole passage, unexpectedly appeared in a very shiny, tall black hat ... He likewise stuck his hands deep into his pockets, and walked the deck with his nostrils dilated, as already inhaling the air of Freedom which carries death to all tyrants, and can never (under any circumstances worth mentioning) be breathed by slaves. An English gentleman who was strongly suspected of having run away from a bank, with something in his possession belonging to its strong-box besides the key, grew eloquent upon the subject of the rights of man, and hummed the Marseillaise Hymn constantly. In a word, one great sensation pervaded the whole ship, and the soil of America lay close before them.[20]

In America Martin Chuzzlewit undergoes a chastening experience, and is cured of his selfishness (the central theme of the book) in a painful process taking him to the door of death.

The coming of the railway brought the age of the coach to an end. The first track was laid by George Stephenson between Stockton and Darlington in 1825, and the line laid between Liverpool and Manchester in 1829 ensured great publicity for the new means of transport. The railway was, thus, already in existence when Dickens began to write, but had not yet become a universal system for transport. The great changes continued into the Thirties, when Dickens wrote his first works. Like many new ideas, he embraced the invention of the train wholeheartedly, and even promoted the interests of the railway lobby in the *Daily News*, a new radical

---

[19] *Martin Chuzzlewit* (London, 1968), 116.
[20] *Martin Chuzzlewit* (London, 1968), 253.

newspaper that first appeared in 1846. This paper was financially backed by famous 'railway-kings' as Joseph Paxton and George Hudson. Dickens himself was editor, such for only one month, after which he resigned advancing, amongst other reasons, the paper's dependence on railway interests.[21] The role played by the train, and especially that of the laying of track, is described in Dickens's novels in such a way as to suggest that he saw the dark sides of the new invention. That he came to see it as a symbol of destruction and death, rather than as a sign of progress and power is most clearly expressed in *Dombey and Son*. The first instalment appeared in 1846, ten years after the success of Pickwick's mail coaches. In this book, Dickens describes, in detail, the devastation caused in Camden Town (a district of London) by the laying of the railway line. He knew Camden well, having lived there in 1822 with his parents when he was 10 years old, after the family had left Chatham for London. When his father ended up in Marshalsea prison for non-payment of debts, little Charles lodged with a Mrs Roylance of Little College Street, Camden Town. Many years later, she was immortalized as Mrs Pipchin in *Dombey and Son*: 'a marvellous, ill-favoured, ill-conditioned lady, of a stooping figure, with a mottled face, like bad marble, a hook nose, and a hard grey eye, that looked as if it might have been hammered on an anvil without sustaining any injury.'

Dickens's descriptions of the changes to Camden Town and to the fictitious Stagg's Garden, where the Toodle family lived,—a 'stag' was a speculator in railway shares—are particularly interesting. On 11 October 1854, he wrote an article on the same subject for *Household Words* (the paper he edited), entitled *An Unsettled Neighbourhood*. It gives us an opportunity to compare Dickens's writing as journalist with his fiction. As is only to be expected, Dickens allows himself much more leeway when he is not bound by physical reality. In the novel, he compared the destruction caused by the laying of the railways with an earthquake:

> The first shock of a great earthquake had, just at that period, rent the whole neighbourhood to its centre. Traces of its course were visible on every side. Houses were knocked down; streets broken through and stopped; deep pits and trenches dug in the ground; enormous heaps of earth and clay thrown up; buildings that were undermined and shaking, propped by great beams of wood ... Everywhere were bridges that led nowhere; thoroughfares that were wholly impassable; Babel towers of chimneys, wanting half their height; ... Boiling water hissed and heaved within dilapidated walls; whence, also, the glare and roar of flames came issuing forth; and mounds of ashes blocked up rights of way, and wholly changed the law and custom of the neighbourhood.[22]

Within this context the train is depicted as a remorseless monster, as the symbol of Death. Mr Dombey takes the train to Leamington Spa, a fashionable watering place, to try to help himself get over the death of little Paul Dombey, the pride and joy of Dombey and Son. He wants to put the death of his son behind him, but by getting into what for many people was a hellish machine, death continues to accompany him. The journey reflects his shattered hopes:

> He found no pleasure or relief in the journey. Tortured by these thoughts he carried monotony with him, through the rushing landscape, and hurried headlong, not through a rich

---

[21] Cf. Peter Ackroyd, *Dickens* (London, 1990), 477.
[22] *Dombey and Son* (London, 1968), 62.

and varied country, but a wilderness of blighted plans and gnawing jealousies. The very speed at which the train was whirled along mocked the swift course of the young life that had been borne away so steadily and so inexorably to its foredoomed end. The power that forced itself upon its iron way—its own—defiant of all paths and roads, piercing through the heart of every obstacle, and dragging living creatures of all classes, ages, and degrees behind it, was a type of the triumphant monster, Death.'[23]

Dickens continued this with three sentences describing the train, and each ending with the same exclamation: 'like as in the track of the remorseless monster, Death!'

So proud Dombey heads straight to his next fateful destination. In Leamington, he will meet the equally tragic Edith Granger, more or less sold to him by her grotesque mother Mrs Skewton, Cleopatra.

The sinister description of the train anticipates the second confrontation with death. Now Dickens goes further than a comparison as a metaphor. He gives a realistic and detailed picture of death caused by the train. Scholars, studying the Victorian age, have already frequently pointed out that the morals of that period did not allow Dickens to write as freely about sexual desires and instincts as today. Without doubt, Dickens felt restricted by this taboo, especially since 'he had such a strange insight into the secrets of the human heart', as his daughter Kate said. He has only been able to hint to his readers of the darker impulses of passionate natures, the fate of Little Emily, abducted by Steerforth, the prostitute Martha from *David Copperfield*, and Nancy from *Oliver Twist*. There is, however, no trace of such restraint when he describes physical aggression and violence in *Dombey and Son*, where the train is not only compared with death, but is the actual cause of the death of the treacherous Carker, who after a wild chase through France and England, is crushed by a train. Here follows the description of the end of Carker's journey and of his life, seen through the eyes of Dombey, the man whom he had betrayed:

> He heard a shout—another—saw the face change from its vindictive passion to a faint sickness and terror—felt the earth tremble—knew in a moment that the rush was come—uttered a shriek—looked round—saw the red eyes, bleared and dim, in the daylight, close upon him—was beaten down, caught up, and whirled away upon a jagged mill, that spun him round and round, and struck him limb from limb, and licked his stream of life up with its fiery heat, and cast his mutilated fragments in the air.
>
> When the traveller, who had been recognised, recovered from a swoon, he saw them bringing from a distance something covered, that lay heavy and still, upon a board, between four men, and saw that others drove some dogs away that sniffed upon the road, and soaked his blood up, with a train of ashes.[24]

Five years to the day before Dickens died, the horror of his imagination became reality when he was involved in a train accident, one of the worst in the young history of the railway. The first part of the train, in which Dickens, his mistress Ellen Ternan and her mother were sitting, crashed through a bridge; their carriage teetered over the edge of the bridge but they were able to escape unhurt. Many people were lying dead or dying under the bridge. As long as possible, Dickens assisted in the rescue operations. This incident haunted him for the rest of his life,

---

[23] *Dombey and Son* (London, 1968), 280.
[24] *Dombey and Son* (London, 1968), 779.

making his daughter Mamie say: 'My father's nerves never really were the same again ... we have often seen him, when travelling home—to Gads Hill—from London, suddenly fall into a paroxysm of fear, tremble all over, clutch the arms of the railway carriage, large beads of perspiration standing on his face and suffer agonies of terror.' And sometimes, when the memory became too much for him, he left the train at a station half-way and walked the rest of the way home.[25]

As with everything else in his life, Dickens dealt openly with this experience by discussing it with his public. A few years earlier he had begun to hold public readings which brought him both unimaginable fame, and unexpectedly large sums of money. It can hardly be coincidental that shortly after the accident, he began to arrange a reading of the murder of Nancy by Bill Sykes. Though he had considered the idea before, he had been afraid that it was too horrible to launch upon the public. But, perhaps as a result of the train accident, this horror no longer seemed to bother him. Again he was extremely realistic, adding in the margin of his script the words 'Terror to the end', as a stage direction for himself. The deliberate bludgeoning exaggerations are particularly noticeable when we compare the text of the lecture with that of *Oliver Twist*. These excesses, emphasised further by the novelists's acting, are typical of the older Dickens, who had personally experienced the threat of death.

His public reacted exactly as he had expected: women fainted and a fleet of ambulances was necessary to supply first aid. Contagion of hysteria was imminent. The audience felt an almost irresistible impulse to scream. After such a performance, Edmund Yates wrote in his diary:

> Gradually warming with excitement he flung aside his book and acted the scene of the murder, shrieked the terrified pleadings of the girl, growled the brutal savagery of the murderer ... The raised hands, the bent-back head, are good; but shut your eyes and the illusion is more complete. Then the cries for mercy, the Bill! dear Bill! for dear God's sake! uttered in tones in which the agony of fear prevails even over the earnestness of the prayers, the dead dull voice as hope departs, are intensely real. When the pleading ceases, you open your eyes in relief, in time to see the impersonation of the murderer seizing a heavy club and striking his victim to the ground.[26]

Dickens, wrapped up in this scene, became obsessed. He could hardly write about anything else in his letters, and according to his friends and family, this was what eventually killed him, the endlessly repeated murder: Terror to the end!

We have come a long way from Mr Pickwick, travelling through the lanes of England. As Dickens was laying aside the innocence of his youth, the coming of the train sounded the death-knell of the mail coaches of his early writing. With the arrival of the train, rural England, with its winding roads and post inns where the coach horses were changed, vanished for ever. All this made way for what Dickens saw as the more mechanized England, which he personified in the characters of Mr Rouncewell in *Bleak House*, of Daniel Doyce in *Little Dorrit*, and in his novel *Hard Times*. He not only perceived the inhuman and violent side of

---

[25] Cf. Peter Ackroyd, *Dickens* (London, 1990), 963 ff.
[26] Cf. Peter Ackroyd, *Dickens* (London, 1990), 1039.

industrialized society, but also saw this change of the world as a reflection of changes happening within himself. It seems no coincidence that his 'railway novel', *Dombey and Son*, marks the end of what critics call his youthful phase. 'The Wheel of Time was rolling for an end' for Dickens, too, a more tragic and gloomy end than he was willing to admit. In later years he may have looked back with astonishment on his first creation: Pickwick, who remained youthful in outlook and never lost his lust for life, while his creator grew older.

Dickens's readers, too, can be roughly divided into pre- and post-railway readers. The latter are most admiring of the mature Dickens, who descends into the darkest recesses of the human soul, where few writers before or after him have been able to penetrate, the former love the indestructible optimism of Pickwick, old Wardle, of Sam and Tony Weller, the sparkling genius of the early Dickens that still fizzes 150 years later. These Dickensians are actually Pickwickians, because they always return to Pickwick. Chesterton was the greatest exponent of this group (in which I would also humbly include myself). And it is significant that in the last sentences of his personal Dickens biography—'personal' because it is as much about Chesterton as about Dickens—, he creates a picture of travellers approaching the end of their journey, of the 'Wheel of Time rolling for an end'. This is what he says:

> The hour of absinthe is over. We shall not be much further troubled with the little artists who found Dickens too sane for their sorrows and too clean for their delights. But we have a long way to travel before we get back to what Dickens meant: and the passage is along a rambling English road, a twisting road such as Mr Pickwick travelled. But this at least is part of what he meant; that comradeship and serious joy are not interludes in our travel; but that rather our travels are interludes in comradeship and joy, which through God shall endure for ever. The inn does not point to the road; the road points to the inn. And all roads point at last to an ultimate inn, where we shall meet Dickens and all his characters: and when we drink again it shall be from the great flagons in the tavern at the end of the world.[27]

---

[27] G. K. Chesterton, *Charles Dickens* (London, 1906).

INDEX

Besides personal and geographical names, this index contains titles of anonymous writings, names of legendary people and references to maps.

BRILL'S STUDIES
IN
INTELLECTUAL HISTORY

28. BOUCHER, W.I. *Spinoza in English*. A Bibliography from the Seventeenth-Century to the Present. 1991. ISBN 90 04 09499 7
29. McINTOSH, C. *The Rose Cross and the Age of Reason*. Eighteenth-Century Rosicrucianism in Central Europe and its Relationship to the Enlightenment. 1992. ISBN 90 04 09502 0
30. CRAVEN, K. *Jonathan Swift and the Millennium of Madness*. The Information Age in Swift's *A Tale of a Tub*. 1992. ISBN 90 04 09524 1
31. BERKVENS-STEVELINCK, C., H. BOTS, P.G. HOFTIJZER & O.S. LANKHORST (eds.). *Le Magasin de l'Univers*. *The Dutch Republic as the Centre of the European Book Trade*. Papers Presented at the International Colloquium, held at Wassenaar, 5-7 July 1990. 1992. ISBN 90 04 09493 8
32. GRIFFIN, JR., M.I.J. *Latitudinarianism in the Seventeenth-Century Church of England*. Annoted by R.H. Popkin. Edited by L. Freedman. 1992. ISBN 90 04 09653 1
33. WES, M.A. *Classics in Russia 1700-1855*. Between two Bronze Horsemen. 1992. ISBN 90 04 09664 7
34. BULHOF, I.N. *The Language of Science*. A Study in the Relationship between Literature and Science in the Perspective of a Hermeneutical Ontology. With a Case Study in Darwin's *The Origin of Species*. 1992. ISBN 90 04 09644 2
35. LAURSEN, J.C. *The Politics of Skepticism in the Ancients, Montaigne, Hume and Kant*. 1992. ISBN 90 04 09459 8
36. COHEN, E. *The Crossroads of Justice*. Law and Culture in Late Medieval France. 1993. ISBN 90 04 09569 1
37. POPKIN, R.H. & A.J. VANDERJAGT (eds.). *Scepticism and Irreligion in the Seventeenth and Eighteenth Centuries*. 1993. ISBN 90 04 09596 9
38. MAZZOCCO, A. *Linguistic Theories in Dante and the Humanists*. Studies of Language and Intellectual History in Late Medieval and Early Renaissance Italy. 1993. ISBN 90 04 09702 3
39. KROOK, D. *John Sergeant and His Circle*. A Study of Three Seventeenth-Century English Aristotelians. Edited with an Introduction by B.C. Southgate. 1993. ISBN 90 04 09756 2
40. AKKERMAN, F., G.C. HUISMAN & A.J. VANDERJAGT (eds.). *Wessel Gansfort (1419-1489) and Northern Humanism*. 1993. ISBN 90 04 09857 7
41. COLISH, M.L. *Peter Lombard*. 2 volumes. 1994. ISBN 90 04 09859 3 (Vol. 1), ISBN 90 04 09860 7 (Vol. 2), ISBN 90 04 09861 5 (Set)
42. VAN STRIEN, C.D. *British Travellers in Holland During the Stuart Period*. Edward Browne and John Locke as Tourists in the United Provinces. 1993. ISBN 90 04 09482 2
43. MACK, P. *Renaissance Argument*. Valla and Agricola in the Traditions of Rhetoric and Dialectic. 1993. ISBN 90 04 09879 8
44. DA COSTA, U. *Examination of Pharisaic Traditions*. Supplemented by SEMUEL DA SILVA's *Treatise on the Immortality of the Soul*. Tratado da immortalidade da alma. Translation, Notes and Introduction by H.P. Salomon & I.S.D. Sassoon. 1993. ISBN 90 04 09923 9
45. MANNS, J.W. *Reid and His French Disciples*. Aesthetics and Metaphysics. 1994. ISBN 90 04 09942 5
46. SPRUNGER, K.L. *Trumpets from the Tower*. English Puritan Printing in the Netherlands, 1600-1640. 1994. ISBN 90 04 09935 2
47. RUSSELL, G.A. (ed.). *The 'Arabick' Interest of the Natural Philosophers in Seventeenth-Century England*. 1994. ISBN 90 04 09888 7
48. SPRUIT, L. Species intelligibilis: *From Perception to Knowledge*. Volume I: Classical Roots and Medieval Discussions. 1994. ISBN 90 04 09883 6
49. SPRUIT, L. Species intelligibilis: *From Perception to Knowledge*. Volume II. (in preparation)
50. HYATTE, R. *The Arts of Friendship*. The Literary Idealization of Friendship in Medieval and Early Renaissance Literature. 1994. ISBN 90 04 10018 0
51. CARRÉ, J. (ed.). *The Crisis of Courtesy*. Studies in the Conduct-Book in Britain, 1600-1900. 1994. ISBN 90 04 10005 9
52. BURMAN, T. *Spain's Arab-Christians and Islam, 1050-1200*. 1994. ISBN 90 04 09910 7
53. HORLICK, A.S. *Patricians, Professors, and Public Schools*. The Origins of Modern Educational Thought in America. 1994. ISBN 90 04 10054 7

54. MacDONALD, A.A., M. LYNCH & I.B. COWAN (eds.). *The Renaissance in Scotland*. Studies in Literature, Religion, History and Culture Offered to John Durkan. 1994. ISBN 90 04 10097 0

55. VON MARTELS, Z. (ed.). *Travel Fact and Travel Fiction*. Studies on Fiction, Literary Tradition, Scholarly Discovery and Observation in Travel Writing. 1994. ISBN 90 04 10112 8

56. PRANGER, M.B. *Bernard of Clairvaux and the Shape of Monastic Thought*. Broken Dreams. 1994. ISBN 90 04 10055 5